Unpublished Fragments

from the Period of *Dawn*

(Winter 1879/80–Spring 1881)

Volume Thirteen

Based on the edition by
Giorgio Colli and Mazzino Montinari
First organized in English by Ernst Behler

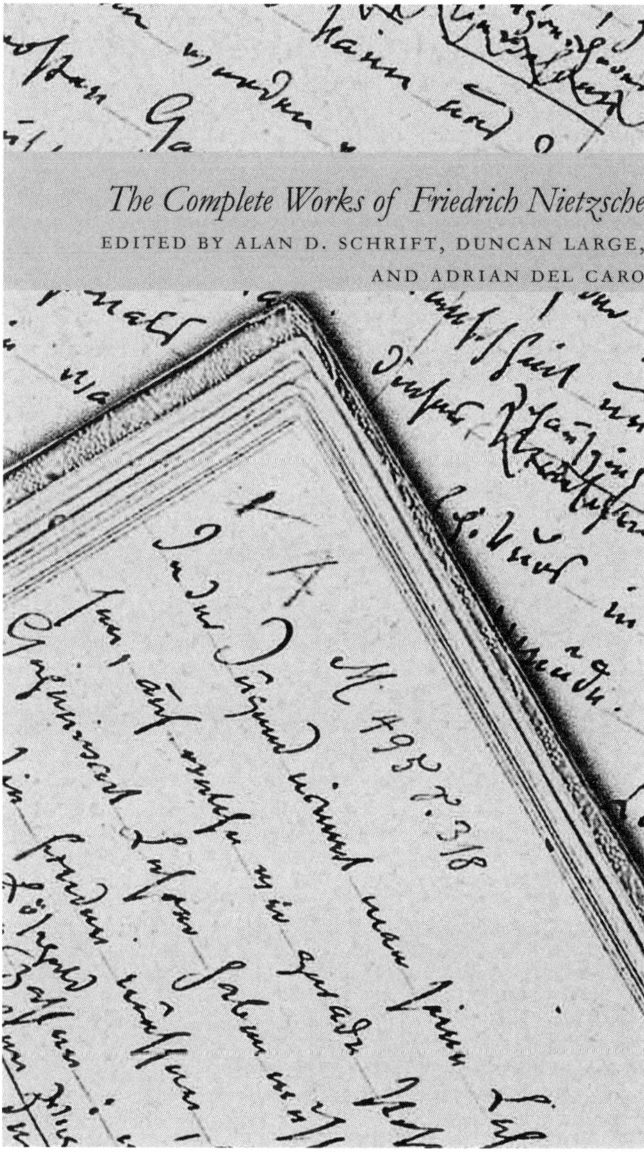

The Complete Works of Friedrich Nietzsche

EDITED BY ALAN D. SCHRIFT, DUNCAN LARGE, AND ADRIAN DEL CARO

Friedrich Nietzsche

Unpublished Fragments
from the Period of *Dawn*
(Winter 1879/80–Spring 1881)

Translated by J. M. Baker Jr. and Christiane Hertel
Afterword by J. M. Baker Jr.

STANFORD UNIVERSITY PRESS
STANFORD, CALIFORNIA

Stanford University Press
Stanford, California

Translated from Friedrich Nietzsche, *Sämtliche Werke: Kritische Studienausgabe*, ed. Giorgio Colli and Mazzino Montinari, in 15 vols. This book corresponds to Vol. 9, pp. 7–439, and Vol. 14, pp. 625–44.

Translated by J. M. Baker Jr. and Christiane Hertel
Afterword by J. M. Baker Jr.

Critical edition of Friedrich Nietzsche's *Sämtliche Werke* and unpublished writings based on the original manuscripts.

Printed in the United States of America on acid-free, archival-quality paper.

CIP data appears at the end of the book.

Contents

A Note on This Edition

This is the first English translation of all of Nietzsche's writings, including his unpublished fragments, with annotation, afterwords concerning the individual texts, and indexes, in nineteen volumes. The aim of this collaborative work is to produce a critical edition for scholarly use. Volume 1 also includes an introduction to the entire edition, and Volume 19 will include a detailed chronology of Nietzsche's life. While the goal is to establish a readable text in contemporary English, the translation follows the original as closely as possible. All texts have been translated anew by a group of scholars, and particular attention has been given to maintaining a consistent terminology throughout the volumes. The translation is based on *Friedrich Nietzsche: Sämtliche Werke. Kritische Studienausgabe in 15 Bänden* (1980), edited by Giorgio Colli and Mazzino Montinari. The still-progressing *Nietzsche Werke: Kritische Gesamtausgabe*, which Colli and Montinari began in 1963, has also been consulted. The Colli-Montinari edition is of particular importance for the unpublished fragments, comprising more than half of Nietzsche's writings and published there for the first time in their entirety. Besides listing textual variants, the annotation to this English edition provides succinct information on the text and identifies events, names (except those in the Index of Persons), titles, quotes, and biographical facts of Nietzsche's own life. The notes are numbered in the text and are keyed by phrase. The Afterword presents the main facts about the origin of the text, the stages of its composition, and the main events of its reception. The Index of Persons includes mythological figures and lists the dates of birth and death as well as prominent personal characteristics. Since the first three volumes appeared, important corrections and additions to the 1980 edition of the *Kritische Studienausgabe* have been noted, and these corrections and additions have been incorporated into the translation that appears here.

ERNST BEHLER AND ALAN D. SCHRIFT

Unpublished Fragments
from the Period of *Dawn*
(Winter 1879/80–Spring 1881)

[1 = N V 1. Beginning of 1880]

1[1]

On superstition.
On praise and blame.
On the permissible lie.

1[2]

Esteem for compassion (proceeding from the side of those who are its object?)

Monogamy

1[3]

Do humans deem themselves bad as a consequence of their *immorality* or their *morality*? — Or as a consequence of both and many other things?

1[4]

How should one act? So that as much as possible what is individual is preserved? Or so that as much as possible the race is preserved? Or so that as much as possible another race is preserved? (morality of animals) Or so that life as such is preserved? Or so that the highest species of life are preserved?[1] The interests of these different spheres diverge. But what are highest species? Is the level of intellect or is goodness or power decisive? With regard to these most general standards for action there was no reflection, let alone agreement.

1[5]

As far as friendliness and benevolence are concerned, Europe does **not** stand on the heights: that testifies *against* Christianity.

1[6]

To strive for *universal* happiness is insolence, and silliness.

1[7]

The bad the sick the uneducated human is a result whose continuation and influence must be curtailed.

1[8]

Always to think *of others* is the most damaging tendency (to be active *for* them is almost as bad as to act *against* them, it is a violation of their sphere. What brutality the usual upbringing is, the parental intervention in the children's sphere!

1[9]

Morality (just like the art of poetry) is strongest among nature peoples[2] (their boundedness by customs) Among the most highly cultivated nations customs are mainly what is most backward, often ridiculous, here the exceptional human is always immoral.

1[10]

Assuming that to sacrifice oneself for others is *more esteemed*, one does it then: but because it is *esteemed*. Instinctive!

1[11]

Devil worship Spencer p. 31[3]

1[12][4]

Education continuation of procreation. The whole of life is adaptation of the new to the old.

1[13][5]

Napoleon's *presentable* motive: "I want to be superior to everyone." True motive: "I want *to appear* superior to everyone."

1[14]

The greatest problem of the coming age is the eradication of moral concepts and the cleansing from our representations of moral forms or colors that have crept into them and are often difficult to recognize.

1[15]

The "murderer" whom we condemn is a phantom: "the person capable of murder!" But that is all of us.

1[16]

The capacity for joy is crippled by the desire to be equal.

1[17][6]

The barbarism in Christianity.

2) Remainders of devil worship etc.[7]

1[18]

When one takes such extraordinary pleasure in one's works and exalts oneself on their account, one demotes oneself within the hierarchy of spirits: for how one judges other works and persons does not count for much anymore. One has not withstood the great trial by fire of righteousness and must no longer wish to sit on the judgment seat.

1[19]

If it is not prohibited: "thou *shalt* not murder!" — for whole periods of time the inner feeling has no objection to murder.

1[20]

Whoever has experienced the pain of speaking the truth *in spite of* his friendships and honors, will certainly shrink from new ones.

1[21]

There are quite intelligent people who believe that if they obstinately shut their eyes before a thing, it is no longer in the world.

1[22]

Is there anything more important and effective than to regard every person of one's acquaintance as a difficult process through which a *specific kind of well-being* might assert itself: only when this well-being has been achieved is a balance attained between him and the rest of us; from that point on he shares his joy and yet does not intrude into the sphere of others, he stands as a strong tree among other trees, in the freedom of the forest.

1[23][8]

NB. *Benighted and superstitious people* believe 1) — — — 2) — — — 3) — — — in contrast with the enlightened

1[24][9]

Compassion without intelligence is one of the most unpleasant and disturbing phenomena: regrettably, on its own compassion is not at all clear-sighted, as Schopenhauer would have it.

1[25]

No more tepid and dull sensation would be possible than if all people imagined themselves being one with one another or even simply the same. The most spirited sensation, that of amour-passion, actually consists in the feeling of greatest difference.

1[26]

Because Christianity is uprooted, our youth grows without education.

1[27]

Society must learn to tolerate more and more *truth*.

1[28]

Humans who might burst with poison and jealousy for others preach benevolence for animals

1[29]

A new culture — that should not be merely feigned!

1[30][10]

Just now when the lamentable comedy of reconciling art with Christianity is being staged again, to remember Schopenhauer! very much to his honor that he never —

1[31]

The need to speak out about every matter that torments us — made God always seem present to the Christian; for cruder, less imaginative natures the church created his deputy, the confessor. *Why* does one want to speak out? Because a desire is there, a violation of the other whom we task with hearing, feeling, and bearing our suffering — God as scapegoat must also be confessor.

1[32]

I know someone who so thoroughly spoiled himself with the little breath of wind of his "freedom" that the idea of belonging to a *party* causes him to break out in a cold sweat — even if it were his own party!

1[33]

Our task is to cleanse culture, to grant the new saplings[11] light and air and in the belief that once opposites are overcome, very much more energy will be there.

1[34]

Whether a person is to be killed for the good of society? The murderer disturbs security, the free spirit endangers the soul for all eternity. The cantankerous disturb comfort

1[35]

Immoral actions make for the *moral* way of life in certain cruder cultures. — They are still present in our *organs*. We murder, steal, lie, dissemble, etc. even in the highest matters.

1[36][12]

Our later valuations are formed by analogy with the habitual ones, just as a house once begun is expanded — i.e., — — —

1[37]

As long as these sentences somehow still sound paradoxical to you, you have not understood them: they should seem superfluous to you and all too evident.

It is impossible to think too casually about that.

1[38]

Free spirits seek *other forms* of life, inestimable! moral humans would leave the world to wither away. The experimental stages of humanity

1[39]

An astonishing amount of *pain* is suffered in vain at the testing stations of new ways of life and usefulness — there is no helping it; may it at least help others! so that they recognize what a failed experiment was undertaken here.

1[40]

To act according to habit is "to imitate oneself," the nearest and easiest thing — *without* the motives for those past actions repeating their effect.

1[41]

The innovative s⟨pirit⟩ must have *time* and may not become too accustomed to *regularity*.

1[42]

Certain bodily-mental conditions are supposed to come from God and the devil, then also the ethical conditions (God is at work in us "the devil rages in him" etc.)

1[43]

Morality as *obstacle* to innovations. The innovator who is too lazy invents the machine and the animal: the ambitious one invents the states, the dissembler the dramatic spectacle etc. — The reasonable human lives on the attainments of innovators.

Ethical is taking the reasonable course of action whose purposes and means are approved.

Merely ethical: there humanity languishes nothing is invented.

1[44][13]

Where *stimuli* are needed, the purposeless overflow of power is no longer there; the power one wants to restore — but the overflow?

1[45]

One is active because everything living must be in motion — *not* **for** the **sake** *of pleasure*, thus *without purpose*: even though there is pleasure in it. This motion is *not* imitation of purposive motions, it is different.

1[46]

Supposing that through science an end were put to very many *complacent* representations and many a comfortable laziness, its effect would appear unhealthy. But against that it must be reckoned that science does away with a great deal of discontent and namely the terrible ideas of all evil philosophies and religions that we are evil through and through and face hard penance.

1[47]

Only with respect to their *common usefulness* has it been possible to call habitual actions moral and thus stamp them with the highest human rating — in themselves they are very poor and almost "sub-animal."

1[48]

To describe a matter

1[49]

Immoral persons are those who have freedom of movement without purposes, or who walk old paths with different purposes.

1[50]

Up to now between the 2 main motives the fear of pain has had overwhelmingly greater effect than the pursuit of pleasure. We knew far too few pleasures and far too many dangers. — Here the backwardness of the human being becomes evident on the whole, according to whether the motives of fear are more crudely refined or faded and eclipsed by the motives of pleasure.

1[51]

An *accidental* encounter between two words or of a word and a spectacle is the origin of a new thought.

1[52]

People who have much of the *accidental* and like to wander around, others who only walk on *familiar paths* in pursuit of purposes.

1[53]

Genius like a blind sea crab which perpetually gropes in every direction and *occasionally* catches something: yet it does not grope in order to catch, but only because its limbs must be in motion.[14]

1[54][15]

Actions undertaken with an *unexpected* outcome, for an *other* purpose— e.g., an animal that guards its eggs as *food* and suddenly faces its fellow beings.

1[55]

Whoever is practiced in splendid moral attitudes should be reckoned among the tricksters, caprice tight-rope walkers, fire-eaters, and other artists who are there for the working masses, they have a such an appetite for the improbable and eccentric; I have always found the best persons in their best actions somewhat ashamed and short-winded. There is a way of being a moral flirt through which the whole fellow becomes suspect. Virtue without shame before oneself is nothing but a ruse.

1[56]

Change of valuation e.g., *contempt* for the superstitious and their objects.

1[57][16]

To do the good, the excellent, without expecting praise for it, to be too proud to accept praise for it, and to keep ready a scornful eye for the all too impudent who nevertheless praises, and to accustom everyone in one's surroundings to this manly practice; but to grant the need to be praised to the more feminine and artistic natures and there to let it stand because such natures do their best not out of pride but out of vanity. — That is right! If *only* we felt it to be equally *right* in times of full strength, that certainly would be no objection. For the tired and sick a little praise as spice or narcotic might be necessary. — I do not distinguish here between just and unjust praise, nor between just and unjust reproach: the latter we should not only let stand but provoke and encourage; by virtue of comprehensive and always resounding reproach, be it just or unjust, we rise above ourselves, for thereby we see ourselves as we appear, and indeed to uncorrupted eyes.

1[58][17]

One learns presentable motives.

1[59]

An altogether conscious egoism would dispense with those pleasures that emerge through imaginary motives or because we wish to see only *one* motive among the many.

1[60]

"All humans are sinners" is the sort of exaggeration, like "all humans are mad," that physicians could encounter. Here differences of degree are ignored, and the word and the feeling which the abnormal extreme degree has awakened are transferred to the whole related life of the soul of the middle and lower degrees. By falsely embedding an abnormality at its core, one has made humanity horrible.

1[61][18]

Ingenious and *purpose-driven* natures — opposition.

1[62]

To grasp how little worth moral actions have, how little unworthiness immoral actions — how great by contrast the intellectual difference between them — to receive this clarification of the acting person's motives elicits the greatest astonishment.

1[63]

Principle: in the whole of human history until now no purpose, no rational secret direction, no instinct, but chance, chance, chance — and many a favorable one. These are to be set in the light. We may not have any false confidence, and least of all continue to rely on chance. It is in most instances a senseless destroyer.

1[64]

When a people remains fixed on particular moral judgments, it becomes narrow, ossified, isolated, old, and finally meets its end because of that.

1[65]

Moral judgments are most assuredly pronounced by people who have never thought and least assuredly by those who know humankind. It is nothing to praise and to blame.

1[66]

Voluntary actions — that is actually a negative concept — actions which do not occur involuntarily, not automatically, without purposes. The positive thing that one feels in this is an error. "Involuntary" is actually the positive concept. Strictly speaking, arbitrary actions are *two involuntary* actions which are temporally joined together, a movement in the brain upon which follows a movement of the muscles without being its effect.[19]

1[67]

To maintain the greatest multiplicity in conditions for human existence and not to make people uniform with a moral codex — this is the most general means of preparing for the *favorable* chance occurrence. — Up to now humanity has set no aim for itself that it wished to reach in its entirety — perhaps that will happen someday. For the time being, since the end is wanting, there are no discernible means to it. Meanwhile the greatest possible mass of such individuals should be produced who enjoy individual well-being — what is mutually implied — the most general

1[68]

Morality is the legislation of those who knew themselves shrewder than their company and who thought for them. They made often difficult demands incontestable by drawing in the will of the godhead.

1[69]

So there are no blameworthy *actions*, instead praise and blame apply only to human beings, not things.

1[70]

Every living thing is in motion; this activity is not for the sake of particular aims, it is just life itself. In its movements humanity as a whole is without purposes and goals, there is in this from the beginning no will: nevertheless it would not be impossible at some point for the human to embed a purpose: just as certain initially aimless movements by animals function to serve their feeding.

1[71]

In its victory celebrations a victorious army almost expires, the victor marks the day black and does not recover for a year from this strain — but the street urchins of all genders and ages are happy. It must nevertheless be conceded that ⟨there are⟩ cheaper ways of making them happy and indeed much happier.

1[72]

Christianity learned a lesson from the Old Testament to the extent that it sought to become a world religion. World-denying Christianity did not need the Old Testament.

1[73]

In our schools Jewish history is taught as sacred history: Abraham is more to us than any figure out of Greek or German history: and what we feel in the Psalms of David is as different from what stirs us in reading Pindar or Petrarch as home is from the foreign. This draw to the products of an Asiatic, very distant and very peculiar race is perhaps one of the few phenomena amidst the disorder of our modern culture that stand even above the opposition between education and lack of education:[20] the strongest moral aftereffect of Christianity, which appealed to persons rather than peoples and therefore, without the least malice, handed the religious text of a Semitic people to people of the Indo-Germanic race. But if one considers to what lengths non-Semitic Europe went in order to make a place right close to its heart for this foreign little Jewish world, to cease wondering at anything in it, instead to wonder at itself and at being taken aback — thus in nothing perhaps did Europe so overcome itself as in this appropriation of Jewish literature. Present-day European feeling for the Bible is the greatest victory over the limitations of race and over the conceit that for each person only what his grandfather and grandfather's grandfather said and did is really valuable. This feeling is so powerful that whoever now wishes to adapt a free and more discerning stance toward Jewish history must first take pains to emerge from an all-too-great nearness and familiarity and again to experience the Jewish as something foreign. For to a considerable degree, Europe has had to embed itself in the Bible and by and large has had to do something similar to the English Puritans, who found their Sundays, their customs, their contemporaries, their wars, their small and large turns of fate recorded (prophesied) in the Jewish book. — But what does the European say when asked about the priority of ancient Jewish literature over every other ancient literature: *"There is more morality in it."* But that means: there is more of that morality in it which now is recognized in Europe: and this in turn means nothing else but: Europe has adopted Jewish morality and deems it higher, better, and more appropriate to the present morality and understanding than the Arabic, Greek, Indian, Chinese. — What is the character of this morality? Are Europeans really *by virtue of* this moral character the first and dominant people on the globe? But what is the standard for measuring different moralities? Moreover, non-Europeans like the Chinese do not even acknowledge that Europeans marked themselves off from them through *morality*. It may perhaps belong to the essence of Jewish morality that it considers itself the first and the highest: it is perhaps a conceit. One may well ask: is there any such thing as an order of rank of moralit⟨ies⟩? Is there a generally valid canon defining morality regardless of people, time, circumstances, level of knowledge? Or is the degree of adaptation to knowledge perhaps the ingredient of all moralities which makes possible an order of rank in moralities?

1[74]

How much happiness is there in self-sacrifice for a beloved sect, etc. (one takes pleasure in being despised, insulted — how does that happen?

1[75][21]

The harmful side of religion has often ⟨been⟩ highlighted, I would like to show for the first time the harmful side of morality and to counter the error that it is of any usefulness to the senses.

1[76]

To the false supposition of causal relations in areas where there is in truth only a succession many illusions about morality owe their emergence.

1[77]

To curse science because occasionally its method hurts would be as smart as to curse fire because a child or a moth has burnt itself on it. Indeed, only moths and children burn themselves nowadays on science — I am thinking of the enthusiasts.

1[78]

The judgment of very hard-working and industrious eras on the value of life sounds always very desperate: one thought about life when one could no longer work and was tired. The Greeks thought better of life, after all they were a people of leisure: they worked in fact as a recreation from leisure, and their reflectiveness came from fresh strength.

1[79][22]

"In the *eyes* lies the soul:"[23] the habitual kind of movements and muscle contractions around the eyes betray what they are mainly used for: thinkers have a direct clear or penetrating look; the anxious person is afraid of *really* looking; the envious person has a sidelong look and wants to snitch something. Even when someone does not want to see in service to these dispositions, the eye's attitude still reveals the habit.

1[80][24]

Inventive people live *very differently* from actively engaged people; they need *time* for purpose-free, unregulated activity to set in, experiments, new paths, they grope more than follow the familiar paths like the usefully engaged.

1[81][25]

Eventually the art of artists must be subsumed in the human need for festivals: the hermetic artists exhibiting their work will have disappeared: they will then stand in the front row among those who are creative with regard to pleasures and festivals.

1[82]

Schopenhauer, the last to represent the ethical mean⟨ing⟩ of existence: he appends his powerful trump card without which he gives nothing to us and which in the eyes of one class of his readers strengthens his credibility as much as the same weakens it in the eyes of another class.

1[83][26]

Some show spirit, others give proof of it, others still show it but do not prove it, but the many do neither and believe they are doing both.

1[84][27]

The meager handful of knowledge which present-day education bestows on the cultivated already seems to be too much for these narrow and clerical minds, they become fearful it might diminish art and the same could no longer conduct itself so conceitedly as no doubt presently happens. — The critical conditions that emerge within those rare persons in whom science stirs a powerful fire should truly not be bespoken by such narrow minds[28]

1[85]

We find the weakness of fear contemptible in the person who knows that wine is bad for them and who drinks wine nevertheless.

1[86]

Morality has inhibited knowledge inasmuch as it inhibited desire for it, it set rules for action and awakened the belief that knowledge is not necessary to figure out the most expedient action.

1[87]

Some philosophers match past conditions, some present, some future, and some unreal.

1[88]

In some eras the individual stood higher, was more common. Those are the *more evil* times, the individual was more visible, one dared more, one harmed more, but lied less.

1[89]

The illusion about valuation (general esteem) and likewise false valuation are the origin of many non-egoistical actions.

1[90][29]

Morality, an **Asian** invention. *We depend upon* **Asia**.

1[91]

To use and *recognize* chance is called genius. To use the expedient and familiar — morality?

1[92]

As useful and unpleasant as a well-oiled *keyhole*

1[93]

Fearfulness poisons the soul.

1[94]

New paths should not be tried ⟨if⟩ our heart is not considerably bolder than our head: otherwise eats away — — —

1[95]

No one is capable of a crueler revenge than those souls without pride, those poetic and sensitive souls who suffer continuously in concealment and out of fear appear mild and quiet — I am thinking, e.g., of Racine.

1[96]

The entire past era is that of *fear*. One learns things as they are in others' heads, one learns how they are valued, one does the same with regard to the means. One is afraid of differing, of standing out. Our skills are what serves *others* and affords them pleasure. — Our greatest pleasure is to please others, our constant fear is not *being able* to please them. — This has *tamed* solitary animality.

1[97]

Whoever has a dominant *passion* experiences in the exceptional act a pang of conscience, e.g., the Jew (in Stendhal) who is in love and puts aside money from his business for a bracelet,[30] or Napoleon after a generous act, the diplomat[31] who for once was honest etc.

1[98]

Spencer always presupposes the "equality of human beings."

1[99]

In action too there are such inventive, always experimental persons who will not banish chance from themselves (Napoleon).

1[100][32]

Acquired value judgments diminish pleasure and consequently capacity for life. Times of "equality" are dull and cause fear of the future. —

The pleasure in being judged by others is now almost the most powerful pleasure of all.

1[101][33]

What is habit? — *Practice.*

1[102]

"But no one will notice" — but no one plants in you what you do, and then your habit of concealing and keeping to *yourself* grows, finally one can tell both in you after all.

1[103][34]

The little bit of scientific knowledge now on the earth already makes them fearful and anxious so that prophesies of doom grow loud. And this disgraceful scientific education!

1[104]

The hidden, *i.e.*, the most frequent actions compel us finally to our visible, infrequent ones, without our awareness of compulsion.

1[105]

Among Christians the same ideas still rule as among the savages — cf. Spencer p. 52[35] and Roskoff.[36]

1[106]

Spencer[37] confuses systems of morality "how should one act?" with the emergence of morality. Absence of insight into causality is important for the latter.

1[107]

Wherever a frightening power commands and orders, morality emerges, i.e., the habit of doing and omitting to do as that power commands, upon which the good feeling follows of having escaped danger: whereas in the reverse case conscience stirs, the voice of fear before the approaching, of discontent over what has been done etc. There are personal powers, like princes, generals, superiors, then abstract powers like the state society, finally imaginary beings, like God, virtue, the categorical imperative etc.

1[108]

Tragic jesters

1[109][38]

In every action there is 1) the true motive that is concealed 2) the *presentable* acknowledged motive. The latter proceeds from us, from our joy, from our individual being, we *place ourselves individually* thereby. But the former pays regard to what others think, we act as everyone acts, we *present* ourselves as individuals but behave as species-beings.[39] Droll! E.g., I seek a position 2) "I owe it to myself to make myself useful" 1) "I want to be respected by others on account of my position."

1[110][40]

The generation of offspring is not altruistic. Here the single animal follows a desire that is often its ruin. Self-sacrifice for the brood is self-sacrifice for one's own kin, one's neighbor, for the offspring, etc., thus also not altruism.

1[111]

The same things are *done* over and over again, but human beings cocoon them with ever new thoughts (valuations)

1[112]

To distinguish motives and the mechanism — and in that case the expression motive is misleading, they do not set into motion — rather once they are in motion, the mechanism's movement ensues.

1[113]

The unhappiness of the evildoer — i.e., he is afraid of bad consequences or nausea and satiety etc., not conflict of conscience.

1[114]

One should use even the slightest contact with human beings to practice one's sense of what is righteous and benevolent.

1[115][41]

When we are in a certain physiological condition, then what others thought of us the last times we were in it enters into our memory. There must be a release mechanism in the brain for each condition.

1[116]

There are people who do not know how to communicate their not quite customary thoughts in any other way than by releasing their anger on everyone. That means though bringing one's opinions to market at a bit too high a cost. But when there are often such odd fellows, a prejudice arises against all uncustomary opinions, almost as if anger, irritation, calumny bitterness baseness would have to be their necessary attendants.

1[117]

Habitual actions (in certain circumstances called "moral") are mechanisms without consciousness, as little moral as the action of a wound-up musical clock. Neither "free" nor with "intentional sacrifice," nor "for others" — but pleasant and useful and therefore labeled with the highest rating.

1[118]

Faced with the single person we are full of 100 considerations: but *when* one *writes*, then I do not understand why one does not step forward with the utmost honesty. That is real recuperation!

1[119]

On the whole only very moral persons have troubled themselves with morality, mainly with the intention of enhancing it. Is it any surprise that in the process immoral and average people have remained virtually unknown! Moral people have fantasized about them and often planted their fantasies into people's heads.

1[120]

Attempts at an extra-moral view of the world too lightly undertaken by me in the past — an *aesthetic* one (veneration of genius —)

1[121]

Whoever acts so is superstitious etc.
Whoever pretends is superstitious[42]
Whoever *does both* is a *Christian.*

1[122]

Schopenhauer's theory is unpsychological. Truly suffering or care-ridden people are without compassion. When we chew the cud of all the past misery humanity has suffered, we become ill and weak. One must avert one's gaze. Only happy people are suited for history.

1[123]

False concept of *genius* in the present age: the wild intellect is revered and the domesticated intellect despised, i.e., one is *tired* of morality.

The consequence of morality is the *sand.* Critique of morality up to now by demonstrating its results in the future.

Necessity of *anti-moral* theories.

1[124]

There is music which so thoroughly imitates the impression of visible things that it can be recommended to all those who have ears *in order to see.*

1[125][43]

To will, i.e., I imagine the outcome of an action
this outcome has this or that value for me
this valuation has these or those causes
the outcome conditions this or that action as means,
known to me ⟨from⟩ my experience and
many more besides that I cannot be conscious of.
So what do I will
Intention: why do I will
Motive: what drives me to this valuation?
The intention aims at something that has a value for us.
How do I reach the goal?
The motive is the cause of the valuation

1[126]

We always forget the most essential because it is what lies nearest, e.g., spontaneity while playing, the perpetual *fumbling and groping of movement.* The *consequences* of every motion instruct us.[44]

Words continuously hover before us, from which thoughts are formed. In the eye countless figures continuously — — —

1[127]

The fewest **actions** occur according to purposes, most are only **activities**, movements, in which a force is discharged. The results which emerge at the end of their course bring us with frequent repetition to the idea of cause and effect, i.e., we arbitrarily generate a representation and its valuation, and with that the mechanism is involuntarily set into motion whose result corresponds to our will.

1[128]

There are much more elevated *actors* who *play* the statesman, the founder of culture, the moral prophet (women who play the lady in waiting etc.): once one figures this out, one ceases to be vexed by them and enjoys yet another pleasure.

1[129]

The *moral* has created a very sublime form of **pleasure**-sensations. Immorality is **useful** as well as the m⟨oral⟩.

1[130]

Orient

Europe immoral,
Schopenhauer's bad taste for the Buddh⟨ist⟩ holy men — better the Brahmins
Stoicism is Semitic
Europe poor in morality

[2 = N V 2. Spring 1880]

2[1]

On the servitude of spirit (we transfer the processes of political tyranny and servitude onto the realm of spirit

2[2]

The weeping person wants others to weep with him, in this way he exercises power and enjoys himself.

2[3]

To live ethically and thus to choose the hard way of life may be good, but if from that, as it seems, the demand always arises that life must absolutely have an ethical final meaning, then we should refuse to tolerate it, for then it would be the source of the greatest impudence.

2[4]

Many make up a theory of action and speak constantly about it, but never act accordingly. It is their homage and compromise before morality (English people). In this way Catholic priests come to terms with God, their devotion is all the greater, the more godless their life is. Only *then* do they feel well. — Others also deal with that contradiction, but feel bad about it. Others have the — — —

2[5][1]

Strongly sensual humans only gain their *intellectual* force with the *receding tide* of their nerves: that gives their production its *melancholy* character.

2[6][2]

The love of one's neighbor is the love of our *representation* of the neighbor. We can love only *ourselves* because we know ourselves. The morality of altruism is impossible.

2[7]

The feminine appears in Bach religiously timid and almost nunnish; I am thinking, e.g., of some veiled chaste laments, like those of a nun (Bach's Preludes

2[8]

where we do not know what we alone actually *are capable of,* we speak of "will." The perfect insight speaks only of *must.*

We have a clear overview only of *a few* powers necessary for a deed.

Every deed (act of will) is an experiment as to whether our judgment (in the will) was correct.

2[9]

Most philosophies are devised to modify grievances for perception such that they are transferred into the world's necessity — whereas the ill humor and grievance are fugitive!

Philosophy belongs in the struggle against pain, is thus destined for demise!

2[10]

For one *single* person the reality of the world would be without probability. But for two persons it becomes probable. The other person is namely a conceit of ours, altogether our "will," altogether our "representation": and we are in turn the same in him. But because we know that he must be mistaken about us and that we are a reality notwithstanding the phantom of us he carries in his head, we infer that *he* too is a reality notwithstanding our conceit about him: in short that there are realities outside of us.

2[11]

The *imagined* world (we mostly love and hate fantasies not realities, persons).

2[12]

Description of *marriage* for the purpose of knowledge — St{uart} Mill (Comte)[3]

2[13][4]

Law of the world's dark phases

2[14]

In the living world (beginning with the plant) as much *individuality* as possible seeks to unfold itself. It is now greater than ever, on the *whole*.

2[15]

Lack of selfishness is what humanity suffers from.

2[16]

Only *moral* humans feel pangs of conscience: the misery of the immoral ones is a fiction.

2[17]

Respect, pleasure in the *diversity* of indiv⟨iduals⟩! Pleasure in the foreignness of nations and cultures is a step toward this (the "Romantic" —)

Only the fable-humanity, as it haunts people's minds, is equal and molds real humans to equality (each according to its image) This "fable" is to be eliminated!

2[18]

The fine arts and the novel are on the right path!

2[19][5]

there is much *more* morality (latent)

Mor⟨al⟩ h⟨umans⟩ affirm in emotion the morality of the *penultimate stage*, *effective* morality. This is *by far overestimated*

2[20]

Our life must become *more dangerous*.

2[21]

How can modern humans secure for themselves the advantage of *absolution*, make an end of the pang of conscience? In the past it was said: "God is merciful:" it cannot be helped, now humans must be!

2[22]

Mourning the dead — they are not unhappy! hence egoistic

2[23]

The more *insights* and reason I have, all the more belief in freedom decreases, not much choice lies open to us

2[24]

With the help of science every human can allow his originality to *progress*

2[25]

Lack of restraint in mourning as in love is the way of common souls.

2[26]

In Russia absolutism

in Germany one seeks what Richelieu {seeks} for France

in France one experiments with 25 forms of the constitution in 100 years.

2[27]

Path and entry into culture!

2[28]

A Corsican considers begging immoral, living as a bandit not; killing by vendetta even becomes moral. Pride! as standard.

2[29]

100 deep solitudes together make up the city of Venice — this is its enchantment. An image for humans of the future.

2[30][6]

Dramatic music is a means to the arousal or enhancement of affects: it does not want to give pleasure in the music itself, like music for connoisseurs and enthusiasts (chamber music)

Because it wants to convince of something *external to it*, it belongs to rhetoric.

2[31]

Through the words hovering around us we come upon thoughts. —

2[32]

Who will want to read this? God does not know, neither do I.

2[33]

Southern music. Haydn apparently felt about *Ital⟨ian⟩* opera as Chopin {did} about an *Ital⟨ian⟩* barcarole.[7] Both created music of longing by using truly Ital⟨ian⟩ music.

2[34]

Why does it seem contemptible to us that someone lets himself be flattered publicly, such as an old man by youths? Because he spits in shame's face: shame wants that such a grandiose desire as that for flattery should not be satisfied at all, or only in secret: that outsize nonsense is a disgrace to common human reason.

2[35][8]

By virtue of knowledge about pain, one can reduce it. Actual compassion only doubles the pain and is perhaps itself the source of the inability to help (in the case of the physician). — But why does the knower help? Because not to prevent an evil that one can prevent is nearly as bad as doing it.

2[36][9]

"Picturesque Morality"

Effect-morality is violent, an eruption that must repel so much accumulated immorality (e.g., cowardly surrender to unjust lords, etc.). Checking justice on a small scale, though constantly, is less pathetic *for others* and for ourselves. Similarly absolute abstinence more effective than the relatively small kind

2[37]

A dietetic prescription given and we do not follow it: immoral (because unreasonable, because harmful to oneself). But "one does not want to harm oneself": it is an illusion: self-harm

so because we do not want to harm. — But on what ⟨account⟩ do we not want to harm? — Out of habit *now* — and out of fear *originally*.

2[38]

No one knows exactly what he is doing when he begets a child; for the wisest it is a lottery game. And the human being is supposed to be *free*! even though he does not owe his existence to an act of reason!

2[39][10]

Shared knowledge of suffering —

If one truly suffers through compassion, one bears one sorrow fewer. Only if one knows about it but does *not suffer* can one act for the sake of one's neighbor like the physician.

Those who *know* about it and are glad (the gods of cannibals and ascetics[11])

2[40]

Hopefully there are still enough of those who know what an Olympian laughter is: it comes about when someone is relieved that others do not share his taste.

2[41]

Incapable of seeing blood — is that moral?!

2[42]

to yield to pain is a pleasure (Napoleon)

2[43]

Public lecturers
(against restaurants and the press.)
Decline of the theater.

How is Greek to be learned?

In the evening the soul becomes confused.
Lack of moral education, no accounting for the day.

2[44]

The second old age, the life in Hades, even with the undignified greed for life that old people have.

2[45]

How is the dehumanized human to be thought when the human is the de-animalized animal?

2[46]

People with an *unstable equilibrium*, their dangerous trifles in morals and health.

2[47]

Morality: we invest our actions with an imaginary *value* (depending upon the *outcome*) the sensation of the *no-longer-slave*! upon everything he stamps the seal of new freedom. Strongest feeling of *change* when the slave can do what he *wants*

2[48]

Fatigue unavoidable — thus pleasant!

Why states of ill humor, embarrassing, dangerous?

2[49]

Morality, *if* necessary responsibility, then only actions that have proceeded from the clearest mind, the most superficial whose motives we *can* know. "Why have I done this?" As for those that arise out of disposition responsibility is impossible, because we do not know the motives. To that extent behaving morally would always only mean behaving superficially, without passion and emphasis, i.e., "responsibility" is a showing off. Where we *feel*, we are irresponsible, hence "immoral"?

The belief in freedom *suffices*, for morality: the illusion.

2[50]

It is hard to do something offensive to those whom we revere most highly, even though in that case we would only honor their weaknesses, were we to refrain from the action.

2[51]

Shame on all parties! They falsify friendship, the purest devotion, the strongest love of truth — their perpetual activity is counterfeiting. The most important human is not far from a scoundrel and slanderer when he wants to found a party.

2[52][12]

Altruism is not intended for other *individuals* but for imaginary *equal* beings. It is impossible to help the individual because one cannot recognize it. The unrecognizable — that is one's neighbor.

2[53]

Among foreigners one can hear that Jews are not yet the most unpleasant thing that may come their way from Germany.

2[54]

Atrophy of the nerves and its philosophy.

2[55]

Mor⟨ality⟩ in the service of physiological functions.

2[56]

The "possibility of an external influence, the capacity-for-being-conditioned" does not exactly presuppose "freedom" but rather "conditionality."

Two unconditioned things cannot act upon each other.

2[57]

Perfect knowledge would not have let the concept of "freedom" arise and thus would have prevented the moral evaluation of deeds. If there were no immoral actions, there would be *no morality*.

2[58]

H⟨umans⟩ must have their daily annoyance.

2[59][13]

Those who are presumptuous out of earlier habits, who do not notice it anymore (and yet do not resemble the proud because their gestures accents, etc. are different ones)

2[60]

Some want to be taken for presumptuous, because it is still better than being taken for a poor depressed devil.[14]

2[61]

We get to know the habits and opinions of others, *not* individuals. Thus, later in life we also do not come to terms with individuals, i.e., we do not treat ourselves as individuals.

2[62]

Hard physical labor like that of porters oarsmen peasants is badly paid, the one who does it scorned. The tradesman exacts so high a price for his surplus of intelligence; even in the worst conditions higher races like, e.g., the Jewish do not easily fall on such extremely hard times as to have to hire themselves out as physical machines.

2[63]

The emotions are a physiological counterpoise.

2[64][15]

Someone who *empathizes with* something thereupon values it more highly, indeed he wants it to be restored, e.g., the religious (F. Schlegel)

2[65]

What matters is that a virtue be *attained*, *not* in what way. Good fortune should be the outcome: it is a question of learning a difficult mechanism so that it becomes as easy for us as a game.

2[66]

Each action, each thought, each impulse contributes to the happiness or unhappiness of your future; they build your *disposition*, your habits, there is nothing indifferent. Your logical carelessness will have to be repented. Disposition is the great cistern; clear consciousness is the means to having finally a clear disposition — though perhaps only in the 3rd generation.

2[67]

Moral actions are means whose purposes have been lost sight of and whose attainment is in itself now already an enjoyment.

2[68]

There is no proper organ of "memory": all nerves, e.g., in the leg, remember earlier experiences. Every word, every number is the result of a physical process and solidified somewhere in the nerves. Everything that has become organized onto[16] the nerves lives on in them. There are cresting waves of excitation where this life enters into *consciousness*, where we remember.

2[69]

Whoever now assumes an equivocal view of Christianity immediately sees himself abandoned by the best stricter nobler society.

2[70]

The conscious experience of the single individual is too short a chain and does not extend to his end.

2[71]

The vain person stops at the means to the goal and becomes enamored of it so that he forgets the purpose.

2[72]

There is so much superfluous suffering and vexation and misery in the independent classes because so few can take pleasure in the effect that they have — in consequence of a false way of life, false profession, i.e., in consequence of a superfluous dependency.

2[73][17]

Repulsive! Someone approaches us with words of praise so as to win us over, i.e., he wants to take possession of us because he believes that we will offer the one who praises an open house. But the one who praises sets himself above us, he wants to possess us — it is our enemy.

2[74]

Love of neighbor

2[75]

I confess it is pleasant that not all good thoughts on the subject are already stated in it

2[76]

no longer conscious thinking between mother and child

2[77]

the *faut⟨e⟩-de-mieux*-man[18] Dühring

[3 = M II 1. Spring 1880]

L'Ombra[1]
di
Venezia.

3[1]

Preface.

When I recently made the attempt to acquaint myself with my earlier writings, which I had forgotten, I was shocked by one feature they share: they speak the language of fanaticism. In nearly every case where there is mention of those who think differently, that bloody way of tattling and that delight in malice become conspicuous which are the emblems of fanaticism — ugly emblems, on account of which I could not have endured reading these texts through to the end, had the author been only a little less familiar to me. Fanaticism spoils character, taste, and in the end health as well: and whoever wants to restore these three together from the ground up must reckon with a protracted course of treatment.[2]

Having said that much, and at that not the most edifying thing about myself — as the custom of the preface does not in fact recommend but nevertheless permits — I may at least hope to have assured that my newest thoughts, which I share in the present book, will *not* be read *without caution.*

3[2]
1. We are more likely to perish from our strengths than from our weaknesses; for with respect to these we live reasonably, but not with respect to our strengths.

3[3]
2. At the same time one way of seeing the world is always coming to an end in us and another is growing: for our confused education acquaints us simultaneously with different ones, and each seeks to grow in our soil.

3[4]
3. We show our love of the truth most clearly in the treatment of what *others* hold to be "truths": in this way it is revealed whether we really love the truth or only ourselves.

3[5]
5. These are the descending degrees of compassion: *first*, compassion with one's own (child, product, property, wife, servant); *second*, with what we desire to possess; *third*, with what is similar to us; *fourth*, with what is familiar to us. The feature distinguishing compassion from suffering is the embitterment that our property, or something resembling property, is being harmed. The suffering of what is hostile to us is pleasant as the sign of the diminished hostile force: in the foreign, in what is dissimilar to us, almost pleasant because it seems almost hostile to us, whereas the similar and familiar arouses in us a feeling that is related to the feeling for property.

3[6]
8. A coming age, which we want to name *the colorful* and which will conduct many experiments with living, will have these properties: *first*, restraint with respect to last decisions (that is, as soon as one has recognized how these have acquired their extraordinary overestimation, they are no longer meaningful to us); *second*, the prejudice against all customs and against

everything binding in the way of customs; *third*, a greater honesty in the letting-become-visible of so-called evil qualities.[3]

3[7]

10. It is a prejudice that the appropriate diet is also that which for the human is natural and from the outset pleasant; originally, though, much likely tasted bad and what necessity urged to eat was to him "unnatural"; but in the course of adjustment attraction and pleasure entered in. And so it is with many things having nothing to do with nutrition: the first thing is the compulsion to do it: the pleasure in it is belated and often late-born.

3[8][4]

11. The presumptuous person poses as proud, but pride is precisely free of pretense (in contrast to the vain person); to this extent presumptuousness is the hypocrisy of a kind of absence of pretense, and wherever it is masterfully simulated it is confused[5] with pride.

3[9][6]

12. We still may strive for all kinds of pleasures, but should be very mindful of those which necessarily entail displeasure and exhaustion; these are, depending on the kind of human, the numbing and shattering pleasures of enthusiasm, compassion, ecstasy, wrath, vengeance or of alcohol, opium, sexuality, etc. In the end we will name and strive for as the most valuable pleasures neither the highest nor the weakest but rather the middling: that is, those that last and do not entail displeasure and yet are more intense than the weakest. To this extent Plato and Aristotle are right to see in the pleasures of knowledge that most worth striving for[7] — provided that they wish to express thereby a personal experience and not a general one: because for most humans the pleasures of knowledge belong among the weakest and stand well beneath the pleasures of the meal.

3[10]
13. Before we learned to understand physiological conditions physiologically, humans[8] believed they were dealing with moral conditions. Consequently the moral realm has shrunk extraordinarily — and will continue to shrink: just as religion in the life of the ancients was more encompassing than in the life of Catholic Christians, and as the Protestant in turn has reduced once again the sphere of religion.

3[11]
18. Nature is evil, says Christianity; should not Christianity thus be a thing against nature? Otherwise it would surely be, according to its own judgment, something evil.

3[12][9]
21. In human passions the animal reawakens; humans know nothing more interesting than this regression into the realm of the incalculable. It is as if they were all too bo⟨r⟩ed by reason.

3[13]
22. What one owns, one supports, aiding and caring; what one loves, desires, that is, wants to possess, one supports even more vigorously, because possession has not yet disappointed, not yet sated. The feeling of *love* presupposes the feeling for property.

3[14][10]
25. We can only ever help our neighbor insofar as we assign him to a category (the sick, prisoners, beggars, artists, children) and in that way *demean* him; there is no helping the individual.

3[15]
26. In Risano (Dalmatia) fallen girls were stoned; as late as 1802, the Austrians prevented such an act; at the head of a crowd the father had just picked up the first stone. In the Saharan city of Biskra each girl from a neighboring people lives for a while from prostitution in order to enrich herself thereby; the profit

is then handed over to the parents and it would be considered immoral, unforgiveable in fact, if someone did not express her piety in this way.

3[16][11]

27. Since compassion redoubles the single sorrow in the world, a hundred- or a thousand-fold in fact, it ought to be called the highest virtue in the eyes of such gods as cannibals and ascetics have.

3[17][12]

30. The faultfinder draws a line between himself and us; he is not partial to us and does not wish to take us in: he leaves free, whereas someone who praises wants to take possession of us. Let him pay heed who wants to know himself and still remain independent.

3[18][13]

32. The image of the neighbor as it always hovers before us is either the product of a fullness that demands discharge or of an emptiness that wants to be filled — it is always a physiological condition for which we have no proper and characteristic word.[14]

3[19]

33. What is new in our present attitude toward philosophy is a conviction no other age has had: *that we do not have the truth*. All earlier people "had the truth": even the skeptics.[15]

3[20]

34. How did it come to pass that, in the history of Christianity, in the end even the witty, indeed even the rich-in-spirit, went over to the poor-in-spirit,[16] among whom and from whom it was born? Christianity as a great mass movement of the Roman Empire is the elevation of the bad, uneducated, oppressed, sick, deranged, poor, the slaves, the old women, the cowardly men, on the whole all those who would have had cause for suicide but did not have the courage for that; they fervently sought a means of making their lives bearable and worth bearing, found it, and

offered the world their new kind of happiness. A happiness of such origin was the greatest paradox of antiquity; education back then was too enamored of paradox not to find it attractive. "Salvation comes from the Jews" — that was a phrase[17] against which no sophisticated ancient held out for long. "Let us then give the Jews a try" — so sounded the inner voice through which *spirit* was called to the side of the great movement.

3[21]

35. In the metabolic circuit of our bodily and psychic functions our neighbors furnish the occasional causes for furthering physiological occurrences that are necessary to us.

3[22]

37. When a person yawns — and that after all is something unpleasant — and another yawns too, then we have a simple example of the phenomenon of compassion. But would the *principium individuationis* thereby really have been breached?[18]

3[23]

38. That morality which is most strictly demanded, honored, and sanctified by everyone, the foundation of social life: what else is it but that dissimulation which people need in order to be able to live with one another *without fear*? (So that the single person presents himself as the other's equal and lets himself be used, just as he uses that other.) The greatest part of this dissimulation has already passed over into flesh, blood, and muscle; we no longer sense it as dissimulation, as little as we think of words of greeting and polite gestures as dissimulation: which they nevertheless are. The commonest kinds of dissimulation are: *first,* one assimilates to one's surroundings, one conceals oneself in them as it were; *second,* one imitates another human who enjoys respect and success, and dissembles as something higher than one is. In the first case one follows custom and becomes "moral," in the second case one follows authority and becomes "faithful": at all events one no longer arouses fear — for we have now many "peers."

3[24][19]
43. We come to know the ambitions and opinions of others before our own; those become organized onto us by long practice. When we later become more independent, we always still relate all conscious judging and acting to this acquired foundation, comparing or contesting, rebelling against it or reconciling ourselves with it.

3[25]
45. Morality and civilization seek "less pain," but not "more happiness."

3[26]
46. A heart full of valor and cheer needs from time to time a bit of danger, otherwise the world becomes insufferable to it.

3[27][20]
48. The dramatic musician[21] must, not only as poet but also as musician, be an actor and through and through an actor. This inexorably separates him from the true poet and the true musician; he is in comparison with each of them of a lesser genre. But as *actor* he can rise to brilliance and the same rank as they.

3[28]
53. In the end the one gives to his actions a presumptuous character through a kind of interpretation, the other behaves presumptuously from the beginning. The first, who doesn't rein himself in and only at the end of his action casts a glance at others, has more pride than the other, yet knows the essence of pride less well than the other.

3[29]
56. That which one does not know one cannot love, otherwise one loves something else, namely a phantom, and this is the usual. Love is certainly something else altogether than a means of cognition.[22]

3[30][23]
67. In order to fantasize about compassion, like Schopenhauer, one does not have to know it in oneself from experience. Where a person's shortcomings lie, there his ideals become fantastic.

3[31]
68. Three times Germany has exerted an influence on France; in the third century it brought savage customs and barbaric ignorance; in Montaigne's era it brought a second, belated Middle Age and religious wars; and in this century it brought German philosophy, Romanticism, and beer.

3[32][24]
70. His bright head often drove him onto lonely paths where he was rid of humans; but his heart was too anxious for this and pounded unbearably against his ribs. When he yielded to his heart, he mingled again with humans and now his head felt miserable.

3[33]
74. Everything we do for ourselves we do for the sake of others; but also everything we do *for* others we do for the others' sake. — But this is no "altruism"!

3[34]
75. Imitation, aping, is the authentic and oldest human trait — to the degree that we only eat dishes that taste good to others. — No animal is so much ape as the human being. — Perhaps human compassion belongs here, too, insofar as it is an involuntary internal mimicking.[25]

3[35][26]
77. The most bashful girls will present themselves half naked if fashion[27] so decrees, and even wilted old crones don't dare resist such a decree, as clever and good as they otherwise may be.

3[36]

78. Strength of will, which some people and cultures possess to a higher degree than others, consists in our having approximately the *same number* of ingrained internal mechanisms and valuations: so that as soon as one valued thing emerges in representation, the corresponding mechanism immediately performs its part. Other humans and eras lack such a quantitative congruence of mechanisms and valuations. They generate many more valuations from which nothing more comes than those which have an "effect," as they say. In this it is always to be noted that valuation is never the cause of an action; rather, through an old association the mechanism automatically is set in motion when a valued representation has risen in the brain: it is a regular succession, not cause and effect, as little as, for example, a word is the cause of the concept which at its sound appears in us. — Willing ages were until now always poor in thought, but this is not inevitable.

3[37]

79. The appearance of being and solidity in the individual, the appearance of voluntary actions, the appearance of an absolute character in the actions, the appearance of an absolute value of certain actions (that is, of an infinitely highest value) — these four mistakes have contributed most to the advancement of morality.

3[38][28]

80. Why religious faith can no longer stand upright has often been shown; but no one as yet has shown why faith in morality has also become unbelievable.

3[39]

81. Marriage gives occasion to different kinds of humans for different kinds of moral heroism: I do not know whether its highest value is not to be sought there. Some would not enter into marriage even with the most beloved person if the church withheld its blessing, and others, conversely, would forgo marriage

if it were contingent upon ecclesiastical confirmation; others again find an occasion for heroism in the thought that a marriage, once made, is insoluble, whereas George Sand pressed her strictest and most moral feelings into the demand that marriage *may* only last as long as the bodily union of both spouses is bound to a state of psychic rapture about each other.[29]

3[40]
82. The error in ecclesiastical absolution (and often enough in punishment by the state) lies in the fact that here once is supposed to be turned into never.[30] If the memory of guilt no longer torments, then the ingrained internal mechanism takes effect much more easily and there is no obstacle anymore to a replaying of the old song. For this reason pious adulterous women among Catholics, who daily sin and daily have themselves absolved, are no rarity.

3[41]
83. One should invoice the indescribable discomfort that productive persons so often spread around themselves when one calculates the joy and elevation that humans owe their works. Their incapacity for self-control, their envy, the ill will and insecurity of their character are as likely to make them evildoers of humanity as they might otherwise be its benefactors. Especially the relationship of geniuses to one another is one of the darkest pages of history. Veneration of genius has often been unconscious devil worship. One should calculate how many humans have ruined their character and taste in the company of a genius.[31] Great humans without works are perhaps more needed than great works for which one must pay such a price in human souls. But for the time being one hardly understands what a great human without great works is.

3[42]
84. Schopenhauer had defined his fame too early and was not proud enough to develop further against his stated principles.

He feared for his fame and preferred relative infertility to the shame of having to contradict himself.

3[43]

87. Whether one praises or blames, one becomes fearful in doing so. With blaming we wish to make ourselves feared, with praise we wish covertly to take the other in, to reconcile the other with ourselves or to align ourselves with the power we fear. — But only the rarest praise, the rarest blame is honest, that is, simply expresses our fear of a person; instead, most often we express our fear of others differently than we feel out of fear of a second person. Usually praise and blame is a form of fear crossed by fear.

3[44]

91. The morality of men diminishes with age; as children we are most moral because without fear, surrounded by love and ignorant of presumption. For that reason, the morality of women, who live all their lives in circumstances similar to children's, rather increases than decreases with the years.

3[45]

93. What we expect, we call right and proper; what amazes us, what seems wondrous to us, we praise or blame. The first feeling of amazement is fear: praise and blame are a product of fear. By contrast, the right and proper leaves us content, is for our feeling neutral and corresponds to health. — That which everyone expects of themselves and others in every situation, thus what is customary for an entire culture, is not customary though for another culture and arouses its amazement, awakens praise and blame, and is thus in any case felt too strongly. Cultures do not understand that which belongs to the health of other cultures. The expected, the customary, the healthy, what is neutral for feeling, these make up the greatest part of what a culture calls its morality.

3[46]

94. Supposing one always expects evil, the unpleasant surprise, then one is always in a hostile tension, becomes unbearable for others, and damages one's own health: such natures die out. On the whole, only the more contented and more hopeful races have survived. — Whoever always expects the bad becomes evil, that is, hostile, suspicious, restless; this is the effect of pessimistic ways of thinking.

3[47]

95. Science, which wants to abolish praise and blame, wants to eliminate surprise and lead humans always to expect the proper and right; in the end they are supposed to say to themselves, even when a volcano erupts: it is proper and right, it can't do otherwise; what is there to wonder at?

3[48]

96. Where we feel that we do something with an excess of strength, there we feel free; where the action itself delights and is not only done for the sake of a delightful purpose, there the feeling of the freedom of willing emerges: we do indeed will a purpose here, but the purpose does not entirely rule us, it only provides an opportunity for our strength to play with itself, we know there are many more opportunities for that; because we judge the purpose to be somewhat casual and slight, we do not feel ourselves its slaves, that is, we feel ourselves willing in relation to this purpose but also free before it.

3[49]

99. On people to whom much happens suddenly, whether from outside or inside, everything that can be quietly expected has a humanizing effect; thus, for example, every habit that governs them and their society: for what is habitual requires no swift action, no quick rule. Sudden impulsive action is just as semi-savage as sudden impetuous being overcome by affects; for such states the moral consists in the habitual, calm, expectant,

reflective. In other ages, where by contrast there is a surplus of these qualities, the passions and impulsive actions seem more moral; it is as if thereby the people of these times were granted a look into nature, so that they come to feel freer, bolder, more excited; they thus regard the sudden as the humanizing element, just as those earlier ones thought the opposite.

3[50][32]
101. Are there humans who admire the affects, despise reasonableness, and put ⟨aside⟩ moral valuation? Among acting humans certainly not; here and there, though, an artist will find morality and reasonableness not picturesque enough: he wants humans with strong contrasts.

3[51]
102. Moral judgments are means of discharging our affects in a more intellectual manner than happens with gestures and actions. Scolding is better than a blow of the fist or spitting; flattery (praise) better than petting or licking (kiss); the curse transfers to a god or spirit the vengeance that the animal itself takes out on its enemy. By virtue of moral judgments, the human being lightens his mood; his affect is discharged. Already the use of modes of reason affords a certain easing of the nerves and muscles;[33] moral judgment emerges in those times when affects are felt to be troublesome and gestures too crude a relief.

3[52]
103. The sudden affects are what over time makes humans ugly. Christianity unleashed the sudden affects, consequently —

3[53]
106. The common Catholic folk, who know nothing of voluntary restraint but a great deal about the involuntary kind — which is why they worship life's pleasures — see in the saint an opposite manner of acting, of which they grasp nothing: they believe in the saint, *quia absurdus est*.[34] In our Protestant lands,

where especially now moral education is almost lacking or proceeds in a completely thoughtless manner, one has nearly the same respect for the saint. One thinks of asceticism as of something superhuman, forgetting thereby that asceticism belonged to every ancient morality, even the Epicurean.[35]

3[54]
107. We do not first acquire insights into things and humans, but rather valuations of things and humans; these impede the access to real knowledge. One would first of all have to overthrow all value judgments through a radical skepticism of value in order to have a clear way ahead.[36]

3[55]
108. The fine court culture under Louis XIV required in many aspects Stoicism; many emotional storms had to be locked up in the heart, much exhaustion concealed, much pain disguised by cheerfulness. For our lazy contemporaries this way of life would be too strict.[37]

3[56]
109. It is the way of the Jews to take advantage of their chances in relation with others by stepping closely up to them while letting it be sensed that they know they are doing just that. This makes them forward; of course, we all want to be unapproachable and appear unbounded; Jews work against this individual and national fantasy of being beyond grasp and are very much hated for it.

3[57]
110. Epistemology is the pastime of those astute minds who have not learned enough and who suppose that here at least anyone can begin anew, that here "self-observation" will suffice.

3[58]
113. When despite every effort to oversee it we no longer can oversee the good that we owe to a possession, then love emerges:

an overflowing toward something boundless; love lacks knowledge of the entire value of a thing or person, because no scale is large enough to contain ⟨it⟩. One brings forward for comparison all the highest one knows; when we love, we think continuously of the highest of every kind, and because it always occurs ⟨to us⟩ simultaneously with the beloved object we also likely confuse it with that object.

3[59]
114. Instead of wishing that others know us as we are, we wish that they think of us as well as possible; we desire then that others deceive themselves about us: this means that we are not proud of our uniqueness.

3[60]
115. The stunted condition of many people is grounded in the fact that they are always thinking of their existence in the minds of others, that is, they take seriously their effects und not that which is having the effect: themselves. Our effects though are conditioned by that upon which an effect must be made, thus are not in our power. Hence so much disquiet and vexation.

3[61]
116. Dreary and bitter thoughts are not even possible without physiological causes. In order to become the great accuser of the age or the whole of life, our liver must first be prepared.

3[62]
117. Our first passionate decisions for or against, with which in our youth we give the ship of our life a direction, are usually the proofs of bad education, immature taste, and the lack of reflection in which we have lived up to then.

3[63]
121. The great full open eye belongs to the one who habitually wants to oversee much at once, such as the child who is often

astonished, the lover who would like to embrace all his happiness with his glance, the thinker who has many important things before him and wants to order them; others who think much about small things, have a focused sharp eye, they wish to see as exactly as possible, as though they were following an insect's movements, so too the suspicious. Terror looks wide-eyed because in it lies astonishment, fear changes the direction of the sharp glance very rapidly, wondering from where danger is coming.

3[64]
122. Our valuations determine our way of life (residence, profession, company, etc.), and our way of life determines how much or how little we feel a pain or a desire, not only in the finer and most spiritual matters, but all the way down to the most corporeal. Whoever alters valuations, also indirectly alters the kinds and degrees of people's pleasure and displeasure.

3[65]
123. Among the means of consolation for passionate, unrestrained characters belongs tragedy; it counsels to expect calm and inner freedom *only* beyond the world — thus it temporarily removes such natures' moral dissatisfaction with themselves, for it seems to say: not to be capable of the impossible should not cause grief.

3[66][38]
125. Everything we now call immoral was once moral sometime and somewhere. What guarantee do we have that it will not once more change its name?

3[67][39]
128. There is a comic definition of the comic: it is supposed to be, according to Vinet, the naïveté of sin.[40]

3[68]
129. Society must become so sure of itself that it can tolerate a fair amount of crime without on the whole becoming

disturbed thereby; similarly, the state must be so prudently and enduringly founded that much clumsiness and folly among its servants will not essentially harm it.[41]

3[69][42]

130. The moral judgment of humans and things is a means of consolation for the suffering, oppressed, internally tormented: a kind of revenge-taking.

3[70]

131. For a millennium it was not possible for the most free-spirited minds to imagine a non-religious form of thought; now we possess the same, but are incapable in turn of imagining an extra-moral form of thought; later humans will perhaps have this as well.

3[71][43]

132. Science continually gives commandments, for example, for health and upbringing: it justifies them by reference to the harmful effects of their neglect: so also did earlier legislators of morals justify their commandments, except that the consequences of their neglect were not supposed to be the effects of natural causes but rather arbitrary punishments from God. With respect to the consequences of actions popular morality does not know natural causality, only the miracle.[44]

3[72]

133. Anyone for whom the common prejudices do not begin to sound paradoxical has not yet reflected enough.

3[73]

134. It is to be regretted that Jesus Christ did not live longer; perhaps he would have become the first renegade of his own teaching, perhaps[45] then he would even have learned to laugh and cried less often.[46]

3[74]
135. The means of consolation devised by beggars and slaves are thoughts from malnourished, tired, or overstimulated brains; Christianity and socialist fantasizing are to be judged accordingly.

3[75]
136. *First*: to do away with punishment; *second*: to do away with sin; *third*: to do away with moral measuring and weighing.

3[76]
137. It seems that many crimes stem from the same force from which the pessimistic way of thinking stems; they are the discharge of this force in actions.

3[77][47]
138. How much sickness there still is! How much exhaustion from excessive exertion! How much evil boredom! — and in all these conditions one thinks and judges, about oneself, about one's fellow humans, about the value of all existence. Consequently: how much pessimism must there still be![48]

3[78]
139. What? The truth is supposed to be simple?[49] — the truthful person is simple, but the truth is very, very complicated.

3[79]
140. In the most extraordinary conditions humans deem themselves closer to the truth, in the highest excitations they ascribe to themselves superhuman capacities — and yet such conditions and excitations are the least suited to knowledge of an object, but in fact humans see here visions, specters, seventh heavens and hellish abysses. Thence religion, thence most metaphysics —. And science should be required to *reconcile* itself with these monstrous brainchildren of semi-madness?

3[80][50]
141. We have forgotten the wild animals: for millennia, waking and sleeping, humans thought of them.

3[81]
143. In the future there will be: 1. innumerable facilities to which we temporarily consign ourselves to have our souls cared for; here our anger will be combated, there sexual lust, etc.; 2. innumerable measures against boredom; at any time we will be able to hear public readings and the like; 3. festivals in which many single inventions are united for the total purpose of the festival, for those who celebrate a festival must have coinvented the festival; 4. individuals and whole groups will swear never to draw upon legal assistance.

3[82][51]
145. The amount of spirit humans expend in combating ills they lack in the invention of joy; that is why humanity on the whole has not advanced to a higher level than means of consolation; perhaps science will finally succeed in eliminating the monsters, and ultimately it will have to eliminate the means of consolation as well, which in the long duration of their existence have themselves become monsters.

3[83]
146. Pessimistic representations inhibit the expression of gestures, encourage dissimulation, namely that of frightening distortion (in order to arouse fear); they command the excited soul not to become audible in language, in short, they make the human ugly in gesture and sound. — Contempt along with fear make ugly.

3[84]
148. What culture now demands, not to express our emotions, is the long-term effect of fear: humans should not see what goes on inside us, which presupposes that it is always something

bad or that we thereby give good openings to our enemies. Courtly dissimulation, stoicism within a controlled decorous performance of gestures, proceeds from evil presuppositions about fellow humans: they must not get to know us, it would be to our harm.

3[85][52]
149. In order that the species-preserving drive, the behavior of parents toward their offspring, not be seen erroneously as the beginning of a whole new chain of motives, the so-called non-egotistical, let these hypotheses be introduced: the lowest species-preserving drive shows itself in that some species of fish keep watch over their eggs and ward off the enemy.[53] I surmise that here, as in other cases of the animal world, the parents consider the eggs and their offspring food that one must protect and preserve; in many cases the animals actually live on them. Those species that have most assiduously cared for and watched over this kind of food have the best prospect of reproducing, and the habit of caring for the eggs and the young is passed down ever more strongly, in the end as a powerful drive in itself whose original motive is forgotten.

3[86][54]
150. Sympathy increases when pleasurable feelings are its predominant result; it decreases when it carries with it more pains than pleasure. At the continuous sight of suffering beings compassion continuously sinks, yet one becomes the more sensitive to another's suffering the more shared joy one has. — The most compassionate humans are those who have much inner joy, they are hurt by everything conflicting; the unfortunate and the belligerent are hard.

3[87]
151. Who then has so tinted the world, so dipped it in these glowing lights? It was humans of spiritual convulsions, of the most extreme terrors and raptures, the deepest dejection: medicine

men, tragedians, saints, etc.; they were feared; one believed them because that is what they wanted, for they were terrible.

3[88]

152. Animals of the same species spare each other in multiple ways, not out of a wonderful instinct of compassion, but because they assume a similar power in each other and treat each other as uncertain prey; they seek to live on other kinds of animals and to abstain from *their own*. From this the habit is formed of leaving each other alone and, finally, rapprochement and the like. Already the intention to attract young females or males can dispose animals not to appear fearsome but harmless with respect to their own species. In chivalrous ages the male becomes all the more decorous and gracious towards all women the prouder and more fearsome he appears to all men; only so does he attract the female.

3[89]

153. That extravagant and fantastic pathos with which we have appraised the strangest actions is paid for in the absurd indifference and contempt we bear towards inconspicuous and everyday actions. We are crazy about rarity and thereby have devalued our daily bread.

3[90]

154. Most have spirit only when they are in a warlike frame of mind, in attack, fear, defense, revenge; but as soon as this state wanes, they fall into torpor. It takes a great deal of spirit to have any left for times of well-being.[55]

3[91]

155. What has existence cannot want to come into existence; what has no existence also cannot. Hence there is no will to existence. This is a bad and nonsensical arrangement of words. One could understand though: will to a longer, or higher, or different existence. — Will is the representation of a valued

object connected with the expectation that we will take possession of it. "Struggle for existence"?[56]

3[92]

156. If the old *ius talionis*[57] were not still effective, one would certainly not execute the murderer, but instead, following the tenet that honor is worth more than life, much rather the slanderer,[58] the calumniator. In the same way painful mutilation and the like are a much greater form of suffering than dying; accordingly, the cruel person would have to be executed rather than the murderer, likewise the unscrupulous doctor, midwife, etc. Finally, insofar as the author of many deaths is more pernicious than the murderer, all princes, ministers, agitators, and journalists by whom a war has been stirred up and advocated would have to be executed; I naturally mean the unjust wars, but I will be told that there are no unjust wars.[59]

3[93]

157. Moral prescriptions stem from ages in which nature, peoples, and humans were much less well known than they are now. Ignorance and false assumptions have been co-sanctified by the solemn inviolability in which morality lives.

3[94]

158. When we say: this is useful, that is harmful, this statement must prove itself in its consequences, that is, it is continually tested and accordingly refined or rejected. Conversely, if we say: this is moral — then we believe we have said something that does not need to be proven by its consequences, indeed cannot be proven. For that reason, what is harmful is preserved for so long under the label[60] "moral."

3[95]

159. Some all-too-timid statesmen may do what they will, a stain will always remain on them: as some cannot break open an egg without dirtying themselves.

3[96]
160. Life for the future — that is a consequence of the morality in which all of life, that is, the sum of all present moments, becomes a folly and hunt and inconvenience. Life for the others — a consequence of the morality in which others are arbitrarily regulated and the human himself yields without hesitation to all his mental and emotional weaknesses for the sake of his good goal.

3[97]
161. To what extent has morality had *harmful* effects? Insofar as it despised the body, in the asceticism of duty, courage, diligence, loyalty, etc. Namely in that canon mixed up with religion that the procuring-of-pleasures-for-oneself is displeasing to the godhead, the procuring-of-suffering-for-oneself pleasing. One taught to suffer, advised against enjoying oneself — in all morals (that of Epicurus excepted), which means that morality was until now a means to disturb the physiological foundation of the human in its development — it lay in the weak nature of morality that it did not destroy this foundation; it was a terrible throw of the dice in this great game of dice. We must unlearn conscience, just as we have learned it. — On the whole the great preserving force that maintained preponderance over morality was that which they called evil, the striving of the individual to assert itself without regard to doctrines, to feel comfortable, to seek its enjoyment, to subordinate proximate needs to the more distant, whereas morality not only distinguishes these as higher and lower needs but teaches to despise and often condemn the latter (the so-called sensual pleasures).

3[98][61]
162. The more the feeling of oneness with one's fellow humans gets out of hand, the more uniform humans become, the more strictly they will feel every difference to be immoral. Thus, the sand of humanity necessarily emerges: all very similar, very small, very round, very tolerable, very boring. Until now Christianity

and democracy have driven humanity farthest on the path to sand. A small, weak, gloaming little feeling of well-being spread uniformly over everyone; an[62] improved Chineseness carried to the extreme, would that be the last image humanity could offer? On the path of moral development to this point, unavoidable. A major reflection is necessary, perhaps humanity must make A break with its own past, must perhaps direct the new canon at all individuals: be different from all the others and rejoice when each is different from the other; the crudest monsters have actually been exterminated under the rule of the prevailing morality — this was its task; we do not thoughtlessly want to go on living ruled by fear of wild animals. So long, all too long, it was said: one like all, one for all.

3[99]
163. To say about everything that happens: God would not allow it, if it did not benefit me — from this heavenly childishness humanity could already have gone to ruin several times. Fortunately, there were always humans who were not Christian enough to reassure themselves so childishly.

3[100]
164. If general happiness were to be the goal of every single action, then the single person would have to forgo actually executing a single action all his life: the consideration, whether his purpose would actually correspond to the highest good of all present and future humans,[63] would consume his whole life. Christianity named the neighbor the target of our actions and left it to God to determine who should become our neighbors; anyone to whom this religious way out is not open ought to say though: with respect to the actions I execute, I do not have to put up with any neighbor as object but look for those to whom my actions are most suited, to whom they *can* actually be of service. For that of course we would have to become acquainted with our neighbor as well as with ourselves, and that could again consume our whole life.

3[101]
165. Rules for how to act are all the more beyond discussion, the more the actors' insight is subordinated to that of the one making the rules. Since besides him no one knows exactly *which* consequences he expects from the actions, those consequences which in fact follow from the rules are then also beyond discussion. Thus the religious human surrenders to God's commandment, the moral human to the moral law — an inheritance from times in which there was a chief and blindly obedient followers who saw in him their reason and without him had none.

3[102]
166. The metaphysical pessimist who flees enjoyment and security and attributes to misfortune and suffering the highest value — namely to enlighten about life's lack of value — how could he have compassion when another suffers? He could only rejoice in it, just as he would have to refuse compassion if he were in need; on the other hand, were he to find the other in a state of joy, he would be distressed for him and seek to spoil his joy — so Schopenhauer's practical morality should sound. Compassion, as Schopenhauer describes it, is, from his standpoint, the real perversity, the most profound of all possible stupidities.

3[103]
168. I cannot explain how it happens that the Jews of all peoples have brought moral dignity to its highest level, in theory as in practice. Only they have succeeded in a Jesus of Nazareth; only they a holy God, only they the sin against him. In addition the prophet, the redeemer — those are their inventions.[64]

3[104]
169. What the Romans hated in the Jews was not the race but a kind of superstition they found suspicious, and specifically the energy of this belief[65] (the Romans, like all southern peoples, were lax or skeptical in matters of faith and only took practices

seriously). What offended them in the Jews is the same as what offended them in the Christians: the lack of images of the gods, the so-called spirituality of their religion, a religion that shuns the light, with a god who cannot let himself be seen, this awakened suspicion; even more what was murmured about the Easter lamb, about eating of the body, drinking of the blood and the like. — In summa: educated people of that time thought Jews and Christians were secret cannibals. Then they were thought capable of honestly believing crazy things, the extent of the Jewish and Christian capacity for belief was for the Romans contemptible; it was the Jew in Christ who above all demanded faith; the educated of that time, for whom all philosophical systems were at loggerheads, found this demand for faith insufferable. "*Credat Judaeus Apella*"[66] (Horace).

3[105]

170. Christianity considers 1. a fundamental improvement of the human being possible without improvement of their knowledge, without improvement of their social conditions; 2. it wants abstention from the world but not advancement of the world; 3. it prefers suffering and gloom and awakens suspicion of well-being; 4. it prefers faith to knowledge and incomprehensibility to understanding and makes people suspicious of reason; 5. it ignores gender, class, ethnicity, these distinctions are inessential to it; but when these distinctions are tied to states of emergency, then it finds the preservation of these distinctions desirable for the sake of the emergencies and their salutary effects; 6. it presupposes the deep depravity of all things and humans and sees ruin as imminent; it does not want to halt this ruin, it wants to spoil the world as much as possible for itself. — Were we to imagine Christianity, taken in its full strength, as dominant, were we to imagine that no powers worked against it, then it would in short time bring about the ruin of the human race: it robs the human of health, pleasure, confidence, plans for the future of the world (thus activity). Some Church Fathers concede this consequence: they see no reproach and objection here.

3[106]
172. Christian compassion, altogether different from that of the Indians and their disciple Schopenhauer, emerges in the context of the thought of eternal damnation of the other, about God's disfavor, about the lack of faith, about pleasure in worldly things, about the abundance of devilish deceit which envelops, unbeknownst to him, the non-Christian, for example, the unbaptized barbarian: it is pity for the appearance of happiness or for the error with which the other laments his misfortune, compassion for ignorance and error then, not for pain — so actually not com-passion.[67]

3[107]
173. Nearly everywhere on earth a church, a temple stands or stood, a miracle once took place, which is to say the mushroom of sacred architecture shoots up wherever religious humans encountered a little madness. Has one ever built in a place where a great truth first dawned on a human? Probably not; but why even, such a truth wants to be criticized, not worshipped.

3[108]
175. The poet *seems* continually to open new entryways to a new or better knowledge of nature and human matters: even before we have yet quite grasped that what hints so excitingly here is a will-o'-the-wisp, another is fluttering before our senses. The similes, the metaphors of the poet are not at all given by him as such, but rather as new, until now unprecedented identities by virtue of which a realm of knowledge seems to open itself. The less has been established so far about what is really true and proven in nature, all the stronger the poet's effect is, all the stronger his dramatic art of representing for a time the discoverer of nature. The question to what extent something a poet says is true is a piece of pedantry. All its value lies just in this, that only for a moment it *appears* true, and this holds for his whole world view, his moral order, his moral tenets, as much as his parables, his characters, his stories. To want to confirm

an earnest opinion appropriate to science by pointing out that some tragedian said something similar is foolishness: in matters of knowledge poets are always in the wrong, because as artists they want to deceive and as artists do not understand at all the striving for highest truthfulness; if they by chance say something true, their authority is not suited to awaken belief, rather mistrust. It is such a delight that the drive for the will to know occasionally plays with itself and hops from one twig to another, adorned with lovely notes and colorful little feathers— and we should be fools and expect an oracle where a bird is singing and warbling?

3[109]

176. Here an action is valued because it costs the agent much effort, there because it costs him little effort; here because it is so rare, there because it conforms to the rule; here because the one judging thinks it impossible for himself, there because the one judging thinks it altogether impossible (a miracle); here because it counts as useful, there because it takes no consideration of use; here because humans care in this way for their best welfare, there because in doing it he is not concerned for himself; here because it is duty, there because it is inclination; here because it is done without inclination, there because it is instinct; there because it is utter reason — and all of that is occasionally called moral! Now one applies at once the standards of the most diverse cultures and thereby is capable of appraising nearly everything as moral or immoral, just as one wills, that is, according to our good or evil will toward fellow humans or ourselves; morality is now the great topology of praise and blame — but why always praise and blame? If one could renounce that, then one would also no longer need the great topology.

3[110]

177. Gloomy seriousness, tension, and fear are common to all passions: in them is no excess of life, indeed it seems as if there were not enough of it.

3[111]
179. Now one seeks above all to preserve human life: this lends to our culture the appearance of cowardice and of the old man's craving for long life; in earlier times, when one could lose life more fortuitously than now, it belonged to the essence of virtue that one lightly tossed life away and considered so many things as of higher worth.[68]

3[112][69]
180. Modern life wants as much as possible to be protected from all dangers: but with the dangers much liveliness, high spirits, and stimulation are lost; our crude remedies are revolutions and wars.

3[113]
181. With alms one maintains the condition that works as the motive for alms; so one does not give out of compassion, for compassion would not want to maintain the condition.

3[114]
182. Excess of force seeks conflict and thereby becomes evil; yet here being evil is only means (for the purpose of discharge)[70] and therefore more harmless than in the weak person, who is evil in order to hurt.

3[115]
183. If one wants to claim that the German was preformed and predestined for Christianity, then he may not lack for impertinence, for the contrary is not only true but also evident. How should the invention of two excellent Jews, Jesus and Saul, the two most Jewish Jews that perhaps have ever been, make precisely the Germans feel more at home than other peoples? (Both claimed that the fate of every human and all eras, before and after, along with the fate of the earth, the sun, and the stars, depended on a single Jewish occurrence: this belief is the Jewish non plus ultra.) How does the highest moral subtlety that a

rabbinical and no lazybones' intelligence honed and which first succeeded in the invention of the holy God and the sin against him, the feeling of lack of bondage and servitude in a boundlessly honor-hungry little people, its expectation of the savior and fulfiller of all hopes, the priestly hierarchy and more folksy asceticism, the everywhere palpable proximity of the desert and not that of the bears' forest — how does all that accord with the lazy but belligerent and rapacious German, with the sensuously cold lover of the hunt and beer-drinker who has not advanced farther than a middling tribal religion and one thousand years ago still had not unlearned the slaughtering of humans on sacrificial altars?

3[116]
184. Not moral decline — this was limited to five to ten cities of the vast empire — but rather the fatigue, which had set in everywhere because it was believed the goal had been reached with respect to culture and governmental forms, led the old world into the snare of Christianity; humans would rather expire than know themselves at the end; living out life to the end as life's unique purpose is an unbearable thought for them; one was tired of oneself and the world: Christianity made everything interesting again, in that it upended all value judgments and placed a court of judgment behind the end of all things.

3[117]
185. Christianity appears as an epidemic panic; it was prophesied that the earth would soon expire. Similar thoughts wound themselves around the thought of this fearsome danger — why ruin? on account of our sins? so perhaps a court of justice? and where an advocate? etc. In the end it seemed generally most expedient to appear before the place of execution in the customary ancient manner, that is, in the most miserable and pitiable condition imaginable. This picture of the ancient accused is later retained by the anchorites — they want to be ready at every moment and the idea of the judgment suddenly breaking

in caused them to think up everything through which a human being appears lamentable; like a Roman praetor, God should not endure treating such a stunted and woefully suffering being as guilty. Christianity knows only the undignified culprit.

3[118]

187. The poet lets the drive intent on knowing *play*, the musician lets it *rest* — should both really be possible side by side? When we are totally given over to music, there are no words in our heads — a great relief; as soon as we hear words again and make inferences, that is, as soon as we understand the text, our feeling for the music has become superficial: now we relate it to concepts, we compare it with feelings, and practice symbolic understanding — very entertaining! But with the deep peculiar enchantment that gave respite to our thoughts for once, the colorful twilight that extinguished the mental day for once, it is over. — As soon though as one no longer understands the words, everything is in order again: and this fortunately is usually the case; after all, in fairness bad texts are preferable to good texts because they do not draw attention to themselves and want to be ignored. — Opera wants to engage our sight at the same time, and because among the mass of people their eyes are larger than their ears, which says a good deal, opera music is directed at the eyes and is content to blow characteristic clarion calls as soon as there is something new to be seen — beginning of barbarism.

3[119]

189. A girl who sacrifices her virginity without the man having solemnly sworn before witnesses never to leave her side is not only considered imprudent: she is called immoral. She did not follow custom,[71] she was not only frivolous but disobedient, for she knew what custom commands. Where custom does not so command, a girl's behavior in that case is therefore not labeled immoral; indeed, there are regions where it is called moral to lose one's virginity prior to marriage. — The core of

the blame then concerns the disobedience, this is immoral; is this enough? Such a girl is considered contemptible — but what kind of disobedience is it that is being despised? (The imprudence is not despised.) It is said of her: she could not control herself, that is why she disobeyed custom; then it is the blindness of desire that is despised, the animal in the girl. To that extent one is also saying: she is unchaste — for with that one cannot mean that she is doing the same as the woman pledged in marriage and whom one does not therefore call unchaste. — Accordingly custom commands that the discomfort of the unsatisfied need be borne, that desire be able to *wait*. Immoral means then here the inability to endure discomfort in spite of the thought of the prescribing power. *A feeling* is supposed *to be wrestled down by a thought*, more exactly: by the thought of fear (whether fear in face of the sacred custom or in face of the punishment and shame that custom threatens). In itself it is in no way shameful, rather natural and right, that a need be *immediately* satisfied; consequently, the truly contemptible thing in that girl lies in the *weakness of her fear*. To be moral means: to be susceptible of fear in a high degree; fear is the power by which the community is preserved. — If, on the other hand, one considers that in other respects every original community utterly needs the fearlessness of its members, then it follows that what in the case of morality absolutely should be feared, must command fear *in the highest degree*; which is why morality has introduced itself everywhere as *divine* will and has retreated behind the fearsomeness of gods and demonic means of punishment: so that to be immoral meant *not* to fear the infinitely fearsome. — Of someone who denied the gods one expected anything; it was therefore the most frightening human that no community could tolerate: because he tore up the roots of fear from which the community had grown. It was assumed that in such a person the sway of desire was unbounded: one thought of every human without this fear as boundlessly evil. — Complete fearlessness though goes back to a lack of imagination; the evil human in this sense will always be a person without imagination. Good people's imagination was always an imagination of fear, an evil imagination — another kind was not yet known. Evil imagination was supposed to hold down evil desire, that was the old moral law; the constant rule of fear over desire constituted the moral person. From this emerges asceticism as the sign of morality: to be able to endure, wait, keep silent, fast — that is, for example, the morality of the Indians. — The relative security of the community derived from the ability often and strongly to set unpleasant images before the soul by virtue of which one could abstain from the immediate satisfaction of painful needs. These are images of punishments and shame, and above all, the more indefinable, more uncanny punishments of gods and spirits: whereas in secular justice the punishments' deterrent effect may not be the first thought (mainly they are a matter of fines by virtue of which a damage is to be redressed). Even the prospect of secular justice's most painful punishments, of death by torture and the like, does not remotely have the effect in savage times of the prospect of divine and spiritual punishments: back then one feared death much less than today and was practiced in and proud of the ability to bear torture; to hold one's lust for revenge, plunder, sexual pleasure in check for such reasons would hardly have been considered manly; it is different when one is threatened with madness, furies, rash, white hair, with sudden old age, with night terrors: the threat of such punishments is effective. In short, the fear on which morality rested back then was superstitious fear: *to be immoral meant to be without superstitious fear*. — The more peaceful the condition of a community is, the more cowardly its citizens become; the less they are accustomed to bearing pain, the more will worldly punishments already suffice as the means of deterrence, the more quickly religious threats prove to be superfluous. Peace then suppresses religion, imagination's vague means of fear are no longer needed; for the anxiousness before the state's familiar punishments and civic contempt is already great enough. Among highly civilized peoples even the punishments might finally become highly superfluous means of fright; already the fear of shame, the quaking of vanity is so perpetually effective that henceforth immoral actions cease. — The refinement of morality increases with the refinement of fearfulness. Now fear of the unpleasant feelings of other humans is almost the strongest of our unpleasant feelings. One would only too gladly live so that one no longer does anything but what gives others *pleasant* feelings and no longer enjoys anything oneself in which this condition is not also fulfilled.[72]

3[120]
190. We understand only the smallest part of that out of which every action is composed, and the long chain of closely interlocking nervous and muscular operations involved is even completely unknown to us. So we take action then to be a momentary act of the will, just as a Hebrew writer says of God: he commands and there it stands; that is, we make magic of it and as magicians feel free. Our ignorance plays the pleasant trick on us of preserving our pride. If what we want does not work out for once, it must be owing then to a hostile being, which, once again by magic, places an obstacle between our will and the deed. To will the good and to do what is wrong — the one puts that off on the devil, the other on sinfulness, a third sees in it punishment for the guilt of earlier stages of life: almost all interpret it morally and demonically. In short, after we gave up the savage's belief in *miracles as the rule of nature*, the same belief fixed itself on our psychological processes; here the miracle still holds as the rule. In truth, to want something means to make an experiment in order to learn what we *are capable of*; about that only success or failure can instruct us.

3[121][73]
191. Some show spirit, others conceal and prove it.

3[122]
192. Universal happiness or universal love of neighbor are *results* which *perhaps* can be attained through the continuous growth

of morality (but perhaps not!). To let nothing of human achievements lapse again and always to maintain the respective level of humanity, that is perhaps a *consequence* of universal morality (a side effect); but what drives humans to moral actions, now *is driving*, are not those results, even less these consequences, also something other than that which originally generated the recognition of moral predicates. The origin of morality cannot lie in the moral. One should not then confuse: *first*, results of morality; *second*, consequences of morality; *third*, motives for moral actions; *fourth*, motives for the emergence of moral concepts. And yet in morals up to this point one thing, the "principle," is supposed to suffice for such different services.

3[123]
193. We honor where we do not understand; for example, with old customs, with words that get spoken with a ceremonial tone, etc. But we should reserve judgment where we do not understand, so that the hollow tower of reverence not grow even higher on earth: our spiritual world still looks very Egyptian, desert and colossal pyramids in it — and in the pyramids, mostly inaccessible, a wretched corpse.

3[124]
195. Plato had to live to see the refutation of the doctrine of the Ideas by[74] a brighter and more capacious mind than he was: and the refuter had until recently been his disciple. As long as thinkers treat their insights as their products, as long as that ridiculous paternal vanity rages in them, refutation will be the philosophers' crown of thorns — how many have already had to wear it! — whereas a friend of truth, that is, an enemy of being deceived, that is, a friend of independence, should exclaim about a refutation: I have escaped a great danger, I almost strangled myself in my own noose. One can congratulate so fierce and dictatorial a tyrant as Schopenhauer that he did not guess how passing the triumph of his philosophy would be and how soon all the gems of his invention would be[75] recognized as mirages.

3[125]
196. As soon as conventional wisdom imagines it, there is one more thing between heaven and earth;[76] but as soon as a truth is recognized, the number of such things decreases and a number of putative stars fade. Not right away of course! But just as is said of stars whose light rays only reach us long after they have perished, so errors spread their radiance long after they have been refuted. Considering the brevity of a human life, one error is quite sufficient to bathe many generations[77] completely in light; when its splendor finally fades and dies, they are long since gone and have not known the ultimate bitterness there is: to see the star expire.

3[126]
197. To let an evil occur that one can prevent is nearly the same as to do it, for that reason we rescue the child at play running towards the open well, remove the stone that has fallen onto a smooth path, place upright a chair that is about to fall over — None of this out of compassion, but because we wish to avoid doing harm. We have *accustomed* ourselves to that; whatever the motives for this habit may be, we now act according to habit and no longer according to those motives.

3[127]
199. Some words of a foreign language we cannot pronounce, indeed not even *hear* correctly; some things we cannot see if we have not learned to see the parts. Speaking, hearing, and seeing must also be learned; but with our inexact observation of the learning process we believe in all three cases that good will is enough, and presuppose ill will in a young person who fails. How evil has one represented humanity to oneself by displacing its incapacity onto the will.

3[128][78]
201. Europe has allowed an excess of Oriental morality to proliferate within itself, as thought up and felt by the *Jews*.

One will not be the happiest and most prudent people if one indulges to such an extreme in the moral sphere and transposes that into the divine, the humanly impossible. They[79] have often been made captive and subjugated, they have come to know Oriental contempt for the fact that they were persistent in their faith; they have behaved toward this faith like Asiatic peoples toward their rulers, fawningly deferent and full of fear, yet not free of a craving for independence: so they developed a restless, desirous, secretly self-indemnifying imagination, the breeding ground of that sublime accusatory morality and savage heroism that makes itself known in their devotion to their commander God just as in their contempt for themselves. By virtue of its Jewish descent Christianity gave Europeans that Jewish discontent with oneself, the idea of inner disquiet as human normality; hence the Europeans' flight from themselves, hence this unheard-of activity; they stick head and hands in everywhere. Moreover, Christianity succeeded in causing the purely Oriental countertypes, the anchorite and the monk, to appear as advocates of a "higher life" in Europe; in this way it has expressed a false criticism of all other life and made what is Greek impossible in Europe. The Athenians indeed felt themselves to be the most restless Greeks: but how calm, how full of themselves and other good things they appear next to us! They knew no one above themselves and did not need to despise themselves.

3[129]

202. What then is the imagination? A cruder, unpurified reason — a reason which in comparisons and categorizations makes crude mistakes, is unsteady in tempo, and led back and forth by the affects' leadings strings: a wild and picturesque kind of reason, the mother of pseudo-knowledge and of "sudden illuminations" (where the splendor of an idea is confused with the light of truth); both reason and imagination are generative, but the latter is more easily fertilized and brings many more monsters and moon calves into the world. Reason is an imagination

which has learned by injury, by virtue of increasingly better seeing, hearing, and remembering.

3[130]

203. The universal commandment of all customs and morals declares: reflect and fear, control yourself, dissimulate.

3[131][80]

204. For the darkening of the world becoming visible at times there is the following occasion: *first*, the crossing of cultures, out of which much ugliness emerges; the constant sight of the ugly makes somber; *second*, the moral fantasy of Christianity[81] which has left human actions with only evil predicates and wanted to make a glorification of life, humans, actions truly impossible; if one may never glorify, one becomes somber; *third*, the barbaric and animal-like, which temporally does not yet lie far enough from us; *fourth*, fear of the individual and suspicion of the same because society is no longer sure of itself; *fifth*, fear of the natural which has replaced the earlier fear of nature; *sixth*, the comparison of life to imaginary beatitudes of which Christianity and the poets have spoken; *seventh*, the exaggerated feeling of responsibility[82] which does away with every indifferent, small, and harmless thing and in each case wants to have us act so that we can withstand an accuser.

3[132]

205. Has morality really given humans more happiness or unhappiness? And even when we replace happiness with "more painlessness and lesser pains," we may still remain doubtful; it is the product of those times when to harm another with deed and judgment brought a far greater satisfaction than to do someone good by those means: the age when one believed in evil divinities. The pleasure in hurting through moral judg ments always strengthened the tendency towards harmful and cruel actions and thus itself became the instigator of greater pain than moral judgment is capable of.

3[133]
206. Moral and religious judgments have this in common: *first*, the belief that they possess knowledge of human nature and human inner life; *second*, both deny having a merely local and relative value: wherever they appear they behave as absolute, perennially valid judgments; *third*, both believe in approaches to knowledge different from those that science has; *fourth*, both imagine beings that do not exist, the religious judgments gods, the moral judgments good and evil humans and the like; *fifth*, both hate examination and speak of shamelessness and worse if one wants to see them naked; *sixth*, they are each other's companion, they have allied themselves with each other in order to support themselves, and when one separates them, then never completely: the ones live on in the others.

3[134][83]
207. Polite (pretty), gentile, chivalrous, distinguished, noble, *généreux*, *courtoisie*, gentleman — this designates the qualities in the upper caste that were observed and imitated; hence a good part of morality probably derives from the instincts of *this* class, as from the personal pride and the pleasure in obedience to a superior who confers distinction; they despise downwards, they revere upwards and among their equals, but they themselves demand respect from all the world (the world above, in the middle, and the underworld), they pretend to be the better half of humankind. In German by contrast the simple man was formerly the bad[84] man: so far went the distrust of anyone who did not possess the more artificial manners and expressions of good society.

3[135]
208. Christianity (and not only the Catholic Church) continues to present itself as if it demanded everything, but it is very contented, very thankful, if it receives only *something*. In this modesty now even the best Christian is, measured by Christian standards, worse than a heathen; he wants neither to live *for*

his faith nor to die *with* his faith; he is content when both are given alms.

3[136]

209. To feel strongly, to be able to let a strong feeling last long and to play many melodies on one string — that defines the great pathetics among the great writers, to whom Schopenhauer too belongs: they are distinct from the philosophers, although Schopenhauer counted himself among these: for they do not want to know at all costs but rather to sing *their* song at all costs.

3[137]

210. Christianity *emerged* from Judaism and from nothing else, but it grew into the Roman world and sprouted fruits which are both Jewish and Roman. This cross-bred Christianity found in Catholicism a form in which the Roman element came to be predominant: and in Protestantism another in which the Jewish element dominates; this is not because the Germans, the bearers of the Protestant creed, are more closely related to the Jews, but because they are farther removed from the Romans than the Catholic population of southern Europe.

3[138]

211. Moral ideas are stimulants and spices for whose sake we more easily perform the necessary actions; without them these actions would be repulsive or boring to us.

3[139]

212. *Not* to think of the other, to do everything strictly for one's own sake is also a high morality. The human has so much to do for himself that he is always careless when doing something for others. Because so much is done for others the world looks so incomplete.

3[140][85]
213. Is not our freethinking to be understood as an exaggerated, one-sided behavior that has lost its counterweight? Is not the artist frequently thrown from his center by his artistic creativity? Are not self-concealment, self-forgetting, self-denial the dangers of the fruitful solitary man?

3[141]
214. It is seldom that someone who has become famous has not just thereby become cowardly and foolish; the followers latch as[86] a mass onto his weaknesses and exaggerations and have an easy time convincing him that herein his virtue and his destiny are to be seen. Has a great man ever been recognized by his contemporaries for that which makes him great? Has a famous man ever been the enemy of his followers? — Schopenhauer became crazed with his fame before he had it.

3[142]
218. The greatest mass of evil is done out of weakness and sickness in order to procure for oneself the feeling of superiority (by doing harm), as a substitute for the feeling of physical power. Weakness and sickness, though, mainly have their roots in ignorance.

3[143]
219. When others' pleasure hurts us, for example when we find ourselves in deep mourning, we hinder this pleasure, we forbid children then to laugh, for example. Conversely, when we are happy, then others' pain embarrasses us. What then is sympathy?[87]

3[144]
220. Equality causes each person's happiness to decrease but paves the way to everyone's freedom from pain. At the end of their goal of course the loss of happiness would stand next to the freedom from pain.

3[145]
221. Lying and dissimulation, which within the community are cultivated to produce equality, yield in the end a free surplus that discharges itself in the generation of poets and actors. Let us think how much pleasure a community takes in bragging, cursing, sleights of hand, and similar original arts.

3[146][88]
226. Love of the fatherland decreases when the fatherland ceases to be unhappy.

3[147]
227. Fanatics have indeed no moral but instead intellectual pangs of conscience; they take vengeance on all dissenters for the fact that they themselves at bottom and secretly and under a wrathful feeling of pain — think differently.

3[148]
228. Nature[89] uses the brain in order to relieve the lower body of one function and vice versa.

3[149][90]
229. There is no immediate, instinctive fear of death; one flees the pain standing at death's gate, the unknown to which death leads and which it itself is; we still want to enjoy ourselves often, that is why one wants to live, that is why one also bears suffering. The drive for self-preservation, too, is a piece of mythology.

3[150]
230. Here are humans who would like to make the whole world drunk with music and imagine culture would come then; until now though something else than culture has forever[91] come after drunkenness.

3[151]
232. Happiness lies in the increase of originality, which is why other times than ours may have had more of it. — Science is the means through which to prove the necessity of education to originality. — If descent and the *così fan tutti*[92] make for morality, then morality is the impediment to happiness. The teaching that morality is the right means for a life without pain is certainly the product of very painful times. — When originality wants to tyrannize, it lays a hand on its own life principle. To take pleasure in another's originality,[93] without becoming its ape, will one day perhaps be the sign of a new culture.

3[152][94]
233. No mythology has had more damaging consequences than that which speaks of the subservience of the soul to the body.

3[153]
237. Morality has a picturesque effect when it has been long dammed up by immorality.

3[154]
238. The intellect of present-day humans would probably suffice to create an organized solar system out of a chaos, but perhaps it lacks the necessary time for that and above all the chaos; certainly the world would be infinitely farther along if the human intellect instead of chance had been permitted to do as freely as it liked; it would also have saved billions of years.

3[155]
240. Whoever appeals to custom nowadays as the basis for their way of acting is practically saying: I am superstitious, or: I am tolerant — but previously it meant: I am prudent and good.

3[156]
241. The goal of Christian morality is not earthly happiness but earthly unhappiness. The goal of the practical Christian

who stands in the world is not worldly success but rather no-longer-having-to-act or even failure. That unhappiness and these failures are the means and steps to detachment from the world. Is there still Christianity? It seems it has already reached the end point of its detachment from the world, namely beyond the world. But before it departed it painted its scripture on the wall,[95] and this has not yet disappeared: the world is contemptible, the world is evil, the world is perdition.

3[157]
242. A reduction of moral feeling is taking place: all of this feeling's factors, which stem from illusions, from veneration where there was nothing to venerate, from the accrual of respect because criticism of the respected was missing, from the neighboring twilight of religion — all of this will gradually get subtracted and the result will be that the obligation of morality for the foolish will decline. From this arises the task to strive with every force for the decrease of the numbers of the foolish.

3[158]
243. Our present education is certainly something miserable, a fetid bowl in which nothing but insipid chunks float in a jumble, chunks of Christianity, of knowledge, of art, on which not even dogs could eat their fill. But the means of opposing this education are hardly less miserable, namely Christian fanaticism or scientific fanaticism or artistic fanaticism from people who can hardly stand on their own legs; it is as if one wanted to cure a lack with a vice. In truth, though, present education appears miserable because a great task has arisen before it on the horizon, namely the revision of all valuations; but that requires, even before all the things can be laid on the scale, the scale itself — I mean that utmost fairness of the utmost intelligence which has in fanaticism its mortal enemy and in the present "well-rounded education" its ape and master of ceremonies.

3[159]
245. If in every place where the Christian imagines his God at work we replace God with chance, then we get an overview of how much the Christian in the sum of his action empties the world of spirit and exposes it to chance (for example, when in illness he refuses the doctor). Religions have *extended* the realm of chance, that is, they have limited spirit's time and power. — As long as we act morally, we allow the chance that we were born in this country surrounded by these humans to become a law for us and withhold ourselves from spirit, which only seeks the individual best.

3[160]
246. We mayflies do not want to behave all too dangerously and anxiously with our thoughts; with them, after all, one can no longer bring the soul of another into eternal danger — which the Middle Ages believed. The principle of freedom of thought and the press rests upon unbelief in immortality.

3[161]
247. Whatever the level of civilization, the condition of society, the degree of knowledge may be: for the individual a kind of *happy* life is always possible — that is what religion and morality want to show him from near at hand and recommend. Whether the feeling of happiness, and of the same unmixed with sorrow, really *grows* with the increase of knowledge, improvement of the social condition, easing of life, is to be doubted; for with this growth powers are always lost or weakened to which the erstwhile feeling of happiness was primarily owed: the security and extension of life, on whose attainment the modern world prides itself so much, have perhaps been purchased rather through *decrease in the feeling of happiness* than through increase. To promote culture *for the sake of the happiness of individuals* — that would accordingly be a very dubious and perhaps foolish thing! — but if we are ever somehow in a state of happiness, *then we cannot do other than* to

advance culture! The new high level of self-confidence, satisfaction in our strength, cessation of the fear of others, longing for their closeness, wrestling with them in a good sense, the surplus of wealth, tools, children, servants of which we become aware — in sum: every kind of feeling of happiness drives us into the paths of higher culture and on them forward. Need, by contrast, causes us to regress, makes us defensive, distrustful, in morals superstitious and overly rigorous. Culture is the gradual *consequence of the happiness of innumerable single persons*, not the intention of these single persons! — The more individual the single person becomes, the more productive for culture his happiness will be, even if its duration should be shorter and its intensity less and more refracted than the happiness on lower levels of culture. If one wanted to deny promotion of culture to the happy person in order to maintain happiness in general at a high level, that would be as foolish as forbidding the silkworm[96] to spin for the sake of silkworms' happiness. What *do we have* from happiness of every kind, if not just the obligation to make something of it for the best of culture? — Happiness can*not* at all be maintained, neither high nor low, if one wanted to thwart its necessary *expressions*. Hence: culture is the *expression of happiness*. —

3[162]
248. The emergence of the categorical imperative is nothing significant. For certain most prefer an unconditional order, an unconditional commandment to a conditional: the unconditional allows them to leave intellect out of the game and is more suited to their laziness; often it also suits a certain tendency to persistence and pleases people who boast of their character. In general, it belongs to the realm of blind military obedience to which humans have been bred by their princes: they believe there is more order and security when the one rules absolutely, the other obeys absolutely. So we also want the moral imperative to be categorical, because we believe that in this way it best serves morality. We want the categorical imperative: that

is, an absolute lord should be created through the will of many who fear themselves and one another: it shall exercise a moral dictatorship. Were it not for that fear, no such lord would be necessary.

3[163]
249. The works of German genius do not keep well when they travel abroad: like Italian wines they must be drunk on the premises.

3[164]
250. It is the European form of moral idealism to poeticize moral ideas so loftily and refinedly that when humans look back from them upon their deeds, they feel humiliated. This[97] kind of idealism agrees excellently with a profit-seeking, ruthless, ambitious life; the[98] minute of humility is the advance payment for a life that has nothing to do with that idealism.

3[165][99]
251. What have philosophers not fantasized about the happiness of those who have overcome the world! What wonders did Schopenhauer talk himself into about that condition in which the human is no longer inconvenienced by his sexuality.

3[166]
253. Presence of mind: that is, the ability ⟨to⟩ allow one's words and actions to be dictated by circumstances — thus an ability to lie and to be hypocritical.

3[167]
254. When the lie matches our character, then we lie best.

3[168]
257. There were gods who willed misfortune, others who protected against misfortune, still others who consoled in misfortune.

3[169][100]
259. Where morality is at its greatest, there intellect perishes. The assumption that our neighbor deceives us where he can, keeps our mind in a state of tension, and this can happen with mischief, as in Italian cities, without our bearing a grudge against the neighbor.

3[170]
260. Honesty demands that instead of indefinite moral words of noble sound, as they usually are, we mention only the recognizable and dominant elements in the mixture by name, despite the fault of incompleteness and despite the fact that these dominant elements sounded evil until now; but at least in this way a false halo is destroyed. A thing should be named *a potiori* and not *a nihilo*.[101]

3[171][102]
261. How should one act? So that the single person is by all means preserved? Or so that the race is by all means preserved? Or so that through our race another race is by all means preserved? Or so that as much life as possible is preserved? Or so that the highest species of life are preserved?

3[172]
262. The perfect morality is that of justice, which gives to each thing its own and knows nothing of reward, punishment, praise and blame. In every complete cognition this perfect morality is realized, every exercise of cognition is an exercise of this morality, and if even cognition concerns itself with the most dangerous critique of moral actions, it is nevertheless far removed from undermining it. In the moment when a cognition occurs, the cognitive subject is morally absolutely perfect; in a deficient cognition moral faults are usually involved, such as impatience, injustice, envy, arrogance. — But let us not conceal it from ourselves: there is none other than deficient cognition!

[4 = N V 3. Summer 1880]

4[1]
263. The people, or more precisely the few people accustomed to visiting the theater, take it as a fable and offer the most solemn assurance that it is nothing less than myth, and all serious, and not without philosophical secrets

4[2]
264. We require of music that it should be *fairy tale-like*, strange, incomprehensible: earlier times had no idea of this kind. Certainly festive merry sociable heartfelt solemn! but — — —

4[3]
265. Every age has its storyteller of Thousand and One Nights. Ours is now Wagner; they are things that one does not believe, does not think possible — but very much enjoys seeing in the theater once in a while as if they were true.

4[4]

Moral Prejudices.

4[5]

WHAT IS TO BE UNLEARNED.

4[6][1]
2. All progress by individuals is rendered useless again by the chanciness of marriages, for which reason humanity is a lost cause. And supposedly God binds marriages!

4[7][2]
7. Illusions have also bred *needs* in people which the truth can*not* satisfy.

4[8][3]
Byron says, "if Coleridge had not *spoiled* his fine talent with transcendental philosophy and German metaphysics, he would have become the greatest poet of his time"

4[9]
10. In cultivated times moral regulations become more and more indefinite, just as the idea of God becomes more and more faint. More and more ground is wrested from morality (wherever success becomes controllable and cognition sets in, the moral standard leaves off). There morality flees into the "ideal," etc.

4[10]
11. How much illusion the human needs in order to live well!

4[11][4]
12. Where we no longer understand we become solemn. This benefited morality.

4[12][5]
How should one act? *To what end* should one act? But the more ambitious, the more *arbitrary* the decision becomes: all the more must it be *made* artificially authoritative. Making ends and means pathetic, the less clear they are in themselves.

4[13][6]
21. The *proof* for morals does not lie in their consequences but in the accidents affecting a community. When they are struck by misfortune, they believe they have either committed offenses or must adapt themselves to new customs.

4[14]
23. Custom does not apply to him who is outside the community. Here fear of the individual, compassion for the individual, appears. Within the community he who suffers is the object not of compassion but of suspicion that he has probably done wrong. Illness is demonic. — Toward the enemy compassion emerges on the basis of contempt, a person not to be feared.

4[15]
24. The virtue of Buddhists is: to add to your own suffering another's suffering (while all is filled with suffering). The virtue of Christ: to take the punishment of sin upon himself, and the virtue of the Christian: to suffer *voluntarily* following his example (not compassion —) These are the beginnings of morality with the purpose of *individual consequences.* This is progress. The **superstition** that guilt can be *redeemed* through suffering — a mysterious event, not deterrence, not revenge, rather purgation from the stain. —

4[16]
25. That new morality arises when the community and state no longer live in fear of enemies and *morals slacken*, i.e., the individual, the immoral, emerges. Now the *individual consequences* are moved into the foreground, the superstitious ones at the head.

4[17]
28. Two individual moralities, a) one lives in order to become fully *like* the type envisioned by the community ("like one's father," Spartan saying) or b) one lives in order to distinguish oneself among one's peers. In the first case differing from the type is something perceived as a defect, and the objective is difficult. In the second case similarity is thought of as easily achievable, it does not yet confer honor.

4[18]
29. In Germany we have unbridled respect for immature and uncultivated talents, we call them "geniuses"; we are very susceptible to spirit's picturesque effect, it is the taste for the wildly romantic. Perfection, grace and freedom of the spirit are not "enjoyed" — we speak there of esprit, etc.

4[19]
30. The madman, the cripple as *jester*. Don Quixote's frightful example. Hephaestus on Olympus.

4[20]
32. A thing's value is augmented when its veneration accumulates, i.e., when we lose sight of its use to the individual and envisage *how many* individuals it has served very well (or seems to have). It is now credited with more powers —

4[21][7]
33. The *naïveté* among the Germans! Even though all those uncultivated talents have put on an act with that! In France it was ruined by the court, in Germany by the geniuses (even Beethoven)

4[22]
The problem in the time of the Greek tragedies was: how could these *gruesome* things actually happen when their perpetrators were heroes and no criminals? This was the great exercise in Athenian psychology.

4[23][8]
The propensity to hideous topics: rape, incest, etc. — to what end?

4[24][9]
Awkward gestures and dismissive words are felt as an insult when someone would like to speak from the deepest feeling, e.g., "don't pay me any compliments."

4[25]

The woman who murders her child acts out of fear of disgrace and makes the greatest sacrifice to that fear. If society did not despise and revile, the child would remain alive. Adam Bede.[10]

4[26]

Concealment of the deed as *moral* originally — for society it should be done away with: just so concealment of the wrongdoer.

4[27]

Morality's value can only be defined by *measuring* it against something, e.g., against use (or happiness); but even use must be measured against something in turn — always relations — absolute value is nonsense.

4[28]

Reason as *cause* of moral feelings — and the influence of moral feelings *on* the *development* of *reason*!

4[29]

The form of address "sir" shows how much *all* humans are flattered by submission and how each wants above all to be considered *proud* and dominant.

4[30]

Schopenhauer, so far removed from negation, was yet decent enough never to feign it and not to turn it into finery, which ambitious artists do right off because they hope thereby to gain an advantage. Playacting with ascetic and miraculous subject matter surely is a *piece of personal* hypocrisy.

4[31]

Rhetoric an art like architecture — function is the first norm (and as soon as it is *recognized* as art, it suspends the effect of its function or puts it into question. Or the reverse?) We are not supposed to *think* about the function but be unwittingly led to the point where it is useful to us.

No! The *rhetorician* and the *actor* are to be compared: 1) aims at an effect 2) represents an effect.

4[32]

Shakespeare and Aeschylus, the many-sided dramatists, *bow* before the one-sided[11] higher humans, the poets of their time. Goethe bows before Shakespeare — *not* before the theater-poet but rather, as a follower of Rousseau, before the *nature-infinity* in him.[12] It is a period taste.

4[33]

Alas, the human intellect! Alas, "genius"! It is not so very much to have created a *Faust*, a Schopenhauerian philosophy, an Eroica![13]

4[34]

To be *just* — nothing! Everything fluid! In order even to *see* we need planes, limitations!

4[35]

The fact is the eternal flow. The state endeavors to make out of its citizens something of lasting character, morality something stable out of each individual — *Memory* is the basis for this apparent stability (from day to day, from generation to generation), *contempt* for change *taught*.

4[36][14]

The blind mole descends from the one that sees well — effect of darkness on ocular nerves.

4[37]

In morality even the era of hypotheses has not yet occurred: it is now to be endorsed; the range of possibilities from which morality *could* have its beginning is to be exhausted now by imagination. I am making the start; very skeptically!

4[38]

Someday "*inheritance*" will just be considered another hideout for obscurity and mythology: for the time being it still counts for something.

4[39]

The way in which the h⟨uman⟩ *depends* in spirit on his fellow humans is very *paradoxical* and not at all self-evident.

4[40][15]

Goethe prided himself on how much effort was required in order to resist Voltaire's view of nature.[16] — He was in error, and that marks him as reactionary.

4[41]

In Schopenhauer genius's homage to the good was a nice pose.

4[42]

The human, astonishingly fearful, attempts something new only by necessity. If it succeeds, he repeats it until it becomes a custom, and pronounces it sacred.

4[43][17]

Will contemplative people not necessarily misunderstand the active? Can much insight be expected from them with respect to history? But there are *active people who have returned*: this is their business.

4[44][18]

The greatest happiness, as Plato and Aristotle recognized, does *not* lie in intuitive knowledge (Schopenhauer's ingeniousness), rather active dialectical understanding is the source of this happiness — Besides, these are subjective judgments that herein lies the greatest happiness — but I am thankful for such subjects.

4[45]

Humans living in solitude often torment themselves to an astonishing degree over their character: but ⟨it⟩ is not character, rather solitude, from which they suffer. Let anyone who does not wish to accept this go back into the stream of the world where "one's character is formed": whereas solitude consumes it. Let us become accustomed to intercourse with the dead; that preserves character. No, one should only enter into solitude with a *formed character* — not too early!

4[46][19]

To relinquish the world *without* knowing it, like a nun — this yields a fruitless, perhaps melancholic, resigned solitude — but *vita contemplativa* should have nothing of renunciation, instead it should be the choice of such natures for whom the *vita practica*[20] would be a renunciation, renunciation of themselves.

In the end the *vita contemplativa* does not need to be *solitary*: even conceivable in marriage.

4[47]

Seen in the mirror, someone who has drunk strong coffee does not only look livelier, but he also sees his image more spiritedly (sees more of it than otherwise)

4[48][21]

To prostrate oneself before a god, to put oneself at his mercy, even to be blissfully happy about his alms, to fawn on him like a dog — that has qualified as the *highest task* of humanity! As a result, *love* as a *moral principle* has for all time become somewhat suspect. What once was given to a god, that now to a genius, a prince; a woman — —

4[49][22]

For me Richard Wagner wears — too many fake diamonds,

4[50]

It is not the non-egoistical action that has emerged (through forgetting) from heredity, but the **continuous** *thinking of others* as the measure of our actions.

4[51]

We do so much for the sake of others, nearly everything, that the actions in which we think uniquely of ourselves are exceptions: *egoists* are the greatest exceptions.

4[52]

Even the (Chinese) virtue of politeness[23] is the result of the thought: I do others good *because* that then benefits me — yet so that this *because* has been forgotten. But benevolence does *not* arise in the stated way through forgetting. — Politeness, though, is still a neighboring concept. The Chinese have *realized* a sense of family (children *toward* parents[24]), the Romans more that of fathers to the family (duty

4[53]

κρεῖττον τ'ἀγαθὸν ἀληθείας,[25] say the neo-Platonists,[26] i.e., the useful is more useful than the truth — naturally. If the preservation and advancement of happiness is the ultimate task, truth may have to take care how it will withstand error in the contest with it. In the end though humanity will have to *adapt* itself to the truth, as it adapts itself to nature, although an omnipresence of loving powers may have been a *pleasant* belief. Then there will be much *less* deceptive hope and disappointment and the occasion for *solace* rarer than now.

4[54][27]

Philosophers now as window-dressers of science, they arrange nature to great effect.

4[55]

Tenets: there are no purposes in nature, there is no mind except among humans and human-like beings, there are no miracles and no providence, there is no creator, no lawgiver, no guilt, no punishment.

4[56][28]

Luther denies that God might take pleasure in "the celebrated spiritual works of the saints" — somewhat malignant. Only in the 10 Commandments.

4[57][29]

(Baum⟨ann⟩ 243) Luther: to have something that the human heart may *trust* in everything, i.e., to have a *God.* According to Thomas Aquinas the human, on account of the defects he feels, needs a higher being to which he can subordinate himself and which can help and lead him: God.[30] — Both believe there must be a God because humans *need* him. So too Fräulein v⟨on⟩ M⟨eysenbug⟩, life would not be endurable if everything ultimately had only a physical meaning. In truth it is the converse: **because** we are used to believing in God or the ethical meaning of existence, we presume "the human being" needs them, otherwise it is not possible to live. — Besides, from that would follow at most "*necessary* representations" — which would not make a God or the ethical meaning of existence necessary.

4[58][31]

Among *contemplative* natures, 1) the religious have done the most to make life difficult for practical humans; 2) artists are usually intolerable as persons, and this should be subtracted from what is gained from their works; 3) the philosophers were something of both kinds with the dialectical mixed in, through which they became boring for the practically minded; 4) the thinkers — — —

4[59][32]

Luther vented his rage on the *vita contemplativa*, after his monk's life had miscarried and he felt incapable of being a saint; vengeful and opinionated as he was, he went over to the side of the *vita practica*, the farmers and blacksmiths.[33]

4[60]

I believe that many of us, if with their abstemious, temperate morals their meekness their sense of justice they could be transplanted to the semi-barbarism of the 6th–10th centuries, would be revered as saints.

4[61]

Alas, the *deep humiliation* that seizes me when I hear the spa society speak, or enter a dining room full of young men, or take a newspaper into my hands.

4[62]

Let us suppose that a good physician came among savages and allowed himself to be treated as a sorcerer, how far superior would he be to all sorcerers! Just so every good historian now to each prophet![34]

4[63]

Purposes are most often unintended but very desirable outcomes with which we retrospectively justify before reason our way of acting.

4[64]

Not to let perish something that has existed for a long time — a cautious practice because all growth is so slow and the ground itself so rarely suited to planting. To *bend* the existing powers to different effects!

4[65]

Theatrical music (— not "dramatic music") ruins musical taste, just as theater itself impairs pleasure in poetry (missing are solitude, nature, true life surrounding us, it is an extravagance and an assembly of idlers), without atmosphere.

4[66]

The mixed *impure* character of artists: ambitious and ruthless, in furious rivalry with everything that is esteemed, yes, everything that is sound and estimable, and unhesitating with respect to the means, calumnious, vicious — entirely like *Napoleon*, but with *him* we feel we are in an honest atmosphere, because he knows what he wants and is not deluded about himself. Speculation on the masses, on enthusiasts of every sort, this fear of the mind and of moral⟨istic⟩ science (Napoleon did not suffer talk of any kind about de Tracy and Cabanis[35]) — everything that would offend the best followers' and fanatics' instincts gets scented out and discredited, branded as object of hatred even in the *art motif*, and the reverse: fanaticism, the mortally furious love preached *through art*. Totally content in their own lives, they profess the most extreme fanatical *virtues* (like chastity, holiness, unconditional loyalty) — in this way everything becomes a school for fanaticism, art, opinions, followers.

4[67]

All morals and laws are aimed at planting *habits*, i.e., at abolishing the question of why? for a great many actions, so that they are done instinctively. In the long run this is a great *encroachment on reason*. Then "acting out of habit" is acting out of convenience, on the next impulse, at the same time a fear of the unusual, of what others do, an *encroachment upon the individual*. To breed a race with strong instincts — that is what a morality wants.

4[68][36]

"Moral feelings" the Germans say, "moral judgments" the English. "Compassion" does not belong for St{uart} Mill, e.g., among the moral phenomena, rather among those of "amiability," it is the stuff of "sympathy"; and the chief Stoics even labeled it immoral. For the feelings there is no "thou shalt," rather only "I must": but what becomes of duty when the human tells himself, "I *must* do this whether I am supposed to or not," "I *can*not do otherwise."[37] The German admires this, in Luther, for example: *not* how someone forces himself, bows *under a law*, rather how *despite* every commandment and prohibition someone is true to *himself*, i.e., in Germany *individual* action *is admired*, likely because for the timid and obedient German it is so rare.

4[69]

If I say: "I like this person, I sympathize with him," according to Schopenhauer that is supposed to be moral! And antipathy again the immoral — as if one did not for *the same* reason feel sympathy for the one person and antipathy for the other! As such the moral person would necessarily be immoral! — On the contrary, having-sympathy-and-antipathy has *never* been accounted to morality, it is a kind of *taste* — and Schopenhauer wants us to have the taste for *anything that lives*? That would have to be a very crude and raw voracious taste that is content with everything!

4[70]

When an idealist in practical affairs is not by instinct a skeptic, then he becomes vanity's fool and, in the end, takes himself for the son of God.

4[71]

It is the human's interest to name what he has wrested from his own self-interest and sacrifices to the general best interest with the highest possible language; those who sacrifice little insist most strenuously on pompous moral oratory. The one to whom it comes naturally wants it to be spoken of *in simple terms*, possibly a bit too modestly: in that way it does not catch anyone's eye and can be practiced *quietly*. The best have an interest in diminishing the moral value of words.

Others require moral, exalted attitudes, those semi-actors whose worth lies in what they *signify*, not in what they *are*.

4[72][38]

When a person whose life is filled with adultery and lewdness glorifies chastity, he has every reason to do so: for with it his life would have been more dignified; he knows Eros as nothing other than a wild insatiable and dissolute demon. But to him for whom it is something else (for an Anacreon), for him chastity is also nothing so honorable in itself.

4[73]

Just as nature does not proceed according to purposes, so the thinker should not *think* according to purposes either, *i.e.*, not want to seek, prove or refute anything, but, as with a piece of music, *listen*: he takes away an impression, *according to how much* or *how little* he has heard. This impression emerges from a comparison of impressions from music one has previously received, one has to understand this kind of language; the more refined the understanding, the *greater* the *pleasure* **and** *displeasure* in it. The crude person enjoys life like music *of every sort, essentially as enjoyment* and *pleasure*. — The *refined* art pleasures as well as the more refined insights must be paid for *dearly*, i.e., too often by enduring disappointment, discontent. — The quantity and frequency of musical enjoyment diminishes with the refinement of taste — is this a *counterargument against* music's development and its cultivation? And is it not so with everything, with cognition as well? In what kinds of things does the child not take cognitive pleasure? And how greatly!

4[74]

We should not be astonished if someone were to teach that until now no human has recognized the motive for his actions for since time immemorial an acquired *pseudo-motive* has embedded itself within the real motive. We *see* and *hear* so *poorly* and are moreover so *conceited*!

4[75]

The many cares and vexations of the educated classes, indeed of the most sublime minds —

4[76]

Those drives which stand *in opposition* to the *scorned* ones are designated the *higher* drives. But we scorn what instills no fear, what is to be expected from common people, etc. — Quite different things have been accounted to *higher* humanity, opposed things.

4[77]

The morality which initially does *not* at all consider the happiness of individuals but rather fears it and seeks to dampen it (the Greeks' "measure") wants something that extends beyond the individuals' time, the union of successive generations, namely from the standpoint of the community: the individual is the scapegoat for the collectives "state," humanity, etc. "Only *as a whole* can we preserve ourselves," that is the basic conviction. That is how old men and sovereigns think who want to hand down the community secure to their descendants. "Virtue" here is not a mark of distinction but rather the requisite rule which garners no praise (as in military organizations) *Individual* distinction is only first discovered in Greece, in Asia there were only princes and legislators. Morality for individuals *despite* the community and its statutes begins with Socrates.

4[78]

When morality prescribes valor, loyalty, abstinence outside of marriage, it does not consider its purpose to be the single person's happiness, their mental and bodily health: rather, it sacrifices these to the general good. For morality the slighter humanity of a multitude has a value which it does not hesitate to pay for with the higher humanity of a single person: just so with respect to health, happiness. It thereby proceeds from very unscientific presuppositions about the *means* through which a multitude arrives at happiness, health, continued survival: often enough it errs. The *modifications* of morality are proofs that they have erred and feel it.

4[79]

All moralities thus far have proceeded from the prejudice that we know *for what purpose* the human being exists: hence knows his ideal. Now we know that there are many ideals: the consequence is the individualism of the ideal, the denial of a general morality.

4[80][39]

Many humans are capable only of a very *slight happiness*: it is no objection to a morality that it cannot give them more happiness, as little as it is an objection to medical care that some cannot be cured or are forever ailing. — We need to choose the view of life with which we achieve *our* highest measure of happiness: which may still be very small.

4[81]

By what means have aristocratic families preserved themselves so well in all ages? By the fact that in marriage the young man did not seek first of all sexual satisfaction and so let himself be counseled in the matter and *not* get carried away by *amour-passion* or *amour-physique*[40] into contracting unsuitable marriages. First, in matters of love these were *experienced* young men who got married: and then they had to consider social standing, etc., in short, had to think more of their dynasty than themselves. I am in favor of breeding moral aristocracies again and of conceding a degree of freedom outside of marriage.

4[82]

There is neither action nor way of thought that would be *moral in itself* without respect to what in a country and people is considered custom. Of course, it would be possible for a philosopher to persuade the people of a country to feel differently: thus, to believe in "the moral as such." With that this way of thinking (belief in the moral) has become custom: i.e., here an error qualifies as moral commandment.

4[83]

Cunning deceit breach of promise murder cruelty with respect to community *foes* — is considered virtuous: frequent treatment of foes as distinguishing and glorifying.

4[84][41]

With the supposition of an individual *eternal* life the individualism is extreme, it knows no concern for existing communities, every consideration is meaningless in relation to an eternity: no compromise, no clemency, not a line's width is to be conceded when it is a matter of *that*. Here the *fanaticism* of the individual is at its *height*: on the other hand, we with our 70 years may be milder. What does it finally matter if someone suffers for 70 years!

4[85]

To set up an *ideal*, to place it first, as introduction? Undisturbed in eternal rest, to have an effect through one's example, not through active intervention, not to let oneself become conspicuous, to wish to live not for long but individually, to distinguish oneself through no virtue, at home with no custom, without a fatherland, lightly tied to needs, not carping or disparaging, but *brave* everywhere and always, in recognition acknowledgment, and therefore conciliatory in the deed, without motive, disinclined to grandiloquence and moral judgment, not to be angry at those for whom some of these insights are too ugly and therefore do *not* wish to accompany us farther

— perhaps they are more refined natures, and bravery is no virtue, rather a matter of temperament —

4[86][42]

History appeared as a *reactionary* power after the Revolution (see St{uart} Mill on Coleridge[43]). And now? —

4[87]

The natures who have most vigorously *resisted morality* (surely the individuals!) must still await their *homage*. Thus far *progress* has been seen only on the other side.

4[88][44]

This reflection is not written for —. Cordial and refined participation in human affairs without becoming obtrusive by giving advice.

4[89]

That effect of "redemption" exercised an illusion: enough that a *representation* is capable of giving the human a victory over his adherent, inescapable being and of letting him triumph.

4[90][45]

Humans could be *sized up* according to the level of happiness *possible* at all for each: then again, how much happiness he is *capable* of sharing, how much discontent and misfortune, etc.

4[91]

Humans want to be *active* even more than happy. Hence anyone who gives them something to do is a *benefactor*. The escape from boredom! In the Orient wisdom has come to terms with boredom, a feat so difficult for Europeans that they suspect such wisdom of being impossible.

4[92]

Music's effect on hysterical persons of male and female gender can be enormous and completely unrelated to the composer's achievement. Elemental effects frequently appear in Wagn⟨erian⟩ music. The limits of the pure elements of m⟨usic⟩ are not yet known (mountain air beauty

4[93]

Conscience, insofar as it has essentially produced dull sensations, counts among the scourges of mankind.

4[94]

Note how, for instance, a sudden downpour affects different persons: each interprets the event according to mood and temperament. Our sensations of *pain* only seem to be *weaknesses* of the organism: the same stimuli induce pleasure. There is *nothing in itself unfortunate.*

4[95][46]

"The eye can never have been brought forth by the faculty of seeing." Semper.[47] NB. "A *color* is never brought forth by natural selection or adaptation, instead always only a *shading*, disposition of colors" Semper[48]

4[96]

The inclination to trace all highly valued things and conditions back to a yet higher cause still rules: so that the world of higher things is a reflection as it were of a still higher one. The *depreciation* of a quality seems therefore to come more naturally to humans than an enhancement: "what is perfect cannot *become*, but only perish" is an ancient hypothesis. Recollection of an earlier, better world (pre-existence), or paradise in the beginning, or God as the cause of things — all this presupposes the same hypothesis. "God coming into being" is the mythological expression for the true course of things.

4[97]

"Brain in the foot," mollusks in part: ear in the tail, crustaceans[49]

4[98]

Desensualization[50] in morality and praise of holiness is a lower level than the Hellenic call for moderation. Oriental debauchery cannot help itself. Negation of the world is the consequence of the arrogance of such natures. — Instead of ruling, rather *annihilate* so that there is nothing left to rule: means of the most extreme danger.

4[99]

It is completely false to claim that great minds essentially have judged existence and the human *equivalently*: to prove this equivalence ⟨one⟩ proceeds from the belief that geniuses stand closer to the essence of the world and to that extent ought to say more accurately, i.e., more uniformly what it is. *But* the geniuses have had *individual* points of view — and have transported themselves into these things: which is why they deeply contradict one another and always believe they must annihilate all others.

4[100]

There are so many moralities now: the single person arbitrarily chooses the one most useful to him (for he is afraid of himself), i.e., he must *embrace* the *error*, according to the degree to which he is a dangerous animal. Long ago when people of one race were *alike*, *one* morality also sufficed.

Now humans are very *unlike* one another! There are more individuals than ever, let's not be mistaken! They are just *not* as picturesque and crudely visible as in the past.

4[101]

Since there are more individual standards than ever, so too is the *injustice* likely greater than ever. — The historical sense a mor⟨al⟩ counterforce. Hurting through judgments is now the greatest beastliness that there still is. There is no *general* morality anymore, at least it is becoming increasingly weaker, just so the belief in it among thinkers.

There are enough humans who live *without* morality because they do not need it anymore (like those who live *without* physician, medical care, painful procedures because they are healthy and have corresponding habits)

To live in a consciously moral manner — presupposes fallibility and its pressure and consequences, i.e., we have not yet found the conditions for our existence and are still searching for them.

For the individual, *as long as he* is *no thinker*, morality has a *limited* interest: as long as he is not content, not inclined toward equanimity, he reflects on the causes and seeks moral ones, for as a poorly educated person others are unknown to him. To *shove* the faults of one's constitution, one's character, into morality, to want to be *guilty* of one's disease — is **moral**!

4[102]

When a person has established the customs with which he tolerates his surroundings and his surroundings him, then he is *moral*. As long as he vacillates and no one can rely on him, he is not yet that. The "moral person" becomes "*predictable*," e.g., as partisan: hence much hatred for the "*immoral person*."

4[103][51]

Luther's consolation when the cause did not advance, "demise of the world." The nihilists had Schopenhauer as philosopher. All extremely active people want to let the world go to pieces when they recognize that what they want is impossible (Wotan)[52]

4[104]

We have to be true only to ourselves: to be true to *others* is *self-sacrifice*, and only in the case that there is a natural inclination for it in us, is truth to others also a commandment of nature that wants to be satisfied. — Toward ourselves it is self-preservation, e.g., we have to assess our physical powers *correctly*. In the mental sphere, to trust ourselves with a leap our legs are not capable of is, in the moral realm likewise, occasion for broken bones and the worst pains; our morality has the measure of its ideality in the measure of the power possible for us, assuming that we can increase the latter. All growth must occur gradually, not by leaps and bounds. — How much misery is in the world because we measure ourselves by the rule of an impossible morality! We are not ashamed after all if we are not capable of running like a racer: but in moral matters we are so childish as to chalk up the *lack* of natural conditions to our own *guilt* and *shame*! As if we were our own work! This is really the hypothesis from which that feeling of shame grew.

4[105]

Higher humans are distinguished from lower as higher animals are from lower by their organs' complexity and number. To long for simplicity — i.e., to wish to have it easier!

Today the semi-barbarian is still glorified, namely, by artists: power, feeling, ignorance, natural bearing, and instincts — this is the *picturesque* standpoint, "this species looks good" — now the danger of the sickening and partial atrophy of so many organs is great.

4[106]

Now people like to let themselves be hounded and to hound: even artists choose the spirit of discontent as the muse that inspires them. If one looks at them then in their moments of recreation they are completely empty, they have no energy to spend on it and prefer what is most vapid (even important scholars). It would be very unfair to judge the era by *this* measure: an era does not entirely reveal itself, *let alone* its best aspect, in its amusements and recreation. So let us be tolerant of its art and let us deplore the higher artists to whom the age does not do justice, *truly* not, because it would be unworthy of them! As a youth one judges this wrongly.

4[107]

The moralists took popularly revered morality to be sacred and *true* and sought only to systematize it, i.e., they wrapped the mantle of science around it. No moralist dared to explore its origin: that touched on God and his messengers! It was assumed that morality lived distorted in the vernacular, that it needed "purification." —

4[108][53]

We revere those who in *thought* have broken through the spell of morality. But those who did so in *deed* are disparaged and have bad motives ascribed to them. This is unfair, we should at least ascribe the same bad motives to the freethinkers. — That in *crimes* a great deal of courage and originality of the mind, independence can be proven is concealed. The "tyrant" is in many ways a free, brave spirit, his character no worse than that of the fearful, often better because more honest. Now we generally answer the question whether the Russian nihilists are more immoral than the Russian civil servants in favor of the nihilists. — Countless morals have fallen victim to attacks by freethinkers and free-perpetrators:[54] our current individual way of thinking is the result of all kinds of *crimes* against morality. Anyone who attacked the established order was considered a "bad person"; history concerns itself only with these bad persons!

4[109][55]

Compared to freethinkers, free-perpetrators are at a disadvantage because their egoistic motives become more apparent than the former's. But often freethinkers have found satisfaction of their egoistic motives already in the pronouncement of the forbidden: In this way the immoral is more harmless and thus does not get reviled. With respect to the source it is all one: Napoleon and Christ.

4[110]

According to Aristotle[56] the Greeks suffered not infrequently from an excess of compassion: hence the necessary discharge through tragedy. We see how suspect this inclination appeared to them. It is perilous to the state, takes away the necessary firmness and severity, makes heroes behave like wailing women, etc. — Nowadays we want to *strengthen* compassion through tragedy — good luck with that! But no one notices it is there, neither before nor after.

4[111]

Either one *obeys* as slave and weak person or one is **complicit** *in commanding*: the latter is the way out for all proud natures who *interpret* for themselves every duty as law, which they *impose upon themselves and the others*: although it is imposed on them from the outside. This is the great snobbery in morality — "I ought to do what I *will*" is the formula.

4[112]

Since Rousseau *immediacy of feeling* has been glorified, throwing ourselves on another's breast, expectorating one's anger like one's spittle, etc. Curious that the great sages of morality have demanded the exact opposite! Reserve of feeling — and thence the dignity in the moral person's conduct. There are charming perfect souls whom that suits well because they bear no excess within themselves: but to make a law after the example of a Mozart, that means though — — —; we are no little songbirds. Even good and respectable feelings, expressed excessively and immediately, arouse a repulsion: so everyone at some point has probably wished compassion not kept within limits to hell.

4[113]

Is it necessary to preserve the moral vocabulary? What place does the terminology of alchemy have in chemistry?

4[114]

1) Prejudice: the consequences for which a sanctified moral rule is famed would also be the consequences of other rules: but this one alone is supposed to have the privilege; 2) the consequences ⟨indeed⟩ are not consequences at all but merely a common *post hoc*;[57] 3) the consequences are in truth the consequences of a concomitant that is overlooked, etc.

4[115]

Since each thing that has existed for a while claims a degree of dignity, so we also see Wagnerian art grasping at anything capable of lending it dignity: Christianity, princely and noble patronage, etc.; all too readily it would like a halo, but where are the powers that could confer such!

4[116]

Things that one wants to love lastingly must be set a little beneath their true worth: one may never know completely what they are. Woe to him who exaggerates! He loses every gem: namely, in the event he falls from the hyperbolic frame of mind into its opposite.

4[117]

In moral matters one mustn't go to one's most extreme limits: otherwise, one becomes mired in disgust with morality.

4[118]

Knowledge of one's powers, law of their regulation and release, distribution of the same without using some too much, the others too little, the sign of *displeasure* as infallible hint that a mistake, an excess etc. has been committed — all with respect to a *goal*: how *arduous* is this *individual science*! And in its absence one reaches for the folk superstition of morality: because here the prescriptions are already prepared. But one should look at its success — we are the victim of this superstitious medicine; *not* the individual, rather the community *ought* to be preserved through its prescriptions!

4[119]

What constitutes the value judgments of native peoples no imagination can *divine*, one must experience it. Specific practices and the range of ideas connected to them are *not* to be *constructed*; when we speak of humans' "natural" needs and desires, we think about the matter too simply: intellectual needs, for instance, have been satisfied in highly peculiar ways.

4[120][58]

Often 2 people come together whose morality matches so poorly that the one has a vacuum where the other feels his strength and virtue: they call each other "*immoral*."

4[121]

To revere **more highly** what *goes beyond* necessity, the more dispensable, finery, etc. an age-old drive: a certain *contempt* for what constitutes the organism and life. Καλόν[59]

Greeks, *honestum*[60] Romans — very curious! The extraordinary? Morality wanted to give human actions a meaning, fine attire, a foreign charm, likewise all relations to the godhead[61] — an **intellectual** *drive* expresses itself in this way, life is supposed to be understood as interesting, and before we had science, which made precisely everything pertaining to necessity in the highest degree interesting, we believed we had to raise ourselves above necessity in order to find human beings interesting. Hence the assumption of mysterious demonic forces in them, etc. (Namely, where the satisfaction of natural drives is easy, with great fertility of the soil etc., contempt for the "natural" quickly set in)

4[122]

The *regular* in nature is the predictable, to that we can accommodate ourselves so that it proceeds safely or even *usefully*: so wherever regularity obtains, one has believed in *good* beneficent powers (through a confusion). Evil is the unpredictable, e.g., the lightning bolt. The human is predictable on account of morality, to that extent *good*; the foreign people unpredictable, therefore evil; foreign customs are regarded as evil. The transference of what *to us* is good onto the object, which is now called good —

4[123]

The feeling of sympathy could have sprung from its opposite: fear of and antipathy to the foreign{, the} other is natural. Now the case occurs where this feeling is silent, no fear: we begin to treat *this* thing *like ourselves.*

4[124]

The human being is *not* the heir of *all* the animal world's sympathetic feelings.

4[125]

When the sexes seek and attract each other, the opposite of antipathy arises: here is the home of morality as sympathetic impulses. "To have pleasure with one another" — to desire one another, not in order to devour each other. — Morality as animals' sympathetic behavior stands in relation to the degree of their sensuousness. — Among humans as well? The religions that have esteemed compassion and love most highly have emerged among very sensuous peoples, which is already proven by the fact that they set up the ascetic ideal with respect to sensuousness: a proof that in this regard they felt themselves immoderate and unconstrained (Indians and Jews)

4[126]

The novella has a stronger effect than the performed drama because it equates itself with history; whereas the drama continuously destroys the illusion; supposing *one* actor brings it forth, then another destroys it, and *in any case* so do the theater and the people around us. How lackluster, how unconvincing is Mozart's Don Juan compared to Mérimée's Don Juan![62] Moreover, when hearing a story told we are much more *active* than when we are spectators; the latter elicits much more often the inclination to criticize. Music, as continuous accompaniment, has in all circumstances a distracting and disturbing effect; even the best music too often bores.

4[127]

Sympathy for someone, i.e., not to fear ⟨him⟩ and to expect joy from him. And that is supposed to be non-egoistical!

4[128][63]

To *understand* how another (or an animal) feels is something different from *sympathizing*, e.g., the physician's knowledge and that of the sick child's mother — but the presupposition? It is in no way a recreation of this *specific* feeling of suffering, rather a suffering on account of someone's suffering. By contrast knowledge pertains to the specific kind of pain. "To feel someone's pain" because we have experienced something similar is like the medical *knowledge* of pain — is not actual compassion, which generally suffers with *a person's* suffering and not with a specific pain. The feeling, someone is suffering whom we love, who is in our care or power, is *completely personal*, usually tied to vexation over our powerlessness (with compassion the ability to imagine the nature of the suffering can be very slight).

4[129]

To shield friends out of compassion is considered a weakness and is the opposite of virtue, which bids strictness with oneself where it is a matter of measures for the public welfare.

4[130][64]

In India the highest good is contemplation, the second-highest life according to the caste regulations —

4[131][65]

The passions are "false judgments" according to the Stoics.

4[132][66]

Early Christianity valued most highly *those qualities* that enabled its mission to bring its teaching to the ends of the earth before the imminent end (celibacy and relinquishment of possessions) — *Flight from the world* meant not participating in Greco-Roman life, as this was entirely based on heathen culture. Basic Neoplatonic assumption that we must live for a higher life; the earth seemed too common, likewise culture. This naïve pride! "Removed from and elevated above the earth, touching on the highest world principle in feeling" — a kind of Platonic knowledge — all illusion. The Neoplatonic perspective fused with Christianity, they are the *religiosi*, the higher humans. The Reformation rejected these higher types and denied the fulfillment of the moral religious ideal, it bore a lot of malice and opposition towards the *vita contemplativa*.

4[133][67]

In morality the strictest *theory* is *demanded* of everyone.

4[134][68]

Superficiality characterizes the theoretical life: the practical life is thorough and always proceeds by all *necessary* means to its goal, or otherwise the goal is missed. The thinker by contrast often imagines he has reached his goal and does not register the faulty ways and leaps as such: he has too often and too easily the feeling of success.

4[135][69]

Chastity is only a virtue for the age of adolescence in boys and girls: in itself a perversion because it would destroy the species. As individual rule in the interest of others an exception: namely, where only complete renunciation can save the h⟨uman being⟩.

4[136]

Perhaps in one hundred years humanity, through mastery of nature, will have acquired already much more power than it can expend and then an element of luxury will appear among humans which presently we cannot at all imagine. Assuming the idealism in human goals would not stagnate, magnificent things could be undertaken such as we cannot dream of now. Aviation alone overturns all our cultural standards. Instead of creating works of art, within a couple of centuries of work nature will be greatly embellished in order, e.g., to raise the *Alps* from their first beginnings and motives of beauty to their perfection. Then all earlier literature will reek of the narrowness of small towns. An era of architecture is coming when we will build again, like the Romans, for the ages. The backward populations of Asia, Africa will be used as laborers, the world's populations will begin to intermingle. When we think of the past we will think of its dismal gloom and idle tranquility: fire and excess of strength outcome of the healthy way of life. In order to prepare such a future, we have to segregate the low-spirited the sullen the faultfinders the pessimists and cause them to die out. Politics organized so that middling minds suffice for it and not everyone, every day, needs to know about it. Likewise the economic conditions without the avidity for life and death. Age of festivals.

4[137]

I think it possible that a logically magisterial mind abundantly filled with facts will, with an enormously excited intellect, create an unprecedented mass of successive inferences and thus will arrive at results that will take whole generations of researchers to catch up with: it is also a fantasizing — he will have to atone for it.

4[138]

Among our present-day inductive researchers the acuity and foresight is more ingenious and inventive (more imaginative as well) than among actual philosophers.

4[139]

Prejudice, that in order to judge independently one must represent a high rank, a power, that the lower-ranking also may not be free to think. "That wants to reason, have opinions etc., etc." — — — when one, in his view, too long about opinions[70] — — —

4[140]

Too many miserable and hang-dog souls have reproduced!

4[141]

The happiness of people who let themselves be ordered around (especially soldiers, civil servants): no complete responsibility with respect to the direction of their activity, and a carelessness and harmlessness, requirement of strict fulfillment of duty (which is the nicer name for obedience, its dignity). Prudent Christians, too, have this thoughtlessness. Just so science *unburdens* (irresponsibility)

4[142]

To want to have nothing to do with reality, to seek contact with the true reality in enraptured feelings, to be divergent and without understanding for life: in earlier times "science" had its formulas for that; to it such behavior seemed a reasonable tendency because it believed in the world behind the world. We grant it to the poet when he relates pretty follies from a "possible" world: in the event he himself *despises* our world, he pays for this scorn with his works. But woe to him if he should want to seduce us into "raising ourselves above the world," i.e., into raving action and turning the pleasant deceit of an idle hour into the judge of life! We are now strict about that.

4[143][71]

Have not all "sublime feelings" now become suspect because the false philosophy of enthusiasts has long since aligned itself so closely with them that alongside a sublime feeling a distorted thought, an extravagant point of view almost always arises! Sad. Moreover, aesthetic consideration finds the fantastic thoughts more charming than the rigorous and conventional ones, and all the arts insist as if on a dogma that intellectual eccentricity and sublime feelings live and die together. That there is elevation without fanciful vision, please prove it daily and by the hour! Friends!

4[144][72]

When we explore a moral feeling, we discover finally, upon following its course through imitation, the very strong valuation of a thing or action that has its basis in a theory. Thus, when concepts persuade, subjugate humans and they in turn *measure* something *according* to them: then a desire or an abhorrence emerges as a practical result. This then is directly transplanted without the corresponding motivation and often with a new one imputed afterwards. Where there are moral feelings, either a concept has become second nature[73] or a feeling been imitated.

4[145]

Everyone considers moral what preserves their *status*, the mother what increases her respect, the politician what benefits his party, the artist what will help immortalize his work: and the degree of spirit and knowledge decides *how far* someone drives this interest, whether he declares the reform of the whole world, even its destruction, as the *moral* goal *so that* he may thus best serve the interest of his estate. The prince, the nobleman shares one morality with the commoner, but each calls the other's means immoral. "Morality is always at home *with us*"; the question is how far we extend this "with us."

4[146][74]

Incest, adultery, rape, erotic obsession, to which not only the French dramatists of Romantic taste resorted but also German opera composers — signs of what? This tendency to mythical horrors, from which the Greeks too suffered, is in any case bad taste: bad enough when philosophy requires *that* in order to make its propositions credible.

4[147]

We do not *grasp* what the other wants, annoying ourselves and him: terrible distress in the family is the cause, and in the process, it is the *good* humans who are most vexed because what they do not understand they feel to be alien to themselves, hence *evil.*

4[148]

Since moral judgments and feelings have produced so much misery, namely, pangs of conscience, it must be asked: is this counterbalanced by a greater good? "Humanity exists through them" dubious: the animal species exist without them. On account of moral differences many tribes harbor such a destructive rage against their neighbors.

4[149]

In the most specialized sciences one speaks most determinately: each concept is precisely defined. Most uncertainly in morality though; each person feels something different in each word and according to mood; here upbringing is neglected, *all* words exist in a haze becoming now large, now tight.

4[150][75]

Ennui with humanity is possible, as if it were always the same old farce; for an intelligent being it is a dreadful limitation always to have to know as a human being; there can be an intellectual disgust for humanity.

4[151][76]

Very ambitious persons to whom access to a domain of distinction is closed e.g., military science astronomy medicine, avenge themselves either by scorning and ridiculing these things and their representatives or — they fancy there would be for them a special "king's highway" for arriving immediately at the quintessence. That way they simply imagine clairvoyant powers for themselves.

4[152]

That hot, burning feeling of enraptured people, "this is the truth," this grasping with hands and seeing with eyes among those who have become mastered by fantasy, the groping at the new other world — is a disease of the intellect, no path to knowledge.[77]

4[153]

First principle: fulfillable and nearby ideals: thus, individual ones!

4[154]

"You need only be martyrs, then you will be certain of your cause" — thus sounded the voice of seduction with which one triumphed over the demands of morality. A resolve like that for having a tooth pulled!

4[155][78]

Without *bodily* perfection — is then a spiritual or moral one possible? — What vigilance when in a sickly condition, how urgent the sifting through. Besides, convalescence has perhaps too much of the rapture of health for *its* insights, too, not to be somewhat suspicious.

4[156]

The shipwrecked man who sees land and would much prize being on land, but cannot swim — what use is it to him to *want* to get to land? It is not a matter of our will when we achieve little, but rather of our strengths or the lack of practice: above all of knowledge of our strengths: there is much we would otherwise not *want* at all.

4[157][79]

The spirit "the human in the human being," Philo. (for whom all true being is removed from reality and only those graced with pneumatic revelation partake in it)

4[158][80]

The Jews felt the earthly to be the weak, transient in comparison with the exalted one enthroned in heaven — in "most humble submission"

Purely spiritual being is a Greek, *not* Jewish invention. But the heavenly and earthly world is Jewish.

The Jews do *not* believe in *unfulfillable* ideals, the "heavenly tablets" (related to the Platonic ideas) are fully realized, heavenly wisdom manifests adequately in the law. Not so Plato.

4[159][81]

Hellenistic: receptive to revelation through abstention from meat and wine. Such requirements are *not* necessary for the Jewish.

4[160][82]

Through the Essenes the Hellenistic breaks through.

4[161][83]

The bodily resurrection is *Jewish* dogma. The dead person keeps flesh and blood. Both share in the blessed life. With the resurrection a martyr hopes to recover the bowels torn from his body (2 Macc.)

4[162][84]

"What the flesh desires is opposed to the spirit πν⟨εῦμα⟩[85] and what the spirit desires is opposed to the flesh," Paul. "Sin dwells in my flesh" and the flesh then works upon spirit and heart, the inner person.

The connection between death and sin! Because all died, all must have sinned.

4[163][86]

According to Philo the first human being is of highest perfection, wholly wise: he falls in yielding to sexual desire, quite voluntarily.

4[164][87]

Jewish and also Pauline: there is a religiously adherent guilt without knowledge and will

a violation of the law establishes guilt, which is to be atoned for (the regulations concerning Levitical purity and impurity)

According to Philo sin is: the *conscious* yielding of νοῦς[88] to the evil character of the bodily — that is Greek.

"The flesh must be eliminated,"[89] Paul.[90] The resistance of the inner man merely with *knowledge* of the law and *joy* in the same does not suffice, wholly impotent. (He therefore did *not* think that knowledge and valuation suffice for effective willing.)

The proof for Paul was the vision at Damascus: the radiance of God in the countenance of Jesus.

He took on the sinful sensual body of the human being; the human sinful flesh. That is ἁμαρτία:[91] *before* the appearance of the law it rules the πνεῦμα ἀν⟨θρώπου⟩[92] *without* the latter's knowledge, after the appearance of the law *with* its knowledge, and begets the παράβασις.[93] In Christ though a πνεῦμα Θεοῦ[94] that held ἁμαρτία captive. In killing, destroying the σάρξ[95] of Christ, God destroyed, condemned ἁμαρτία to death. The triumph over the σάρξ *not* through the earthly life of Christ, rather *through his bodily death.* — Through *baptism* what has happened in Christ happens in the baptized as well. The effect immediate. When his σάρξ has died, then he is free from sin. The radical extirpation of sin! We have become one with Christ, with the "life-giving spirit" — ergo immortal, and the resurrection just as Christ has risen from the dead.

The human who is filled with πνεῦμα is righteous and *holy.* And Luther? The body of flesh is not gone — but *dead.*

The fact *that* Paul exhorts proves that the σάρξ is exposed to ruin. The dying away of the σάρξ is *inexorable.*

Therapeuts,[96] Essenes,[97] later the Ebionites[98] leave the mortification of the senses to the individual.

For the stretch of time until the parousia the Christian will be bound to the σάρξ.

Paul knows 1) no resurrection of the flesh 2) no resurrection of the unredeemed.

4[165][99]

Since the feeling of sin and depravity is imaginary, there are also antidotes with which it can be nullified. Living constantly in an idea of the contrary, of having become one with God. In general, every strong, missionary, ready-for-death, martyr-like existence is an expedient against moral desperation: i.e., *restoration of an enormous pride*, the leap from the depths into the height. "Righteous and holy" not at all or all at once! Instead of reform the miracle of perfection.

4[166][100]

All religiously productive natures have had visions and raptures. That is proof against the health of the religious.

4[167][101]

The cosmic position of Jesus, the redeemer of nature. Yearning for completion, often without finding expression, sighs. The remnant of *sarx*[102] is removed entirely, we become "sons of God" — in the resurrection.

4[168]

As morality is a sum of prejudices, it can be *nullified* by a prejudice.

4[169]

The feeling of having become completely good is just as producible as that of being completely depraved. It is a question of an interpretation, an adaptation.

4[170][103]

Fanaticism a means against self-disgust. What does Paul have on his conscience? The σάρξ[104] led him astray into impurity, idolatry, and thaumaturgy (φαρμακεῖα), enmity and murder, drunkenness and revelry (κῶμοι). All *means* to the *feeling of power*.

4[171][105]

If through Christ's death the law has been satisfied, we can feel *emancipated* from it.[106] The anti-divine principle is destroyed when the fleshly body of Christ perishes:[107] not only is a debt settled — but "guilt" as such is expelled from the world.

4[172][108]

In the four main letters[109] the labor of thought wrestling with Judaism.

4[173]

Nowadays we would treat the inclination to religious ecstasies with laxatives.

4[174][110]

How is the feeling of excessive *enhancement of power* brought forth in the human being? Brahmins: by conceiving of potent gods and imagining means to take them captive and treat them as tools.

(or: by magnifying great humans into something gigantic and setting them forth as earlier stages of oneself.

4[175]

The feeling of power? Asceticism as a means to it (unification with God, intercourse with the dead, etc.). Dying-away-to-the world is already pride.

4[176]

The feeling of power insofar as one belongs to a strong chief, family, community, state — foundational to the establishment of moral obligation; we submit ourselves *so that* we have the feeling of power. — Whoever has grown averse to the fatherland, in moments when it is in danger still recovers his spirit of sacrifice: he does not want the feeling of powerlessness.

4[177]

Transition from the feeling of powerlessness to that of power very *pleasurable*: hence often the deepest humiliation sought. David, *so* that afterwards —. Perhaps Jewish?

The *secret* pride of the *slave*: religious

E.g., the demarcation from the animals; of the earth from the stars.

4[178]

With regard to a drama the Germans want people to grasp *what* is happening, the French *why* it is happening; they are more reasonable, the former stop at the viewing and the pleasure.

4[179][111]

The first effect of happiness is the feeling of power: this wants to express itself 1) toward ourselves 2) toward humans 3) toward representations of things 4) toward imaginary beings. *To annihilate, deride, bestow gifts.*

4[180][112]

Mastery of nature, the *idée fixe* of the twentieth century is Brahminism, Indo-Germanic.

4[181]

Actors' genius. Is it conceivable that someone can put forward such nonsense? — I myself put it forward at one time. *Dulce est desipere in loco. — Sed non hic locus.*[113]

4[182]

We should not believe we refute the claim that morality is superstition by saying morality is, and particularly has been, eminently useful: hence a very useful, perhaps indispensable superstition.

4[183][114]

Today the feeling of power one aspect of science: not the individual for himself ("philosopher") but as member. Princes and peoples serve this aspect. — Perhaps it is possible to surpass Brahminism. What are the means for increasing the independence of the individual? The feeling of higher beings?

4[184]

At all times humans have striven to acquire the feeling of power: the means they have devised to that end are almost the history of culture. Now many of these means are no longer *possible* or no longer *advisable.*

4[185]

He feels, she feels, it feels — man, woman, and child.

4[186][115]

"The Indian gods are not the givers of gifts: all wealth, all earthly happiness proceeds from the sacred acts, from the hymns, indeed from their meters." W⟨ackernagel⟩[116]

4[187]

The tradeoff in return for the moral limitation of the individual is the enhancement of his feeling of power (as member of a community, later of a higher, more spiritual humanity, of an order[117]) By virtue of moral action one can *perform magic.* To perish with the feeling of power — a special trick, to triumph in dying ("to shake off material being," etc.)

4[188][118]

The impersonal spiritual nature of God is Greek, the Jews had the God of their people, the God of the covenant, a personality. The Christians vacillate, but more Jewish.

4[189][119]

Cyprian[120] "all virtue exercised outside of the Church, even martyrdom, is worthless."

"rock-solid convictions and fearless certainty in the face of death" Christianity is supposed to have brought to the ancient world.

4[190]

Plato essentially a pantheist, but in the guise of the dualist.

4[191]

Spirits and narcotics as means to the feeling of power. The intoxications of the arts, of festivals, of beauty, of duty

4[192][121]

To know that so and so many persons die with us as our necessary entourage, or as wives, etc. — yields a feeling and expression of *power*, which in turn makes future victims *proud* to be subject to someone so powerful.

4[193]

The art of flattery before God, princes, women has forfeited some of its value; people nowadays wish for willing — or unwilling — loyalty, and scorn menial bearing: that way it is more aesthetic.

4[194]

According to whether the feeling of weakness (fear) or power prevails, pessimistic or optimistic systems emerge.

4[195]

It is shrewdest to limit oneself to matters where we *can* gain a feeling of power *which* is recognized by others as well. But their *ignorance* of themselves is so *great*: they are carried away by fear and awe to regions where *only through illusion* they can have a feeling of power. If the veil is torn asunder, *envy* appears.

4[196]

To have one's power, in which one does not believe oneself, proven from the outside — hence through fear in subordination to the judgment by others — a subterfuge of vain humans.

4[197][122]

The great passion of p⟨ower⟩ (Napoleon, Caesar), one must thereby appear vainer than one is, *want* it, in order to satisfy the feeling of power among the instruments (nations). Power for me and my people and not only the feeling *inside* us but power visible outside of us. Because such a power satisfies the strongest and most elevating feeling, here history proceeds on its *great path*: the conquerors are really the main thing, the inner processes of the nations, their questions of pressing need are secondary, *i.e., are always perceived as such*: the peoples want wine *more* than bread.

4[198]

The power of science is now building up a feeling of power such as humans have not yet had. Everything through themselves. — What then is the danger? Which would be the greatest presumption, *assuming* that science remains just science?

4[199]

The bubble of imaginary power bursts: that is the cardinal event in life. Then the human retreats angrily, or shattered, or stupefied. Death of the most beloved, collapse of a dynasty, disloyalty of a friend, untenability of a philosophy, of a party. — Then one wants *solace*, i.e., a new bubble.

4[200]

To have a pointed, two-edged, provocative little phrase for everyone: those are the ones who like it when the oxen run faster, and lend a helping hand. But there are the foolhardy who want to drive everyone insane in order to enjoy their strength's effect.

4[201][123]

The so-called commensals[124] do not eat their hosts but often use them as a means to provide themselves with beneficial nourishment. Here we have protection with the aim of nourishment.[125]

To have something lively around one that does not frighten — could recommend their offspring to animals. That they want to be fed is guessed. The feeling of possession, of dominance, then causes the parents to appear very irritated when one wishes to separate their young from them. Socialization of animals is probably just as old a thing as care for the young.

Just as *parasites* settle on many animals which cannot get rid of them, so too on humans — they are distinct from servants in that they live on the host, with or against his consent, would perish without him: many women. Formerly free life and for that purpose multiple organs which then are no longer necessary for the parasitic life: they degenerate and become *vestigial* organs.[126] Is there something similar among humans?

4[202]

These wars, these religions, the extreme moralities, these fanatical arts, this party hatred — that is the great playacting of impotence which brazenly alleges for itself a feeling of power and wants, for once, to signify strength — always with the relapse into pessimism and misery! You lack *power over yourselves*!

4[203][127]

I recommend to you the temperance societies, not as if you had a strength in need of being curbed, but so that you not drink too many *alcoholic beverages* which for a few hours give you a feeling of power and in the long run self-loathing.

4[204]

Ascetics attain an amazing feeling of power; the Stoics likewise because they always have to present themselves as triumphant, unperturbed. *Not* the Epicureans; they find happiness in the feeling not of power over themselves but of fearlessness with regard to gods and nature; their happiness is *negative* (as according to E⟨picurus⟩ pleasure should be) Compared to the feelings of power the yielding to pleasant sensations is almost neutral and weak. The Epicureans lacked the ascetics' mastery over nature and the feeling of power flowing from that. Knowledge back then was not yet constructive, instead it taught adaptation and quiet enjoyment.

4[205]

Even from the history of morality the feeling of power is supposed to flow: it is automatically counterfeited, the human is thought of as splendid, as a higher being with qualities animals do not have. Nearly all writings are *suspect* of flattering *the human.*

4[206]

If through science we wish to restore to humans their pride, such as they used to carry off from wars, then science must *become more dangerous*, require *more sacrifice*: to reveal oneself

4[207][128]

The gods were created, *not* only out of fear: but when the feeling of power became fantastic and discharged itself in persons.

4[208][129]

Luxury is demeaning for the man of knowledge. It is not simply dispensable for him, but *represents* a life different from the *simple* and *heroic* — and to that extent has a disabling and conflicting effect on the imagination. We are not "at home." Proclivity to luxury goes to the depths of a person: the superfluous and immoderate for the eye and ear like water in which such a person feels content.

4[209][130]

The conjurer seems to represent a *new causality* we do not yet know; that *elevates*! Just so the poet through his images and figures.

4[210][131]

Of *love* only humans with little experience of it have spoken so emphatically and longingly. *Universal* love of humanity would be unbearable: if not one but hundreds longed for us and took pains as lovers now do, then everyone would call for the return of the times *without love*. Feeling of power as the basis for wanting to help is already dangerous because it presupposes the person who lets himself be helped.

4[211]

Wherever one positions oneself in history, it was always the moment of a deep ferment when new concepts triumphed over old ones: it is not only so today.

4[212]

An age of transition: that's what everyone calls the present age and everyone is right about that. Though not in the sense that the word is more suited to this age than to any other. Wherever we step in history, we find ferment, the old concepts in conflict with new ones; and humans with a keen scent who used to be called prophets, but who only felt and saw what was happening to them — knew it and usually were very fearful. If it continues this way, everything will fall apart; well, then the world must go to ruin. But it has not gone to ruin, the forest's old trees broke, but a new forest always grew back and in every age there was a decaying world and a world coming to be.

4[213]

If only the artists knew how much imagination every greater insight presupposes, how much must ⟨be⟩ conceived and flourish only to be mercilessly cut off! We are an orchard: do you believe then it is so easy simply to annul the most graceful inventions and hypotheses? We are almost cruel to ourselves, but for the sake of the fruits that you and everyone shall have! — Goethe knew what it takes to be a scientific person: he is an ideal in whom all human competencies unite like all the streams in the sea. Why do you judge him by the standards of laborers of the mind? After all, we do not judge you according to your pigment-grinders and theatrical extras.

4[214]

The Germans have experienced the drunken acuity of the Hegelians who presumed to explain Goethe through boastful posturing,[132] and the repugnant narrowness of Wagner's disciples who made out of each of their master's weaknesses a dogma and a demand that here everyone be weak.

4[215]

Means of consolation: to have *more* to endure than everyone else, that gives a feeling of privilege, of power.

4[216]

How can the feeling of power 1) be made more and more substantial and not illusory? 2) be divested of its effects which injure, suppress, belittle, etc.?

4[217][133]

Whoever "speaks in tongues" has no clear awareness of what he is saying.

4[218][134]

The heart as Jewish concept, unintelligible, darkened, blinded, hardened, too enchanted by flattery, or the opposite: its functions are the affects: the Old Testament assigns the capacity of νοῦς[135] to the heart: only God can look into the heart. The fleshly heart: in the affects the innards are at work. It roughly corresponds to the Schopenhauerian "will"

4[219][136]

Paul believes in a heavenly corporeal matter which the resurrected body receives.[137]

Paul feels that among the Corinthians he appeared very timid on the outside.[138]

"The paradoxical mortal fate is the knot of the riddle, here one has to be able to figure out God's decree." At first the death of Christ argued *against* Messianic promise: but the miracle on the road to Damascus proved it.

Freed from the σάρξ,[139] filled with πνεῦμα,[140] we are no longer under the law. The law places the ἁμαρτία of the σάρξ in its utmost force before our eyes, thus making it unbearable. "To be in the flesh" means "to be inside the law." To die to evil is to die to the law. — What a profound hatred Paul bears towards it here!

Paul declared the law abolished through *several* proclamations, that to him was the most important point. Whatever a Christian now did, he *no longer* had to measure it by the law; it was dead, like the σάρξ. One of these proclamations: Christ had fulfilled the law.

In the feeling of divine *forgiveness* and *grace* the one argument, the other in the feeling of the innermost spiritual union[141] in Christ through baptism. "From faith and through grace" — the law was to provoke transgressions in the first place.

Christ's death would be impossible in the divine decree if a fulfillment of the law *could* at all occur: "If justification came through the law, then Christ would have died to no purpose."[142] To let oneself drift on the current of the spirit, to surrender entirely to it without consulting one's own will —

The law is the reason I have died. But thereby I have also died to the law. *Even if* a Christian sins, then no longer against the law, he is outside it "I live no longer as *I*, but Christ lives in me. What I still live in the flesh, that I live through faith in him. If I now wanted to take up the law again (so as to submit myself to it), I would make Christ into an accomplice in sin."

ἁμαρτία[143] is still there, but it can be overcome: whereas under the law ἁμαρτία cannot be overcome: the sin-abetting law is annulled (namely, the *natural* necessity of sin is annulled)

Sin now as weakness and imperfection against the sacred God — now as automatic diabolical principle.

pp. 204–5 state the acuity of the matter.

4[220][144]

As soon as something counts as true, any more refined understanding comes to an end, e.g., for its edification all of Christendom has read its Paul word for word, sentence for sentence, but has *not at all* grasped the true dialectic, the conflicting thought processes, his true distress and crux; thus, the suffering and struggling Paul: he was dead, i.e., he spoke inspired, as God's mouthpiece.

4[221]

Whoever dedicates his ear to a single genre of music no longer knows in the end how repulsive it sounds: moreover, he no longer knows how to tell the finer and good things from the weak and overwrought and enjoys less in the detail than one would think, though on the whole of course he has the feeling of power — *his* music is the best music and is altogether good music: though the opposite of both is true. Whoever loves only himself can experience bliss out of the worst taste and can make a law from it, a tyranny: *le mauvais goût mène au crime.*[145]

4[222]

When the Don Quixotism of our feeling of power rises one day to the level of consciousness and we awaken — then we *grovel* like Don Quixote — dreadful end! Humanity is always threatened by this ignominious *self-denial* at the *end* of its striving.

4[223]

I want to bring a stop to art's fanatical presumptuousness; it should not pretend to be a cure; it is a momentary balm, of slight worth to life: very dangerous when it wants to be more.

4[224][146]

In ancient times the Greeks thought of milk and honey as the fare of the gods — those were not times for wine-drinkers. For the Germanic gods, mead was the drink that granted immortality: there we have the drinkers. The Soma of the Indo-Aryans an *intoxicating* drink only encountered in sacrifice. Thus: brought together in the mind are intoxicating drinks and the sensations of immortality and deliverance from suffering. With the enjoyment of the Soma all mortal suffering will cease for mortals at the end of time, they cross over to the bliss of the gods. — The delight in milk and honey: Ninon de Lenclos to be remembered, who was intoxicated already by a soup.[147]

4[225]

Dionysian — for us wine is something very sober. And so we look for the cause of the Dionysian *apart* from the wine and take its effect for at best a symbol. On the contrary! Wine's effect was the novelty, something that could only be grasped as a new life and new godhead — *thereafter* other phenomena were understood symbolically.

4[226]

The epileptic twirling mania, which befell the hysterical women of Greece, was compared to the frenzy from wine.

4[227]

If all the tears shed at every moment on earth were to flow together, a strong stream would steadily flow through the "field of calamity."[148]

4[228]

Everything is vain and transient, nothing worthy of enduring effort; enjoy then the moment, calamity will come after all. — Solomon[149]

4[229]

To drive misfortune out of one's mind through fierce work, fierce pleasure. Epicureans.

4[230]

not wishing to see a bad thing, not to admit its existence, to deny it, reinterpret it, to stake one's intellectual honor on its denial — a means of consolation.

4[231][150]

Paul was a fanatic and honor guard of the law who wanted to satisfy it: but that did not work! The σάρξ![151] And then the law itself, that provoked transgression! — He begrudged it with a deep hatred: to see it *annulled* through C⟨hrist's⟩ death was his triumph; the *invincible* enemy of this tyrannical man was defeated.

4[232]

Wine had a different effect on the Greeks than on our inebriated brains. "Undiluted wine causes insanity," they said.

4[233]

False inferences: "I value people slightly, consequently they value me highly." "I do not fear people, consequently they fear me" — but the *inverse* inferences are equally false. To infer here is precisely what is false: it is as when a child infers: I close my eyes, consequently the others do not see me.[152]

4[234]

Geniuses who cut out a part of their followers' brains, as one would from chickens, so that these then, half-drunk and unsteady, perform the reflex movements of adoration.

4[235][153]

Christians forgot how to *read*, and how much had antiquity, in its philologists, endeavored to learn it! But the Bible!

4[236][154]

Once it was thought, where there is wine, there is God. Where exaltation is, it is still thought God is present. Alas, exaltation is like wine: alcohol and narcosis.

4[237][155]

Misfortune of humanity and reason for its slow progress is that the *elevating* and *stimulating* things have been valued more highly than the *nourishing* ones.

4[238]

When humanity sinks for us in value (e.g., with sickness), our respect for its institutions sinks as well; "the sick person is a rogue" and the saint as well!

4[239]

Do not say that boredom afflicts them: they do not want to be baited by anything because their will to power does not know how to be sated — all else is nothing in comparison.

4[240][156]

In case of a crime: the terrible abasement in the feeling of power, to turn from an irreproachable into a disreputable family. The thought of enemies no longer torments. Nor pangs of conscience!

4[241]

Essence of art: a harmful function is exercised *without* causing harm. Most pleasing paradox.

4[242]

Rákóczi March[157] the most beautiful in the world.

4[243][158]

Now they already tolerate the truth about the most recent past because generations do not found their own views on past ones and are *honored* to do so — instead they oppose theirs to the earlier view and so have their feeling of power from independence.

4[244][159]

The great statesmen share their people's imagination — by that means they are great, i.e., efficacious: one senses among the people that they bring forth the feeling of power which one craves. One people wants power with splendor and mili⟨tary⟩ success, another wants it with cunning and diplomatic superiority.

4[245][160]

The great sovereigns and conquerors speak the pathos-ridden language of virtue as a sign that it is commonly recognized among humans by virtue of the feeling of power it gives. The dishonesty of *every* politics lies in the fact that the grand words, which everyone must proclaim in order to identify himself as someone possessing p⟨ower⟩, *can* not be congruent with the true conditions and motives.

4[246][161]

Alas, it is impossible to *effect* anything with the language of truth: rhetoric is necessary, i.e., the old habit, to be *moved* only by specific words and motifs, governs and demands the disguise of the truth.

4[247][162]

I disregard the interest and vanity of the single person and of peoples: but the need to sense power in oneself, to let squandering, sacrificing, hoping, trusting, fantastical feelings well up *from it* — that drives great politics as the mightiest stream. There one acts against one's interest, against one's vanity (for one may have to serve like a slave in order that the nation may have a feeling of power, or put one's life, one's wealth, one's honor at risk) (Virtue).

4[248][163]

One may not even offer peace and enjoyment to peoples without a laurel wreath around them: as if *in the feeling of power* it were permitted to be easy and cheerful but otherwise not: even as if it were a duty so to present oneself because that way one appears powerful.

4[249][164]

Counterfeiting of the feeling of power and payment with counterfeit coins is the greatest human ailment. Peoples are deceived in this way because they *seek* a deceiver: a stimulating wine for their senses, not good nourishment. Governments are the means of giving that feeling to the people: men chosen from among the people give much less of it than brilliant conquerors, bold conspirators, old legitimate houses: they must have something intoxicating about them.

4[250]

Meanwhile wars are the greatest stimulants to the imagination, after all Christian raptures and horrors have grown dull. The social revolution is perhaps still something greater, which is why it is coming. But its success will be slighter than is thought: humanity *is capable* of so very much less than it *wills*, as became apparent with the French Revolution. When the great spectacle and the thunderstorm's intoxication are over, it becomes clear that in order to be capable of more we would have to have greater strength, more practice.

4[251]

Christianity triumphed as a strong wine triumphs; antiquity got drunk because it no longer felt strong and glad and had become accustomed to great excitements. Faced with the

Roman imperium the idea of the world coming to an end looked extremely fantastic and intoxicating.

4[252][165]

Really it was consistent for Paul to say that through Chr⟨ist's⟩ death and union with him through baptism the σάϱξ[166] is dead and our body therefore another body, the heavenly body. But it was not possible to say that, although in single moment⟨s⟩ he believed it perhaps: but *no one believed him*! If the union was not complete, then — *how* does it become so? Faith and baptism not enough. Why only with the resurrection? In imitation of Chr⟨ist⟩! Three days of *decomposition*?

4[253][167]

To partake in the splendor, glory (fame) of God, to become sons of God — that is of course a goal! There is no modesty anymore! There must just not be too *many* of them, otherwise the honor is too slight! *That* is being taken care of!

4[254][168]

Natures like Paul arrange all experiences according to the logic of their passion. The appearance at Damasc⟨us⟩ was preceded by the thought: "Supposing the Christians were right" — and he had presaged its advantages for his personal plight — above all it was a new attempt, and the aversion to his condition up to then had become too great. So he saw "Christ" — how did he know it! Why did he believe it when the appearance said it? "*Why* do you persecute me?" — it is *not reasonable*, said the prudent Jew to himself.

4[255][169]

Paul as proselytizer of the *heathens*: for that it was necessary "to be released from the law" — proudest task — — alas, the *Saint* Paul! With him we see right through to the bottom!

4[256]

To obey, to do more than is one's duty, to reject praise, to be proud of integrity: *German*. Now vanity has become all the rage among us, and regrettably some of our outstanding thinkers and artists have taken the lead: each wants to mean more than to be and "advertises" himself.

4[257]

Why does culture make *weak*? Carthage succumbed to the less cultivated Rome, the high Arabic culture succumbed, etc. Because in culture the fantasy-satisfaction of power is esteemed too highly and achieved too easily: so that the true power grows weak (power over oneself, etc.)

4[258][170]

How did Christianity raise itself above the idea of a "fulfilled Judaism," of a Jewish specificity, whereas the nation maintained that its ideal was not yet fulfilled? — That is actually Paul's personal history, who felt driven *away* from Jews and Jewish-Christians — he wanted nothing more to do with the law. That one might become a Christian without first becoming a Jew — was *his* invention — By the way it was an error: Christians became Jews after all.

4[259]

So should one live in the world as though one had to *carry out* the commandments of a *higher spirit world* and had nothing else to do? This could happen out of interest or out of vanity or out of a feeling of power (out of the conviction that one *belongs* to this spirit world and is fulfilling one's own *needs*). But if one *no longer believes*? Then our interest, our vanity, our feeling of power *directly* guides our action, no longer indirectly. For all older moralities, however sacred they may be deemed, have originated from *inferior knowledge*; they *may* no longer rule.

4[260]

Our life should be an ascent from plateau to plateau, but no flight and fall — the latter, however, is the ideal of fantasts: higher moments and times of dejection. This bad indulgence debases the greatest part of our own life; at the same time, we learn to scorn other humans because in our ecstasy we do not see them: it is unhealthy, for we have to pay for the moral aesthetic excesses. With a deep-rooted indisposition and inner ill humor, the dose of exaltation has to become ever stronger; ultimately, we become indifferent to its value and make do with the strongest *stimulation*. Decline. — This process is observable in the history of every art: the classical age is where ebb and flow make a very fine difference and an agreeable feeling of strength is the norm: what arouses the deepest upheavals is always *absent*: their production belongs to the period of decline.

4[261][171]

They believed in Napoleon because they needed a helper and someone reassuring; Paul believed in Christ because he needed an object that concentrated and thereby satisfied him. Luther fought against the clergy because his earnest attempt to become its ideal expression had failed, now appeared to him altogether impossible and impossible for anyone. On account of his experiences he was suspicious of the whole *vita contemplativa*: he believed in the *Bible* because he no longer wanted to believe in the Pope; he put it into everyone's hands and taught the *universal* priesthood — he simply *hated* the priesthood.

4[262]

In the deepest distress, wailing and screaming prone in one's chamber — and then these people come in, like glaring daylight: shrieking and covering one's face: oh, these people! oh, these people!

4[263]

To move around as if transformed, with a different heaviness to one's feet, burdened with a weight so that one is always on the brink of collapsing, the sounds of other people come as if from a dense fog, their depths sound like flowing hollow-roaring water, it is *bright*, and withal the sensation of night.

4[264]

To have served loyally and conscientiously a regime which proves in the end to be mean and fatal — and no longer capable of turning back, no longer right and left — what bitterness! To see oneself trapped in the snare of one's unsuspecting virtue! To be conscientious and to reap as the certain reward the contempt of those who despise the regime, i.e., of the best! There holding out can be more heroic than escape and struggle and the surrender of security and possessions.

4[265]

There are ideas which have the task of wine: they elevate, entertain, encourage, but enjoyed in quantity they produce intoxication and, enjoyed often, a need without whose satisfaction life becomes bleak and insufferable.

4[266]

Moral prejudices are still indispensable: it is regrettable that we still cannot dispense with them, for the strengthening they provide supports most securely the weakness and want of force against which they are taken as a medicine.

4[267]

To spare the honor of a beloved by posing as someone almost unknown to her in a circle where she is the subject of talk, and now to hear her affronted in a way that one cannot avenge, so as not to ruin her reputation — hideous!

4[268]

Whoever has felt the claws of those pretty cats that crowd around great artists is no longer of the opinion that the genius improves the character of his environment.

4[269]

Why is it that common people, namely in the Orient, are happy and calm? They lack the false fantasy-satisfactions, the spiritual ecstasies and disenchantments; they live spiritually tempered. *Not* the *spirit* but *spirituality* is the danger.

4[270]

What acts upon present-day Germans as *intoxicating* may be seen in W⟨agner's⟩ themes; what acted that way upon earlier generations in Schiller's themes. One should think of Corneille.

4[271]

May I put in a word! For me all truths are unvarnished truths[172] — consider my early writings.

4[272]

Suicide practiced on a whole era of our life, our experiences — everything should be dead — and everything should be forgotten — everything should have been *otherwise* than it was! Paul.

4[273]

Language has become *unclear* because such great *vagueness* has run rampant in the *definition of concepts* and the *demand* for firm definition is not planted. Hence the task is clear.

4[274][173]

Alas, the depreciation of simple joys! The Greeks started that; to content oneself with ἀναγκαῖα[174] is slave-like. Things should proceed *merrily*! The common people are right! — Luxury rules in the intellectual sphere; that is our disease. The truth is: you live like slaves in overworking yourselves, in your social constraint; you use intellectuality as *intoxication*: and it ill becomes you.

4[275]

In every era the humans who have artistic needs, but above all a deep, ponderous temperament, fall to the deep, earnest artist and sanctify him by attributing to him their virtues: he gladly complies. But nothing is *proven* thereby for the artist.

4[276]

The soul filled with repulsive experiences, repul⟨sive⟩ anxiet⟨ies⟩, then we must of course demand of art something different, purgation, a jolting, forgetting.

4[277]

Reflection and inventiveness with respect to *elemental stimuli* (in music and colors, etc.) belongs to the philosophical character in our time: just as truth to nature belongs to painters. One goes as far as one can and is radical.

4[278]

they scorn form: as if this music were of the slightest interest, if it did not, *contradicting* the demand of form, inscribe itself on the background, did not stand in relief against it!

4[279]

All the things an artist needs in the way of opinions, sympathies, antipathies, habits, excesses in order to give himself breathing space in which to feel his productivity grow, need not concern us at all: as little as the soil concerns us when we eat bread. If he demands though that we share all that with him in order fully to enjoy his art, the answer is that the enjoyment of the greatest work of art does not outweigh a single eccentric judgment, a dislocation of our position. The work of art does not belong to the bare necessities;[175] clean air in one's head and character belong to the necessities of life.[176] We should free ourselves from an art that sells its fruits too dearly. If an artist cannot bear bright good air, if he must enter misty caves and limbos in order to fertilize his imagination, so be it: we do not follow. Likewise, if he needs hatred and envy in order to maintain strict loyalty to his artistic character. An artist is not life's leader — as I said earlier.[177]

4[280][178]

To imagine what another feels when we do this or that — thus to calculate our advantage or disadvantage from the conjectured advantage or disadvantage for another, to which our action leads him — that is *ingrained* in the animal realm's methods of self-protection and attack. To imagine the effect on another and to do something for another's sake — the greatest schooling! of cognition! Instinctive compassion has led the least to this, rather by *fear* and *its* imagination: and their result has been accepted by hunger (as the starting point for the attack on another being). To guess from his gestures how someone feels, whether he wants to flee or attack and the like — that could not have been learned without the intellect being *stretched to the limit* by *necessity.* Compassion comes late, after everything has been learned, it *does not stretch* the *intellect*; it is fairly unproductive for knowledge of the human being.

4[281][179]

Love fantasizes about the other: its secret impulse is to discover as much beauty as possible in the other, or to *think* him as beautiful as possible. So illusion is rather an advantage here. *Fear* wants to guess what the other is, what he is capable of and wants: illusion would be the greatest disadvantage. Hence knowledge of the *true* human has been furthered much *more* through *fear* rather than through love (compassion).

4[282]

I know that swelling breast, that smiling down upon earthly things, that hot stream, the proud stride, that glowing, despising, and hoping eye —[180]

4[283]

When one considers how much pain one must assume, how much pain one has to cause oneself, how mistaken it would be to choose immediate satisfaction: then it follows that also in relation to other humans we must inflict pain and may not immediately satisfy, i.e., compassion should not rule over us, rather our insight into usefulness must *rule over* comp⟨assion⟩.

4[284]

Men establish marriage in order to have the feeling of p⟨ower⟩: women as well (to be independent). But both are mistaken. Love is no reason for marriage, rather an objection to it: a deep feeling conceals itself.

4[285]

I have always composed my writings with my whole body and life: I do not know what "purely intellectual" problems are.

4[286][181]

Plato became impatient, he wanted to be finished. And why? His feeling of power wanted satisfaction, that strong political drive. The brevity of our life demands that at some point the summit finally comes into view and the goal is reached: otherwise we would forever remain in suspense and that o⟨ne⟩ cannot endure for want of patience. Individually *necessary* the appearance of truth.

4[287]

Plato did not keep to Socrates's course, Heraclitus's first impressions suggested Pythagoras was the secret, jealously regarded ideal.

4[288][182]

When the ancients speak of necessity: ἀνάγκη,[183] they mean the realm where things happen arbitrarily (accidentally), where not every cause must be followed by its effect. Only the teleological realm, where the godhead lets its traces become visible, constitutes an exception: the mind brings *into* it order and regularity. — Conversely the moderns, who see in the mind the principle of freedom, in nature constraint.

4[289]

People used to believe they could arrive at the cause of a thing by *generalizing* its qualities: and that the most universal generalizations ought to be the cause of all things. Hence perfection as such ought to exist as essence from which the virtues and virtuous humans are to be explained.

4[290]

I know so little of the findings of science. And yet this small amount already seems to me *inexhaustibly rich* for the illumination of darkness and the elimination of earlier ways of thinking and acting.

4[291]

In the yielding and defiant feeling of youth we latch onto precisely those teachers and men whose capacities are alien to our own and who rise up in areas where we sense our deficiencies. Thus, by taking sides we triumph over the chance of having been born poor and inferior in precisely this or that. Later we stick to our *strengths*, because only here can we capably work, build, and do we want to become masters.

4[292]

The more we grasp *how* our value judgments have emerged, the more their value diminishes and the need for new valuations results. The study of first and last questions, for example, loses its ponderous meaning when we see through how many errors we have *hung* our present condition and eternal salvation upon it.

4[293][184]

That Schopenhauer's teaching on the Schopenhauerian "will" so easily insinuates itself lies in the fact that we have already been drilled in its *essence* — through the Jewish concept "heart," as it became familiar to us through Luther's Bible. The feeling that something is easy for us and ties in with already existing feelings qualifies for us as *testimony* of the truth.

4[294]

When someone has taken one of those great *flights into the higher realm* of spirits and been able to *represent* it, humanity then makes the attempt to absorb it: i.e., many attempt to fly in the same direction and only late does the desire subside. Such are fashions in a grand style, namely for the most ambitious. Such was the way people once *traveled* and sought *adventures.*

4[295][185]

The sciences represent the higher ethics, by comparison with the solvers of the world-riddle and system-builders: moderation, justice, abstinence, placidity, patience, valor, simplicity, reserve, etc.

4[296]

Art, *too*, has fantasy-satisfaction: and this is more innocent and innocuous than elsewhere because beauty implies the standard of *measure*, furthermore because the muses say: "we lie."

4[297]

What prompts us to such rash generalizations that we imagine the person according to one trait and positively no one wants to leave his picture of another unfinished? *Fear* and the habit of fear: "he exhibits this trait — what if he were always this way: Let us assume so *for the sake of caution*, namely, when it is a dangerous trait!"

4[298]

The animals who draw everyone's eyes to themselves through a dreadful *colorfulness* nevertheless are very much left alone: they all have a malign weapon, venom and the like[186] — parable.

4[299][187]

When we perform an action with a *feeling of power*, we call it moral and sense freedom of the will. Actions performed with the feeling of powerlessness are seen as of unsound mind. Hence the accompanying mood determines whether something belongs in the moral sphere, is "good or evil." Hence this perpetual search for means of bringing this condition about: it is the *human condition*!

"To do evil with power is worth more than doing good with powerlessness," i.e., the feeling of power is more highly valued than any use or repute.

4[300]

they are enthused in their youth just once and are enduringly grateful for it, while they grow *more distant* from the objects of this enthusiasm: but piety *hinders* their *critique*. Sanctification proportionally *increases* as the time of enthusiasm grows more distant and we feel removed from its objects. "What once *elevated* us so much *must* have been the *truth*." "Now we stand at a distance and can no longer examine it: but back then we were fully at home with it." The delusion that what elevates must be true and that whatever is true must elevate is a consequence of the contempt for the earthly material as the unreal and of ⟨the reverence⟩ for the spiritual and the beyond as the *true* world, from which all impulses that elevate emerge.

If the story of Christ had taken place in this century, whoever believed in what now many still believe of it would be considered *insane*.

4[301][188]

All Greeks (see Plato's *Gorgias*) believed the possession of power as a tyrant to be the most enviable happiness: its nefariousness presupposed.[189] *All* were concerned to thwart the emergence of this happiest one, and if he existed, to hinder or eliminate him.[190] The highest happiness, in which everyone believed, was wholly invested in the *feeling of power*: this condition treated though as the absolutely unethical (hostile to ethics, i.e., individual, egoistic). The happy one was loathed and feared: in his recklessness he spares no one. In their eyes omnipotence would be perfect ruthlessness and devilishness, namely not the desire to harm but the sacrifice of all for the tyrant's pleasure. *Just so* does the tyrant of the spirit proceed now, he is the happiest and most unconscionable.

To be just {is} a continuous sacrificing, only to be endured in anticipation of *acclamation* by society (i.e., of a feeling of power): being just *without* this success would be the most horrible fate. This is Greek thinking. But to have the reward of justice, acclamation, without being just (without these efforts and sacrifices) appeared to be the greatest good fortune. The practical way out (since that toward tyranny was usually closed off) was: the *appearance of justice*: just as Napoleon in words and actions applauded, yes rewarded nobler motives and thus gained for himself their splendor. Equality of citizens is the means of preventing tyranny, their mutual surveillance and suppression. If one had the ring of Gyges,[191] each and every one would be unjust. — Evidently these equals wildly fantasized about the tyrant's happiness, that was the covetousness of their fantasy; in tragic drama it is still the expression of the great paradox, "to be king" and "unhappy"; "not even to envy the King of Persia." The feeling of power is thought to be enough to outweigh by far all hardships of governing, all fear, etc. (Xenophon's *Hiero* is the Socratic paradox that the happiness of the tyrant does not amount to much!)[192] To say that the virtuous person is the happy person — that sounded *insane*: abstinence was such a bother! In the end there remained nothing but the

Stoics' *pride* in virtue; king and wise man is: the new feeling of power: there is nothing with which to *subjugate* him, he rules. — Every philosophy had its imperious aspects: the Epicureans triumphed in having conquered the Acheron and the fear of death, the fear of nature: hence in being lords over nature.

4[302]

Plato's main reproach is not directed at the Sophists but at the *poets*: they guide youths, who are **disposed** to **something higher**, onto the path of political ambition — whereas *he* would like to guide them onto the path of philosophical ambition. The *ordinary way* to satisfy the feeling of power is the deep shadow that Plato sees: he wants to show another way. Now the reproach could be repeated, but in reverse. Philosophers, like poets, satisfy youths' pride — *they dissuade them from science.*

4[303]

Devised for myself and written down for those who are just as capable of heartfelt and sensitive engagement with human matters as they know themselves free of the importunate desires of the reformer and moralizer — so might these thoughts — — —

4[304][193]

Mill on the Plato⟨nic⟩ philos⟨opher⟩ who, like the gods, is exalted above the earth and lives in contemplation of true things. P. 67.

4[305]

The order of *rank* of thinking minds is yet to be created.[194] Until now philosophers have been treated too much like artists, their talent for description, their imagination, their capacity for coloring treated as proof of their genius: but the degree of their justice, self-restraint neglected: in fact they have been judged extra-morally. *Their effect* was decisive, and whoever touched the most receptive humans, those whose thanks rhythmically welled up over their lips,[195] qualified as the greatest: thus as the *inspirer of youth*!

4[306]

Alas, those wretched ones who believe humanity *before long* might become *too clever*, and that would be the end of *their* influence, *their* renown!

4[307][196]

All those beings devoured by their passion, Werther, Tasso, Tristan, Isolde, call to us: be a man and do *not* follow me![197] — and so also call those with philosophical passion, who individually desire highest power through knowledge, alchemists as well as Platonists, etc.

4[308]

The impulse to self-sacrifice passes for good. In itself it is *not*: how should doing harm to anyone at all (in this case oneself) in itself be good? And besides, this harm is so superfluous! Nothing more than an instance of the craving for power and self-spite that knows no reasonable way of satisfying itself.

4[309][198]

"Will to urinate," i.e., there is, in the first place, a pressure and urge; second, a means to relieve oneself of it; third, a habit of making use of it once it is transmitted from the brain to the hand. In itself that pressure and urge has nothing to do with that discharge of the bladder: It does not say "I will" but "I suffer."

4[310]

Schopenhauer's teaching is a concealed teleology, but that of an evil and blind being bent on purposes neither admirable nor lovable. If among earlier teleologists it appeared as though the head of the universe and the brightest most just knowledge in it had created the world and humans — whereby it was not graspable why both did not turn out somewhat more reasonable and just — with Schopenhauer the universe's lower abdomen seems to be the root of things: and its appetites only invent an intellect for themselves in order to build better nests with its help. One is as wrong as the other: the latter though is opaquer because it speaks of willing without assuming from the outset an intellect that could represent *what* is willed: there is no such willing into the blue (or into existence!), it is an empty word.

4[311]

Vita contemplativa.
Hints and Signposts
toward it.

4[312]

On the Life of Thinkers.
Moral Questions.

4[313]

Vademecum Vadetecum[199]
Thoughts on Individual Morality.

4[314]

Moral Prejudices.
The Feeling of Power.

4[315]

Redemption.
What is to be unlearned.

4[316][200]

Just as robbers and great boxing champions behave toward soldiers, so do *philosophers* toward *men of science*. Of course: the former were made into *heroes*, the latter into *geniuses*!

4[317][201]

In *men of science* the virtues of soldiers and their kind of cheerfulness live — they lack ultimate responsibility. They are strict with themselves, with each other, and do not expect praise for doing good. They are more masculine and have a predilection for danger, they have to prove themselves *capable* of risking life for the sake of knowledge: they hate grandiose words and are harmless, and a little foppish.

4[318][202]

I will speak of h⟨umans'⟩ greatest disease and want to show that it emerged from the battle against other diseases: that in the long run the apparent remedy produced something worse than what it was supposed to eliminate.

Will my readers tolerate a single thought, and this in hundreds and hundreds of turns of phrase and illuminations? Yet this is a necessity for the general health, and harder things have been undertaken in its service than reading a book that is far from entertaining.

4[319]

rapturous, girlish sensations of so-called bliss, dreams of converted and rescued dissolute rakes,[203] faithfulness to the point of leaping into the water,[204] and the beloved himself something terrible, uncanny, a man of unknown crimes, but a perpetrator without guilt who is at the same time a concealed god and prince[205] — all in a very charming natural setting — those are now the diversions of the *iron* Germany. — Evil harmonies, raging rhythms and unspeakable chromatic wailing, the alternation between all musical keys as emblem of the inconstancy of all things under the moon — thus *reality* is described.

4[320]

Hungarian Rhapsody II[206] — such a *good* piece of music and at the same time such a *boisterous* one, as if God had become possessed by the devil.

4[321]

The "insights at one stroke," the "intuitions," are not any kind of cognition but rather representations of a heightened liveliness: as little as hallucination i⟨s⟩ tr⟨uth⟩.

4[322]

Self-conceit, the feeling of power, is often entirely innocent and behaves like a child, without knowing about good and evil.

4[323]

Formerly someone considered it wondrous *how far* he had come on his own; today by contrast we rather underestimate our own contribution and see only *what has affected us*.

[5 = Mp XV 1a. Summer 1880]

5[1]

He[1] needs to sow hostilities so that he may stay famous and become even more so. Do not believe him, he knows fully well that he deceives. He needs the fanaticism of friends and enemies in order to deceive himself.

5[2]

The holding on to deep terrible rapturous sensations, exploiting the depths for —

5[3]

German dramatic acting is to be ruled out, enough that it satisfies the Germans. Things are different in Vienna where they have never spurned learning from the Italians and the French: just as Austrian composers have done.

5[4]

There is a great artist: yet he[2] wants to appear greater than he is. And so we say with every fifth moment of his art: he is presumptuous, he pretends to something that befits those higher than he is: he poaches on them and is not honest with respect to himself — he lacks not greatness but naïveté, which is why he is so seldom at ease: the tension is too great.

5[5][3]

Desire! That is nothing simple, elementary! Instead a need (pressure urge etc.) is to be distinguished and a means of allaying the need known from experience. Thus there arises a link between need and aim, as if the need *wanted to reach* that aim from the outset. There is no such willing at all: "I desire to urinate" is just as mistaken as "there is a will to the chamber pot."

5[6]

It is very difficult to maintain a cheerful disposition when we tread our own and new paths. We cannot know what we are *worth*, for that we have to believe others; and when they *can* not judge us correctly, precisely because we strike out on unknown ways, then we become suspect to ourselves: we require cheerful encouraging acclamation. Otherwise solitaries become *gloomy* and lose *half their prowess*, and their works with it.

5[7][4]

Oh, I know you, you secret liars, I see you standing at the crossroads and deciding for the path leading to ecstasies hopes raptures stupors: I see you take on that mien, as if you wished to deceive yourselves by telling yourselves it is the more difficult, harder path, it is the humbler, narrower path, it is the lonelier more disparaged path — at the bottom of your hearts you know better, you are not truthful enough to act as you pretend, yet still truthful enough to sense a pang in yourselves. The pious and the enthusiasts are precisely the conscience-ridden humans.

5[8]

And when it concerns the decision about your life, how can you entrust yourselves to someone, whether it be a Christ or Plato or Goethe! But your faith must be so blind, so unconditional, so fanatical for you to drown out the song of your bad conscience, for you to boost your morale with the energy of your sounds and movements. Oh, you actors playing to yourselves!

5[9]

Fine, we let ourselves be made sad by the music and sigh like a willow in the wind — but then suddenly with cheerful laughter we shake all that off and exclaim: the music was capable of that, sorrow and tears *without cause*! To live in feeling without knowing the causes for the feeling! And now off into the real world and our soul is freer and has already atoned for its sickness.

5[10]

To arouse feelings — bad music can do that too. But that it produces such in *you*, who easily experience music as mindless or extravagant or mendacious or histrionic — that constitutes its value.

5[11][5]

We are so grateful for the good and so little spoiled, we count a musician who has made nothing but bad music and one hundred single measures of the first and most beautiful order, among the great musicians.

5[12]

To remain standing before the fate inside us, like Schopenhauer, but not therefore to give shape to his "insights": with our intellect we must vault ourselves over our character into the expanse and height.

5[13]

Humans should already have within themselves the norm according to which they should have to act — the colossal absurdity is still believed to this day! The conscience! It is an aggregate of feelings of affinity and aversion regarding actions and opinions, *imitated* feelings we encountered among parents and teachers!

5[14]

The counterfeiting of truth *in favor of the things* we *love* (e.g., God even) — most accursed bad habit among enlightened minds, whom humanity is used to trusting and who *thus* corrupt it, hold it captive in the delusion. And often it was such a difficult sacrifice for you, *sacrificium intellectus propter amorem*![6] Alas, I too sang its praise! W⟨agner⟩ i⟨n⟩ B⟨ayreuth⟩

5[15]

Whenever music brings us a feeling, then reason must say nevertheless: there is no cause for these feelings, we are being *deceived*. It is the same as with yawning, we yawn *along*, without cause.

5[16]

Struggle not against stupidities, rather against conceits: elimination of imaginary things from the minds: Don Quixote Cervantes

5[17]

The general characteristic of the age: we know what no other age has known, there were and are myriad different valuations of the same things, and perhaps the number is increasing, the more the number of independent humans increases (formerly, independent cultures corresponded to them). But the more various the valuations, the more humans can *exchange* with one another; the intellectual and spiritual interchange increases. We *learn to understand* others in order to know what we can offer them, what we can demand of them. — Care to be taken that no imaginary things get smuggled in whereby the value of all the true ones gets falsified. This is in the *general* interest.

5[18]

Sensations referring to unreal things are *unjustified*, without a right to existence: because only real things have a right to sensations and with the intrusion of fictitious ones their right is curtailed.

5[19]

Art's dangerousness consists in habituating us to imaginary things, indeed in ascribing to them a higher valuation: in preferring the half-truths, the *dazzling* ideas, in short, in letting the brilliance and effect of things stand as proof of their quality, indeed of their reality. "To perfection belongs reality," this error in reasoning has been made very often. "What we strongly admire must be *true*"

5[20]

Nothing interests me more than when someone takes a detour by way of distant peoples and stars, only finally to relate in this way something about *himself*.

5[21][7]

A human can endure the most horrible contempt (like the Jews), but he must derive the feeling of p⟨ower⟩ somehow (as Jews do from money)

5[22]

Art's value is that here for once we let the *upside-down world* be right side up,[8] untrue true, for recreation (the untrue as true, the unfounded as founded, etc.).

5[23][9]

For K⟨öselitz⟩: your youth lacked recognition and success, such as the experience of a regular course of education from semester to semester (?), etc. In its course you let a scattering prevail over you, just as if this ego had not sufficed you. The genteel young people grow up amidst social success: this becomes the basis of their further endeavors, the serene feeling, as it were. — You have diverged from the customary path in order to take the right path: but with that there are always pangs of conscience — G. Sand

5[24]

Christianity gave each person the right to take himself unspeakably *seriously*: he is an "eternal being!" a "genius," a "personality"

5[25]

Our task is to plant the correct feeling,[10] i.e., that which corresponds to true things and correct judgments. Planting does *not* mean restoring: for they have never existed. Let us not be deceived by the phrase "natural or real feeling"! That signifies "popular," "ancient," "general" — it has nothing to do with the truth. Only on the basis of *correct* feelings can humans *understand* each other lastingly and across all distances. For that *new* valuations are required. First of all, a critique and elimination of the old ones. What is to be *unlearned* is now the next mass[11] to be worked on.

5[26]

Valuations based upon an *incorrect* foundation wage a destructive war against one another, though perhaps all still work together towards *strengthening* certain basic representations. For that reason, they cannot be left to themselves but must be attacked. NB — The action into which they draw the human being serves to produce false standards over and over again — the devil gets painted on the wall and in the end, one is *governed* by the same feelings that one struggles against. Hence: one should *not* struggle *much* against them!

5[27]

Schopenhauer's teaching contains at its inner core the principle: we are guided by our *appetites*: *not* by our profitable and reasonable interests, let alone our virtue and wisdom. The world is appetite.

5[28][12]

Martyrdom is evidence for truthfulness and pride.

5[29]

The feeling of happiness has two forms: the feeling of power and the feeling of surrender: the latter is that of fatigue and relaxation.

5[30]

The chaos of incorrect feelings, anarchy at times, are transitional stages: to be brought about for certain groups.

5[31]

Correct feelings will still be highly varied: and what they have in common is that they include no imaginary factors, i.e., what gets *weighed* is *real*: the *scales* vary, not what is weighed.

5[32]

In many things one will for a long time *not* be allowed to *have feelings*, because here *nothing certain* has been said as yet. Necessary here to stake out end points!

5[33]

Once faith in Jesus Christ was recommended for the redemption from sins. But now I say: the means is: do not believe in sin! This cure is *more radical*. The erstwhile cure wanted to make one delusion bearable through another.

5[34]

Only it is not so easy *not* to believe — for we ourselves once believed in it and the whole world believes, or at least seems to believe in it. Not only do we have to relearn, but to *rehabituate* our valuations — *practice* is needed!

5[35]

"Accept *my* art: for then you Germans have an art which is comparable to that of other nations, '*the* German art' — at first indeed only '*one G⟨erman⟩ a⟨rt⟩*' but now it shall be *proven how* just this art corresponds to the character of the Germans, has grown from it, topics thoughts music, etc." — This is Wagner's way of tending to *his* fame: he wants one *nation* to advocate for him and incorporate him into itself and its "fame." This game has never yet been played so openly — which is why until now it has not succeeded. Later, when Wagner is dead and his writings forgotten, something like that will be possible. In the meantime, composers of all nations are seizing upon his music and before long it will no longer sound like German music but rather like "music." — It ⟨is⟩ the music of the *grand opera*.

5[36]

Wagner courts being named the *German* artist, but, alas, neither the grand opera nor his character is specifically German: which is why he has not as yet become dear to the populace, but instead to a class of refined and over-cultivated people — the circle to which, say,[13] in the last century Rousseau appealed.

5[37][14]

In France Christianity has attained its most consummate types: the Quietists (Francis de Sales): they stand higher than Paul. Fénelon the consummate Christian on an antique foundation. Pascal — — —

5[38]

The satisfaction of the drive should not become a practice in which the race suffers, i.e., no selection occurs anymore, rather all mate and beget children. The *extinction* of many orders of humans is just as *desirable* as any kind of procreation. — And through this close relationship with a woman one is supposed to let his whole development be thwarted and disrupted — for the sake of that drive!! If one did not even find such close friendships useful (in the highest sense)! The "completion" of the m⟨an⟩ by the woman to make a full human being[15] is nonsense: *from that* there is nothing to be deduced, either. — Rather: only to marry 1) for the purpose of higher development 2) and in order to leave behind the fruits of such a humanity.

— For everyone else concubinage will suffice, with prevention of conception. — We must make an end of this gross frivolity. These geese shall not wed! Marriages ought to become *much rarer*! Walk through the large cities and ask yourselves whether this rabble ought to procreate! Let them go to their whores! — Prostitution not sentimental! It should *not* be the sacrifice that is made to the ladies or the Jewish purse — rather to the improvement of the race. And besides one should not misjudge this sacrifice: the whores are honest and do what they like and *do not ruin* the man through the "bond of marriage" — this strangulation![16]

5[39]

The Italian painters have retranslated the "sacred story" so beautifully, discovered all the moving scenes of the family, all those moments where an important person makes a moment *unforgettable* for several: before each of their paintings we can shed tears. Only where the sacred wretchedness begins, there we no longer *em*pathize — the knowledge of its consequences holds the *counterweight.*

5[40]

[+++] more valuable to look for the so rarely *well-rounded* humans who are not monsters with protuberances and presumptions.

5[41][17]

Just do not press unbidden one's opinions! Let them be stated and dispatch a little bit of laughter after them; no genius has yet existed whose opinions would not have been dispensable.

5[42]

We have to learn to think differently about geniuses. I would not know why fertile humans should not conduct themselves quietly and unassumingly (Moltke) or rather — it is contrary to all fertility to throw one's person thus into the fray of opinions and oneself to be full of desires that make us restless, impatient, and deprive us of the solemnity of pregnancy. I can still tell from every measure what ailments the musician has: his wanting-to mean-more, his rejection of the rule, his underscoring of what he does better than others, every pettiness is perpetually *co*-productive once the genius-folly rages in him. By contrast m⟨en⟩ like Moltke.

5[43][18]

[+++] to be able to promise: and *if* the occurrence of an appearance is merely as certain as this one, then it makes no difference whether we say "I will," "I shall do" instead of "it happens," "it is done." Just so medicine men once promised natural events with their "*I will* that the sun shine, that it rain," and some day we will recognize that willing in relation to ourselves is also such a prejudice. — So does duty rest upon a prejudice? Upon an unjustified pride?

5[44]

Are representations really motives of our actions? Are they not perhaps merely forms under which we understand our actions, something on the side that the intellect generates during such actions as are noticed by us at all? Most actions are not noticed and pass by without intellectual enticement. I mean even: the intellectual action, the actual neural process of a thought is something essentially different from what becomes noticeable to us as a thought: our representations of which we have knowledge are the smallest and poorest part of those we have. The motives of our actions lie in the dark, and what we *believe* to be motives would not suffice to lift a finger.

5[45]

Language bears major prejudices within itself and maintains them, e.g., that what is signified with one word is also one process: will, desire, drive — complicated things! The pain in all three (as consequence of a pressure an urgen⟨cy⟩) gets transferred into the process "for what?": the pain has nothing to do with that, it is a common mistake by association. "I have such a longing for you" No! I have a need and I believe you can satisfy it (a *belief* is inserted) "I love you" no! in me is an enamored state and I *believe* you will allay it. These object-accusatives! A belief is implied in all these words for feelings, e.g., will hate etc. A *pain* and a *view* with regard to its alleviation — that is the fact. Likewise where there is talk about purposes. — A vehement love is the *fanatical* stubborn *view* that only such and such a person can allay my need; it is faith that makes us happy and unhappy,[19] occasionally even in possession still strong enough to withstand any disappointment, i.e., truth.

5[46]

We must study then the urgent conditions of humanity, but their views, *how* the same are to be resolved, must still be figured in: —

If we alter the view⟨s⟩ about the means of relief, then we alter humanity's "longings" "will" "desire." Hence: alteration of the valuation is alteration of the will. — Should it turn out that humanity suffers most of all from the impossibility of fulfilling its will, then it is to be examined whether the essential pain, relieved by other means, perhaps does not entail an unfulfillable will: that therefore the ideals of humanity are fulfillable and another valuation of everything unfulfillable must arise.

5[47][20]

When someone is always *surprised* by his own actions (like the wildly passionate), thus cannot anticipate himself, then he doubts his *freedom*, and then there is often talk of daemonic influences. Thus the *regularity* with which certain representations and actions occur in us leads us to the belief that here we are free: to be able to calculate, to know in advance! i.e., omnipotence is derived from the omniscience of God — a common error in reasoning. The feeling of power in the intellect⟨ual⟩ sphere that appears with foreknowledge illogically gets linked with what is foreknown: *as prophets* we fancy ourselves to be miracle workers. The fact is: "in such and such a case we usually do that." The appearance is "such and such is the case: I want now to do this." Willing is a prejudice. Something happens in and through us, and I know beforehand what comes from it and highly appreciate the fact that this occurs. Nevertheless, this happens without our freedom and often contrary to our superficial knowledge: we say then in astonishment "I cannot do what I will." We only observe our essence *from outside*, even our intellectual essence: all consciousness merely grazes the surfaces.

5[48]

You are looking for "bad conscience"? You will find it among people of cowardly sentimentality who deny the truth for the sake of love.

5[49]

What happens most frequently is lying to oneself. The intellect⟨ual⟩ conscience is weak and the *other* c⟨onscience⟩ stronger. Cleansing and strengthening, not annihilation of both is necessary.

[6 = N V 4. Autumn 1880]

6[1][1]

Compared to the Brahmins we know humanity only in a state of massive slackening of its feeling of strength and of its belief in itself: even among our proudest philosophers.

6[2][2]

Humans whose drive has become immoderate only through long abstinence, so that they then lose control over it in equal measure, e.g., Lord Byron[3] with eating.

6[3][4]

The history of science shows the victory of the nobler drives: there is a *great deal of morality* in circulation in scientific practice.

6[4]

Which drives constitute the individual? At a certain level of stupidity i⟨ndividuals⟩ ruin one another. Just so with an *atrophy* of the basic drives and their substitution by altruism. With certain qualities of other i⟨ndividuals⟩ one must feel the opposite or strangeness or not feel them at all: or harmonic accompanying notes or fundamental movements, by which our movements first receive a measure. The "music of individuals" "counterpoint." Can be charming: parallel movement, the convergence of two lines in an angle, etc., the arabesque of the line that often teasingly touches the other straight line and instantly leaves it. I intersected with W⟨agner⟩: we ran towards each other with great fervor, there was a flash, and then apart again with the same speed, ever more.

6[5]

One reaches an upper limit of one's dishonesty: and there we become hateful to ourselves and, turning the mirror *towards* ourselves now even take pleasure in the sight of the ugly, for thereby we take revenge, or experience disgust at the satiety of intoxication by illusions. — *Drive for truth*!

6[6]

The Greeks suffered most of all at the sight of ugliness, the Jews at t⟨hat⟩ of sin, the French at the sight of the inept, insipid, brutal self — which is why *they idealized the opposite* — and this ideal transformed them in turn. Revenge for the suffering — motive for the representation of the gods and artistic models. The lack of enchanting sensuality turns German painters into enthusiasts of the sensual. Suffering from the heat of passion has turned the Italians into devotees of cold artificial formalism: and into devotees of the Virgin M⟨ary⟩ and Christ. Schopenhauer idealized compassion and chastity because he suffered most from their opposite. "The independent human" is the ideal of the most dependent and impressionable. — These are the *unfulfillable ideals*, genuine false phantasms: their sight *enraptures and humiliates*: this hybrid state is telling for humans of the unfulfilled ideal. It is their zenith: they *repose* then *above* their essence, with a contemptuous gaze downwards.

6[7]

Often a drive is misunderstood, falsely interpreted e.g., the sexual drive, hunger, the desire for fame. Perhaps all of morality is an *interpretation* of physical drives.

6[8]

In that hour when we do not know how wicked and how good we are to ourselves and both seem to us infinite —

6[9][5]

more liar than devious.
hard in words, fearsome at bottom.
tyrannical and cowardly at once, like Nap⟨oleon⟩

6[10][6]

Oh, what authority, what magic science exercises on passionate spirits! They surely see in it a wonderful magic and turn into fantasts here.

What a nice pillow doubt is for a well-formed head![7]

6[11][8]

the chasm that separates us from him who wants to acquire money, worker, craftsman, artist, not to be denied: bequeathed ages ago.

6[12][9]

"it takes *time* to make oneself love: and even when I had nothing to do, I had the vague feeling that I had no time to lose." Napoleon.

6[13][10]

Napoleon made novels and "measured" his daydreams afterwards "by the compass of his *raisonnement*."[11] "Through *thought* I flung myself into an ideal world"

6[14][12]

"I have always loved analysis, and when I was seriously in love I dissected my love piece by piece"

6[15][13]

the time and circumstances were not favorable to his *good aspects*, they did not allow them to *develop*.

6[16][14]

"The person whom one *must constantly bribe*," Napoleon said of Savary; he trusted him unconditionally because he had completely isolated him from all respectable people and knew he had him in his hand.[15]

with respect to the *intellect*

the perfect servant of his master, Duroc (Duc de Frioul): cold reserved impenetrable, he never thought beyond his duties, he did not flatter; perfect exactitude, a faithful mirror of the surroundings for his master and of the master for his surroundings; no friends, no need for entertainment, no pleasure in examining whether his master be a great man or not, indifferent to everything, no boredom, no enthusiasm. Dry cold, entirely personal without passion with respect to others, clever and skilled in certain circles.

6[17][16]

"It befits only youth to have patience: for it has the future before it" says Napoleon. "Everything had to be done in this (Ital⟨ian⟩) army, persons and things"

6[18]

The useful can be no final goal, no principle of morality, nor can the pleasant (which kind of pleasantness is to be preferred?) the final goals cannot at all be reached at once through concepts: we can always only *envision* goals to the extent that we have *drives beforehand*. How far our drives can grow no one knows.

6[19][17]

the dry and icy tone of the discontented

6[20]

the shameless form of market crying[18] with which our age surpasses all others. Never did an Athenian artist —

6[21][19]

"In France one never knows how to take an interest in things when one takes an interest in persons."[20] Napoleon. The habits of an old monarchy accustomed you to personifying everything. You do not know how to take anything seriously, "except perhaps equality. And they would gladly forgo that if everyone could flatter himself with being the first. Everyone must be given the hope of elevating himself"

6[22][21]

Napoleon said the time in Egypt was the most beautiful of his life, for it was the most ideal. Everything he dreamed of he was able to carry out. Civilization was not in his way.

6[23]

Main difference: Before some people hovers a model condition of things outside them, where these things play upon them as it were in a most pleasing way (politicians, socialists, etc.) Before the others a model condition of themselves where they play upon external things and humans in a way most pleasing to themselves: the latter the ideal of productive nat⟨ures⟩, the former that of those onerously laboring: they prefer to be passive beings! The ones tyrants and the others slaves. The first do not doubt, once they become so and so, that they will elicit from the world instrument the most glorious notes: and the latter do not doubt that when everything is securely ordered and made *free* from the individual (the ruler), everything will be predictable and they will have nothing but pleasing *impressions* of life. "Ex-pressive and im-pressive humans"

6[24][22]

"What did the revolution produce? Vanity. What will it end? Vanity once more. Freedom is a pretext."

6[25][23]

He suddenly ended his *role* as a *bonhomme*[24] and added a command with the dryness of a master who will not let pass the opportunity to command.

6[26][25]

Napoleon's weak side: he could not endure the thought of defeat in any respect. Because his soul was without *nobility* and he did not know the great feelings which transcend a bad fate, he turned his thoughts away from this weak part of himself: instead, he fixed his mind on his admir⟨able⟩ ability *to aggrandize himself through success*. His fortune was his personal superstition (*Je réussirai*![26]) and the cult, to which he felt himself obliged for the sake of the same, legitimated in his eyes all the sacrifices he was to impose on us.

6[27][27]

"The resistance to crime is so innate in us that we very easily believe in the *necessity* in which he who committed the crime found himself."

6[28][28]

To exchange weak devotion for the real fear which he inspired: one admired the boldness of his game.

6[29][29]

"You have seen other times: I, I date from the time where I began to be something" Napoleon

6[30][30]

"I have no hatred, I am not capable of doing something out of vengeance: I simply remove what annoys me!" said Napoleon with regard to the execution of the Duke of Enghien

6[31]

Our drives run riot in the tricks and artifices of the metaphysicians, they are the apologists of *human pride*: humanity cannot get over its lost gods! Supposing this passion consumes itself in rage: what a state of fatigue, of pallor, of dimmed glances! The greatest distrust of the intellect as the drives' tool: the afterbirth of pride is skepticism. The tortuous inquisition of our drives and their mendaciousness! It is a final vengeance, in this *self-pulverization* the human is still the god who has lost himself. What follows upon this violent skepticism? Exhaustion, the second exhaustion, an age of senility: the entire past is dimly felt, despair itself becomes history, and in the end the knowledge of all these things is still a sufficient stimulus for these old men.

This entire history is being played out in ever fewer heads. But among everyone else the loss of faith becomes notorious — and now ensues: the suspension of fear, authority, trust, life lived for the moment, for the crudest goals, for the most visible: an *inverted* movement begins. Trust is still greatest in that which is ⟨most⟩ opposed to the earlier goal! A trying and experimenting, a feeling of irresponsibility, the pleasure in anarchy! *Prudence* has taken the place of pride. Science enters into *its* service. A more common species of humans acquires authority (instead of the *noblesse*[31] or priests): first the merchants, then the workers. The masses emerge as dominant: the individual must *dissimulate* as part of the masses. — Now some such are still being born who in earlier ages would have belonged to the ruling class of priests, nobility, thinkers. Now they oversee the destruction of religion and metaphysics, nobility and individual-significance. They are epigones. They must *give* themselves a meaning, *set* a goal in order not to fare badly. Let deceit and secret retreat into what has been overcome, service in nocturnal temple ruins be spurned! Just so service in the market halls! They seize upon the parts of knowledge which are not furthered *by the interest of prudence*! Just so the arts, to which the modern[32] spirit is averse. They are the observers of the age and live behind the events. They practice making themselves free from the age and understanding it only like an eagle that soars above it. They limit themselves to the greatest independence and do not wish to be burghers and politicians and owners. Behind all the proceedings they reserve the individuals, educate them — perhaps one day, when the vulgar frenzy of anarchy is over, humanity will need them. Shame on those who now importunately offer themselves to the masses as their saviors! Or to the nations! We are emigrants. — We also want to be the bad conscience for science in the service of the prudent! We want to be ready! We want to be the mortal enemies of those among us who take flight into hypocrisy and want reaction! — It is true, we are descended from princes and priests: but just for that reason we honor our ancestors because they *overcame themselves*. We would disgrace them if we were to deny what is greatest about them! What then do the princes and priests of the present age who must and want to live through self-deception matter to us!

6[32]

The same insecurity and skepticism the boatman has with respect to his crossing, whether it will succeed, whether it has been undertaken at the right moment, we must have with respect to all duties. I am *not* absolutely obliged, I don't have it so *easy*. We experiment with our virtues and good deeds and do not know for sure that they are the necessary ones with respect to the goal. We must raise doubts and question all moral rules. Moreover, they are so crude that no real action corresponds to such a rule: the real is much more complicated.

6[33][33]

Napoleon was serene, he secretly enjoyed the small constraint that the new ceremonial produced among all of us.

6[34][34]

"To be a stranger to every intrigue: almost a fault at court. What princes least[35] forgive: that someone in their service observes some means of slipping away from their power"

6[35][36]

"There is not enough pomp there: it would not throw dust in your eyes," Napoleon said to Monsieur de Rémusat when the latter submitted a plan for the décor of the new imperial reign

6[36][37]

"I, solely of my own accord, am the entire revolution." Once he achieved his character, he took care not to destroy anything useful to it. He wanted to dazzle and benumb the French, by all means at once. He loved the pomp of the ancien régime, he believed that in this way the parvenu became even better concealed.

6[37][38]

"*Vengeons nous, par en médire*"[39] Montaigne

6[38][40]

"It is always only a very small number of humans who allow themselves to blame success" Flattery carries off the victory over criticism.

6[39]

Music has no sound for the raptures of the spirit; if it wants to render the condition of Faust and Hamlet and Manfred, it leaves spirit aside and paints emotional states that are highly unpleasant without spirit and not fit to be seen; it coarsens and paints discontent and misery, perhaps with *musical* spirit; but how dreadful is this art when it indiscriminately paints what is ugly: what torments are peculiar to the sounds, the obtrusive sounds! — Is that because among musicians a fine and well-defined spirit is generally rare? Because they never isolate feeling in themselves and do not know its refraction and colorfulness in the flash of inspiration? They must coarsen all states, translate everything back into the inhuman, as it were: as if thoughts and words were not yet invented. This is moreover a great enticement: there is primordial nature in music: it belongs to the age when one revered landscape's savage nature and discovered high mountain ranges. To a society that is not mature enough for spiritual pleasures, that is even too intellectually impoverished for painting and has generally already squandered its mental powers when it sets about to *amuse* itself, only the appeal to the feelings and senses remains: and in these the musician offers the most decorous amusement. Already more common is the pleasure of the theater, with its counterfeiting of human events and the crude charm of direct imitation of exciting scenes. One step farther: and we have for recreation the arousal of the drives through drinks, etc. — The poet stands higher than the musician, he makes higher demands, namely, on the whole human being: and the thinker makes still higher demands: he wants all of the fresh, gath⟨ered⟩ strength and does not summon to enjoyment but rather to the wrestling match and to the deepest renunciation of all personal drives.

6[40]

I loved the man,[41] how he lived as if on an island, how he *shut* himself *off* from the world without hatred:[42] so I understood it! How distant he has become to me, as he now, swimming in the current of national greed and national spitefulness, would like to meet the need of these present *peoples*,[43] stupefied by politics and money greed, for religion! I once thought he had nothing to do with the moderns — I was apparently a fool.[44]

6[41][45]

When Napoleon became cheerful he assumed garrison mores and was without moderation.

6[42][46]

"Chance always remains a mystery for mediocre minds and becomes a reality for higher humans." To determine the part of chance with mathematical precision in advance: "one decimal more or less can change everything." "Mediocre people are brought to a certain prominence through circumstances which they have not created"

6[43]

"*Pour être un véritable grand homme, il faut réellement avoir improvisé une partie de sa gloire et se montrer au-dessus de l'événement qu'on a causé.*"[47]

6[44][48]

"Tacitus a skillful writer but seldom a statesman"

6[45][49]

"When politicians are truly skillful, they understand how to make themselves masters of their passions, for they go as far as to *calculate* their effects"

6[46][50]

"the statesman, a perfectly eccentric personality, always alone on the one side with the world on the other." While he observes things and lets the often so dissimilar threads run evenly through his hand, paying the greatest attention — how can he amuse himself with sparing certain convenances of feeling which for ordinary humans are so important! (Blood ties, affection, etc.)

6[47]

The energy of the tension (between love and hatred) never greater than with Christ. He had more than all of mankind.

odium generis humani[51]

6[48]

The feeling and happiness of submission — to be explained by the end of fear, commencement of security (*not* by the fem⟨inine⟩ drive)

6[49]

Power	: to contradict	Foundations of logic. A > < B
Surrender	: to consent	A = A

power urges to recognize difference.
surrender wants to posit equality.

6[50]

My goal is not for everyone, nevertheless it is communicable, on account of *similar humans* as well as because those *opposed* will gain strength and pleasure from it to formulate their essence for themselves, too, and to realize it as working spirit. I want to help all who seek their model by showing *how* one seeks a model: and my greatest joy is encountering the individual models that do *not* resemble me. The devil take all the imitators and followers and panegyrists and admirers and devotees!

6[51][52]

"the military glory which lives for so long in history is that which for contemporaries most quickly expires." Napoleon after the greatest moment of his power (the Peace of Tilsit)

6[52][53]

Napoleon saw in war the means to benumb us, or at least to reduce us to silence.

6[53]

The sexual excitement in rising sustains a tension which discharges itself in the feeling of power: to want to dominate — a mark of the most sensual people. The waning tendency of the sexual drive manifests itself in the decrease of the thirst for power: preservation and nourishment and often the pleasure in eating emerge as the substitute (parental drive is to preserve, order, nourish, not to rule, but rather to provide well-being for self and others). In power inheres the feeling of gladly doing harm — a profound irritation of the whole organism which constantly wants to take revenge. The most lustful animals are in this condition the most malign and violent, self-obliviously subject to their drive.

6[54][54]

Love as a passion is *desire for absolute power* over a person: (e.g., to want to be the unique object of thoughts and feelings). The person in love barely sees the remaining world and sacrifices every other interest to this thirst for power. To believe in being loved entails a deep satiety: "we are felt as absolute power!"

6[55][55]

We must *separate* the aphrodisiac stimulus and the consequences of its satisfaction for the continuation of the species: the expression "sexual drive" contains a prejudice

6[56]

The reabsorption of semen[56] into the blood is the strongest nourishment and perhaps most of all produces the impulse of power, the agitation of all forces to overcome obstacles, the thirst for contradiction and opposition. Up to now the feeling of power has risen to the highest level among abstinent priests and anchorites (e.g., among the Brahmins)[57]

6[57]

The feeling of the desire for *submission* is perhaps *feminine* — and both sexes are capable of both feelings, but each has its own particular excess. God knows with what peculiarities of the sexual female function it may have to do that her sensual stimulation is not essentially expressed as will to power: to be controlled, to serve; they feel weaker through love. The nourishment of the ovary demands strength.

6[58]

Whoever is capable of deep feelings must also endure their intense struggle against their opposites. One can, so as to rest wholly in oneself free from suffering, wean oneself of just the deep feelings, so that in their weakness they also arouse only weak counter-forces: which in their sublimated thinness likely get *ignored* and give the human the impression he is completely in harmony with himself. — *Just so* in social life: if everything is supposed to proceed altruistically, then the contrasts between individuals must be reduced to a sublime minimum: so that all the hostile tendencies and tensions, through which the individual preserves himself as individual, can barely be noticed anymore, that means: individuals must be reduced to the palest shade of the individual! Thus, equality prevailing by far! That is euthanasia, entirely unproductive! Just as those humans without deep feelings, the amiable, calm and so-called happy ones, are also just unproductive! The value of science is to be a huge counterforce: perhaps bad logic and fanciful thinking always ignite anew in opposition to it! — Perhaps this is necessary!

6[59]

Humanity has no goal, just as little as the dinosaurs had one, but it has a *development*: i.e., its end is *not more significant* than any point along its way! NB. Consequently, we cannot define the good so that it would be the means to the "goal of mankind." Would it be what extended this development as far as possible? Or what would yield the highest culmination point (between rising and falling, becoming and passing away)? But this would once again presuppose a measure for the culmination point! And *why* as long as possible? This too presupposes a good e.g., the pleasure of existence. — As much pleasure as possible as goal? But one cannot even direct one's individual life by that, for we do not know the sources of pleasure, the drives, in relation to their innermost needs e.g., whether a maximum of pleasure does not presuppose a tremendous displeasure? — Or a *minimum* of displeasure in the development? — Toward that everything now strives — but this also means as weak a development as possible, a general self-weakening, a faint leave-taking from humanity thus far, up to the boundary where the animals become our masters again! Feeble stupor is moreover no ideal capable of calling forth great sacrifices — and yet a tremendous renunciation would have to be required, if humanity were to rise to this level! But this could well be the *end* one day *without* being a goal of striving! Or else a stray star will take pity then on humanity!

6[60]

the highest degree of individuality is reached when in the greatest anarchy someone founds his realm as recluse.

6[61]

the thirst for power is telling for the ascending path of *development*, the thirst for surrender for the descending. The pleasures of old age all have at bottom this surrender to things, thoughts, persons: the upward striving person dominates. — The sick person anticipates the tendency of old age.

6[62]

We *always* sense the outside world *differently*, because each time it stands in contrast with the prevailing drive in us: and because as something living this drive waxes and wanes and is nothing abiding, so in the briefest moment is our sensation of the outside world always *becoming* and *ceasing*, thus changing.

6[63]

Judgment is something very slow in contrast with the perpetual infinitely small activity of the drives — so the drives are always there more quickly, and judgment always arrives only after a *fait accompli*: either as effect and consequence of the drive impulse or as effect of the *co-excited opposite drive*. Memory is stimulated by the drives to deliver its material. — Through every drive its counter-drive is also excited, and not only this one, but like overtone strings still others whose relation cannot be designated with so common a word as "contrast."

6[64]

We painfully sense that someone scorns us. In a high frame of mind we look over and back upon this painful sensation as something remote that hardly pertains to us anymore, the sensation of the same almost becomes *knowledge of it*: nearly all things of which we have only this sensation of knowledge seem to us remoter and outside us, the underlying suffering or pleasant drive is barely perceptible to us anymore. But it *must* be in there, memory registers only facts of the drives: it learns only what is transformed into an object of a drive! — Our knowledge is the most weakened form of our drives' life: hence so powerless against the strong drives.

6[65]

In matters of the spirit anyone is great who, as the great exception, feels objects of knowledge strongly and who comports himself toward distant objects just as toward the near, so that they can hurt him, arouse passion, exalt, in short, so that they become fused in him with the strongest drives. (Honesty, for example, would no doubt be curiosity pride tyranny gentleness magnanimity courage in relation to things which for most remain entirely cold and abstract) Passion for abstracta and the inability to keep an abstraction remote and indifferent to oneself makes for the thinker.

6[66][58]

Humans tortured by a preacher of repentance, like a deer that entangles itself in a trap and dies in a furious frenzy.

6[67]

My **task**: to sublimate all the drives so that the perception of the strange goes very far and yet is still intertwined with enjoyment: the drive to honesty with myself, to justice toward things, so strong that its *joy* outweighs the value of other kinds of pleasure, and those, if need be, are sacrificed to it, altogether or in part. There is indeed no disinterested contemplation, that would be complete boredom. But the *tenderest* emotion suffices!

6[68][59]

Napoleon hated nothing more in the world than someone's exercising the capacity to judge in relation to him, or only having the capacity at all.

6[69][60]

she lacked serenity (Mad. de Staël): according to Rémusat "*une privation sans remède pour le bonheur et même pour le talent.*"[61]

6[70]

the I is not the disposition of one being toward several (drives, thoughts, etc.), rather the ego is a plurality of person-like forces of which now this one now that one stands in the foreground as ego and regards the others as a subject does an influential and determining outside world. The subject point leaps around; we probably sense the degrees of the forces and drives like nearness and distance and interpret for ourselves as a landscape and plain what in truth is a multiplicity of quantitative degrees. The nearest denominates "I" more for us than the remoter, and, accustomed to the inexact designation "I and *tu*,[62] everything else," we instinctively turn the *predominant* momentarily into the *whole ego* and place all the weaker drives perspectivally farther off and make of them a *whole you*[63] or "it." We treat ourselves as a plurality and carry into these "social relationships" all of the social habits we have with respect to humans, animals, regions, things. We feign, cause anxiety in ourselves, create parties, stage court scenes, ambush ourselves, torment ourselves, glorify ourselves, make of this and that in us our God and our devil and are as insincere and sincere as we are wont to be in the presence of society. — Trace all social relations back to egoism? Fine: for me, though, it is also true that all egoistical inner experiences can be traced back to our ingrained, acquired attitudes towards others. What drives would we have that from the beginning would not bring us into a posture towards other beings, nourishment e.g., the sexual drive? That which *others* teach us, want from us, command us to fear and pursue, is the original material of our spirit: alien judgments about things. Those furnish us with our *image of ourselves*, by which we measure ourselves, are well or ill content with ourselves! Our own judgment is only a *continuous production*[64] of combined alien judgments! Our own drives appear to us under the interpretation of others: while they are all basically pleasant, yet through acquired judgments of their worth they are so mixed with unpleasant associated feelings, indeed some are now felt to be bad drives: "it pulls in a direction where it should not" — whereas bad drive is actually a *contradictio in adjecto*.[65] — What then does *egoism* mean! *Within ourselves* we can be once more egoistic or altruistic, hard-hearted, generous, just mild untruthful, want to harm or give pleasure: the way the drives contend with each other, the feeling of the I is always strongest just where the preponderance is.

6[71]

Indescribable disgust when our educated class fantasizes about the necessity of an ideal education and a renewal of religion! this mendacious rabble that wants to become religious again with music and acting and gets into its head, just as soon as its heart begins again to tremble, to abandon all sense of mental honesty and to plunge head-first into the mystical mire. Altogether the thought of a generation grown stupefied and servile by politics and greed for money!

For whether one serves a Napoleon or the nationality principle, both lead to slavery and in the end to self-disgust: Good luck to religion! Good luck to the artists who do not have the inborn decency of a free spiritual attitude! I once thought: we are another sort, of another provenance; nothing was more foreign to me than to *proffer* myself to *these* currents of nationality and the tendency to mysticism! I saw them — I was nauseated then, and now, on their account. To be alone! to live apart! was always my device. What do I care that those who then appeared to me like-minded in this respect now all *proffer* themselves *there*! Here the spectral fingers of the spiritualist and the mathematical-magical trickster, there a brain-scorching cult of music, there the reawakened treacherousness of a persecution of the Jews — witness the general exercise of hatred

6[72][66]

"Those who come to visit me will pay me an honor: those who do not come will render me a pleasure."[67] Augier

6[73][68]

Napoleon after the first Italian campaign, to a journalist: Remember in the reports of our victories to speak *only of me, always of me*, do you understand?

6[74]

All moralists are at one in the general tendency as to *where* action ought to strive and what the welfare of humanity is — *I* find them ruled by one drive and therein full of prejudice. The rule of altruism seems to *me* to be ruining humanity — a process of dying away, euthanasia: — perhaps moralists thus serve the general development: but they *expect* something *contrary*! I want to establish egoism and that wise insight which *reluctantly* meddles in the other individual's business and affairs: only through necessity are we altruistic.

6[75]

All moralists share common assessments of good and evil, depending on respective sympathetic and egoistic drives. I find good what serves an end: but the "good end" is nonsense. For everywhere the question is, "good for what?" Good is always only an expression for a *means*. The "good purpose" is a good means to a purpose. Every end — — —

6[76]

The virtue of cleanliness. NB. Root of the drive to beauty

6[77]

A system of life that is supposed to rest upon inclinations alone — altruism. But then fate would need to play on us solely with chords — that would mean doing away with the unreasonableness of existence and turning it into human reason. And so that each would hear only harmonies, everyone else would have to be like him and have no other conditions — but in that case inclination would become weak and finally unnecessary because everything would already *tender itself* without striving.

6[78]

When noble independence is lost, all talents become *feeble* — whether under Napoleon's tyranny or altruism: end of the geniuses!

6[79]

"With only a taste for the real we are not good for anything, neither on a farm nor in a palace"[69]

6[80]

Our relation to ourselves! With *egoism nothing* at all is said. We turn all habitual drives, good and bad, toward ourselves: thinking about ourselves, feeling for and against ourselves, the struggle inside us — never do we treat ourselves as individual, rather as a duality and plurality; all social practices (friendship revenge envy) we honestly practice on ourselves. The animal's naïve egoism is completely altered by our *social training*: we cannot feel at all anymore a uniqueness of the ego, *we are always among a plurality*. We have split ourselves asunder and always split ourselves anew. The *social drives* (like *enmity envy hatred*) (which presuppose a plurality) have transformed us: we have transposed "society" into ourselves, in small, and to retreat into ourselves is not flight from society but often a painful *continuous daydreaming and interpreting* of our processes following the schema of earlier experiences. Not only God but every being we recognize, we take, even without names, into ourselves: we are the cosmos, *insofar as we have grasped or dreamed it*. The olives and the storms have become a part of us: likewise the stock market and the newspaper.

6[81]

Our *waking life* is an *interpreting* of inner drive processes aided by the remembrance of everything felt and seen: an arbitrary picture language of them, like dreaming of sensations when asleep.

6[82]

How life for others emerges! With a servant, who at first thinks of his master's interest under compulsion and penalties; gradually that occurs to him sooner than his own, because he has noticed that his well-being depends on that of his master and on his good humor: in the end he tends to it like the gardener to the plants, they are continuously before him, familiar, easy, assuaging, the reason for his joys and sorrows. So the groom to his horse, the scholar to his topic, the father to his child, the merchant to his money. We forget the motivating thoughts and live according to the ingrained feelings of the pleasant customary — that is supposed to be moral! Certainly it ⟨is⟩ pleasant for everyone, masters and servants, and therefore it is much *praised*; consequently, much *fanciful thought* laid around it so that it might appear to be something august!

6[83]

When our drives are equally strong and pull us toward opposed goals, that struggle and that urgency arise which moralists place so high. Actually, for many, virtue is worth nothing if it does not make for such a struggle, i.e., we want the opposed drives to be equally strong! A Laocoön who crushes his serpents! An *attitude*[70] of pathos!

6[84]

Much benevolence among those who easily forget a misfortune, who are easily excited and calmed, incapable of lasting emotion, of earnest reflection, expansive, somewhat indiscreet.[71]

6[85]

l'entraînement de ma destinée,[72] said Napoleon.[73]

6[86]

Sublimity of the soul! Most often it is exaltedness![74]

6[87]

"strict in their principles or in the feelings their imagination had produced"[75]

6[88]

the effective writers prove that words are only allusions, that nothing may be completed and that in this respect writers have advantages over painters.

6[89]

the geometer Ampère: *je crois que le monde extérieur a été créé tout simplement pour nous être une occasion de penser.*[76]

6[90]

Napoleon was a dreamer, taciturn, awkward in interactions with women, but passionate and overpowering although alienating in his whole person when he was young. Then bouts of a gloomy and threatening jealousy.[77]

6[91]

Uniformity in mood, mildness and natural serenity make for the happy private life. The final reason: *to be moved deeply by nothing.* It is called philosophy when this indifference manifests ⟨itself⟩ not only in relation to what interests others, but in personal tribulation.[78]

6[92]

Her imagination was fired up by the duties laid upon her; she prescribed herself the most painful sacrifices precisely because she had the misfortune of not loving her husband. She took care to please him as if she had loved him.[79]

6[93]

Non consilia a casu differo, destiny drives them, their intentions are weak.[80]

6[94]

Napoleon knew how to cross from the deepest calm into the greatest anger if it seemed useful to him.[81] "My anger has never risen higher than here," he said to the Abbé de Pradt, pointing to his neck (*cou*).[82] "He finds a means of feigning his passions even though they truly exist," said Talleyrand.[83]

6[95][84]

Napoleon had emotional attacks, shed tears, but afterwards it always made for ill humor in him. "If my blood does not pulse with its constant slowness, I run the risk of going mad." According to Corvisart he had a slow pulse. But he complained about *intraitable*[85] nerves. He maintained he could absolutely not understand what it would mean "to feel his head spinning"

6[96][86]

He took a secret pleasure in causing fear and making people tremble. For: "restlessness excites zeal;" he avoided showing himself pleased by persons and humans: "*une petite terreur de détail*[87] always lay in the most secret interior space of his palace."

6[97][88]

He gave the impression of constantly hating rest, both for himself and for others.

6[98][89]

If a social gathering's conversation was proceeding calmly, he would suddenly change the tone with an imperious word and put the conversation partner back in his place before him, namely, in his fear.

6[99][90]

The truly fortunate one is he who conceals himself from me in the depths of a province and when I die the world will emit a loud phew!

6[100][91]

When he paid for a service, he let on that he was purchasing a new one. He never wished to bring his wife's debts in order so as to preserve occasions to trouble her.

6[101][92]

Napoleon's mother was of very mediocre intellect.

6[102][93]

romantic imagination joined with dryness of the heart in Louis Bonaparte. "His feigned virtues give me just as much trouble as Lucien's vices," Napoleon said of him.

6[103][94]

La Fontaine: "*Et la grâce plus belle encore que la beauté.*"

6[104]

Wild animals are supposed to learn to look away from themselves and to seek to live *in* others (or God), forgetting themselves as much as possible! They are better off so! Our moral tendency is still that of wild animals! They are supposed to become tools of great machineries external to them and rather turn the wheel than be together with themselves. Morality until now was the demand *not to be occupied with ourselves*, by displacing our capacity for reflection and robbing ourselves of time, time and strength. To work ourselves to the ground, tire ourselves, bear the yoke under the notion of duty or the fear of hell — morality was immense slave labor: with fear of the ego.

6[105]

A time would be conceivable when humanity, in order to preserve the species — and that after all is supposed to be a duty! — would have to throw off all forms of higher life and limit itself to ever lower ones because the former turn out to be too costly and sterilizing: as an old man must renounce his best activities in order to live. But what! is life then a duty! nonsense! you physiologists! humans have become so pathetic that even philosophers do not notice the deep contempt with which antiquity and the Middle Ages treat this "self-evident value of values, life!"

6[106]

The principal achievement of *work* is the prevention of idleness among common natures, also e.g., civil servants, merchants, soldiers, etc. The main objection to socialism is that it wants to afford the common natures idleness. The idle commoner becomes a burden to himself and the world.

6[107]

the night chills of a beloved woman

6[108]

I propose a model:[95] if it charms you, then you will have to imitate it. Not the aims, rather the satisfaction of the already existing drive compels to this or that morality. *Not* reason! unless in the service of a drive!

6[109]

Out of what pathetic elements German socialism consists in its *leaders* can be seen from the fact that none has demanded total abstinence from alcoholic drinks — and yet this plague is much more fateful than whatever social pressure!

6[110]

the evil drives are by no means unpleasant, rather evil *and* good drives are pleasant. They become *unpleasant* only through 1) excess and 2) in being inhibited by other drives. If we are dominated for example by the view of the shamefulness of sensuality (as the basis of the marriage drive) or by the view of its evil consequences in the afterlife, then the drive becomes for us unpleasantly mixed, indeed it can be felt as something purely disgusting. Just so the inclination to compassion can be felt as pathetic weakness and unpleasant. Thinking immoderately has the effect of pain, even for the enthusiast of thinking; the *excess* is a *coerced* manifestation of the drive, i.e., the *inhibition* of a (tired) drive bent on expiring — hence also inhibition of development. All development *pleasurable*.

6[111]

genius the product of *fortunate accidents*: its conditions cannot be known in advance. Pure encouragement, in the sense of morality up to now, by no means creates a genius and fertility; morality knows nothing about the education and use of evil drives and accidents, praxis all the more. It is impossible *intentionally* to promote geniuses — for that one would have to know them through and through. Women, in their intention to promote, usually ruin them.

6[112][96]

What a dreadful condition earlier! Even in morals uncertainty of knowledge and perennial dangers! That was a calm impartial way of yielding to thought and the truth!! under the scourge of the fear of hell! Or in the fear of sinning against eternal love, of doubting revelation!!

6[113]

The paradoxical virtue e.g., magnanimity, admired as miracle and much revered!

Otherwise those who feel the force of a drive and whose imperiousness proudly resists it, who therefore suddenly change into the opposite.

Otherwise they who *expected* more from satisfactions and, disappointed, avenge themselves on the drive.

Otherwise: to feel weak cowardly awkward before the fear of death and in self-*contempt* to do the opposite of what the fear of death advises.

6[114]

the motives of the legislators of morals for a law and the motives' *transformation* in those to whom the law is given NB

6[115]

The *ostensible* effects of moral feelings, while their *appearance* is itself already an effect of the becalmed nervous system, etc., not the source of the calm NB.

6[116][97]

All humans are at pains to lend to their duty an *unconditional* character: they feel degraded by the thought that they sacrifice themselves out of *fear* to a human being, prince state party, and *subordinate their* intell⟨ect⟩ to the intell⟨ect⟩ of another: they wish for a *no longer humiliating superior power* to exist which commands them so ⟨to⟩ subordinate themselves, an absolute duty, a word of God (e.g., be obedient to the powers that be). Even now moral philosophers still seek *definitively* to give ethics a foundation: *without this*, they feel, one has no right to great pathos, to nice poses as politician and socialist. "We must have a being to which we can unconditionally entrust ourselves," says Luther, i.e., we want to be able unconditionally to trust ourselves and to set our actions over against the world as beyond questioning and absolutely exalted. Vanity!

6[117][98]

That which often compels us (and indeed with the feeling of consent, *even though* it is no pleasant compulsion!) we name *duty*. Through frequent practice emerges from that a *pleasant habit*: and then it is a deception still to speak of our duty. But this almost always happens. Nearly everyone represents his occupation as an unpleasant thing; because of his self-overcoming, i.e., because of his *power* he wants to be admired. There is so much *false displeasure in existence*! Likewise, so many false amenities among princes women feasts idlers travelers Christians the virtuous peoples parties philosophers writers: they exhibit their "happiness," mainly in order to do harm, to arouse envy thereby.

6[118]

The attempt to resolve all moral drives in the religious dr⟨ives⟩: God commands and *for his sake one does something*. That is no longer moral. That one fears or loves God is not a consequence of morality, rather a *consideration of advantage*. This is the Christian standpoint. There are supposed to be only religious actions, all motives are egoistic, and religious action itself is done out of egoism. Or: *every action is evil. Thus, the religious as well. Therefore predestination*! The Quietists say to the contrary: I no longer act on my own behalf, rather on God's behalf.[99] What a low-water mark for self-knowledge! What dishonesty that takes! Let it be measured by the woman who says, "I do everything for the sake of my beloved!" It is not true! Yes, even this "for the sake of my b⟨eloved⟩" she does in order to follow *her* drive and not *his*. For then she would behave as he does: which is impossible. She can only act according to the image of the beloved that *she* makes for herself: *her* product certainly does not become = the beloved, but rather a piece *of her*.

6[119][100]

In each smallest moment there is in us an absolute necessity to what happens. If we could recognize this, then for each instance we could substantiate it with the name of unconditional duty, if we wanted by all means *to lie* ourselves *free*! We say: I want, where we ought ⟨to say⟩: "I must": and we would predict what is about to happen with the mien of a soothsayer and hero of duty. This would be the apex of mendacity. Fortunately, we *never* know that causality: and "I will" means always "if I can." "It is my duty" means: "provided I have the power, it will be possible." To command the sun to rise when it is just rising, that is the freedom of our virtuous people. When we feel that a commended and favored motive is at work in us, then to say "I will!" (is supposed to mean: "I command myself") — — —

6[120]

since all our actions are absolute necessities, and equally absolute unknowns for us, so is each "you shall unconditionally" spoken into the wind. We can neither do otherwise than we must, nor can we control in each single case whether what has occurred was what we were supposed to do.

6[121]

The unpleasant individuals, suffering on their own account, shall be inclined toward the state, society, altruism! And the pleasant, self-confident individuals shall have the *opposite* drive, **away** *from that morality*! NB NB

6[122]

Skepticism has its parallel: "rather go hungry than eat something disgusting." The views of authorities have become disgusting to us — rather starve *to death*! This is a rare passion: skepticism is a passion.

6[123]

Knowing that "this is healthy, this preserves life, this harms the descendants" — is still by no means a moral regulative! Why live? Why by all means live gladly? Why descendants?

— Assuming this would all be more pleasant than the opposite, to die, to be sick, to be isolated without descendants: perhaps something would be more pleasant than these comforts e.g., the feeling of one's honor or an insight or a sensual pleasure, for the sake of which we should have to choose dying or illness or loneliness. Why preserve the species? We are referred to the *drives*: but there is *neither a drive to self-preservation nor a drive to preservation of the species*. Not to be could seem *more valuable* to us than to be:[101] then physiological ethics has nothing to say. Or we could seem more valuable to ourselves than the state, society, humanity. What then determines this appearance of value? A drive. Morality can only command — i.e., prevail by causing fear (thus with the help of a drive), or it can legitimize itself with the aid of another drive — morality always already *presupposes its* immediate soundness and persuasive force; it *comes when* the drive and the valuation of a certain kind *is already there*: This holds for every ethics. Also, a drive to live individually *is there*: I think in its service. Others, who do not have it, will not be able to be *obliged* to anything by me. "Duty" is the thought through which one drive makes itself sovereign over other drives — always with a befuddling of reason! with a bribed servant![102]

6[124]

"Arrange yourself so that you have the greatest possible happiness from your qualities," that is foolish! For without any command: *everyone achieves* just this, they may live as they choose — namely, must! That they attain, want to acquire, unlearn, reject regulations and knowledge of what is advantageous, all this is a necessary operation of their nature. Morality *can do nothing but set up, like art, images of the human being: with the chance that they have an effect on this one or the other.* Strictly speaking, morality cannot prove them. "Higher" and "lower" — those are already illusions under the impress of a moral paradigm. For these images work like stimulants, ignite a drive and *seduce the intellect* into *serving* it. Now our intellect *is* already at a certain level, likewise our taste: hence we will reject very many images, they disgust us: in a given moment of our powers *we can* not but *follow the example of these images*! This psychological compulsion often *appears* to us as "duty:" the feeling of unconditional necessity, the expression of causality. The inner "must." E.g., with respect to basic multiplication, as *thinkers* we sense the mechanism as duty, just as with A = A: humans of simple intellect do not feel the compulsion here. This subjective feeling of compulsion is naturally only subjective. Many persons have *in nothing* such a *strict* feeling. But the disgust which befalls us at the sight of maggots is a compulsion: we embellish for ourselves such a compulsion with the word duty, where we know precisely that countervailing compulsions are there. (??)

6[125]

"Become a more reasonable freer more feeling, more perfect human, strive for the perfection of your species"? What to ground this law on? On the advantage of the individual or the collective.

Some say: all abilities develop in that those that are means and organs are subordinated to those constituting the proper human end. Our nature is complex: we must distinguish in it facts of a lower and a higher order. But how am I obliged to follow a goal of the species if by chance the usual order of ends and means is reversed for my individual? E.g., if I have more of an inclination to the pleasures of the flesh than those of the spirit, and having my own head and bit of intellect is exactly the means for my cravings? Here one helps with metaphysical ideas: the true nature of the human, his spiritual vocation, and the like.

"You may will a goal *if* you can." Without this condition: that means giving to the human being an unconditional capacity, a force without condition. An unconditional duty implies an unconditional ability to fulfill it: otherwise it is a duty for another being than me, a duty suspended in mid-air. — Whoever speaks of duty and freedom presupposes metaphysical principles.

6[126]

It is untrue that religion should have provided morality — the converse! We prove religion true or untrue *with* morality.

6[127]

Our moral drives urge the intellect to defend them, and to take them absolutely, or to found them anew. Our drives to self-preservat⟨ion⟩ drive the intellect to prove morality relative or void. This is a *battle of the drives* — played out in the intellect. The drive to honesty steps in between alongside the drives to self-sacrifice, pride, contempt: *I*.

6[128]

"to bear the bliss, the *sorrow of the earth*"[103]

6[129]

Our nervous age pretends that a permanent excitement and imbalance of mood distinguishes great humans: they know nothing of the steady deep powerful currents streaming toward one destination: they babble and roar and do not feel the wretchedness of this moody excitability.

6[130]

The intellect is the tool of our drives and nothing more, it will *never* become *free*. It is sharpened in the struggle of the various drives and thereby refines the activity of each single drive. In our greatest righteousness and sincerity is the will for power, for the infallibility of our person: skepticism exists only with respect to all authority; we do not want to be duped, not even by *our drives*! But then what actually does not *will* there? A drive for certain!

6[131]

How a tree can develop is only demonstrated through a fine specimen. Without such one has no notion of wanting to drive it beyond the conventional size and is content. Distinguished humans make others discontent with themselves: — — —

6[132]

like sand between the teeth

6[133]

I hear the sound of jealous tomcats, in these envious utterances

6[134]

The moralist who wants to *found* a morality is driven to declare a final purpose. "*If* you want to be healthy, then you must be moderate. But you must want to be healthy: for it is a condition for being happy or for fulfilling one's goals or etc." Behind each goal a new goal shows itself: and the moralist ends by *having to* declare the purpose of existence. I could say: there is no purpose to existence, hence a morality for the sake of reaching a purpose for existence is not possible. But one believed in such purposes: and consequently one could found a morality with demands. In the end manners and customs of life arise *inevitably* and exercise a compulsion when it is *unpleasant* to resist it.

6[135]

"Duty" means: to want a goal not for another's sake but for its own sake: thus an absolute goal. The categorical imperative: a command without conditions. *It* was what Kant grounded a metaphysics on: for if there is an unconditional goal, then this can only be the perfect or the infinite good: if there were still something more perfect, or a higher good, then it would not be an unconditional goal. Thus, a metaphysical assumption to be made, following Kant!

6[136]

"What is the good for a being? The completion of its goal. What is a being's goal? The development of its nature." Nature, goal, good of a being — three questions which logically follow upon one another: so that the good is defined through the goal, the goal through nature. If one knows human nature through observation and analysis, one can derive the good, the goal, the law of the human from it. For the good entails the thought of obligation. Vacherot.[104]

That means: the goal of the human is the development of his nature, to be human and not horse. That is nothing! There one helps oneself with the "true nature,"[105] a nature as it *is supposed* to be for him, not as it is.

6[137][106]

One drive is stronger than another and makes it its victim e.g., when a mother cares for a child and goes hungry. *Totally wrong* to see, with *Spencer*, in this the care for the brood and already in procreation an expression of the altruistic drive: it is not that it is another that makes a difference. One sacrifices to one's vengeance e.g., one's own child. Or one sacrifices to one's child one's vengeance — depending on which feeling is stronger. *Making sacrifices* has nothing altruistic about it.

6[138]

Whoever thinks and feels very differently goes to ruin, he cannot reproduce. Hence there could be a limit to the degree of individuation. In times when individuation is felt *painfully*, as in ours (and as in *all* previous *moral history* of humanity), the drive to it is poorly transmitted. In times when it is *pleasurably* felt, it easily drives itself too far and creates the most extreme isolation (and thereby hinders the general fertility of humanity). The more *similar*, the more fertility increases, each finds a satisfactory female: thus *overpopulation* as a consequence of morality. The more dissimilar, the more —

6[139]

Our models are constructed according to what in us, if we were to achieve it, would give us the most enjoyment, and what, on the other hand, we consider *possible* to achieve (within the scope of our strengths and our situation). An *overview* of our pleasurable sensation, and of our strength and the process along with conditions is the presupposition — a lofty feat of the intellect: most often it will have to be a *distortion*! That is why most let themselves be *given* a model: and the *compulsion besides* to reproduce it ("duty," a kind of *imagined strength* instead of a recognized one). Failing one's model and failing its reproduction causes a lot of severe dissatisfaction — this type of painting also rarely has masters. One makes sketches one's whole life in an attempt to attain a reproducible model: we shape it according to what we have achieved and decree ourselves as the model — often out of despair.

6[140]

Formerly one asked: is the thought true? Now: how did we come upon it? What was its driving force? Let's discover it —

6[141][107]

Begetting is an often-occurring incidental result of one way of satisfying the sexual drive: *not* its intention, not its necessary effect. The sexual drive has no necessary relation to procreation: occasionally that outcome is also attained through it, like nourishment through the desire for food.

6[142]

The refinement of intelligence also refines our malice, and the pleasure in the intellect gives us in the end pleasure in the refined malice of others as well. Progress consists in the degree to which the human can endure malice *without suffering*.

6[143]

Christ bore not only God but Satan too in his bosom: that is the counterclaim with this moral hyper-idealism: the absolute damnation of the human being, the *odium generis humani*.[108] — For humanity to feel worthy of such a sacrifice by a god, one had to despise humanity to the depths and degrade it in its own sight.

6[144]

morality is a sum of errors that have been fused onto the drives, so that when the mistake is spoken the drive is stimulated — variably, by the way, and without *concordia*.[109] These errors relate to human action from the point of view of what is praise- and blameworthy: and behind praise and blame lies the presupposition that we know the human's *purpose* and, likewise, that we know the *kind* of action and that we believe in the *freedom* of a⟨ction⟩: likewise, that we believe in the identity of humans or of certain groups, thus with equivalent duties and actions: that one know what serves that final purpose, what not. These are mere presumptions of the intellect. But the *drives modified* thereby want their satisfaction, and this *sprouts systems of morality, too*; ever new attempts subsequently to find these drives in harmony with the truth — whereas naïve humans measure all other insights by the moral drives concerning their *truth*. The basic prejudice is: — "the moral alone is true."

6[145][110]

NB NB. There is no drive to self-preservation — rather to seek what is pleasant, to avoid the unpleasant explains everything that is ascribed to that drive. There is also no drive to want to perpetuate the species. All of that is a mythology (still with Spencer and Littré[111]). Generation is a matter of desire: its result is propagation, i.e., without propagation neither this kind of desire nor any kind of desire would have preserved itself. Sexual desire has nothing to do with the propagation of the species! The enjoyment of nourishment has nothing to do with preservation!

6[146]

To be demonstrated that a) love b) parental love c) sense of truth d) justice are of egoistic provenance. In any case, the presupposition is that in all humans the sensual image of the world is almost the same, that this kind of error has *passed itself on* with the highest force.

6[147]

We are capable of creating *many forms* out of all our faculties, or even the absence of form. There is a certain artistic *freedom* in the representation of our models which we can attain.

6[148]

"Moral law, duty, moral freedom, inviolability, absolute respect for the person" — all forbidden to *us*, one may not nourish oneself with that. Likewise purposes of humanity, purpose of the individual — that is not determinable from outside of him: it is an *assumption*, a more or less arbitrary *program* — arbitrary with respect to the material, the contingent material of his self-perceptions. —

6[149]

There is nothing good, nothing evil in itself. The "general truths" of morality wanted to form humans *identical* to one another — through errors deeply tied up with the drives. Just as the patriotic error makes them alike within the limitation of love and national hatred.

6[150][112]

"The true nature of the human being" — forbidden turn of phrase!

6[151][113]

I am no means to a purpose — in nature there are neither means nor purposes.

6[152]

It is nonsense to conceive ourselves as causes — what do we know about cause and effect!

6[153]

Pleasure and pain: is it true that the most individual being *would have the greatest pleasure from himself*! Yes, and *even more* when it is surrounded by the stimulus of purely individual beings. "But how to prevent them from intruding on each other's spheres?" But why prevent! There must be enmity in order for the i⟨ndividual⟩ to come out altogether grandly, all evil affects must be there. Morality thought further! But the increasing knowledge, the increasing pleasure in one another, the superior mien with all bad experiences, the resources of full individuals in emergency situations, in the struggle with the unalterable! In the end: there is just one *time* for the *flourishing* of individuation — and perhaps humanity **must** be ruined by morality.

6[154][114]

"Thou shalt not kill"[115] — but we perpetually kill the thoughts and products of others, it is necessary, perpetually we let something in us die so that something else may live. How the life of the human goes hand in hand with a perpetual letting die away: humanity must always *slough its skin*.

6[155]

The sexual drive takes the large steps of individuation: important for my morality, for it is anti-social and denies general equality and the equal worth of human to human. It is the *type of individual passion*, the great education in that: the *decline* of a people takes place to the extent individual passion *wanes* and the social reasons in marrying *prevail*. — The difference of the sexes is not fundamental; generation is not essentially sexual and does not belong to the *essence of the living being*. It is a very strong expression of individual desire, the higher the beings are, *the stronger what is individual in them becomes*.

"Generation is the repetition of a cell through itself, an extension and reproduction"[116] a kind of *repleteness*, where a part of the complete and richly nourished mass separates itself and often a continuation of the nourishment follows, even after the separation.

Generation is a consequence of nourishment.

6[156]

The root of understanding is A = A? no! A = B, the belief that two equal things are there. The highest development of reason goes in the direction of *denying this* and thus of doubting and limiting oneself.

6[157]

Is the final goal pleasure or duty? this is how everyone now understands the problem. Some say it is logical identity.

No action that is at all *possible* is *incongruous*, illogical in the sense of mathem⟨aticians⟩ physicists engineers.

6[158]

As soon as we wish to determine the purpose of the human being we presuppose a concept of the human. But there are only individuals, from those known *thus far* the concept can only be gained by *stripping away* the individual; — thus to set up the purpose of the human would mean thwarting individuals in their individuation and bidding them to become *general*. Should not conversely every individual be the attempt to *attain* a *higher species than the* **human being** on the strength of his most individual things? My morality would be this, to *remove* more and more from the human his general character and to specialize him, to make him less intelligible to a degree for others (and thus into an object of experiences, wonder, instruction for them)

6[159]

Develop all your powers — but i.e., develop anarchy! Go to ruin!

6[160]

Our love for the ideal is the last enhancement of the drive for nourishment (likewise self-love love of property, the need for power, for means to life and health). L⟨ittré⟩[117]

6[161][118]

The development of the sexual drive up to the level of human love, compassion, self-sacrifice — not a hostile feeling, rather the highest feeling of humanity. Littré. *Non*! *Non*!

6[162][119]

Recognizing the identity of one human being with another — ought to be the foundation of justice? This is a very superficial identity. For those who recognize individuals, justice is *impossible* — ego.

6[163][120]

The progress of morality would consist in altruistic drives prevailing over egoistic ones and likewise general judgments over individual ones? Is now the locus communis. *I* on the contrary see the individual grow when he represents his well-understood interest over against other individuals (justice among equals insofar as it recognizes and furthers the other individual *as such*); I see judgments becoming more individual and general judgments shallower and more stereotyped. *I* see the altruistic drives at their strongest in the crude egoism of animals (it is a species of affirmation of one's own desire); the altruistic drive is a *hindrance* to the recognition of the individual, it wants to make and have the other be *like* us. I see in the state's and society's tendency a hindrance to individuation, a formation of the homo communis: but the common and *same* human is only so much in demand because weak humans fear the strong individual and would prefer *general attenuation* to development toward the individual. I see in the present morality the glossing over of the general attenuation: just as Christianity wanted to weaken and level strong and intellectual humans. *Altruistic morality's tendency is the smooth mush, the soft sand of humanity.* The tendency of *general judgments* is toward the commonality of feelings, that is their poverty and feebleness. It is the tendency toward the *end of humanity*. The "absolute truths" are the instrument of leveling, they eat away the characteristic forms.

6[164][121]

the sexual drive, urges humans away from other humans; it is a furious egoism and *no* source of social feelings — not altruistic!!

6[165]

The young being is dependent on its progenitor, similar to him, intelligible to him, entertaining, his work — even more, it is 1. *nothing hostile*, 2. nothing alien, 3. nothing dead: these last *negative* reasons may *have created* the stimulus *for* the young being in the first place. There was so little or nothing in the world which in these 3 points resembled it.

6[166]

Honesty with respect to property compels us to say that we consist of stolen parts and that herein our sensations are too blunt and unrefined. The individual has a false pride with respect to materials and colors: but it can *paint a new picture*, to the delight of the connoisseur — with that it *atones for* its *misappropriation of the world's goods*. To grasp our existence such that we have something in exchange to offer — *not* as *"guilt"* but as advance payment and debt! We nourish ourselves on everything; it is right that we give something back for the nourishment of all. (Christ was not refined in this feeling, he imparted as his own what others before him had devised)

6[167]

We suffer and disparage things and humans! A nice way of taking vengeance! by way of *damaging* our judgment! We are the ones who exact vengeance on ourselves when we disparage and do harm to the other. We muddy our soul, accustom it to *false seeing* — and finally — —

6[168]

Noble: means to belong to an elite, to be an exception. To sacrifice oneself for others is a craving whereby one becomes an exception. With respect to everyone else who does the same, though, one is not noble, but *common*. Among the "good" the good is not valued as individual but instead as the rule and for that reason is *not admired, not praised*. — Some yearn for a community where what is most individual about them is sensed as rule, where it ceases to be most i⟨ndividual⟩. Others are furious at the prospect of becoming common in such a way. The first suffer the fate of their uniqueness, the others enjoy their uniqueness. Others do not notice it at all.

6[169]

Two interests in things: 1. to know what they *are* 2. what can be made from them.

6[170]

On the whole, I have, as if swimming blind in water, approached by turns the sustenance I require: sharpening of the intellect, afterwards upswing and sacrifice of the self, afterwards justice and independence, then prudent mildness towards everything independent, etc. *Not* through judgment: rather excess always drove me onward and the new taste did me good. Pain taught me to value the scattered pleasure in its existence, the party taught me solitude: the scholar in me propelled me to understand the artist, etc.

6[171]

Goethe's cautious attitude toward music: very advantageous that the German inclination to obscurity did not receive yet another artistic backing.

6[172]

the pleasant shudder at the sound of bells

6[173]

These people act entirely egoistically, but their moral judgment is trained immediately to see everything from the point of view of the laudable and virtuous: they are consummate in their dishonesty with themselves and in society present the "good conscience." Others are more aspiring, but their judgment is subject to pessimistic habits, they interpret everything egoistically and they *despise everything* egoistical. Their noblest actions leave behind in them a residue of disgust. They are those who believe in a *virtue that does not and cannot exist*! They are honest but have nothing but torment and self-disgust from their honesty: because their feeling of pleasure is limited to actions of which they know themselves to be incapable: but they conclude these actions should be *possible* for others: *which is not true*. He who said, "I have fulfilled the law" was certainly not very ambitious in his interpretation of the same and no brooding person.

6[174]

"Thou shalt not steal!"[122] But where does property actually leave off? A thought, an impulse, a point of view, a picture's, building's, person's expression — is that not all property! And all of it we continuously steal. We hoard all things and suns in ourselves, we carry away *for ourselves* everything that is there, yes, that once happened. We do not think of others at the time. Every *individual* human keeps an eye on what he can set aside for himself.

6[175][123]

The higher nature is more irrational than the common, and has some pleasure and displeasure drives *so powerful* that they are hardly believable. With respect to these their thinking sometimes comes to a stop or enters *wholly* into their service. One speaks of *passion*: its satisfaction is more important to it than life. But so too the drinkers the sensualists the vengeful. It must be the *object* of the passion that ennobles it and makes it the sign of the higher nature. Not eating drinking sensual pleasure: rather things *seldom strongly* felt e.g., thoughts, knowledge, the weal of a city, a state, humanity, the salvation of the soul, the happiness of others. Thus, something that ordinarily leaves us *cold* is here object of passion — that makes the higher nature: its taste aims for exceptions. It is the *individual taste* which stands out here: *such* a passion cannot *be grasped*, as little as the individual can be grasped. The higher nature has a *singularity of passions*: it is not common, consequently not predictable. In this its irrationality is great; it makes the greatest sacrifices to a thing for which it alone has a measure of value: it does not heed others' measure of value. Hence: to have *a singular measure of value* in feeling makes the higher nature: *either* to value other things than are valued *or* to value things otherwise than as they a⟨re⟩ v⟨alued⟩. — Common natures do not believe in the difference in standards, i.e., *they do not believe in individuals*. "I believe in individuals" — thus the higher nature? — And it often deceives itself insofar as it *presupposes* individual judgments and standards in others and does not have that practical knack at hand of understanding them as human beings of a certain level (: like Napoleon, who was one himself.)

A sub-species: *higher natures* who *everywhere* presuppose their own individuality and their standard of feeling, thus their own history — and do *not* recognize the individual, *just as little* as they understand the *common* (e.g., Christ). *They know themselves* not as individual. — The other kind: they know themselves as individual, they understand individuals, but only with difficulty commonness — *this they have to learn*. Perhaps they themselves have the fervor to fathom commonness — it is a possible passion (La Rochefoucauld?)

6[176]

A movement is constantly there toward the formation of species, of human beings with a common stamp: cities state cultures work to that end. Statistics are the proof. The divergent transitional natures (between two species) or the degenerating are the individual natures or the attempts to establish a species within species.

6[177][124]

"One is not what one always is, one is that which one often is." Rémusat.

6[178][125]

So: it is not self-sacrifice that makes the noble person, with that he belongs only in the category of the passionate (as e.g., the raging sensualist sacrifices himself) there are low passions, i.e., common and *higher*: individual ones. The noble person sacrifices here an *individual* passion; what makes him noble is not that he sacrifices himself for others but the rarity of this drive for others — an *individual* particularity like many other particularities that *also ennoble*.

6[179][126]

Christianity *required* in fact nothing but an *intellectual sacrifice*: that Christ be *believed* in. — Whoever sets so much value on others believing in him that he guarantees heaven in return — must have had a terrible doubt? Right?

6[180]

The winged goddess who inscribes your deed on a bronze shield and whom humans worship

6[181]

this one cannot grasp the degrees of kinship, let alone have a fine feeling of obligation to the different degrees! ego

6[182]

The most embarrassing thing for me is having to defend myself. With that I become aware that I first to have to compare my way of being with that of others and that I have to *supply* for it *intelligible motives*: not being accustomed to this I know that I will fail. Yes, every presentation of my image by others causes me confusion. "*That* I am certainly not!" is my feeling; if I wished to express thanks, I would appear to myself *dishonest*.

6[183]

The precept of moderation is an observance of nature; what is supposed to become great and strong must always enlarge its power, like capital, and should not wish to live from it.

6[184]

Our thoughts ought to be regarded as *gestures*, corresponding to our drives, like all gestures. Darwin's theory is to be brought to bear.

6[185]

How severe we are with Calvin on account of one execution! And Christ consigned all who did not believe in him to hell — and people, still more terrible than he, added to that: "with retroactive effect."

6[186]

There is a greedy and breathless way of thinking. Here, too, morality is necessary

6[187]

Independence is no longer a pleasure when the spur to it is missing. — And with the absolute impossibility of a prospect of independence dependence loses its unpleasantness. Just so with the will's lack of freedom — we must break off the spur of the ancient illusion! Then we will be quite happy and content.

6[188]

"The need to maintain illusions about one's *master* because human vanity does not like being ashamed of the one to whom one has *subjugated* oneself"[127]

6[189]

More and more a realm of quite inhuman necessities is revealed! In the end we laugh too at seeing how we once believed we could replace that with our drives and drivelets[128] and understand it, with affinity and hatred, will or purpose, etc. The world as a human-world has become a laughingstock for us: like astrology. To take up our position toward this world as solemnly as possible was the endeavor of all philosophers: the idealists most recently knew how to turn us into the principal matter and the world into a kind of product of ours: as if the mirror said: "without me there is nothing, I am the author." In the end we ourselves are woven into the immense system and move within it: yet enough of the unrecognized still clings to us and *that remains the training ground of our pride*. Yes, since we have relinquished so much of the human's position in the world, a life and death struggle is taking place on this last site for the "supreme rights of humanity." It is our whole *pride* and *all drives* are at its service! The *higher value* of morality is boldly opposed to the entire world law, and human goals are posited as the world's goal. With "good" and "beautiful" and "true" one believes one has proven one's exceptional position, one's divinity: science in the service of the old drives struggles and defends the god in the human, after otherwise having let him go — the free god.

6[190][129]

Napoleon's striving was for power: he would have preferred peace, if *that* would give him increase of power.

6[191]

Never to let oneself be loved, but where one does not feel the impulse to love in return, then to hinder the love of the other, and if necessary to ridicule it, yes to abase ourselves before him! Through nothing do artists (and women!) become more common than by allowing themselves to be loved. We ought to prevent *our* becoming another's ideal: in that way he wastes his strength to form for himself his entirely personal ideal; *we lead him astray and away from himself* — we ought to do everything to enlighten him or thrust him away. — A marriage a friendship should be the means, the rare one!! of strengthening our own ideal through another ideal: we should see the other's ideal *as well*, and from its perspective our own!

6[192][130]

Where have the great souls gone? What is now called that — there I see no more than humans who with a huge expense of strength play a comedy before themselves, want to create an effect for themselves, and with a barely imaginable greed listen for the audience because its applause and idolization is supposed to give them faith in themselves. Their effect on others is a beef bouillon for these beings perennially exhausted by excessive exertion. It is a case history!

6[193]

In France every personal relationship (love friendship) has its daily history. "Constantly changeable" — otherwise boring. For Italians this would be torture, they have the placid trust, like cows — the slightest nuance which they perceive — most would not perceive it — almost does them in. St⟨endhal⟩

6[194]

"Manure works more miracles than the saints" — Sicily.[131]

6[195]

In Germany *all* moral education is lacking.

6[196]

To learn to keep silent and to learn to walk away. Wherever a specific opposition to life belongs and robs our soul of breath, one should walk away.

6[197]

"the feeling of the level and the plumb line that actually makes human beings of us and is the basis for all eurythmy" Goethe[132]

6[198]

There is nothing more foolish than to scorn someone in that which constitutes his professional competency e.g., the scholar's: as the spoiled children, the artists take the liberty of doing.

6[199]

Among composers only S. Bach has real greatness of character.

6[200][133]

the mercantile mind has the great task of implanting in humans incapable of elevation a passion that will give them broad goals and a sensible use of the day, but that will at the same time also *exhaust* them so that it levels everything individual and shields from spirit as from debauchery. That mind is shaping a new species of humans who have the status of the *slaves* in antiquity. That they become *wealthy* gives them influence as long as the intellectually endowed do not recognize their advantage and want to conduct politics. Over time this class of workers *forces* the higher nat⟨ures⟩ to segregate themselves and to form an *aristocracy*. *For the time being* artists and scholars belong to this class of workers, they serve it because they want a lot of money. The incapacity for leisure and passion is characteristic of all of them (*consequently* a great affectation of both among artists because they want to entertain through something unusual). The interest in money forces upon them a political interest, and *this* in turn a religious interest: they must maintain parts of themselves in dependency and respect — hence the *English* bigotry as that of the mercantile mind.

6[201][134]

What is *not inherited* is yet more important for the crystallization of character than what is inherited. A noble character, i.e., *not* to have *at hand* a number of habits, points of view that are easy for others.

6[202]

When we eat go for a walk live sociably or alone, the *high intent of our passion* ought to determine us in it down to the smallest thing, and indeed so that it ⟨has⟩ taken reason and science into its service and with deep fervor retrieves from it suitable directives. Not blindly to follow one's drives, however great: but to draw upon all prior knowledge: only *so* does one think highly enough of oneself: everything *known* thus far is worthy of serving your passion. Whoever easily *comes to terms* with science or becomes fanciful in its use lacks the depths of unfailing respect for his passion, for which no sacrifice is too great. To base our being upon the whole world of humanity's previous experience! — You take sides and practice love and hate — if you had more respect for your work, if you *seriously* thought of it as an important matter, then you would be stricken with horror at *thus blinding* your judgment; you would have to question knowledge with fervor and become *honest* about yourselves. Passion drives us out of our calm again and again: our ideal wants ever higher affirmations and sacrifices, and thereby constantly to increase and *cleanse itself*. — You are in love with yourselves, but it is a transitory whim, a small bit of sexual drive; you also suspect as much, that one must satisfy whims with whims, you are only *arbitrary*! *Or* you are *ambitiously enamored* of your ideal and do everything for it that causes a stir and respect *among humans*; your passion requires *publicity*; for all that in your stillest and most secret parts you grow bored. You accomplish your work but the *mirror-image of yourselves in* others' *heads* is the goal standing *behind* the work, it is a magnifying glass, which you hold before others' eyes when they look towards you! — Many do their work respectably, as they have become accustomed with strict teachers, they speak of the feeling of duty and demand duty — but they have a pang of conscience, for they *should only* do *something extraordinary*![135]

6[203]

Not that we want to help and benefit humans: no, that we *take pleasure in humans*, that is what is essential about so-called good humans and morality. It is the new, the latterly achieved. With this pleasure our "good actions" are a matter of course: if we do not fear them and are not hostile and still have countless relations to them, then these can be no other than such as increase our pleasure in them, i.e., we endeavor to advance them in the striving for stylized individuality, or at least to eliminate the appearance of the ugly (suffering). Love for humans?? But I say: pleasure in humans! And for this not to be pointless, we must lend a hand so that we have what delights us. — It is evident: honesty with ourselves and recognition of the other nature, the development of taste which requires the appearance of *handsome, joyful* humans must come first. Here a *selection* takes place: we seek out those who give us pleasure and support them and flee from the others — that is the right morality! The tendency must be to *make* the wretched malformed degenerate *die out*! Do not preserve at any cost! As fine as the ethos of grace towards those unworthy of us is and help for the bad and weak — on the whole it is an exception, and with it humanity would become common on the whole (as e.g., through Christianity) One ought always to build upon the natural drive: "To give pleasure to him who delights us, and woe to him who galls us." We do away with the wild animals, and we breed the tame ones: this is a great instinct. We *ourselves degenerate* at the sight of the ugly and upon contact with it: Raise up protective dams! Level it down to a usability! and the like.

If we only consort with those whose contact delights and elevates us, then groups and strata will form which in turn stand in a respective relation of nearer or more distant estrangement. This is *very good*, a necessary structure of society, out of honesty!

6[204][136]

In themselves the drives are neither good nor bad for feeling. But then a hierarchy is formed in that the satisfaction of some is bound up with fear, and these stand *lower* in feeling than those which are pleasurable. In moral judgment this difference in degree becomes a *contradiction*. If a drive is *always* satisfied with the feeling of the forbidden and of fear, then an *aversion* to it emerges: we consider it now *evil*. We have inseparably tied to it a secondary feeling; a *unity* has emerged. "An evil action." Whoever feels nothing is forbidden to him and does everything he wants knows nothing of good and evil. Whoever feels much is forbidden and does none of it, feels himself to be *good*: regardless of who forbids, whether someone exerts authority over us or *we ourselves*! — the perfect human forbids himself a great deal (infinitely more than *others* can guess!) and therefore feels himself to be *good*: that is the artfully tamed and reinterpreted nature: for it is in a state of becoming, and it is not a matter of building or tearing down *once* — it is a hanging garden.[137]

6[205][138]

By no means ought we to remain in circumstances where our petty irritations are daily exercised — that is the most powerful reason for dissolving a marriage, a party, a friendship, for giving up an office. If you are great in solitude, then know that elsewhere you will ruin yourself. Powerful kindness — where this mood takes hold of you, there you are at home with yourself — and there build your house!

6[206]

I do not speak to the weak: these want to obey and everywhere race toward slavery. In face of relentless nature, we still feel ourselves to be relentless nature! — But I have found strength where it is not sought, in simple, mild, and accommodating h⟨umans⟩ without the least inclination to rule — and conversely to me the inclination to rule has often appeared as an inner sign of weakness: they fear their slave's soul and cloak it in a king's robe (in the end they become the slaves of their followers, their reputation, etc.). Powerful n⟨atures⟩ *rule*, it is a necessity, they will not lift a finger. Even if during their lifetime they bury themselves in a garden house!

6[207][139]

Fault in the Sorrento landscape. — Olive tree more beautiful than the orange.

6[208]

Temperance movement necessary for Germany: the great majority of crimes are connected with alcohol, and likewise suicides!

6[209]

Up to now no German artist has had enough intelligence to *explain* his practice: the cleverest have only understood how to gloss it over, as if they had a bad conscience: in fact, they have *spoiled* their effect by throwing their dull-wittedness into the balance; as a result their works sank somewhat and exercised an influence on lesser imitators. If the *tendency* of an art is grasped as personal exaltation or apology or game of hide and seek, then many will avail themselves of it who have a need to glorify or conceal their nature.

6[210]

Actions which are felt for a long time to be exceptional and bring *honor*, finally become practice and then qualify as *respectable*. Likewise honesty with respect to everything real could one day become a matter of respectability and the fantast fall out of consideration as improper.

6[211]

In this century the French have acquired a taste for painting (through drawing) which was absent in the previous century. The Italians have lost their ear for song, the Germans have learned political passion, the English have placed themselves at the cutting edge of science.

6[212]

Our drives often contradict each other, which is nothing to wonder about! Rather, if they were harmoniously released, that would be odd. The *external world* plays on our strings, little wonder that these are often dissonant!

6[213][140]

After Austerlitz the war was more the result of his system than the nature of his taste: — — —

6[214]

Young people whose accomplishments do not measure up to their ambition look for something to tear apart in revenge, mainly persons, classes, races, who cannot very well retaliate: the *better* natures make outright war; the addiction to duels is part of this. The better is whoever chooses an opponent who is not his inferior in strength and who is estimable and strong. Thus the struggle against the Jews has always been a sign of the worse, more envious and more cowardly nature: and whoever takes part in that now must bear within him a goodly amount of the vulgar way of thinking.

6[215]

The end of all great thinkers and artists whose honesty with themselves has continuously decreased is somber. They miss living out their lives joyfully and flowing into the other world.

6[216]

Humans' beliefs as *necessary* as their actions — but not therefore "true for them"! Only a stupendous way of going beyond ourselves and assimilating other ways of thinking gives us the possibility to distinguish between true ⟨and⟩ false. The *ideal*! A belief that is independent of every personal element and whose limit is precisely just "the human." These are the opinions that must be *most useful* to "the human," his strict relation to things (whose fool he no longer is.)

In the long run mankind must pay terribly for each error — for it to be maintained, a hundredfold falsification of other things must ensue. Such as not-wanting to acknowledge, i.e., deterioration of honesty, decrease of intellect, increase in the dangerousness of life.

6[217]

"ever since 1730 no one anymore had the necessary *passion* and *fantasy* for the colossal bombast of Pozzo and Bibiena." J⟨acob⟩ B⟨urckhardt⟩[141]

6[218]

Among all those who have rendered service in the founding and spread of religions there has been as yet no superior mind, just as little as there has been an honest person. These great mass-passions have been hatched by the crudest minds, *such as have blind belief in themselves, like the animals.*

6[219]

Strength has kindness.

6[220]

the demand for geniuses like that for beef bouillons.[142]

6[221][143]

the mercantile mind and its product

6[222][144]

the taste for *English* landscape architecture — "to imitate free nature with its contingencies" J.B. — is the entire modern taste. The poets want such humans: while another goal is "to make humans subservient to the laws of art." Against the elegiac nature-sentimentality NB I have to disabuse myself of this. "The contrast of free nature which shines into the Italian garden from outside" J.B. Basic condition for the impression. Such *men of style* have the strongest effect in *a semi-wild* environment.

6[223]

With passionate love one can see how much honesty with ourselves is lacking: indeed, one presupposes that and grounds marriage *upon it* (with promises, the like of which *no honest person* can make *to himself*!) So in earlier times with the *loyalty* of subjects to princes or the fatherland, or the church: one solemnly forswore honesty with oneself!

6[224]

We are more inclined to believe about things that which is pleasing to us. Animals, which are less strictly inclined that way, the cautious ones, preserve themselves better. Fearfulness a first step towards honesty.

6[225]

One says "progress," but means development, i.e., becoming and passing away. Even p⟨assing away⟩ we can only perceive as a progression: for it is *tied up with desire*, like all development. Only the *inhibition of development* causes pain.

6[226]

Those pointed creatures who cannot even express their good will without needling.

6[227][145]

Infinite dissimulation is required in order to become a loving person.

6[228]

Value of science and its *appeal*, against dissimulation. If one only takes it half-heartedly one does not understand its heroic charm.

6[229]

If in a superstitious environment and time the thought falls into a child's soul, "you are the son of God," and he is instructed

⟨from⟩ early on through his mother's piety that this God is holy and wants holiness: in addition a mild temperament and a glowing visionary imagination, a self-assurance nurtured by abstinence and solitude: such a one can arrive at the belief he is sinless as soon as he believes himself the son of God and consequently obeys *his own commands* — sublime kind of pride. As lawgiver he is superior to the law, he can show something over and above the law, perfect it: how incongruous for him to do something that runs against his fixed idea! From this height *he longs for love* — humans are to *believe* in him: this is the only thing he lacks, and in return he wants to give them everything that he can e.g., God's grace. Children, the poor, the dumb, the despised, the self-despisers are his favorites. He creates his God after his own image so that he can show love as God: he eliminates and weakens representations that yield another God. His honesty with himself is very slight; neither with respect to his belief in himself as the son of God nor with respect to his knowledge of nature and human being does he have a delicate conscience. He lies to himself, wholly in the service of his passion: what he does not know he does not esteem, he takes himself to be the measure of all things, with the inexperience of a solitary shepherd surrounded only by sheep. His sore point is that humans do not want to believe him, whereas he believes himself: and with this his imagination becomes cruel and dark, and he creates hell for those who do not b⟨elieve⟩ in him. His lack of education shields him from imagining the emergence of a passion and from seeing *himself* objectively for once: he never stands above himself (like e.g., Napoleon). The rejection of his love became for him the most terrible, eternally inexpiable thing on the part of humans — this is a *common* trait. Likewise his suspicion of the wealthy, the mind, the flesh — his kindness and forbearance is brief and wholly egoistical.

6[230]

Among storytellers the more refined avoid intensifying their heroes' experiences into the monstrous, forensic, crude: rather, they tone down and smooth out the events and show what finer natures *already* have to suffer from so little: or that here *their* experiences are only beginning: for crude natures there are no problems here. — To state about one's hero that he is not *non plus ultra*, rather a capable human, distinguishes every good poet. — The demigod-stories require little talent, crude colors — they are told to the *masses*. They are ideal robber- and ghost-stories. — Whoever grows enamored of his heroes and their experiences is not of the first rank — for he must be *poor*. — It is the poor who toil with splendid, captivating topics and heroes, who do not readily believe that others think of them as rich.

6[231]

We do not attain our maximum: for in the period of the most rapid growth all other favorable conditions must be present. We have short trunks and are gnarly.

6[232]

If we also guarded ourselves from blind attacks of love and hate against persons — how much less we would have *to rectify*, i.e., retrace a wrong path! (whereby *our* path has lost time). Greater honesty with ourselves keeps us safe: usually we suddenly *yield to* our checked drives after all, in this love and hate for persons.

6[233]

Christianity has promised the kingdom of heaven to spiritual poverty: but the first educated and ingenious Christian gave to Christianity its dialectic and rhetoric, without these it would have perished from its spiritual poverty.

6[234]

We all have the drives in common with the animals: the growth of honesty makes us more independent of these drives' inspiration. This honesty itself is the result of intellectual labor, namely when two opposite drives set the intellect into motion. With a new affect memory supplies us with respect to a thing or a person the representations that this thing or ⟨this⟩ person earlier, with another affect, stimulated in us: and then *different* qualities display themselves; to let these count together is *one* measure of honesty, i.e., to hold it against someone whom we now hate that we once loved him, and to compare his earlier image in us with the present one, to mitigate, balance the present one. *Prudence* commands this: for without this we, as haters, would go too far and endanger ourselves. Basis of justice: we concede to images in us *of the same* thing a right!

6[235]

The practice of recognizing *several* qualities in a thing, *apart* from our affect, constitutes a series of stable things which becomes ever greater and ever finer. This practice forms a *need*: for the knowledge of things in their multiplicity. Basis of the *intellectual drive*.

6[236]

Honesty with ourselves is *older* than h⟨onesty⟩ with others. The animal notices that it is often deceived, likewise it often must dissimulate. This leads it to distinguish between erring and seeing correctly, between dissimulation and reality. Intentional *dissimulation* rests upon the first sense of honesty with oneself.

6[237][146]

Christ "pious sad and egoistical"

6[238]

What does it mean "*to understand a thought*?" It stirs a representation, this stirs perceptions, these stir up feelings, so at last the stone gives off a dull sound when it has reached the ground below: this vibration of the ground we call "understanding." Cause and effect does not occur here, only association: with this word this representation is customarily aroused: *how* that is possible no one knows. Our "understanding" is something unintelligible, and that final resonance in our drives is nothing more after all than a new great unknown. —

A lie is the excitation of that ground in our neighbor such that a drive awakens in him which he cannot come to satisfy, because the nature of things happens to be another: hence *to excite an unfulfillable need* is to lie.

6[239]

Humans gradually project a value and meaning into *nature* which in itself it does not have. The farmer sees his fields with a feeling of value, the artist his colors, the savage transfers his fear to it, we our security; it is a continuous, most subtle symbolizing and equating, without consciousness. Our eye looks at the landscape with all our morality and culture and habits. — And just so we look upon other *characteristic* qualities: they are for me something else than for you: relations and phantasms, our mutual limits lie therein. — What does justice mean there! The abundance of relations grows continuously, *everything* that we see and experience *becomes deeper with meaning*. At the sight of the sun e.g. — but innumerable old meanings and symbols are also continuously *dying away*, everything is simultaneously emptying — and when we are on the path of justice, then the arbitrary, fantastic interpretations die with which we harm and do violence to things: for their *real* qualities have a right, and finally we must honor this more highly than ourselves.

6[240][147]

Praise of philology: as the study of honesty. Antiquity perished because of its decay.

6[241]

The fateful "*second sense*" behind natural events, experiences, desires, injustice! Poor humanity!

6[242]

The "moral world order" — a kind of astrology.

6[243]

We owe our greatest exaltations, perturbations, the purest heaven to ourselves: we lend from that to works of art and so they become greater, we improve them and occasionally misjudge them in their favor.

6[244]

Honesty in art — nothing to do with realism! Essentially artists' honesty with respect to their abilities: they do not want to lie to themselves, nor to intoxicate themselves — to create no effect on themselves, but to *imitate* the experience (the real effect).

6[245]

If we consider *who* at any given time gains the greatest renown: then it is likely that the most distinguished *minds* will stand in the second or third rank: and the best masters remain unknown.

6[246]

My pathos: to empathize with the dreadful pain of the feeling of sin NB.

6[247]

No one should believe that if Plato were now living and had Platonic views, he would be a *philosopher* — he would be a religious madman.

6[248]

The bad practice in the seeing and *wanting*-to-see of the real has also caused in human relations, in their judgment of one another and themselves, a mythology to emerge, the "moral world."

6[249]

Doubt about what the real is does *not* increase inclination to phantasms: instead, it gradually destroys the good will belonging to the *poetization* of a phantasm.

6[250]

Generally, one considers no action as intelligible unless it is aimed at purposes: and absolutely no movement in the world. For that reason, all earlier thought intended to explain all motion in the world as purposive and purposeful (God). Philosophy's greatest turning point is that action according to purposes was *no longer found comprehensible*; with that all earlier tendencies are invalidated.

6[251]

When we make responsible, then we presuppose the same force in others, and the same knowledge about this force — which after all is mythology.

6[252]

The spontaneous concentration of energy distinguishes humans, not an individual atom. Then the ingrained movements of this concentration, transmitted by inheritance. It is *the same* force that is expended, now through the muscles, now through the nerves.

6[253]

The thought, just as much as the word, is only a sign: there is no question of any congruence of thought and the real. The real is some movement of a drive.

6[254]

Every action is something infinitely different from the pallid conscious image of it we have during its execution. It differs likewise from the conscious image we have in mind prior to the deed (the end of the action = purpose and the path to it); countless stretches of the path that are finally *covered* are not seen and the purpose itself is a small bit of the real *outcome* of the action. Purposes are *signs*: nothing more! Signals! Whereas otherwise the copy follows upon the model, here a kind of copy precedes the model. In tr⟨uth⟩ we *never* know *completely what* we are doing e.g., when we want to take a step or want to utter a sound. Perhaps this "wanting" is only a pale shadow of that which really is already in the process of becoming, a belated copy of our *capability* and acting: occasionally a very false copy, in which we seem *in*capable of doing what we want. Our "wanting" here was a misguided phantasm in our mind, we had misunderstood some sign. — When someone *commands* and we want to do it but find ourselves too weak —? then fear (or love) gave us an impulse with which a lot of force was set in motion. — The *initial* success of the nerve- and muscle-tracts gives the premature representation of capability and from that *results* the premature image of the willed purpose: the *representation of purpose* emerges *after* the action is already *in the process of becoming*!

6[255]

Faith in ourselves is the strongest fetter and the heaviest lash of the whip — and the *strongest wing*. Christianity should have postulated the innocence of the human as an article of faith — humans would have become gods: back then one *could* still believe.

6[256][148]

To beseech "hardness coldness weariness"[149] — torment, when one no longer trusts one's goal in life. "Sublime anger, fitful reproaches"[150]— to fall asleep sobbing — peering out into chill and dread, coldly awakening[151] — "narrow cell of her calamity"[152] — only one glance at the life of another, no more. "All the sympathetic experience installed itself as a countervailing power"[153] — justice to expel one's own pain.

"Need for justice."

"To over-estimate the good of others," blind to the good effects that we call forth in others.

6[257][154]

We must arrive at the point of feeling the impossible unnatural totally-fantastical in the ideal of God Christ and the Christian saints with intellectual *disgust*. The model should not be a phantasm!

6[258][155]

To exchange for every defection of a friend a higher soul.

6[259]

If you have made it your practice to think of others and to do something for them, a good deal remains when it is impossible for you to achieve your goal: namely, to promote that of others. It is good and prudent to have these two strings to play. To comprehend the other and to look closely at *ourselves from his viewpoint* is indispensable for the thinker.

6[260][156]

I discern it in your tolerance for science from 100 paces away: you think you have no need for it, you pride yourselves on being its advocate all the same, even when it contests your opinions: — for you have no such strict feeling for the real that it tortures and torments you to find science in contradiction with yourselves: just as little as you avidly look around to see *what* it all is that is presently being recognized and is on the way to becoming known.

6[261]

Practice in cognition has produced in the end a *need for truthfulness*, which now is a new great power, with dangers and advantages.

Title perhaps: "*the need for truthfulness*."

6[262]

All moral systems which *commanded how the human being* **is to** *act* lacked the knowledge and investigation of *how the human being acts*. But one believed one had this knowledge.

6[263]

The need for activity divides us from Indian wisdom.

6[264]

Even to the finest thought corresponds an entanglement of drives. — The words are as it were a *keyboard* of the drives, and thoughts (in words) are chords upon it. Still, the word's stimulating force is not always the same for the drive, and sometimes the word is almost nothing but a sound.

6[265]

1. Time of the drives without thoughts 2. Time of the drives with thoughts (judgments). Here drives and drive-entanglements are *represented*. The frequent repetition, the approval and rejection of such representations, has a repercussion on the drives themselves, some are practiced intensely, others are taken out of practice and shrivel up. Through prodigious exercise of the intellect *gradually* emerges the *pleasure in its activity*: and from this finally again *pleasure in the truthfulness* in its activity. Orig⟨inally⟩ the intellectual functions are very *difficult* and *laborious*. Imitation is the best, hatred for the new. In the end disgust with imitation, conversely, is quick to arrive and pleasure in the new and in change very great.

6[266]

Humans perish as the result of the *refinement of the intellect*: physically and perhaps morally as well. — We fortunate ones! We are in the *Middle Kingdom*![157]

6[267]

The perfection of a Napoleon, of a Cagliostro enraptures; our criminality has no role models, they have no cheerful conscience. A good robber, a good avenger, adulterer — that distinguished the Italian Middle Ages and ⟨the⟩ Renaissance, they had the *sense for completeness*. With us the virtues and vices are fearful, public opinion is the power of the half-hearted and mediocre, of the bad *copies*, of the patchwork everyman.

6[268]

We do not want to make a *God* of ourselves, we do not hanker after the ideals of *earlier* peoples. Precisely ungodliness, joy in the innumerable individuals with the greatest difference, who will likely be *adversaries*, but like Greeks and Trojans!

6[269]

The passionate bent to help everyone spoils one's own comfort.

6[270][158]

Before people with *great souls* we reveal our *larger* context, and *before them we believe* in it *more* than when alone. That is why we need them. We can *give up* countless little shifting lines of thought — that does good! Others *can* only see these trifles: in their presence we have to own or deny them, in either case without satisfaction.

6[271][159]

With a *great goal* one is above and beyond not only its slandering but also a great crime.

6[272]

To shield a person from *low experiences* is the most beautiful thing — low with respect not to us, but to *him*.

6[273]

A wife as inhibition, a husband as means of degeneration.

6[274]

Rash inclination and disinclination, dissimulation, etc. has been *molded* into our whole organism: gradually truthfulness too can be molded[160] onto it and grow ever deeper roots, with what effects? For the time being it is a moving net of falsehood and deception and their tentacles: entirely animal-useful. The education toward truth — is it an improvement of the animal, a higher adaptation to reality? — Our benevolence compassion, our self-sacrifice, our "morality" rests upon *the same foundation* of falsehood and dissimulation as our evil and selfishness! This is to be shown! The unpleasant, yes, tragic impress of this discovery is initially unavoidable. But at first all our drives must become more anxious more distrustful, gradually incorporate more reason and honesty, become shrewder and thus ever more lose the *reason* for *distrust* of one another: so can one day a greater, more fundamental joyfulness emerge: for the time being this *joyfulness* would only be *possible for the dishonest. Resignation and that heroic pleasure in defiance and victory are the only forms of our joyfulness*: *if we are cognitive beings. NB NB NB*!!! How then does it happen that we struggle against *profound mendacity and dissimulation*? A feeling of *power*, which in our mind's development and operation becomes free, compels us: it whets the appetite.

6[275]

The accursed teacher- and reformer- and preacher-of-repentance-pathos "and our duty commands us to make humans unhappy."

6[276]

The increasing *mendacity* of the pathetic (cf. Lipiner) or of the tolerant (Miss v⟨on⟩ M⟨eysenbug⟩)

6[277]

Taciturn passion with gloomy eyes in Calvin is easily defamed. Grace and spirit in passion is not accredited in Germany.

6[278]

in the form of a tragedy:
1 The path
2 the terrible prospect
3 the respite

6[279]

The fear of death: "I am the woodworm"
loss of the child
loss of honor
disease

6[280]

To what extent it is useful to try to love the enemy? It breaks the unsatisfied feeling and gives a victory *over ourselves.*

6[281][161]

To devise humanity's *highest* goal of death — at some point the task will concentrate on that. Not to live for the sake of living.

6[282]

The ancients thought women in passion capable of what is really inhuman and incredible — in the time of Aeschylus.

6[283][162]

When someone converts to the Jews (according to Tacitus), he must despise the gods, renounce his fatherland, and disavow parents children siblings. The souls of those who die in battle or by execution are immortal (martyr-idea of Christianity). Hence scorn for death. When Caligula ordered his likeness installed in the temple, they took up arms.

6[284][163]

"they eat with no one, sleep alone and refrain, as lascivious as they are, from all foreign women" "even the worst person sent levies and alms to Jerusalem, regardless of the country in which he lived."

6[285][164]

Tacitus speaks derisively of how much the Jews (and Christians) are given over to superstition. Rome went to its extreme when it became Christian: it is a sign of humans' *impotentia*[165] back then, this abrupt switching of horses. Hatred's wrath made the Jews (Christians) interesting in the end.

6[286]

One takes various "best things" from judgment by others (who themselves are very different) and discovers they contradict each other: i.e., one believes *one's* conscience to be restless.

6[287]

In the difficult moment good humans have *no scruples.*

6[288]

A kind of justice: "I have enjoyed his fortune with him. Now also the time of his dishonor and guilt."[166]

6[289]

So to live that our energy is at its *greatest* and *most joyful* — and for that to sacrifice everything. NB

6[290][167]

the metaphysical need is not the source of religions, rather the aftereffect following their demise. We have become used to the idea of another world and miss it (and from this impulse new plants can sprout "*after*-religions"), but what drove us to the assumption of another world were errors in the interpretation of certain occurrences, thus *false judgments by the intellect. The "metaphysical need" is the result,* not origin. Through *want of satisfaction* it can die out! So there is a *need* to hear the bells ring, which has nothing at all to do with the *original purpose* of ringing bells. — We have become used to placing needs at the beginning.

6[291][168]

Against Christianity: the perfect morality is neither possible **nor desirable**. Its value rests upon false views of biology.

6[292]

As moral *judgments* have been passed since time immemorial (as errors about actions), so in any case have *moral sensations, inclinations, disinclinations* been formed from them. These then are *real. But how are they related to the reality of the actions* on which moral judgments are erroneously passed? — The actions upon which among humans moral judgments were first formed are those that are all found among the animals: whose motives therefore did *not* first need to be created. One *imagined* one understood these actions; moral judgments are "explanations of them according to purposes," a scientific starting point. In naming them (evil good just, etc.), one did not doubt that one understood them through and through. Socrates was the first to fall into doubt *whether* he understood them. But he did not doubt that something *essential* corresponded to the *words* good, evil, etc.!

6[293]

"How *should* the human being act?" That is only to be measured against an ideal, either *what* humanity ought to achieve or *what* the individual ought to achieve. *Until now* there were such models as hovered before peoples (in part living, in part imagined) or before religious communities. Or before political parties or ⟨the perfect merchant, soldier⟩, civil servant. Or before philosophical sects. But always until now before majorities. The goal though is: that *each conceive* his model image and realize it — the individual model. In the conception every generative force and youth and manliness required, every insight into his strength, self-knowledge. *At present* it is *not yet possible*!

6[294]

We must not discount our faults and drives in the conception of our model but know how to find their *sublime form.*

6[295]

It can be a tragedy! Our kindness and compassion and — our sense of truthfulness in conflict with each other regarding the opinions of others.

6[296]

A woman who grasps that she inhibits her husband's flight, should divorce — why do we not hear about *this* act of love?

6[297][169]

It stands with thoughts as with bodily movements: I must wait to see *whether* they occur; even when I will them, it depends on whether they are ingrained. Willing here is not the representation of the goal but the representation of logical forms (opposite of a thought, parallel, similar, premise inference, etc.) in the form of the wish. Memory must supply the content — In the instance of a sentence memory seeks to *append* something corresponding to the single words, and our judgment decides whether it fits and how. So the foot tries out any number of positions in the moment of stumbling. We choose from among these suddenly emerging thought-embryos: just as from among the available words we formulate our thoughts. The most essential part of the process takes place beneath our consciousness. *Our* **character** determines whether corresponding thoughts are essentially those of contradiction limitation approval: the emergence of each thought is a *moral event.* — The logical forms thus appear as the most general expression of our drives, affection, opposition, etc. — Down to the level of the cell there are no movements other than such "moral" ones in this sense.

6[298]

Whoever drinks a mouthful of champagne after two days of strict fasting experiences something coming quite close to sensual pleasure. The gaze into nature of a person who has lived for weeks in a dark cave is a visual rapture. And after years to hear our music again! — Only ascetics know what sensual pleasures are.

6[299][170]

The *Christians*, according to Tacitus not found guilty of scorched earth destruction but of *odio generis humani*, "of hatred for humanity." That is true! "As guilty as they were and although they deserved the severest punishments" — "in Rome where everything unnatural and ignominious runs together" "humans hated on account of *shameful deeds flagitia*"[171] (so Christians are defined. They were deemed capable of anything — why? Pessimists

6[300]

Always to act in such a way that we are content with ourselves — here it comes down to the refinement of truthfulness with ourselves. Second, to the standard by which we measure. Thus, a good conscience can be a pronounced sign of commonness and intellectual crudeness: a bad conscience of intellectual delicacy.

If others were not discontent with us, and so much did not go awry, self-contentment would be the rule. The unexpected unpleasant aftereffects disrupt this contentment: with unpleasantness we seek a discharge of our vengeful feeling and thereby mainly strike ourselves. It is *ill fortune* that gives humans their bad conscience, "it could have been different." There we scold ourselves and disparage our acumen and our intentions. If we were not *h⟨umans⟩ of vengeance*, then we would be much *more content*: as in general women are, since in them the feeling of revenge is not as strong. — Conscience then is determined by success: it condemns the intentions after the fact, indeed it *falsifies* intentions after the fact: the whole of a human's immorality and dishonesty is revealed in the trial that his conscience puts him through. A human's bad conscience, just like his good conscience, is as dumb, calumnious, or adulatory flattering comfortable — as the whole human is. One has a *conscience according to one's level.*

6[301][172]

Some are made happy with the secret thought that others, who live according to other principles, should be troubled at their happiness: they want to *refute* others with their happiness. (*Pique-bonheur*)[173]

6[302]

Sudden Christian rigorousness implies inner distress, hence misdeeds committed. — — —

6[303]

From one moment onwards one can misunderstand and rename one's passions — rebirth.

6[304]

One cannot render one's thoughts in words, they fall shadowlike too rapidly be⟨hind⟩ the sensations.

6[305]

However closely we follow with our eyes the movements of boiling water, we grasp nothing more thereby about the *cause of boiling*. So too with actions, if we become clear about the churning web of representations of which we thereby become conscious at all. These are all effects that let us guess at a hidden fire: but it is ridiculous to want to define it.

6[306]

The admiration for the person of Jesus has little meaning if it proceeds from the plane on which Christ placed himself: the profound sinfulness of the human being. What would a Greek from Pericles's circle have thought of that?

6[307]

For someone wishing to attain a model image, pleasure consists in seeing humans who have attained theirs. The impure unclear hybrid constructs embarrass him! That then stands in the place of "good" and "evil" humans!

6[308]

The general public models, according to which up to now moral praise and blame were apportioned, had a one-sided effect and left an abundance of qualities unpraised: one lost sight of the recognition of the individual and the beautiful proportion of forces in him. It was barbaric: to want to work the same model out of *every* material!

6[309]

The representation of exemplary types would be the principal merit of artists: to develop a sense for the unified and proportionate. The artist *selects* and *praises* thereby! The Greeks were great in the pleasure in the characteristic: Thucydides and Sophocles the flourishing of taste!

6[310]

No sooner does one speak of the "not absolute truths" than all enthusiasts desire admittance again, or rather: the good-natured souls post themselves at the gate and believe that they may open to everyone: as if now error were no longer error! What is *disproven* is *excluded*!!

6[311][174]

Tacitus expresses the difference between Jews and Romans thus: "among them everything is sacred which among us is unholy, just as conversely among them everything is allowed which among us is abhorred." This paradox was disseminated by the Christians, they created propaganda, "they are unswervingly loyal and support one another in distress, just as they hate as enemies all other humans."

6[312]

energy wasted through vexation and care, become conscious: becoming small thereby

6[313]

women see in the sciences a vampire near a man.

6[314]

I look with disdain at the pleasant intoxication by alcoholic drinks, the pleasure in play — but the Greeks?

6[315][175]

to beware of myself

6[316]

Shudder and transformation at the sight of a beautiful deed: as among large rocks and sudden enchanting views upon flowering vegetation.

6[317]

Not the action but our judgment on the action (though it be an error) makes our conscience, the private history of ourselves

6[318][176]

It is narrow-minded to construe the Pharisees as hypocrites; they always live with firm trust in their actions, they do not consider them more deeply and truthfully, and among themselves know as a matter of habit only good motives: the others they do not see, their eye is blind in this regard. — Provided one inserted a new eye into them and made them discontent with themselves: now, in that way one would increase the general misery. The actions would remain the same in their effects for others, and thus it would be a superfluous *human cruelty*. This is what Christianity wants.

6[319]

Provided we feel an action to be good, then the whole course of events plays out. What an action is in itself, whether useful or harmful, has nothing to do with it. For that reason, it is so important that the good actions really *can be carried out* and *often*: *otherwise* the moral hell, and the moral as *distant view of the saints* — also calling forth admirable illuminations and colorations!

6[320]

Your morality is a *matter of your fortune*. Your good conscience is a matter of your fortune! Taken by surprise amidst some things and brought out into the public, you would be deeply devastated. That your character improves is a matter of fortune! The small steps and the innumerable small dissatisfactions are the most powerful! | Not only is compassion necessary, but we must create or tolerate *worldviews for the evil* and the unfortunate! | Instead of the confessors we must *put in place philosophies like suns for every type of* human, whereas up to now the highest exemplars have mostly created morals for themselves! |

6[321]

What *others* think of us and know can suddenly crash in upon us. What *we* know of ourselves (remember) is not decisive!

6[322][177]

Those who take no joy in their life and character seek them perhaps in their *spirit*: like Sch⟨openhauer⟩. Whoever is whole though should only be able to be glad of everything at once! And how glad! We all climb our mountain together and do not wish to reach the peak alone! Many a person climbs it as a personality, but his spirit does not befit the situation (e.g., Bismarck).

6[323]

To look upon one's experience as strictly and truthfully as a scientific experiment — one may not fantasize about miracles and "angels surrounding us" and the hand of the Lord: that seems dishonest to me.

6[324]

The *deed* is not blotted out by absolution. The past is not past, our deeds are our being and likewise future doing already belongs to us. Memory decides nothing.

6[325][178]

"To make foolish stunts out of a deep and passionate daydream," as Stendhal says. Is this the work of genius?

6[326][179]

"The ancients did nothing for the sake of *embellishment*, and among them the *beautiful* is only *la saillie de l'utile*."[180]

6[327][181]

Depth and energy of feeling, not to forget; forgiveness is a sacrifice (*not* a casual good-natured letting go of a thought, with *pleasure in* no longer having to bear it.) Italian simplicity, almost coldness as the cloak of these passionate natures.

6[328][182]

In France the *esprit* would like to give itself genius. In Germany genius would like to give itself *esprit*.

6[329][183]

"the strained style"!

6[330][184]

Novella d'Andrea taught in Bologna (14th c.). Teaching from behind a curtain because of her beauty.

6[331]

The *beautiful* seems to us in the end only a state brought about by the generally useful: a profound well-being which breaks forth from all lines and movements of our actions words: a harmony of many utilities coming into resonance.

6[332]

No one as yet has grasped the problem of truthfulness. That which is said against the lie are the naïveties of a schoolmaster, and especially the commandment "thou shalt not lie"!

6[333]

Every flourishing thought finally sprouts its species of luxury, it is its final manifestation. In the arts as in the art of commerce. Every *mature* culture has its luxury. — But show me the inventor of an idea who did not have simplicity and poverty externally as well, also in words. — The luxurious thought writes itself on every vessel, inscribes itself into every gesture (e.g., nobility and simplicity and grace in ancient Athens)[185]

6[334]

The Germans lack *esprit* because they own no surplus of spirit: as soon as they have made use of theirs, they are poor and just sit there. They hate it and nevertheless they feel that without it sociability is a tedious loutishness: — hence "temperament."[186]

6[335][187]

Wanting-to-create-an-effect is a German sickness.

6[336]

In Germany a man of spirit rises *too high* above his fellow citizens and becomes a fool; fog envelops his head. — He degenerates so easily because nothing near him keeps him in check; he shoots forth on all sides and is of an ugly fertility.

6[337][188]

In Germany the *ridiculous* is not terrible for the person who has spirit. For it is not sophisticated people's laughter but that of young asses which defines here the idea of the ridiculous. — This *breeding* is lacking.[189]

6[338]

To *glow* with a thought, to become burnt by it — that is French. The German admires himself and poses in front of the mirror with his passion and beckons to others.[190]

6[339]

Our beliefs: the *skin* in which we cloak ourselves, in which we want to be seen, or in which we want to see ourselves; the most superficial. The scale armor around a person's thoughts. So it seems. On the other hand, this skin is the product of we know not what forces and drives, a kind of *sediment*, continuously detaching itself piece by piece and recomposing itself. — sound images and visual images as hieroglyphs for certain impressions and feelings are the material of beliefs, refinements of the auditory and visual senses and a relation between both.

6[340]

Our consciousness lags behind and notices little at once and in between pauses for other things. This imperfection is presumably the source of our believing in things and assuming something permanent in the process of becoming: likewise of our believing in an ego. If knowledge proceeded as rapidly as development and as steadily, there would be no thought of an "I."

6[341]

It is a limited point of view, but it is how I feel. The *need* ⟨for⟩ *luxury* seems to me to point to a deep inner *lack of spirit*; just as if someone surrounded himself with stage scenery because he is nothing complete, real, but only something that is supposed to represent a thing to himself and others. I say a person of spirit can endure much pain and privation and still be happy; yes, in relation to someone who needs honor and luxury and comradeship, he must be ashamed because in the distribution of goods he has come off too well. I have a deep contempt for a banker. Whoever surrounds himself with luxury, now on occasion he must so position himself that for others' sake he fits in, but then he is also obliged to share and tolerate these others' opinions. I consider liberal-minded daring new views a fraud or a repulsive kind of luxury if they do not press towards poverty and baseness. For me Las⟨s⟩alle, for example, contradicted himself with a kind of white linen.[191] People with such needs should become pious and strive for esteem as magistrates, there is so much good to be preserved and represented. But the *spirit* they should not want to represent! Whoever is spiritually rich and independent is anyway also the most powerful human; it is, for such humane times at least, scandalous if he wants to have still more: they are the insatiable. Simplicity in food and drink, hatred of alcoholic drinks — that befits him, as the drinks befit those who could say, "life would be completely without charm," etc. — I am compelled to an ideal independence: place society region books *cannot* be chosen *highly enough*, and instead of accommodating oneself and becoming common one must be able to be deprived, *without* the silent sufferer's wrinkles.

6[342]

Even in the intellectual sphere, e.g., in the appraisal of beliefs, we do not always put *reasons* forward, but very often an intellectual *disgust* because we see from small signs how dull and myopic and easily satisfied someone is, or how far the self-assurance of the ignorant person or the novice goes. I.e., we judge the method of knowing as: slimy decayed stinking garbage, spat out, chewed over, maggot-eaten, stale, stagnant, musty, etc.

6[343]

"I want this:" we distinguish "object, valuation of the object, and experience,"[192] but at bottom it is *not* an object that we want but a *pleasant condition of ourselves* that we encountered in some connection with the object: and the valuation of the object is an *attempt* to explain what is really a pleasant sensation, in that we *represent* the pleasantness as the *result* of an insight (e.g., eating as the appeasement of hunger, as preservation, etc.): whereas the pleasant sensation is most often not the result of the insight into its purposefulness. "*I want*" means, "I make something pleasant for myself, to the extent I can." We have a familiar condition in mind (e.g., as someone striking, eating); this image we imitate.

6[344]

Memory has causes for morality — and we do not have it in hand! NB.

6[345]

Curiosity, to find out something disadvantageous, likewise in relation to things possible and shameful. NB

6[346]

Chief amusement, to offend others — why immoral? Teasing is only a degree. Here the distinction between moral and immoral is *not* also an antithesis.

6[347]

But then *must* morality, if, according to Kant, it necessarily rests upon freedom, have existed at all? Does not the *illusion* of freedom suffice? And if this illusion is no longer possible, is it then absolutely necessary to uphold morality? *Could it not* have played its role? (against [— — —]

6[348]

I know how wretched you appear next to this sweeping idealism (which takes materialism and skepticism on its back and carries them toward the sun), but — I keep your company and position myself as your equal; what is more, I denigrate myself.

6[349][193]

The subject feeling grows in proportion to how with memory and imagination we build the world *of the same things.* We invent ourselves as unity in this self-created image-world, the unchanging amidst change. But this is an error: we posit signs and signs as identical and conditions as conditions.

6[350][194]

Only what we think of others and what we think of ourselves defines our behavior, *insofar as it is conscious.* Hence the representation of others and of ourselves: these though are the result again of what others have taught and imparted to us. The *interpretation of our conditions* is the work of others implanted in ourselves.[195] Therein morality remains hanging, it is shadow.

6[351]

I spoke vainly for half an hour and at the end was somewhat abashed and tired — but I had wanted to humble myself and give someone occasion to think less miserably of himself with the exclamation: alas, the miserable world! — for he momentarily thought of me in such a way that he was no longer ashamed of himself in front of me; it visibly relieved him.

6[352][196]

the "double laughter" (Epictetus) when he takes on a more elevated position than he could bear and abandons it again. Alas, this too we want to bear, yes, we want to return to appearance and encourage our fellow humans to face their lives by giving them occasion to laugh twice over at us. — We want to reach our goal by detours, and, while we draw near to others, deceive them *for their sake.* — The straightforward paths, e.g., Christ Napoleon presuppose contempt for the human, however far Ch⟨rist's⟩ love for humans went (for the gracious love of Chr⟨ist⟩ is still far removed from wanting to be a sinner for the sake of the sinners)

6[353]

Surroundings in which we let ourselves go are the last thing we should wish for ourselves, a kind of crown for the self-conqueror who has perfected himself and who would like to radiate his perfection. Others become monsters. Caution in marriage. The lack of pathos and form in the family, in friendship, is a reason for the general appearance of sloppiness and commonness — we let ourselves go and let go. (Qualities of conduct not only but also of modern characters.)

6[354]

The actual *impertinence of goodness* I have best observed among Jews. Think of the beginnings of Christianity.

6[355][197]

I have played dice with the prince of the underworld himself.

6[356]

Skepticism! Yes, but a *skepticism of experiments*! Not the indolence of despair

6[357]

The *tension* between the God conceived of as increasingly pure and remote and the human being conceived of as increasingly sinful — one of humanity's great tests of strength. God's love for the sinner is marvelous. Why did the Greeks not have such a tension between divine beauty and human ugliness? Or between divine knowledge and human ignorance? The mediatory bridges between two such chasms would be new creations, which do not exist (angels? revelation? son of God?).

6[358]

Every moment a moral sensation can become so strong that it generates partial sterility, e.g., the drive for truth could kill art and sociable refined intercourse, likewise eloquence. Chastity. Generosity. Diligence. Cleanliness. (Puritans opposed to the theater. Xenophanes opposed to the *agons*.[198] Plato

6[359]

Supposing that our culture had to dispense with piety. It could not generate it out of itself. A certain final inner resolve and appeasement will be missing. More than ever martial and adventurous spirits! The poets have yet to discover the possibilities of life; the *universe* is open to it, not an Arcadia or Campan[199] an infinitely bolder fantasizing by way of knowledge about animal evolution is possible. All our poetry is so petty-bourgeois-earthbound, the great potential of higher humans is still missing. Only after the death of religion can *inventiveness in the divine sphere* flourish again.

6[360]

One thing is necessary: the *isolation* of gifted humans, their self-sustenance, their renunciation of reputation and office, the scorn for all humans and events resulting from great human heaps. A metropolitan *émeute*[200] and newspaper is through and through "playacting," "inauthentic."

6[361]

Our system of pleasant and unpleasant sensations branches out and becomes more refined, and our life of thought as well. For a long time the latter has believed itself to be the *whole* of consciousness and to know the reason for all pleasant and unpleasant things. Naïve people still believe that we know *why* we will. Even *before* an action we are really only able to imagine possibilities for explaining our action according to our respective degree of self-knowledge: but *what moves us*, that we do not yet know even by the deed itself, indeed, never! We *interpret* our action before and after the deed *according to the canon* of our assumptions about human motives. This interpretation can hit upon the right thing, but there is nothing in the interpretation itself that truly motivates or does the deed. To set ourselves a purpose: i.e., to set against a drive a thought-image which is supposed to think it. This is never *completely* the case! The thought-image consists of *words*, is something highly imprecise, it has no levers to cause movements — in itself. Only through association, through a logically inaccessible and absurd relation between a thought and the mechanism of a drive (they meet perhaps in an image, e.g., that of someone giving strict orders) can a thought (e.g., a word of command) "bring about" an action. Really, it is a parallelism. There is *nothing of cause and effect* between purpose-idea and action, this rather is the **great deception**, as if it were so!

6[362]

We think in words! If one knows what words are, how can one believe that thinking can directly bring forth motions! These are nothing but little errors, but our drives are so closely aligned with this region of error, and to each drive corresponds a number of these colorful arbitrary things called "words," that a word is often a signal, not a cause, for motion (as the sound of a horn can bring a locomotive to a stop). The more strictly we apprehend, the more firmly do we set limits to words, they are images in the mirror, even copies of these images! The transition to knowledge of cause and effect can never be made. Our knowing is *describing*, more or less approximately, the exact succession and simultaneity, apparently united in memory into a kind of image (a timeless unity): — — —

6[363]

In the backwoods, where the trees have never heard anything of the city, the boy begins to think over and beyond the city.

6[364]

Infinity! Beautiful it is "to shipwreck in this sea."[201]

6[365]

All drives originally relatively purposive in their effect ("good" *and* "evil"). Morality arises a) when one drive rules over others, e.g., fear of someone powerful or drive to sociable life. There weaker drives must be felt but *not* satisfied. The answers to the why? arising here are as crude and false as possible, but they are the beginning of *moral judgments*, laying down a value difference in actions between necessary admissible inadmissible. To have a drive and feel aversion to its satisfaction is the "ethical" phenomenon. Or, e.g., love for offspring for property, for whose sake one goes hungry, exposes oneself to dangers. Offspring and property are something so pleasant: but if one wanted reasons, it would not suffice to say "they are pleasant" — moral reason is the effort to ignore the instincts and to appear as if we acted according to purposes, thus *willed* our *best*. In fact, the pleasant is usually our best, but *this* best one could not grasp, for that the knowledge of nature and the human was lacking. One construed the "best" *according to* one's assumption about nature and the human. Here belongs, e.g., the salvation of the soul. Or honor. Or a god's commandments. The human always affects to act according to principles — this great comedy goes undetected, he behaves "responsibly." But to the instinctual drives the purpose-concepts are added afterwards and *almost never* strike the moving point. The human machine would almost come to a standstill, if for once only it were guided by the *alleged* motives. Even now still the illusion is very great.

6[366]

The essential is not the *forgotten* motives and the habituation to certain movements — as I *formerly* assumed. Rather the purposeless drives of pleasure and displeasure; one wants the pleasant and *not* because of the advantage to be attained from it, but rather because the action itself is pleasant. The purpose is achieved but not willed. *Those* kinds of pleasurable movements which serve the purpose of preservation are maintained through selection.

6[367]

If he[202] earnestly bade me or I guessed that he very much needed me, I would, against all better knowledge, take his side. This would be my weakness. Better to abandon *ourselves* and those who need us! And we are capable of a great deal of dissimulation: and, consequently, of much reeducation and a *second honesty*.

6[368][203]

Do you feel nothing of the need to be in the right *in opposition to* a person and publicly to attest to it? Has criticism become too easy for you? Is it only that you stand up after the other has? Do you not notice that he wanted to give you his best and that you should accept it, even if it seemed not valuable to you, even harmful? But you act like those who live in self-defense, you are also right. You remain upright with effort, and the other wants to impose something on you that you could not bear. He says: a gift!, you say: a task

6[369]

The life of you civil servants and politicians has something noisy about it, a creek and mill wheels sound around you, they render your thinking feeble with their noise: how should you ever hear your soul's melodies! You are becoming hollow and hard: and superficial! And your "duty" becomes a terror for others and leads them astray, it *seems* a noble self-sacrifice, but it is only self-forgetfulness; from the moment when that little bit of "self" just wanted to become visible: more negligence than sacrifice.

6[370]

Considering that hunting was the main occupation, for many millennia: so, too, our *scientific drive* is nothing else. Just as boys are always on the hunt.

6[371]

Whenever I hear of others' malice against me, then one of my first sensations is a sort of satisfaction: it seems fair to me that people with whom I agree so little, and against whom I have so much right on my side, for their part make a good day of it. I also believe[204] never to fail, in actions and thoughts, to give these others the feeling of their own superiority and a good right to this feeling. For such is the nature of things: we provide much pleasure with our faults and failings, and perhaps more.

6[372]

Before this person and while thinking of him we feel productivity, just like with this landscape, etc., after this nourishment.

6[373]

When we pursue an aim, we would *never* employ the means with full force; but our instincts provide us with the requisite blindness. All men of faith are such instinctive beings, their article of faith did *not* arise from reasons: rather, they have *inner imponderable joy in it.* The *inclination* to thoughts is passed down and tightened, i.e., into thought-drives.[205]

6[374][206]

The human always acts according to the representation that is relatively the most pleasant to him. But this calculation is often very difficult and the exercise in distinguishing the countless degrees too slight, particularly since imagination would have to have the power to set as *complete* future joys and sorrows, like the present enjoyment, which is perhaps already active.

6[375][207]

If I speak about the motives of certain persons, then it is as a point of honor for me. NB.

6[376][208]

I do not want to impose on people a new great burden, but rather relieve them of a burden NB

6[377]

As little state as possible! I do not need the state; I would have given myself, without that conventional constraint, a better education, namely, one tailored to my body, and spared myself the energy wasted in wrestling free. Should things around us become a bit more uncertain, all the better! I wish us to live rather guardedly and martially. It is the merchants who would like to make this worry-free state[209] so inviting for us, they now rule all the world with their philosophy. The "industrial" state is not my preference, as it is Spencer's. I myself want to be as much state as possible, I have so many expenses and proceeds,[210] so many needs, so much to communicate. For all that, poor and without design on positions of honor, also without admiration for martial laurels. I know how these states will go to ruin, on the *non plus ultra* state of the socialists: whose opponent I am, and I already hate it in the present state. I want to attempt even in prison still to live serenely and humanely. The great laments over human misery do not move me to join in the lament but rather to say: *that's what you lack*, you do not understand how to live as a person and have no wealth to set against privation and no delight in rule. Statistics prove that h⟨umans⟩ *are increasingly becoming the same*, i.e., that —

6[378]

In order to reeducate the human: at some point we have to proceed from the fact that *our valuation* of good and bad actions is *false* and arbitrary, then everything has to be examined anew, over centuries, just as it was necessary *for the healing of the body* to reject *all theories* of medicine uniformly! The instincts in this area are to be eradicated; next, respect must be planted for him who *lives experimentally* here — this is the most important species of human, as for the physician the laboratory animal is the most important species of animal.

6[379][211]

1) It is so hard to harm humans! Oh, that it is necessary![212] What good does it do me to hide myself, when I do not want to keep to myself what causes humans offense?

6[380]

To let others, who do not have the same, share in our greatest sufferings and cares, thus only make them suffer — is that not cruel? Did it not arise from the feeling, which with any bad thing that strikes us, wants to see something *suffering*? A fine emanation of revenge? And is not *marriage* and friendship therefore full of danger, because it promotes such cruelty in the transfer of suffering? It is *difficult* not to share a sorrow — therefore we should take hold of the opportunity to live in solitude.

6[381]

I find Schopenhauer rather superficial in matters of the soul, he knew too little joy and suffered little; a thinker should take care not to *harden himself*: whence should he take his material then? His passion for knowledge was *not great* enough to want to suffer for its sake: he barricaded himself. His pride too was greater than his thirst for knowledge; he feared for his reputation, in the act of disavowal.

6[382]

Until now there were glorifiers of the human being and disparagers of the same, both though *from the moral⟨istic⟩* standpoint. La Rochefoucauld and Christians found the sight of the human *ugly*: this though was a moral judgment and they did not *know* another! *We* reckon the human by nature, which is neither evil nor good, and do not find him always ugly where they abhorred him, and not always beautiful where they glorified him. What is the beautiful and ugly here? The complicated-purposeful, which confuses and outwits understanding, the trickster-like therein; then the aptitude for expression and the power of the expression itself: the great arc of his plans and ideals. His history. His way of intoxicating himself. It is a study without end, this animal! It is no stain upon nature, that is something we first laid into it. We have treated this "stain" too superficially. Netherlandish eyes[213] are required to discover beauty here as well.

6[383][214]

Ancient traits: friendship, the oracles, the slaves, *otium*,[215] no sin-gods and no social disgrace. Thucydides is for me the type who stands nearest to me: he takes pleasure in the types, finds that a quantum of good sense belongs to each type, and *seeks to discover this*: that is his practical *justice*.

6[384]

Even if word for word I reflect on what I want to say and do it then with full consciousness, what is spoken is nevertheless a hundredfold richer and *different* (e.g., in the tone, in the pauses, in the accompanying gestures), and the reflected portion is a small part of it. What then is the *unreflected part* of it now, what the *improvised*?

6[385]

Large difference: to want to please another for *their* sake or for our sake. To love ourselves for their sake — why moral?

6[386]

Suicide as the measure of culture: German. The use of soap: English.

6[387]

Some might say and write what they want — there is always something of good music in that. And with others something of bad music. With most the music is missing altogether.

6[388]

The finest *colors* in literature and music are visible and delightful only for calm humans — what do they have to seek in our age!

6[389]

Nowadays the repulsive is *painted very exactly* — why? — There pessimism belongs too. Not degeneration of morals, rather *excess activity* is the reason.

6[390][216]

One suffers from the shame, not from the crime. Few are *subtle* enough to distinguish here.

6[391]

The need to pray, also that to preach penitence, to extol, to bless, to curse, all religious customs break out as soon as a human is filled with pathos: as proof that to be filled with pathos means to take a step backwards. When are we *farthest removed* from that? When we play, show and exchange spirit, are cheerful-serene and at the same time roguish, jesting about anything emphatic in word, tone, drive — perhaps we attain here an *advantage* over our age. The heroic human recovering from the battle and exertion and rancor and ashamed of pathos — and there the priest!

6[392]

The *moral* fanaticism of the ancient philosophers prepared the way for Christianity, far too much importance has been attached to the salvation of the soul. We are profoundly immoral in relation to antiquity, and that is our *advantage*. And profoundly irreligious with respect to Christianity.

6[393]

Natures who do not think *about* themselves at all, but in particular do not like to face certain aspects of themselves (women, e.g., the function of the stomach, let alone the sexual drive) — they interpret all phenomena differently to themselves and do not *want* to see and admit the simple cause. In this way their passion attains something dreamy and, for themselves, mystical; they succumb more easily and more impetuously to it because they think of themselves idealistically. What do unmarried women know of the abnormal sexual drive, in their passion for art and certain of its trends, or in compassion, or in the form of blind devotion to a thought!

6[394]

The love of God for the human being is the dissipation of thought by humans living asexually; something like that could not occur to antiquity.

6[395][217]

The perfect contentment (of Epictetus *and* Christ as well!) with everything that happens — for he can make use of everything. The sage makes use of it as *tool*, only for the unwise is there *evil*. The consequence of course would be that the world owes the sage no amelioration of evil, no elimina⟨tion⟩. He does *not* grasp *evil as evil* — this the consequence of the *doctrine of free will*! Of the absol⟨ute⟩ soul!

6[396]

Antiquity ends with a moral and religious quietism — tired antiquity and the individual, almighty and singularly thinking itself important, it interprets all the world's events with reference to *its salvation*; everything that happens has meaning for *it*. It is *astrology*, applied to states, natural events, social relations and the tile on the roof: everything has a meaning only for the individual who can find it, *apart from this* it is unworthy of the sage's atten⟨tion⟩. The moral-religious use and interpretation of what happens — *everything else* became indifferent and contemptible. Scientific meaning *lost out*!

6[397]

Arise and go, friends, you have already let me speak for much too long. The wind is becoming cooler and brisker, the grass too — this still height is quivering, and evening approaches. Go and do, I ask you, as soon as you come into the valley, a little foolish act so that all the world may see what you have been taught by me here.

6[398]

We are more tormented by our views of the passions than by the passions themselves.[218] — Where humans do not grasp concretely a drive's purpose as necessary for preservation, as with defecation and urination, food intake, etc., then they believe they can *eliminate* it as superfluous, e.g., the drive to envy, hate, fear. And they consider the inability-to-be-rid of it as a wrong, at least as a misfortune: whereas with hunger and thirst one does *not* think thus. *It* should not *rule* us, but we want to grasp it as necessary and to use its force for our benefit. For that it is necessary that we *not* maintain it in its *entire full* force, like a stream that is supposed to drive mills. Whoever does not entirely know it is overwhelmed by it, just as after wintertime a mountain stream comes down destructively.

6[399]

We can give our passions a higher life if we prevent their direct discharges. But at times it is nauseating, e.g., with the sexual drive.

6[400]

The fact was that in Greco-Roman antiquity humans did not suffer intensely enough for their passions, as for their unjust actions; it was mainly suffering such as when one says, "how *stupid* I was to do this!" Something resembling the feeling of sin could only arise among philosophers, on the basis of the pure divine soul and its contaminations: not only a blunder and a true disadvantage, but a feeling of abasement and pollution, an offense to an *august* representation of ourselves.

His view of the passions and evil distressed the philosopher, not so much the evil consequences. But everything was proceeding forwards on one track in *this* direction, Christianity delivered the strongest expression by taking no notice of the real consequences and nearly treating them as indifferent. Thus the effect of acting itself for the organ of action. The ideal of Epictetus: always to keep an eye on oneself like an enemy and persecutor:[219] the martial hermit, who has to defend and protect a precious property from corruption after he has gained it. He does *not* pay attention to humans, he *believes he knows* them, he has *no notion* of the individual's interest: they are the shadows, the true in them is their thoughts and drives, which he has philosophically categorized. In this world of chimeras he lives and fights his battle. *Only* as warrior does he have joy. Just so Christianity takes no pleasure in the human being. But *we* reckon them again as nature and enjoy nature: we are not only just towards all of nature, we find it rich, astonishing, unknown, worthy of investigation. The novel and the psychological observation *out of pleasure in the human* is ours! We forgive ourselves much more, we scorn ourselves much less; there is much that we do *not* wish *away*, even though we occasionally suffer from it. We do not like the terrible simplification of the virtuous human: as little as we want only fertile fields.

6[401]

We can only grasp characters that we can form from out of ourselves, and only *so much of them*. Just as our eye can only see what it has *trained* itself to see.

6[402]

I see a tree and take it for a child. I see facial features very distinctly in conversation, but I imagine them in this distinctness.

6[403]

A triviality which is peculiar to *this* century: God is not to be proven *by the fact* that someone must reward the good and punish the bad. No one believes that this is necessary (as Kant still does). *We think differently about justice.*

6[404]

to marry one's good faith

6[405]

Whoever has not listened to his higher self, but instead serves society or an office or his family, always speaks of "fulfilling duty" — thereby he seeks to appease himself. But in particular he **demands** from others obedience to the existing order: he justifies himself in exercising *authority* by virtue of his mode of action.

6[406]

The new thought enchants me, more and more I unlearn the feeling that it is mine or another's. How silly to be jealous in this! And yet what frightful history in the darkening of truth this jealousy has!

6[407]

The humans with the *mask*, the so-called *personalities* who are not ashamed of showing their masks.

6[408][220]

2) Through yielding goodwill to make amends to oneself for the fact that one pursues a great presumptuous goal: and to be vain with the vain, amorous with the enamored, homely with the homely, and enthusiastic with the enthusiasts. To expiate on the individual the sin we commit against all by deviating, doing harm, etc. Indeed, to welcome it when humans take revenge on us — it is fair with such an exuberant *degree* of deviation.

6[409]

Formerly the will's lack of freedom was proven by reference to the soothsayers. This brought the teaching into discredit when the s⟨oothsayers⟩ came into d⟨iscredit⟩.

6[410][221]

Of a person who is a stranger to us we understand only just the impressions that his form imprints upon us: so we experience in ourselves an alteration of form and understand this negative as positive: we name, e.g., him who is harmful to us *evil*.

6[411][222]

How *cruelly* we reckon our few virtues against other humans and pinch and plague them on this point! I also want to carry on humanely with the sense of truth. NB. As soon as we *drive it too far* and cause it to grow fast, as in a *hothouse*,[223] then life spoils us and humans become *nauseating* to us, yes, we to ourselves!

6[412][224]

Cause and effect are incomprehensible to us because we only become aware of both as negative copies between which there is only a succession. The "body," "the thing" consist in such successions. We do not perceive movements, rather several like things in an imaginary line, we also perceive no *linear* duration; instead, our perception has *conscious moments* (*separated* from one another) and these we set alongside each other, join to one another, and *so construct* a continuous, lasting body out of single sensations. But just as the same thing in movement is an illusion, thus the movement that we construct is in any case something else than the "reality," so too is this formation constructed and fantasized out of several negative impressions on us in any case something else than the reality. It cannot be *complete*, for it consists only of relations to us, and that in us to which it can have no relations prevents a full impression. Even as copy it is not complete. Furthermore, the presupposition is that the thing in *this* moment when it makes an impression on us, is *the same* thing which in another moment (in the "next" — we say and are mistaken) again makes a new impression on us, i.e., a second relation. A tree which appears long, *then* round, then green, etc.

6[413][225]

Three-dimensional space belongs to representation, just like movement, the third dimension "completes itself only in time." We connect planes which become visible to us *one after another* into a unity. As cognitive beings we ourselves are always a new rotating force and so produce a succession, even with solid objects.

We are the moved who revolve around things; **we** *do not stand still*, the inverse of what meets the eye is true.

6[414][226]

"Let us just be natural! Nature is *evil* — it creates an effect all the more" — so the grandees think, who are all impertinent!

6[415]

How weak is the sense of responsibility for indirect or distant effects! The nearby effect by contrast attacks us terribly, and what occurs around us gives us a feeling of culpability, even if it is not our fault. Optics!

6[416]

As soon as we carry justice too far and break up the rocks of our individuality, totally give up our solid unjust point of departure, we give up the possibility of knowledge: then the *thing* is *missing, to which* everything bears relation (also a just relation). Unless we measure everything *according to another individ⟨ual⟩* and in this way renew the injustice — it will also be *greater* (but the feeling perhaps purer, because we have become sympathetic and in forgetting ourselves already freer)

6[417]

they hide themselves in the interior and their exterior becomes mask-like and as if paralyzed. Ah, the look — all *surface*, cold.

6[418][227]

We recognize only the *negative* side of all acting things, their copy and impression on us as it were: not the essence of these things, but *our nature alone* within a determinate *inhibition* and *limitation*!

6[419][228]

Another human is not understood by us other than through the inhibition and restriction that he exercises on us, i.e., as the imprint in the wax of our being. We always only *recognize ourselves*, in a determinate possibility of variation; some humans have no effect on us because here our wax is too hard or too soft. And in the end we recognize the *possibilities* **of our** structural shift, nothing more.

The "human being as such" relates in the same way to all other things: they impress their form on him, to the extent he can receive it, and he knows nothing of them but through the alteration of *his* form.

6[420]

The human's sense of temporal duration and space is certainly different from that of any animal, indeed in this every human will be distinct from every other human. One hour is *never* the same as another hour in another's mind: indeed, also never again for ourselves. But even the average sense of an hour is *for each person different*! and *for all humans together* **different** from that of an ant.

6[421]

The good thought is only an *exception*, most original thoughts are follies. *Customary thoughts* are so highly respected, indeed made obligatory, because they have *proven* themselves in a way, with them the human has not gone to ruin. This "not going to ruin" counts as the proof for the truth of a thought. *True* means "*purposeful for the existence of the human.*" But since we know very imprecisely the conditions for existence of the human, so, too, the determination of *true* and *untrue* can, strictly speaking, only be grounded in success. That on which *I* go to ruin is *for me* not true, i.e., it is a false relation of my being to other things. For there are only individual truths — an absolute relation is nonsense. The way of thinking, the tension and frequency, the objects, the inability to see, to feel many things, is all actually a condition of our existence. Every mistake is harmful to it. Most often then we make mistakes, most often we are continuously somehow sick from our thinking, all we can do is experiment, and what is quite individually necessary to us in knowledge is the exception.

6[422]

What is true in a historical event: everything occurs in heads which mutually see each other falsely and incompletely.

6[423]

Never disclose someone's sins! But break off our interaction!

6[424][229]

What is *noticeable in us* grows or wilts under the influence of the light shining on us from other humans: as if, so to speak, the eyes of humans were necessary sources of warmth and light for us. As noticeable and noticed, growth regulates itself in keeping with others, e.g., our bearing mien. — *Then* what we notice but others cannot know! — and *finally* that which we also do not notice! The boundaries vary, to me *much* is in the *light* which to others is in *darkness* and accordingly *develops* **differently**, e.g., religiosity, sense of truth, sympathy, vice.

6[425][230]

During a solar eclipse, diurnal animals rapidly fall asleep.

6[426][231]

Nocturnal animals only become alert with nightfall. Their eyes are as well developed as diurnal animals'. Why do they only fly around at night? Animals are dependent on light through the agency of the eyes.

6[427]

"It was fashionable for young women, when they met Voltaire, to grow pale, become excited, moved, and even grow ill, throw themselves into his arms, stammer, cry, in short, fall into a state resembling the most passionate love."[232] *Worship*!

6[428][233]

The appropriation of the *past* — how much sympathy, passion, self-forgetting, indeed self-contempt is required in order to let the soul of the past arise again! It is a *beginning*, it comes with an enthusiasm, much spite, and fanaticism. *At the head the Germans* — what that reveals! — To be compared Luther's Reformation (history as well!): aversion to reason, brightness, the want of piety, of tradition, to the lack of stable support.

But history, driven by the motive named, entails an *unintended effect*! The past did *not* prove **what one sought**!

6[429][234]

All the relations that are so important to us are those of *shapes on the mirror*, not the true ones. The distances are the optical ones on the mirror, not the true ones. "There is no world when there is no mirror" is nonsense. But all our relations, however exact they may be, are descriptions of the human, *not of the world*: they are the laws of this highest optic, from which no possibility leads us further. It is not appearance, not illusion, but a cryptography, in which an unknown thing expresses itself — altogether clear for us, made for us, our human stance toward things. In this way things are concealed from us.

6[430][235]

The fly that cannot penetrate the glass

6[431][236]

We do not see the mirror any differently than the world reflected upon it. —

6[432][237]

The human being conceals things from us.

6[433][238]

On this mirror things proceed regularly, again and again one thing follows upon the other — we call it cause and effect, but we cannot *grasp* anything because we see only the images of cause and effect.

We speak as if there were *existing things*, and our science speaks only of such things. But there is only an existing thing according to the *human optic*; of that we cannot rid ourselves. Something coming into being, a movement in itself is completely incomprehensible for us. We *move* **only** *existing things* — therein consists our image of the world on the mirror. If we think things away, then the movement as well. A moving force is nonsense — for us.

If we try to see the mirror as such, then we discover nothing but things. If we want to take hold of the things, we come back to nothing in the end but the mirror.

Our *thinking* is really nothing more than a very refined, interwoven play of *seeing hearing feeling*, the logical forms are physiological laws of sensory perceptions. Our senses are developed centers of sensation with strong resonances and mirrors.

6[434][239]

If we heed the errors into which the senses are most prone to seduce us, then we can anticipate the nature of their basic errors (e.g., the belief in bodies

6[435][240]

A mirror on which things display themselves not as surfaces but as bodies.

6[436][241]

Enthusiasm looks very different in those who must *forget themselves* in order to be happy — self-relinquishment. With them exercise of *consciousness* is *opposed* to the feeling of happiness and they assume that reason and the glow of feeling exclude each other. *To soar with sharp eagle's eyes* — that they cannot do, they want blindness, to be overwhelmed!

6[437][242]

We imagine truth gradually establishes itself — *but only the human being in his relation to other forces establishes himself.* The abundance of the relations is developed: i.e., the abundance of limitations and errors. These are no absolute errors, but rather of an optical kind. We advance science? No, the human! He becomes more solid more durable as a result.

6[438][243]

If life had ever been *lived strictly* according to *some moral system*, then humanity would have *gone to ruin*. Likewise through Christianity. We still live *through immorality*.

6[439][244]

We do *no more* with *knowledge* than the spider with net and hunt and sucking out: we establish our needs and their satisfaction, to which belong sun, stars, and atoms; these are detours to ourselves, likewise the rejection of a god. Over the long term we suffer *harm* from each flawed relation (supposition of a relation). Therefore, our knowledge has no value *in itself*: it is nothing but optical laws (by way of a simile). The human himself, in his five-foot long space, is an arbitrary assumption, *constructed* on the weakness of the sense organs.

6[440]

Imitating (fantasizing) becomes easier for us than perceiving, newly perceiving: so that wherever we believe we are merely perceiving (e.g., movement), our imagination is already assisting, enhancing, and *sparing* us the exertion of the many single perceptions. This *activity* is usually overlooked, we are *not passive* during the effect of other things on us, instead we immediately set our force against them. *The things touch our strings, but we make the melody from this.*

6[441][245]

Our knowing and feeling is like one point in the system: like one eye whose sight and field of vision slowly increases and encompasses more. Thereby *nothing* changes in the real world, but this constant activity of the eye turns everything into a steady increasing confluence of activity.

We see our laws into the world[246] and in turn cannot comprehend these laws as anything but the aftereffect of this world on us. The starting point is the mirror's illusion, we are *living mirror images*.[247]

What then is knowledge? Its presupposition is an erroneous limitation, as if there were a unit of measure for feeling; wherever mirror and organs of touch appear, a sphere emerges. If we think this limitation away, knowledge too is thought away — a grasp of "absolute relations" is nonsense. Error then is the basis of knowledge, of the appearance. Probability, thus degrees of appearance, only emerges through the *comparison of many appearances.* — Language as well is an ostensible and professed basis of truths: the human being and the animal erect *at first* a new world of errors and refine these errors more and more so that countless contradictions are discovered and thereby the number of possible errors reduced or the error carried on. There is actually only "truth" in the things that the human *invents*, e.g., number. He imputes something and afterwards finds it again — that is the nature of human truth. Furthermore, most truths are in fact *only* **negative** truths: "this and that is *not* that" (though most often expressed positively). The last is the source *of all progress* in knowledge. The world then is for us the sum of the relations to a limited sphere of erroneous basic assumptions. The laws of optics are all errors, likewise those of the ear. Assuming there are countless *sensory* points in existence: each has a sphere, *according to whose extent* and *force* it perceives relations, i.e., a sphere of limitation and error. So too every force has its sphere, it works just so far and so strongly and only on this and that, not on another, a sphere of limitation. Actual knowledge about all these spheres and limitations is a nonsensical idea, because here a feeling *without* a "how far," "how forceful," "on this and that" must be conceived: and so too a force *without* limits, and at the same time *with* all limits, which creates *all* relations — that would be a force without *determinate* force, a piece of nonsense. — Thus, the limitation of force, and the perpetual setting in relation of this force to others, is "knowledge." *Not* subject to object: instead something else. An optical illusion of rings surrounding us *which do not at all exist*, is the presupposition. Knowledge is essentially *appearance.*

6[442]

Our actions are, since we are skeptics, experiments, calculations with a few unknown variables — thus very interesting because they are not foolish expressions of our *power*, which annoy us when they fail, instead attempts to receive information about anything at all, through success. We do not let ourselves be tyrannized, neither by our actions nor by our successes.

6[443]

With him his *benevolent* drive *in*creases when his feeling of *power* increases: his joyfulness and his greater responsibility keep him on the lookout for good actions.

6[444]

In the feeling of envy, hate, etc., we all believe that we *know what* envy, hate, etc., *is* — an error! Likewise in thinking: we believe we know what thinking is. But we experience a few *symptoms* of an illness that is essentially unknown to us and believe the sickness *consists* just *in them*. All moral conditions we measure and name according to *what* we *thereby* consciously feel — and even this not *subtly* but quite crudely. — Now we have learned that we fundamentally misunderstand *willing* according to ends. It is therefore also possible that we misunderstand all moral affects; that we already wrongly *interpret* the symptoms, namely, according to the prejudices of *society*, which keeps an eye on *its* advantages and disadvantages.

6[445]

Moral conditions are *physiological* conditions — evident, for example, in love. Nearly all essentially pleasant, essentially necessary for the individual's organism.

6[446][248]

Love, which casts off onto one what is due to many, is nevertheless glorified as an anti-egoistic power: as which, grossly seen, it *appears* and because it wants to do good. Meanwhile: it *withholds* from all remaining persons and things nearly *all interest* and piles it onto one; its effect then is non-beneficial, taken on the whole.

6[447]

The musicians and writers, who always represent something which they are not, the rhetoricians and actors

6[448]

These things you know as thoughts, but your thoughts are not your experiences, rather the echo of others': as when your room vibrates while a carriage passes by. I though am sitting in the carriage, and often I myself am the carriage.

6[449]

The accent on sin has intensified one hundredfold the egoistic preoccupation with the personal consequences of every action and distracted from thinking out the consequences for others. The injustice toward God — thereby the thought*less-ness* about actions and *their general aftereffect⟨s⟩ on humanity* has become immense. The remorse, the pang of conscience! The Christian does *not* think of his neighbor, he is enormously occupied with himself.

6[450][249]

When we do not know how to read a book for the other's sake, how poor will it be! We must feel it like the author — is that moral? — The whole coast with mountains sea and olive trees and enchanting lonely pines, all that we must discover. And so emerging from ourselves we can also associate with humans as their traveler and explorer, *do them good and evil, so that* they show *their own beauty*, sunny or thunderous.

If we remain stuck in ourselves, how are we supposed to grow and become richer! For nourishment we *need* the pleasure in the foreign, just *other nourishment*. The pleasure in the human is necessary for the sake of our *nourishment* —

6[451]

To lift friendship up higher, NB. Emerson p. 149.[250]

6[452]

NB. To take up brotherly feeling with the great spirits and reject rivalry! No isolation!

6[453]

The heart constricts when one observes how people are not at all *ashamed* of their antipathy for something. Whoever hates himself is to be feared, we are the victim of his vengeance. We have to seduce him into self-love.

6[454][251]

The impertinent egoism of *love*, wanting to possess for oneself, wanting to be uniquely prized — it would not have this reputation if it were not so pleasant!

6[455]

Actions are perceived as ethical *only* when their usefulness is *no longer* recognized: thus prescribed, bequeathed, sanctified usefulness. No doubt punishment and reward are signals: but they are not demanded *for the sake* of the punishment and reward, rather because an *authority demands them*, for **unknown** reasons!

6[456]

It is not true that good and bad is the accumulation of experiences with the "purposeful and purposeless." *All evil* drives are *to just as high a degree suitable* and *species-preserving* as the good! NB. against Spencer. Even that which is suitable for the community is not the only criterion. Most important: *blind obedience* where *orders* are issued, and fear crossing over into veneration. Sanctification of the venerated!

6[457]

On the history of
honesty.

6[458]

Confidences
with the nearest friend and the
nearest enemy.

6[459]

The passion of
honesty.

6[460]

The emigrants.

6[461]

Passio Nova
or
On the passion of the honest.

[7 = N V 6. End of 1880]

7[1][1]

Christianity has taught 1) an enormous mistrust toward ourselves 2) and of knowledge of human nature — these advantages we have over antiquity.

7[2]

Only in the depth of night are we entirely ourselves: becoming famous surrounds us with humans and their demands upon us. We must cast our fame into the sea.

7[3]

Christianity has called the *feeling of lowliness* (humility) *good* and made a passion out of it! Thereby raised itself!

7[4]

"At age forty, one is a camel, at seventy an ape." Spaniard[2]

7[5]

We too may have our taste: but it is no longer the eternal, the necessary taste! And every age has *believed* this about its own! Only we may not! An entirely new state of affairs!

7[6][3]

"In the long run one only sees the aspects of nature that are analogous to our way of seeking happiness: the one only the sublime, the other the fine and rare aspects. All else *bores* him." St⟨endhal⟩

7[7]

Inauthenticity is at times only a harsh expression for that passivity by virtue ⟨of which⟩ a m⟨an,⟩ like a woman, only brings children into the world who resemble her father and not himself! Passive artists, like Liszt. Thinkers as well on whom all kinds of reality make a manly impression and likewise infuse with love. The struggle against this passivity is often led by vanity. Then also by the conscience of loyalty, for it is often betrayed. There is a **cunning** *species* of *superior natures* who stand *above* this passivity, allow it a free hand like a passion, yet create *opportunities* for them: thus they acquire experiences to which other thinkers remain strangers.

7[8]

The scourge of sexual desire is not in itself so great if one deems it nothing evil. Just as little as the bowel movement causes us deep mental torment.

7[9]

These thoughts I must pursue, day and night: they assault me in my dreams. I have not been safe from them in the most raging pain. There is no tie of sympathy that would not tear as soon as these relentless ones lay a hand on it. There is something sad, elevating, and sweet about this entanglement — I doubt whether to many humans life has seemed so worthy of affirmation as to me, enveloped by deep melancholy fire and smoke.

7[10][4]

The aversion of Greek art to the terrible: one had enough real evils.

7[11][5]

M⟨ichel⟩angelo *took* goodness and justice from his god and from this made a god of terror and vengeance — he made him *logical.*

7[12]

An office is good: one places it between oneself and humans, and so one has one's quiet and sly hide-out and can do and say what everyone considers his right to expect from us. Even early fame can be utilized in this way: provided that behind it, inaudibly, "our own self can freely play with itself again and can laugh about itself."

7[13][6]

Independence is the renunciation of tyrants to whom nothing is given to rule but themselves. It is the breeding ground of the greatest desire to rule, for we can expand ourselves into something infinite and in turn expand our power to rule upon this infinitude. To let gush one's passions for the infinite so as to become their conqueror!

7[14]

The Germans vacillate between devotion to the foreign and a vengeful desire for originality (vengeance for their shame in hindsight) — and the entirely unobjectionably good Germans, who are productive, have been *mediators* and have worked in a European way (like Mozart and the historians, etc.). — The Germans, as proof that their originality is not a matter of nature but of ambition, claim that it lies in the complete and whopping *difference*: but that is not how Greeks thought with regard to the Orient, nor Romans with regard to Greeks, nor the French with regard to Romans and the Renaissance — and *became* original (one actually *is* not initially! instead one is crude!).

7[15][7]

This entire philosophy — is it more than a drive to prove that ripe fruit, unleavened bread, water, solitude, order in all things taste best to me and benefit me the most? Thus an instinct for a correct *diet* in everything? And a mild sun! There I draw near my kind of sublimity which is not dark and ambitious, but the secret and lonely fluttering of a butterfly high along the rocky shore of a lake, where many good plants and flowers grow? Heedless that perhaps it is the life of one day and that the night is too cold for my winged fragility?

7[16][8]

"Climate or temperament make the *force* of the coil spring: Custom or education give it its *meaning*." Direction!

7[17]

Your cult of strength is anything else but proof of strength, as in M⟨ichel⟩angelo![9] You submit yourselves, you want to drink strength thereby, you are tired of your weakness —

7[18]

Just as the Italians *make* a music their *own* by drawing it into their passion — yes, this music is waiting to be interpreted so personally and gains more from that than from all the art of harmony — so I read the thinkers and repeat their melodies: I know that behind all the cold words a desiring soul moves, I hear it sing, for my own soul sings when it is moved.

7[19]

Plan.

1st Chapter. We believe it is the opposite of a passion: but it feels good, and therefore we begin the struggle *against* the passions in favor of reason and justice. We innocents!

2nd Chapter. We suddenly discover that it bears itself all the marks of passion. We suffer from this insight, we aim for the unclouded eternal still light of the wise man. But we surmise: even this light is *passionate movement*, but sublimated, for the crude unrecognizable.

3rd Chapter. We try to evade servitude, we subjugate ourselves to other passions (art) We seek to kill them through analysis, through derivation of their origin. We discover along the way *how* passions actually emerge, *how* they become *ennobled* and effective.

4th Ch⟨apter.⟩ The repercussion from the outside begins: all that we ourselves have objected to in order to free ourselves, all our errors turn from the outside against us, such as falling out with friends, etc. It is a new and unknown passion. Its bleak bliss! it lets us bear! it effects solitude, it reveals to us the thinkers!

7[20][10]

One of the people I most highly respected appeared to me contemptible from the moment when he, who could have a grasp of the demands experiences tragedies of knowledge, preferred to disparage *science* because of certain effects of knowledge that were unpleasant to him. Only we, who suffer so infinitely on its account, still love it! — What kind of cursed weakness toward oneself and lack of seriousness is that there![11] Not to be hated, just to be despised!

7[21]

Kant: The human being is a moral being: consequently he is 1) free 2) immortal 3) there is a rewarding and a punishing justice: God. — But the moral being is an illusion, thus: — — —

7[22]

One should not purchase the sublime too dearly (like the holiness of God)

7[23][12]

In France originality became dangerous and contemptible and boring (under L⟨ouis⟩ XIV), *therefore* (not from convenience as with the G⟨ermans⟩) the model.

7[24]

1) Differences in acquired judgments that stem from a kind of second nature and are alien or contrary to the first: most often they are somewhat clumsy and bashful, but insofar as they express a victory, we love them almost more than the effortless fruits of our garden (and appraise their value generally higher,

it is what our climate has just barely been able to tolerate, vegetation that appears more *southern* to the one, more *northern* to the other). The force applied here is deducted of course from the cultivation of our first nature! And that is often fine where the latter is already *thriving luxuriantly* by itself! "Justice" is a matter for *overabundantly* endowed humans! Hence for the force that is in danger of being unable to rein itself in! Others would like to pass for such over-brimming nat⟨ures⟩ and like to show themselves untamed: there is for such hypocrites a second more refined finesse! — to let on, through attempts at reining in, that there is something to rein in.

7[25]

In order for an artist or thinker to perfect his way, he probably must have that faith which is an injustice and limitation with regard to the faith of others. For he must see *more* in it and something larger than it is: otherwise he will not mobilize his entire strength. Through the execution's long friction infinitely much is scoured off the enchanting quality of the first thought: hence the enchantment must be much greater than is proper — otherwise it does not last to the end!

7[26]

How is it that Christianity has propagated cruelty against animals in Europe, despite its religion of compassion? Because much more than this it is also a religion of cruelty against humans.

7[27]

So that someone honestly devotes himself to justice in the larger scheme of things, with respect to humans and things, there must be a prototypical process in him: he must sense two powers or several in conflict and wish the downfall of none nor the struggle's continuation. So he experiences in himself the coercions to a *contract*, with rights of the different powers against each other: and also *pleasure in being just* grounded in the habitual respect for these rights. His inner experience radiates outward. Perhaps someone also arrives at such a just disposition proceeding from outside to inside. Mildness is the practice of justice: to see much but not to want to notice it, to tolerate much, but, for the sake of general peace, to look on gladly — it can become a Stoicism that *looks* like an Epicureanism.

7[28]

Greek grace was so strict that today it may appear to us as dignity.[13] And the ancient gravitas of a philosopher or statesman we would barely endure. Our artists, who marvelously pride themselves on beautiful self-indulgence, would look like naughty boys in the eye of the Stoic.

7[29]

Pascal's dialogue with Jesus[14] is more beautiful than anything in the New Testament! It is the most melancholy bliss that has ever been voiced. Since then this Jesus has not been further poeticized, which is why after Port-Royal Christianity is everywhere in decline.

7[30][15]

I can treat myself exactly as a gardener his plants: I can remove motives from myself by removing myself from a location and socie⟨ty⟩, I can place motives near me. I can artificially cultivate or let wither the inclination to treat myself so gardener-like.

7[31]

The unfortun⟨ate⟩ who all at once want to attain virtue through a transformation! And despair at a relapse! Whereas *practice* makes perfect.

7[32][16]

Sympathy and compassion were *difficult* to inspire in savage bellicose times — back then the dramatist had a mission! But in our all too sensitive age the cult of compassion is really the most miserable of all cults — as if there were not much too much compassion! As if even the plot were not guided much more by compassion than by feeling!

7[33]

own "*soul*" I want to say for *individuali⟨ty⟩*
h⟨umans⟩ without their own soul
h⟨umans⟩ without a soul

7[34]

One's own soul.

Kant too, however meager his soul appears next to Pascal's, has a similar ulterior motive with every movement of his head: to dethrone the intellect, to decapitate knowledge — in favor of the Christian faith! And always it must be the *Christian* faith! as if not, were knowledge decapitated, *all* kinds of faith would become accessible!

7[35]

Schopenhauer did not grasp *passion*, but only the general sexual drive and its quirks (but passion is the achievement of the individual, among Italians therefore frequent, among Germans weak). In love the German is *common*.

7[36][17]

Grace is the repose of strong souls. The weak want to be entangled captivated seduced, they find grace ineffective and bland and desire excitants (emotions)

7[37][18]

There are so many kind⟨s⟩ of pleasant feeling that I despair over determining the highest good. Recently it seemed to me to be hovering and flying.

7[38]

The "thing" a simplification. Now if the human wants to grasp himself, he is above all in need of words: if he names so and so many things about the human, he believes in the end he has, *grasps*, the human as the sum of these things.

7[39]

Daily I am astonished: *I do not know myself*!

7[40]

I do not believe that honesty with oneself is something so absolutely high and pure: but to me it feels like a necessity of hygiene. Someone may be what he wants, genius or actor — only clean![19] (H. Heine has something clean about him.)

7[41][20]

The splendid bodies of ancient statues appear beautiful because pleasant, because *useful* (always the thought of war!)

7[42][21]

The small-town "spirit"

7[43]

The elevation of compassion to something *good*, Christian-Buddhist.

7[44]

Things or the effect of things was much higher.

7[45][22]

"How do I matter!"[23] is the expression of true passion, it is the ultimate degree of *seeing something apart from oneself.*

7[46]

Realism in art a deception. You render what about the thing enchants, attracts you — but these feelings are certainly *not* aroused through the realia! You only do not know what the cause of the fee⟨lings⟩ is! Every good art has *imagined* being realistic!

7[47]

With respect to the strongest drive, which ultimately regulates our morality, we must leave aside the question: why? (e.g., who has pride as his foundation)

7[48]

To change the feeling[24] "you must" into "you shall" — that is the trick! The opposite compared to the ordinary human who does not grasp the "you must."

7[49][25]

We must learn from the animal and the plant what *flourishing* is: and accordingly to relearn with respect to the human. Those pale emaciated impotent humans suffering from their thoughts can no longer be ideals. It must have been a *degeneration* in us that *sprouted* such a bad taste. I fight this bad taste.

7[50]

Is there really no escape! Nowhere a law that we do not just recognize but recognize as above us!

7[51]

The attraction of the combated difficulty (Wagner) and the attraction of the defeated difficulty (*still* to express a feeling e.g., love *through the means of* artful figures e.g., Petrarch)

7[52]

Nothing that occurs in reality strictly accords with logic.

7[53]

I am incapable of recognizing any greatness that is not tied to *honesty with oneself*: playacting before oneself instills nausea in me: when I discover something like that, then all great achievements count for nothing to me; I know, they have everywhere, and at the deepest ground, this playacting. — Whereas playacting outwardly (e.g., Napoleon's) is comprehensible to me: probably it is necessary for many people. — This is a limitation.

7[54][26]

Some humans are simpler, but most often though the individual is *unrecognizable* and ineffable. *Consequently*, the *model* is necessarily an illusion! If I do not know the construction materials in terms of mass and kind, what are architectural designs! And how constrained this eternal brooding about the ego makes us! We would have no time for knowledge of the world! And if even this knowledge were first of all the means to cognition of the ego, then we would *never* arrive at the task itself! And ultimately this infatuation with our own model is one more bondage!

7[55][27]

sacred rage (Jews and dramatists), sacred envy (Greeks ἀγών[28]) — affec⟨ts⟩
deemed good (even with Hesiod)

7[56]

What according to strict scientific causal concepts is truly *good* for us (e.g., unconditional faith etc.), that is perhaps no longer possible for us exactly because of the strictness of the scientific spirit! (Against Spencer's harmless faith in the harmony of knowledge and utility)

7[57]

Without noticing it, we enjoy the ⟨most⟩ confident repose in the world, just as though it were providence: in the midst of our cold fatalism we sense a warm air of *older*, religious feelings. Our frightening majority! Thrust into the world!

7[58]

The distinction between *higher* and *low⟨er⟩* with respect to the body and the organs is *not* the distinction of science!

Rather, *the less we see anything* of the function of an organ, the higher we rank it. Or smell! Or feel! *Nausea* decides! on high and low! *Not value*! *Here one beginning of mor⟨al⟩ distinctions is found*! NB

7[59]

The *scholar* under the yoke of 1) the Church 2) the courts 3) polite society 4) the education of *youth* 5) the mercantile-industrial interests 6) the nations — this is his history!

Then the *isolated ones*! Montaigne Stendhal etc.

7[60]

The representation: "this thought *could not be true*!" **shocks** me. "It will not be *considered* true" — leaves me cold, *I presuppose it*: for they do not have to belabor as much time and passion as I do.

7[61]

The mor⟨al⟩ jargon in *our* mouth would insult us or make us disposed to ridicule. Only *actions* are left to us as expression. And in case writings are these actions, —

7[62][29]

How does the model relate to our development? to what we must necessarily achieve? Is the model in the most favorable case an anticipation? But for what then necessary?

It is a *confidently* and *lengthily* elaborated representation of the "I" that is *most pleasurable* to us and works as *motive* for doing and not doing (most people have none!) If it is not feasible, indeed *if it is not executed*, then it is faultily conceived, from ignorance of ourselves. In any case it is a necessary product of all our capacities: with one an empty fantasy, with another a beautiful poem, with a third an architectural design — and here there are again all kinds of taste in architecture. An *attempt* to see and grasp *our infinitely* complicated being in a *simplification*. An image for a "thing."

7[63][30]

Work, now good, at other times evil. The two heroic ages in Hesiod, the reverse, good and evil.

7[64]

Christianity and Judaism: the ideal set outside ourselves, with the highest power and commanding! and rewarding and punishing! — How high everyone must stand in order to achieve this for himself! And *how barely arbitrary* the image of himself must appear to him! May he feel like its creator?! Hardly!

7[65][31]

Is it *possible* to transform conscience into the language of our model for us? *Then* it might work. Very rarely! But this is no objection!

7[66]

The *autonomous human* is very rare. "*The h⟨uman⟩ under bylaws*" and "n⟨ature⟩ itself und⟨er⟩ laws."

7[67]

To feel serenity when we feel embarrassed by our own ceremonial.

7[68]

since h⟨umans⟩ change, the *image of history* changes continuously NB.

7[69]

One praises and blames according to a model (call moral or immoral) First comes the *submission* to a model. Us⟨ually⟩ the one who exercises power over us, and praises and faults according to his will, is the model, it requires the least invention and spirit. Thus: the individuals *positioning themselves as the goal* have initially erected the models. Morality, i.e., "an external model" was there only for the weaker.

7[70][32]

I want to socialize only with humans who have their own model and do *not* see it in *me*. For this would make me responsible for them and a slave.

7[71]

Not to assume a false necessity — that would mean to submit to useless delusion and would be slavish — therefore knowledge of nature! — But then not to *will* anything against necessity! It would mean to waste strength and withdraw it from our ideal, moreover to want disappointment rather than success — NB.

7[72]

I searched through humans[33] and did not find my ideal among them.

7[73]

To be moral, i.e., *to set a goal* and logically deduce from it all our actions. But our nature has *neither this goal*, nor does it have *this same logic*! For that reason, morality entails *deceiving* ourselves about nature, i.e., letting ourselves be guided by it and telling ourselves a tale, as though *we* guided it.

7[74][34]

"The necessity of uncertainty for us: the heart shall beat, the muscles quiver in anticipatory activity. All questions solved except for one: all would cling like wasps to this one point"

7[75]

How a drive, depending on whether one praises or blames it, is considered good or evil, to be demonstrated on the example of *love* (with the Greeks, the ascetic Christians, in Christian marriage, etc.)

All *idealization of a drive* begins with counting it among the praiseworthy things. Sign for the future?? NB

Envy, hate to be improved thereby. To be taken into account how different compassion has become.

7[76]

Animals have feeling of power, i.e., *cruelty* — and happiness of submission, i.e., repose lethargy NB.

7[77]

The Romans called vanity, *honestas*, good and held it up high!

7[78][35]

Apparently everything is now much safer, the world much firmer (because of the many strictly proven truths). But formerly one believed more in error than now in truth; we are infinitely more careful, skeptical, and consequently *possibly more fantastic* than formerly. We can dream altogether different dreams than the earlier ones!

7[79][36]

Influence of flying! — no longer in the plains! On style itself!

7[80]

Generally practiced contempt of the world: all satisfaction here rejected or felt furiously — so all desire of satisfaction throngs into one channel: Life beyond the world!

7[81][37]

I do not tire of Gil Blas: I breathe freely, no sentimentality, no rhetoric as with Shakespeare.

7[82]

When, full of disgust, we turn away from the unsolvable task of ethical autonomy and the untenable task of ethics as a gen⟨eral⟩ law toward knowledge of nature: immediately the problem of duty greets us again: our position relative to things is a moral one, if we really want to *recognize* it: thus an untenable one in the long run! But we can deceive ourselves about this for a long time. We will instinctively turn away from the highest problems and sojourn there where the illusion of moral-*free* knowledge is easy (we use here a morality that has become *natural* for us, as if this were something natural and extra-moral!)

7[83]

the principle "the well-being of the majority stands above the well-being of the individual" suffices to make humankind take all steps back to the lowest animality. For the inverse ("the individual worthier than the mass") has *elevated* it

7[84]

The mor⟨al⟩ judgments about actions *decide* on their morality: this *is* something relatively *external*. Seen from within, actions are other than good and evil. But certainly the m⟨oral⟩ judg⟨ments⟩ can *determine* us to actions and *influence* us in their execution, like an omnipresent police which also does not *do* the actions which it monitors. Entire species of actions can *become extinct* thereby: m⟨oral⟩ judg⟨ment⟩ belongs to the question about the purposeful — have m⟨oral⟩ judgments thus far been in the interest of human development? Which not? Is not rejecting m⟨oral⟩ judg⟨ment⟩ a disadvantage for humankind? But thus far the faith in m⟨oral⟩ judg⟨ments⟩ was there!

7[85]

Living for others an infinitely pleasant respite for strongly egoistical humans (among them belong also the mor⟨al⟩ masochists)

7[86][38]

passionner les détails[39] NB.

7[87][40]

Stendhal: the "good taste" in how to die, to kill a rival, declare bankruptcy, etc., in the time of Mad⟨ame⟩ d'Épinay.

7[88]

Antiquity had the effect of an *attractive compulsion* on the effervescent strength of Renaissance humans. They submitted to the style, felt the vanquished difficulty not to be natural, it was the way to act of strong h⟨umans⟩ who are proud and tyrannical *toward themselves*. Not to be mistaken for the cowardly slave mentality of timid scholars!

7[89]

"*il faut être comme un autre*"[41] once revered and productive, now despised and humiliating for whoever feels accordingly.

7[90][42]

To write something that will have lost all importance in a couple of years — that is impossible for me to imagine. It is probably a sign of limitation. For everything that I myself *survive* I still consider important as a memorial to a state that was valuable to me. I wish my old age surrounded by such memorials.

7[91]

I am *passionately for independence*, I sacrifice everything to it — probably because I have the most dependent soul and am tormented by the tiniest ropes more than others by chains.

7[92][43]

The aversion to strength, deep seriousness, and the appearance of benevolence is modern. *Consequently*, we Germans and I are *ancient*. P. 278, St⟨endhal⟩, Peint⟨ure⟩

7[93]

A king who abdicated from his throne and lived in poverty as a sage; a popular leader who sacrificed his vengeance, etc.

7[94]

The Germans are *indolent* and therefore like to use a model, *it spares thinking*.

7[95]

The *refinement of everyday habits*. Formerly with the priest partially, his gait, his raising his hand, his voice. Then at court: the pleasure in self-control and in not letting one's feelings be noticed (or enveloped in silky fabric) became great. — But what does to refine mean now, serving the ideal! Which ideal! At once we must *have* an ideal! And whence to take it and not steal! — This I mean: an independence that does not offend the eye, a toned down and veiled pride, a pride that pays itself off to others by not competing for their honors and pleasures and by enduring ridicule. This shall refine my habits: never mean and always jovial, not desirous but always calmly striving and flying upwards, simple, yes, frugal with myself, but mild with others. A light sleep, a free calm gait, no alcohol, no princes, nor other famous persons, no women and newspapers, no honors, no company other than that of the highest minds and off and on of the common people — this is indispensable, like the sight of mighty and healthy vegetation — the readiest nourishments that do not bring us into the throng of the greedy and smacking rabble, possibly self-prepared or not lacking in preparation.

Ideals of this kind are the anticipatory hopes of our drives, nothing further. As certainly as we have drives, so do these also work in our imagination a kind of schema of ourselves *as we are supposed to be*, in order to satisfy our drives properly — this is idealizing. The villain, too, has his *ideal*: not exactly edifying for us. It *elevates* him! too!

7[96][44]

How everything has shifted! These followers of Epictetus only thought *of themselves* — now one would almost deny the predicate "moral," in the usual glorification of thinking about others. But it is true: If you have in yourself such an ugly or boring object, then do think about others! Altruism is then very pleasant. — Devotion, becoming unbound from the "I." It seems that humans take little pleasure in themselves when they *look* so far *away* from themselves and deem that the best. Whether — one is more *useful* by *helping* others (still just superficially or tyrannically-transforming) or by creating something from out of oneself that the others like to see, a beautiful quiet self-enclosed *garden* — I do not know. — But one wants to remove from life all *dangerousness, everyone* **shall** help with it!

7[97][45]

To tell the workers that they are supposed to save, etc. is silly. One should teach him to enjoy life, to require little, to be glad, to burden himself as little as possible (with wife and child), not to drink, in short, to be philosophical and to reduce work to the extent that it entertains, to mock everything, to be cynical and Epicurean. Philosophy belongs in *these* circles.

7[98]

For the arts a condition of wildness and of struggling individuals is better than an all too great security —

7[99][46]

The ridiculous does not last. Molière's contemporaries laughed their bitter laughter when they saw someone fail in the imitation of the model.

7[100][47]

The astonishing *ugliness* of American life (in all novellas by Bret Harte[48]), but they can *laugh* and there is naïveté and self-indulgence in everything. Even villainy receives so complete a form and the proximity of wildness and gun shots and sailors invigorates.

7[101]

The Greek virtues are the ideals of such humans as have too much of the *opposite* — they fantasize and exaggerate the value of calm prudence justice valor. The humans who realize this ideal (Epictetus) are *not* prefigured in their gods, rather *their opposite*!

Greek virtue became a matter of ἀγών,[49] one became jealous of one another. *Immobility* as the ideal: in the age when one had already become too *sentimental* and the sorrows and swings too *great* (age of Thucydides). To turn into a statue: whereas the tragedians had let the statue (of the god or hero) become human.

7[102][50]

It is my diligence and my indolence, my overcoming and my indulgence, my valor and my trembling, it is my sunshine and my lightning from a dark cloudy sky, it is my soul and also my mind, my heavy, serious, granite I that in turn can say to itself: "how do I matter!"[51]

7[103]

An interest in things ("the widow of her son") and not in the attraction of things makes the thinker of first rank, i.e., though attraction of things *for other things* = relation, but not that to the human or even to the individual.

7[104]

The *noble* appearance emerges from the fact that the body, for several generations, had the *leisure* to move in keeping with all the demands of pride: thus was not, through the motions of a trade or in order to command common apprentices, forced and accustomed to produce common or humiliating gestures or sounds: common, i.e., not appropriate for our individ⟨ual⟩ and his pride. If pride rose very high, into the most spiritual realm, then English majesty, benevolence and greatness emerge mixed: for the highest pride condescends to the others patronizingly and graciously and does not understand itself other than as ruling and caring. — In our political parvenus precisely this is lacking: we do not believe in their *natural, innate* ruling and caring for others.

7[105]

Strange! I am ruled at every moment by the thought that my history is not only a personal one, that I do something for many when I live in this way and shape and record myself: it is always as if I were a plurality and I speak to it intimately-seriously-consolingly.

7[106]

All these saints are egoists and how could someone not be that who is threatened with hell! It goes beyond all strength and all reason to think of others in such a situation! In Pascal lies the deepest egoism: all raptures are that too.

7[107][52]

This party has the good will even more than the strength for exaltation and expansion: for otherwise it conversely would try to restrain this terrible urge and *suffer* from it.

7[108][53]

The commercial class — it knows how to tax everything without making it, i.e., it understands the needs of the consumer, thus not **him himself** — has a schema for its kind of culture in this: everywhere demand and supply and *accordingly* the value of a thing, of a human! This makes it despicable to me!

7[109]

An ill person's awareness of his illness (and of the public opinion it generates) has completely **changed** (especially with the mental patient) and *consequently also many effects of the illness.*

7[110]

The Greeks did not address themselves to the gods' compassion but to their gratitude, or they promised something. The wretched part of the *beggar before the gods* was not decent.

7[111][54]

Signs of the next century: 1) the Russians' entry into culture. A grandiose goal. Proximity of barbarism, awakening of the arts. Magnanimity of youth and fantastic delusion and real willpower.

2) the Socialists. Likewise real drives and willpower. Association. Unheard-of influence of individuals. The ideal of the poor sage is here possible. Fiery conspirators and fantasts, just like the great souls, find their ilk. — A time of wildness and rejuvenation of strength is coming. 3) the religious forces could still be strong enough for an atheist *religion* à la Buddha, which would glide over the denominational differences, and science would have nothing against a new ideal. But universal human love it will not be! A new human must show himself. — I myself am far from it and do *not* wish it **at all**! It is probable though.

the **individual sacrifice** is too massive with Socialists and others and generates a collective expression! **Generosity**! and the mercantile cold prudence will have its reaction in an absolute contempt for prudence and the respectable: *consequently* a great deal of folly.

7[112]

"Bossuet, a hypocrite full of talent who had a secret rapture in Louis XIV's presence, all kinds of spirits, about which he was so vain, *ravaler*."[55] In Stendhal.[56]

7[113][57]

Impression of the English on the enthusiastic Germans!!

7[114][58]

"The time which the cold human needs to see such truths (the distinctive in the other, rivals, etc.) the genius uses to prepare his successes." NB.

7[115]

Ah, I am tired of having opinions about opinions or even hearing them! I myself want to be right and wrong about things.

7[116]

To understand, insofar as it is possible for anyone — i.e., to delimit a matter as definitely as possible in relation to ourselves so that our form is defined in its contour and we are quite precisely aware of ourselves, how *comfortable* and *uncomfortable* we feel in this definition. Thus, to ask our drives what they say about a matter! On the other hand, to conduct ourselves without drives and pleasure and displeasure, with an artificial anesthesia — that cannot result in understanding, rather we then just grasp the phenomenon with the rest of the drives that are not yet dead, i.e., as feebly and flatly as possible; though in fact we can occasionally ask our drives in sequence, one after the other, about the same matter and compare judgments — e.g., about a woman, a friend.

7[117]

I find in nothing enough joy — therefore I begin to write for myself a book after my heart.

7[118]

(in reference to the *previous* page[59]) universal military capability, the higher valuation of force.

7[119][60]

To stifle *civil courage* was the task of Richelieu and L⟨ouis⟩ XIV (Stendhal)

7[120][61]

Furia francese[62] breaks out, once vanity is overcome by the heat of the blood: sublime follies. Stendhal.

7[121]

Suppuration, fermentation, and *discharge* — disgusting and repulsive — these feelings humans and actions too have aroused through a symbolism. Thus the concept "low" emerged, i.e., disgusting — *moral foundation*!

Then the *easy* is despised — again an occasion to distinguish higher and lower! The strong and the weak next — the *sudden* and the *mundane*, etc. The animal, etc. With all these distinctions of feeling with respect to actions the real relevance for the preservation of life, strict causality, has been disregarded: thus the **real** *meaning of an action*! Instead according to secondary criteria ("pleasant" in various ways) NB.

7[122]

Not for the sake of a goal do we live for knowledge, but for the sake of the astonishing and frequent comforts in seeking and finding it.

7[123]

I believe I represent the pleasures of wisdom and justice too highly — like the Greeks. I am enchanted by all that beckons toward that — probably because I am very passionate! — I am extremely suspicious of the eloquent admirers of passionateness — I surmise they *would like* to represent something. — The Greeks lived in danger: they honored in strength, repose, justice their *respite*, their *relief*, their *festival*. They wanted neither emotion nor — except in tragedy — compassion (because usually they were *hard*).

7[124]

A health full of incomprehensible sudden turns and trapdoors — sustaining a deep suspicion, and every happy hour with an **intentional** *carelessness* and closing one's eyes before the future — otherwise happiness is not possible

7[125][63]

Faust and Hamlet are thinkers with whom German philosophers engage in discourse!!

7[126][64]

This path is so dangerous! I may not call out to myself, just as a sleepwalker who takes a leisurely walk on the roofs has a sacred right not to be called by name. "How do I matter!" this is the sole consoling voice I want to hear.

7[127]

For the *preamble*. What have I done? Provided for my old age: for the time where the soul does not undertake anything new anymore, notes down the history of its adventures and seafaring. Just as I save music for myself for the time when I am blind.

7[128]

I do not like to interact with humans because I cannot see their faces, and without that their speaking is suspicious or incomprehensible for me, or — I alone speak, which afterwards instills shame in me.

7[129][65]

The Christian (especially the *indolent*!) on the *hunt* for his sins — in order *then* to live through the great drama of despair and grace again. A terribly beautiful way to entertain oneself and meanwhile the world can go any way it wants — "eternal salvation" comes first.

7[130]

The veneration of the πόλις:[66] one knew oneself too well not to know how wild and tyrannical one would be *as soon* as the πόλις comes to an end: the revelation of the Corcyrean soul.[67] One venerates strength justice benevolence; *enjoyment* the result of bourgeois peace. The proximity of the volcano made the ancients just *here* so euphoric and sensitive.

7[131][68]

Thucydides and Sophocles representatives of sophistic culture.

7[132]

The ravenous appetite for devoting one's life to something will awaken as soon as there are things that accord with this thirst.

7[133]

Never to hold something back that can be said *against you*! *Promise it to yourself*! NB

7[134]

"No thing is worthy of the effort one invests to achieve it."[69] Stendhal

7[135][70]

A woman with a great soul and a mind not unequal to it, strong enough to fly and fine enough to go through the eye of a needle[71] —

7[136]

Who would now still tolerate Lessing's equally precocious and superstitious Education of Mank⟨ind⟩!

7[137]

Rustic, longing for h⟨umans⟩, vengeful against sociability and its laws, now living deep despair, now sudden intoxication, hidden, tyrannical and overly strict with his equals, sparing with his attention, always driven, without time for leisure, without knowledge about his amiability, without love and pity for himself, glowing in his work and striking the hammer on his marble like an adversary, never actor and as honest in his good as in his evil glances.

7[138]

The *taking-impersonally* of thought is overestimated! Yes, for the strongest natures the opposite is true! But this is how a *bridge to morality* has been built!!

7[139][72]

You are not becoming Don Juans of knowledge because you do not have enough consequence and character.

7[140][73]

"It is no use: in order to feel the perfect repose of ancient sculpture, one needs to be chaste. One must be able to paint the passions in all their vehemence in order to represent that repose." Stendhal

7[141]

I hate the fame that only brings women's love, respect wealth fortune. I don't *want* to be prudent, moderate, wise! Lonely, wild — — —

7[142]

"Shall we value life according to the *length* of foolish days? Or according to the number of strong pleasures?"[74]

7[143]

"How to paint the passions if one does ⟨not⟩ know them! And how to find time for the talent, if one feels them beat in the heart!"[75]

7[144]

Et odoratus est deus suavitatem.[76]

7[145]

"In others we can only esteem ourselves. The judgments by great artists about the works of their rivals are only commentaries on their own style."[77] Stendhal

7[146]

We must know when to let go of our work.

7[147][78]

Does humankind follow the same process as the Greek artists who, in order to express a god, removed from their statues the all too human of the muscles, etc.? removed all *details*? Is the great human a human whose details are *thought away*, by virtue of the compelling deifying power of his *whole*? Is this how virtue emerged, by turning away the microscope of the gaze, thus seeing *less honestly*? Is this how the godhead is formed by the human, by ignoring more and *more* of the human?

7[148]

"The four lines, the design's rough sketch comes first in the invention by the great; the diligent workers by contrast make first of all the minutiae."[79] Stendhal

7[149]

"Ancient pain was weaker than ours"[80] Stendhal

7[150][81]

As long as you find beauty in *Apollo*,[82] you must look for the matching morality: that beauty does not fit Christian morality!

7[151]

Lord Byron Rousseau Richard Wagner were the only object of their own attention — "this bad habit is the leprosy of civilization," Stendhal says.

"Consequently, he *exaggerated* his sufferings."[83]

"Always preoccupied with himself and the impression he made on others." "He did not understand how to transform himself into another, the least dramatic author."[84]

7[152][85]

Byron's pangs of conscience were one more affectation, they became a fashion.

7[153][86]

Not to be ashamed before oneself, like W. Scott's characters. Stendhal. This is *Christian* and very strongly inherited!

7[154]

It is not possible to *live outside of morality*: but for the *cognizant person* morality is *impossible*. Morality as a regulative in the relation of the drives to each other. But from where is this supposed to come! In the end it can certainly only be inspired by a drive that has the upper hand! And who can discover that! (Pride, etc.) From *known nature* we cannot take an impulse. NB.

7[155]

To take the small nearest thing strictly and much to advance the human in the bodily sphere — to see what kind of ethics arises in him from that — watch! Ethical needs must suit our body! — But the athletes!

7[156][87]

I hardly remember the time when I had pangs of conscience. There is almost a balance between my dreaming and my waking: except that my follies emerge in the dream's actions and more so in the day's thoughts — but in the same way. I also think much in the dreams and not much *more reasonably* than now.

7[157]

"Time heals every sorrow":[88] time does nothing at all. Rather it is the satisfactions of many drives that gradually take place and bring oblivion — it is Epicurus's remedy against the great pains: to submit oneself to diversions (the boar hunt with Pascal after the death of a son[89]). The "consolations of religion and philosophy" too belong among these distracting diversions: their value consists above all in the occupation with them and with reflection, etc.

7[158]

The representation that something terrible is chained onto us dyes all feelings differently. Or: to be an exiled god, or to expiate offenses of earlier times. All these terrible secrets about us — made us very interesting to ourselves! but quite egoistical! One *could* not and *was* not *allowed* to look *away* from *oneself*! To lose the passionate interest in ourselves and to turn passion away from ourselves, toward things (science) is now possible. How do I matter! That Pascal could not have said.

7[159]

I want to reach the point where the *heroic disposition* is needed for *devoting* oneself to *science*! NB.

7[160][90]

"*de l'amour*" *symbolice*![91]

7[161]

To be able to force sympathy — is that the delusion of the tyrant? of the cruel? Stendhal.[92] Or is, on the contrary, the craving for sympathy a demand of the lust for power? —

7[162]

You get used to the great restlessness of life, to the mind- and soul-devouring diligence, to the numbness — and in the end believe it is not *possible* to live otherwise — you are just used to it and bear your yoke! It *is* otherwise possible.

7[163]

Loneliness, much free nature
Simplicity and equity
Health
rare and more selective engagement in reading and in friendship
No senseless diligence
Time and mood for elevations of the heart

7[164]

To dedicate your best in strength and time to your best! Nothing best can be forced!

7[165]

They have played the flute for me about the calm happiness of knowledge — but I did not find it, indeed, I despise it, now that I know the bliss of the unhappiness of knowledge. Am I ever bored? Always worried, always a heart beating in expectation or disappointment! I bless this misery; the world is rich for it! Meanwhile I walk at the slowest pace and suck these bitter sweets.

I want no knowledge anymore without danger: may the treacherous sea or the pitiless high mountains always surround the scholar!

7[166]

I never want to provoke contradiction: rather: *help* me to shape the problem! As soon as you feel *against* **me**, you do not understand my condition and consequently my arguments! You must be the victim of the *same passion*!

7[167]

Health announces itself 1) through a thought with a wide horizon, 2) through conciliatory consoling forgiving feelings, 3) through a melancholy laughter about the nightmare with which we wrestled.

7[168]

— the taking all-too-personally of all problems, darkness, bad path, dreadful inn for the wanderer and the entire *eternal* wanderer-misery [+] humans!!!

7[169]

Our passions are the vegetation that immediately begins to cover again the rock of naked facts. The eternal game!

7[170]

Neither good nor evil!!!

7[171]

Yes, we shall be ruined by this passion! But that is no argument against it. Otherwise death would be an argument against the life of the individual. We *must* be ruined, both as human and as humankind! Christianity showed one way, through extinction and renunciation of all raw drives. We also arrive there by renunciation of action, hate love, by way of passion knowledge. Peaceful *audience* — until nothing more is to be seen! Despise us for that, you who act! We shall view your contempt —: *free* from ourselves, from humankind, from thingness, from becoming —

7[172]

I believed knowledge kills strength, the instinct, it lets no action grow from itself. What is true is only that new knowledge initially cannot avail itself of a practiced mechanism, even less a convenient passionate familiarity! But *all* that can grow! although the saying goes, wait for trees that a later generation will *harvest* — not we! That is the resignation of the knowing one! He has become poorer and more feeble, clumsier his acting, as if robbed of his extremities — he is a *seer* and has become blind and deaf!

7[173][93]

Even the connoisseurs still want to admire their morality (their courage their diligence): hence the difficult authors, the artful poets and musicians have so much to study, so much to admire! Marini. With the naïve style, the highest in art, one may not make this pretense; everyone *imagines* it is easy to understand Raphael, and therefore even the one who knows that this is not so will not approach him with such heroic zeal: the grateful audience is lacking for *his* performance!

7[174]

Your soul is not *strong* enough to carry so many minutiae of cognition, so much that is slight and low, along into the height!

You must deceive yourselves about things so that you do not lose your feeling of strength and greatness! Pascal and I are different. — I do not need to relinquish the small, pitiful details — after all, I don't want to make a god of myself.

7[175]

Jewish — a religion of terror, contempt and occasionally grace (like the old patriarchs)

Greek — a religion of pleasure in strength, in one's own perfection, occasionally a religion of envy of those aiming all too high (Agamemnon Achilles)

7[176]

"Insane" such an uncertain boundary, like good and beautiful! and "ridiculous" and

"shamefaced"

7[177]

The honesty of the great men of faith in itself is proven only through the terrible afflictions of their self-doubt: where this is not visible, they are madmen or actors.

7[178]

Let's trust the drives, they will by and by create ideals again! as love perpetually does. And then: from time to time suppress a drive through pride — immediately all the others receive a new coloring. The game can long be continued, like sunshine and night.

7[179]

Science can altogether only show, not command (but when the general command is given, in what direction? then science can provide the means), the general command of direction it cannot give! It is photography. But the creative artists are needed: they are the drives!

7[180]

I yield to my inclination to loneliness, I cannot do otherwise:[94] "al⟨though⟩ I would not have the need" — as people say. But I *have* the need. I exile myself.

7[181][95]

That sudden hatred for what I loved. That shyness and that "how do I matter"!

7[182]

I have taken Mozart to be serene — how deeply melancholy must I be! *Hence* my **desire**!! for brightness cleanliness serenity prettiness sobriety, my hope that *science* will give me all this! It!

7[183]

Now the French and Italians imitate the Germans regarding violence and conscious ugliness in music — these are the necessary counter-colors in order to let the most sublimated heavenly round dances and revelations of paradisiacal enchantments be fathomed in sounds: there the prior physical torment of the ear must not have been slight and — for heaven one only has the right taste after purgatory. The ancients did not know that! They demanded that someone wanting to hear music be in love, or even better, impassioned! Now the best preparatory condition is taken to be: despair, ennui. Having become numb through our own misery and to all misery, we endure the torment — and afterwards are unspeakably grateful to find ourselves moved and shattered! Compassion with ourselves and all who suffer is the happiness this music promises.

7[184]

Pascal's self-deception: he already assumes Christian predispositions. The "evil desires"![96] The meaning of death![97] Yet let us think about death as we do about the death of animals — then the matter is not so terrible. Condemned to death[98] — that is nothing so bad in itself: only with the criminal it gives us such terrible feelings because of the shame. Pascal was not cautious enough, he *wanted* to prove! — Christianity's art of seduction.

7[185]

Christianity has exaggerated the evils of the human condition, i.e., *created* them in the first place. Pascal still does the utmost.

7[186]

The proud and independent person feels deeply embittered by compassion, "rather hated than pitied."

7[187]

It should absolutely not be thought that health is a fixed goal: how often has Christianity preferred illness, and for good reasons! Healthy is almost a concept like "beautiful" "good" — highly changeable! For the *feeling-well* occurs as a consequence of being long accustomed to contrary conditions of the body!

7[188][99]

Alcohol: the Germans, who now have become money-greedy in an impertinent manner, want politics rather than work, and ⟨are⟩ slaves of national conceit — three sources of stultification

7[189]

I have not come to know any persons who instill such a respect as the Greek philosophers.

7[190][100]

Pascal's passion wants to *prove* itself *necessary* for everyone, as the only thing necessary.

7[191]

I have Pascal's contempt and Schopenhauer's curse[101] upon me! And can one be more loyally disposed to them than I! To be sure with that loyalty of a friend who remains honest in order to remain friend and not become lover or fool!

7[192]

Those are aphorisms! Are they aphorisms? — May those who reproach me for that reflect a little and then excuse themselves to themselves — I need no word for myself

7[193]

Pleasure in beautiful gardens and houses, that there are people who have perseverance in this kind of love and that *I* do not have these gardens and houses — double pleasure!

7[194]

The beautiful — by that Americans now understand the quietly-touching. It runs counter to serious business sense and the practical consideration of the consequences, the dryness and the passion of hunting winning and self-reflecting

7[195]

The Germans believe that *strength* must reveal itself in hardness and cruelty, they then submit themselves gladly and with awe: they at once are rid of their compassionate weakness, their susceptibility to all nothings, and reverently enjoy the *terror*. That there is *strength* in mildness and silence, that they do not easily believe. They miss strength in Goethe and believe Beethoven[102] has more: and in this they err!!

7[196][103]

Wagner's followers want to make credible their capacity for exaltation and expansion — in a *sober* age no slight ambition! But it *is* no sober age: so they must go in for excess!

7[197]

The drive to knowledge is still young and raw and, consequently, compared to the older and more richly developed drives, ugly and insulting: *all* were that once! But I want to treat it as a passion and as something with which the individual soul can step aside in order to remain in the world helpfully and conciliatorily: for the time being renunciation of the world is needed again, but not the ascetic kind!

7[198]

Age of Louis XIV: the enchantment of a submission to an *artificial form* felt by *strong* souls such as then existed (they were full of hatred and jealousy among themselves and were not allowed to show it. They took a vengeful pleasure in this constraint that the poet and his heroes be allowed hardly to express their feelings. The "natural" would have scandalized them: what would their artificiality matter otherwise! Just not *peuple*!): that is difficult to savor now![104] Different with the Greeks! who were very loyal to custom and highly cautious about innovation (yet also had the *finest taste* for every little innovating trait!)

7[199]

What do Wagner's followers call a "musical person"? And what about others and formerly! Almost opposites! Thus caution!

7[200]

What I *miss* in myself: that deep interest for myself. I am too much inclined to externalize myself and too easily agree with what surrounds me.[105] I quickly tire in the attempt to behave with pathos. I have never thought deeply about myself.

7[201]

The Germans have had the word "passion" for barely one hundred years — they copied it from the Greek, a translator found it. —

7[202]

The deep yellow of buildings and the black green of cypresses above them — a monastery, and disabled soldiers within.

7[203]

We *seek* the situations that strain our strength to the extreme: but these are often opposites: this person seeks solitude and tries to escape from the mouths of humans. And the other person presents himself to a nation and feels driven mostly by the idea that it wants to honor itself in him — he cannot drive it high enough. A third wants to please his beloved, and since he considers her something incomparable, he can never strive enough. — *Others seek* the situations which allow them to be lazy.

7[204]

I hate those uncouth people who, when we have barely approached them, place their hand upon us with their oafish tyranny as though we were instruments and tools for them. Already the claim that they now believe they know us and are allowed to pass judgment is an impertinence of the worst taste. It is the way of mental parvenus; noble nature is not in their character.

they have no idea of the condescension that is necessary so that we for our part can pay them honor and respect, whoever they may be

7[205][106]

About the *plan*.

A picture of *Hellenism* as the age that produced the most individualities. The perpetual Renaissance!

Polemic against medieval, courtly, liberal-parliamentarian, socialist. I see the socialist bodies forming themselves, unavoidable! Let us take care that also the *heads* for these *bodies* begin to sprout! Those organizations constitute the future estate of slaves, with all their leaders — but over them arises perhaps an aristocracy of *hermits*! *Past* is *the* **age of the scholar** who lives and believes like all others (as a tool of the churches, courts, the commercial parties, etc.)! *Great heroism* is needed again!

The only conquering power in the grand style is Russia (*without* this desire to conquer states are castrated! *That* takes turning excessive force outward!) Consequently, Russia will compel Europe to unify. But socialism takes hold of the ultimate nausea of this state of war without end and bridges the strife of peoples and dynasties! We are moving towards *more savage* times! That is an advantage, for this hyper-nervous present is worth nothing anymore, a cleansing of the hyper-Christian-moral is needed, a *going-to-ruin* and *becoming-powerless* of the elegant weak pampered, etc.!

7[206]

Of the will to power one hardly dares speak anymore: otherwise in Athens!

7[207]

What drove the ancients to become Stoics (since no infernal punishments, no contempt for humans, no divine holiness made renunciation necessary for them)? The terrible *possibility* of great sudden sufferings and the terrible force of their *passions* — they suffered from themselves and from the world of uncertainty (slave and Caesar!). Then the ambition to be the first in virtue — envy. It was a means of gaining notice right up into the courts and being called upon as consolers.

7[208][107]

Pascal promises, in the secret paper, to "sacrifice even his vengeance" to God.

7[209]

Ignorant humans who have seen nothing else make out of their habits a constraint for their surroundings, a law — thus the youth grow up in its *veneration*— that is what is new: in this way custom becomes "moral."

7[210]

To cultivate every passion (in its historic course) so highly that it shows its *individual* flourishing. NB.

7[211][108]

It is in our hands to cultivate our temperament like a garden. To plant experiences in it, to strike out others: to found a beautiful quiet avenue of friendship, to be conscious of secret views upon glory — to have ready paths to all these good spots in one's garden so that it may not fail us when we *need* it!

7[212]

Intellectual magnanimity consists in breaking the thirst for absolute validity and eternal things through insight into the relativity and the *love for the short-lived and changeable* (instead of contempt for it). A piece of cruelty.

7[213]

It is mythology to believe that we will find our true self after we have dropped or forgotten this and that. In this way we unravel ourselves back into the infinite: instead *to make ourselves*, to *create* a form from all elements — is the task! Always that of the sculptor! Of a productive human! *Not* through knowledge but practice, and we become *ourselves* a model! Knowledge has at best the value of a means!

7[214][109]

Apollo and the morality of temperance belong together: whoever were to find Wagner's ideal beauty would have to make it bloated gigantic and nervous.

7[215]

The moral delicacy and the elevated taste in the stories of Jesus perhaps cannot be appreciated by us because we have been inoculated with the belief that here is the highest taste of the good. What would Aristotle feel! And Buddha!

7[216][110]

The Germans submit to impressions without struggle, from weakness — therefore precisely for them a religion of compassion has so little value, because it flatters general weakness instead of resisting it. It was Kant who with his categorical imperative was useful to the German. That weakness has now received its most striking expression in music — the infinite wandering of the soul in pursuit of emotions, the ultimate nervousness as consequence. *We* suffer from it, afterwards. And *what* spices such a sensitive race requires! the coarsest! it is the race of drunkards! Perhaps this drinking has made them so weak and sentimental. — Praise of soldiery, in contrast to artistry and its greed for flattery.

7[217][111]

To reduce the h⟨uman⟩ to *one* eternal ideal — Stoics Christianity Kant Comte — this is Classicism not yet extinct. Absolute morality!

7[218]

I do not perform a pleasant action because its purpose, its *end*, entails a pleasant feeling: it is not the means to this end. Rather the pleasant has so penetrated it that it is immediately pleasant, *not only at the end.* With purposes we humans make ourselves out to be more reasonable than we are! "Why does this dish taste good to us? *Quem in finem*?"[112] No answer! — Wherever our drives speak, the *"purpose"* is a form of boasting!

7[219]

Have you not experienced it? We do our utmost in self-overcoming and emerge like a semi-corpse yet victorious from our grave — and our good friends believe we are in a quite merry and peculiar mood, notice nothing, but believe they have a right to make fun of us? I believe the disciples in Gethsemane did not sleep, but they lay in the grass and played cards and laughed

7[220]

Why do we take pleasure exactly in the most difficult and painful kind of knowledge and art form? Why do we feel ashamed of any shallow and lighter kind? It is pride, conquered difficulties, the *will* to become a *hero* in our own eyes!

7[221]

There is a *Christian* trait in the Old Testament — one understands the emergence of the god of love!

7[222]

Socrates's skepticism with respect to all knowledge about morality still is the *great event* — we have erased it from our minds.

7[223]

Now what then is the real difference between the good and bad with respect to their common drives? Bad people feel their judgment about good and evil to be the same as that of their surroundings and do evil, feeling shame before the judgment by others and before themselves — Contradiction in knowing and doing. Or they dissemble as good in order to have these advantages and in secret the advantages of evil. — This is all nothing! what makes their *nervous system* different so that they *endure* or *seek* this contradiction?

7[224][113]

Love for the brood nothing simple! as is believed! rather product, property, entertainment, something not dangerous, something submissive over which one *rules*, something *warm* — many reasons for *comfort*!

7[225]

The way we make our neighbor safe through social regulations does *not* prove more compassion, but more caution and coldness.

7[226]

The sight of the world only becomes tolerable when we see it through the gentle smoke of the fire of comfortable passions, now hidden as a matter for guessing, now diminished and abbreviated, now blurred, but always ennobled. Without our passions the world is number and line and law and nonsense, in all of it the most repulsive and presumptuous paradox.

7[227]

"We never get to the bottom of things": I say, we never get to the final point of our passions and at most see by means of some *beyond* the others.

7[228]

For Racine to indulge nobly in the passions was already an excess, one must read him with Port Royal in the background.[114]

7[229]

American laughter does me good, this way of coarse sailors like Marc Twain. I have no longer been able to laugh about anything German.

7[230][115]

"Classicism of morality" still rules. To follow one's feelings here: the followers of the 3 unities[116] did that as well.

7[231]

The moral phenomena pass through the history of diseases: first something from the outside, effects of supernatural powers. Then entirely human, but something *by itself*, the "moral." Finally, one recognizes that they are just as imprecisely designated processes as the diseases (about which everyone has their opinion, and the most *expert* stands out by keeping silent) — *that the age of great skepticism has arrived*! There is nothing "moral as such:" they are opinions *produced by drives* and *in turn influencing these drives*.

7[232]

"brought up in supposedly philosophical systems that are only a dark and badly written poetry, but with respect to morality of the highest and holiest sublimity. They have inherited from the Middle Ages not the republicanism, the mistrust and the backstabbing, but a strong inclination to enthusiasm and to credulity. Yet every 10 years they need a new great man who must erase all the others."[117]

7[233][118]

Pascal's principal flaw: he claims to prove that Christianity is *true* because it is *necessary* — that presupposes that a good and true providence exists which in creating everything *necessary* also creates it as *true*: but there could be necessary errors! And finally! Necessity might only *appear* so because one has become so used to the error that it has become imperious like a 2nd nature.

7[234][119]

Pascal's condition is a passion and has altogether the signs and consequences of happiness misery and deepest enduring earnestness. It is, therefore, actually laughable to see him so proud with respect to the passions — it is a kind of love which despises all other kinds and pities the human for lacking it.

7[235]

What are friends to me who do not know where our heaviness lies and where our lightness! There are hours in which we weigh our friendships.

7[236][120]

One gets older, and only with difficulty is persuaded by a region, however famous the names it bears. I have seen flawed lines near Sorrento. The anemic beauty of the Lago Maggiore in late fall which spiritualizes all lines and half makes the region into a vision, does not enchant me but speaks *intimately-sadly* to me — I know the like not only from nature.

7[237]

I have to speak to things, I have been alone too long and without dialogue; I want to flatter them and speak well of them.

7[238]

Character traits of the Germans: 1) they exalt themselves through meditation instead of calming down 2) they die of desire to have a character. Stendhal[121]

7[239][122]

Hope had a different look for the ancients than for us — Hesiod. Likewise *envy*. With other peoples the lie enjoys respect (e.g., still with Napoleon) The capacity for drinking is often honorable among Germans.

7[240]

For Aeschylus the woman in passion was something despicable and horrible, like the animals of the sea — something unpresentable.[123]

7[241]

Judgments about Mozart shift according to the development of music, i.e., they regard his *character and his temperament* — this latter seems to be changing as a consequence of the new elucidation and the contrasts which he receives again and again. A hint for artists and thinkers of *every* kind! Most capable of judgment are individual contemporaries who have *shared the struggle* for everything and the *joy* ⟨over everything⟩ the great creator has given.

7[242]

Plato has depicted the drive for knowledge as idealized aphrodisiac drive: always in pursuit of the more beautiful! The highest beauty reveals itself to the thinker! But this is a psychological fact: he must have had a sensual pleasure at the sight and thought of his generalities which reminded him of the aphrodisiac.

7[243]

The words remain and turn us into fools so that we name various things the same and afterwards believe they are the same (e.g., *ridiculum*[124]).

7[244]

The emergence of the *delimitation* of moral actions from all other actions. Important! Going out to eat is *not* moral: where does indifference end?

7[245]

Contempt and respect have shaped things in the eyes of humans, now one way, now the other. The first causes them to blanch waste away, consequently the attachment to them to die away and the imagination in this domain to become tired or poisonous. The other one conversely.

7[246]

The naïveté of all moralists now! they believe the feelings for others, the sympathetic, are moral in themselves! they notice nothing, that this is only a level of culture which prioritizes *these* feelings in the valuation: others have prioritized others, indeed the opposite! "In itself" moral! — One praises the compassionate, one blames the hard-hearted — now! Even the words are felt with this aftertaste. And yet the Stoics would have praised the inflexible, immovable human on whom no sight makes an impression, and blamed the compassionate! And that was presumably a morality, too! which has accomplished something greater than ours!

7[247]

In England they marvel at how the highest sobriety makes you liberal in matters of morality: Spencer, Stuart Mill. But ultimately they do nothing but *formulate* their moral feelings. It requires something altogether different: really to be able to *feel differently* for once and to have the prudence afterward to analyze this! Thus, new inner experiences, my esteemed moralists!

7[248]

I say too often "you"? But the things speak to me and I answer them, they have spoiled me.

7[249]

The lack of *magnanimity* in the presuppositions of Christianity 1) why must God's justice have a sacrifice? The martyrdom of Chr⟨ist⟩ was not necessary other than with a God of vengeance (who furthermore puts up with a *surrogate*: without generosity!) 2) why is faith in Chr⟨ist⟩ necessary when it is his will to help humans! 3) why the *deus absconditus*![125]

7[250]

The servile idealism of Gellert, the enthusiastic Schiller, Young Germany's[126] lusting after life and action, the painterly-mystical Wagner, the idealism of the underworld-shadows: *mine*!

7[251]

To invent sin and then the redemptive state is the most incomparable achievement of humankind. This tragedy makes the others very pale!

7[252]

May your life be separated from the country road by a high garden wall: and when the fragrance of roses wafts over from your gardens, then the heart of those others may for once know yearning.

7[253]

Have you never blushed as it flitted through your mind that that thing to which you gave your heart is not worthy of your heart? and were you not ashamed immediately afterwards of your blushing and apologized to the beloved thing for your impertinent pride?

7[254][127]

Pascal had no *useful* lives before his eyes, but only wasted ones, it is all an egoistic private matter. That from this sum of activities a new generation is produced, with its passions habits and means (or non-means) of satisfying them — that he does not see. Always just the individual, not the becoming.

7[255]

For many painters *beautiful* was the expression of piety. And since a certain poverty of flesh, a painful attitude could be seen in the pious, they also transfer⟨red⟩ the feeling of the beautiful exactly to these forms. A very long and strict habit would in the end mislead even the sexual sense: which is *very far* from pursuing unconscious expediencies for the sake of what is to be produced.

7[256]

About the *plan*:

By what means has the need for a *firm hold* become so great? Because we have been trained to distrust *ourselves*: i.e., because we may no longer have a passion without a bad conscience! Through this blasphemy against our being the *drive for certainty* outside of ourselves has become so great: 1) religious path 2) scientific path 3) dedication to money princes parties Christian sects etc.: which we must take fanatically, thus *must* falsely understand, so that they accomplish what is desired by us. The Jews had this contempt for themselves and for the human in general!

Goal: 1) however much it is secured, the world is in the end subject to an *individual assessment*: as long as we are investigating, we can often exclude the indiv⟨idual⟩: in relation to that which we ultimately find, there is always a *subjective attitude*! 2) we must think proudly enough of ourselves to take a subjective attitude only toward real things, not toward phantoms! and rather to endure the doubt and the sea voyage than to want certainty too hurriedly! 3) to restore the honor of our *own soul*!

7[257]

As soon as you take recourse to the Christian faith or a metaphysic, at that point where your science leaves off, then you rob yourselves of the strength of heroism: and your scientific character is *deeply abased*! Its highest accent no longer befits you! You are cold and no longer moved, you sacrifice nothing! Hence the despicable sight of the "scholar" — he was without the greatness of final intentions, he did not go to the end, but snapped there and threw himself into the hands of the church or the regiment or public opinion, or poetry or music. He *needs* that renunciation —

7[258][128]

One learns to speak, but one unlearns how to chat, when one keeps silent for a year.

7[259]

Are you then *eager for fame*? I have never believed it. But it occurs to me that I find it unbearable not to be occupied and become one with that which appears to me as the most important thing in the world. — When I did *not* believe this about art anymore, I stepped aside quite cooled, with a kind of *hatred* — it seemed to me like a fraudster who wanted to deprive me of what is most important.

7[260][129]

Pascal believed that the little Périer girl was healed by the real voice of Christ, *cette voix sainte et terrible, qui étonne la nature et qui console l'église.*[130]

7[261][131]

"the Demosthenes of impassionate logic"

7[262]

Comparison with Pascal:[132] do *we* not also have our strength in self-control, like him? He on behalf of God, we on behalf of honesty? To be sure: an ideal, to tear the humans from the world and themselves, makes for the most outrageous tensions, is a *perpetual self-contradiction in the deepest sense*, a blissful repose *above ourselves* in contempt of all that is called "I." We are less bitter and also less full of vengeance against the world, our strength is suddenly slighter; then again, we also do not burn down too quickly like candles, but have the strength of endurance.

7[263]

Their pride was *embittered* by their shyness.

7[264]

The great question, whether there is a circular movement in hum⟨an⟩k⟨ind's⟩ c⟨ulture⟩, small and *large*? We in the *first*?

7[265]

The enchantment of dialectics for a poetic-impulsive and mercurial soul like Plato's. The enchantment of the *dimness* in Christianity for Pascal's bright logical soul — that is difficult to understand

7[266]

The great moral natures emerge in times of dissolution, as *self-restrainers*. Signs of pride, they are the *governing* natures (Heraclitus Plato etc.) in a changed world where they must only govern themselves. Entirely different the morality of submission.

7[267][133]

The pleasure of Molière's society, when someone bares himself and no longer deceives, when the character betrays himself — the contempt at the same time for someone who does not understand how to maintain his role — the deep understanding of all comedic play in life, yes, the belief that the task is to be a comedian and that all that is ridiculous is to be found in a comedian who betrays himself!

7[268][134]

Naïveté is no German trait. But an old French one!

7[269]

Aristotle: "generally humans do evil if they can."[135]

7[270]

In *Inquisition countries* the habitual sinner does not dare withdraw from holy communion out of fear of being denounced, excommunicated, in the end like Jesus suspected of heresy and persecuted by the judiciary — for that reason the laxest casuists emerged there.[136]

If one was too strict, then the integrity of confession was done away with and the confession itself annulled — the powerful means for preserving the Church.[137] (Even with themselves the most rigorous humans are most mendacious).

The ostracism of virtue (of Jansenism).

7[271][138]

To say: "it is God who does this in me," like Pascal, is not to annihilate the human and put God in his place: instead, the grace which he invokes is the *utmost effort of human nature*. He calls God whatever he feels in himself to be exalted and purer.

7[272]

"To withdraw the soul from the world in order to make it die to itself, in order to tie it solely and inalterably to God — that is only possible for an almighty hand."[139] Pascal

7[273]

The Great Condé Richelieu Pascal[140]
Bossuet calls La Bruyère — — —[141]

7[274]

Even in the victories over ourselves a good part belongs to chance: we therefore view the victorious virtuous ones with sharp criticism and occasionally do not find their *spirit* in moral tactics at the same level as their fortune.

7[275]

Napoleon the *power*-greedy provides the type of the Stoic, viewed inwardly: to be elaborated NB. the parts of his character that he has subjugated through seduction he afterwards treats coldly and indifferently despotically.

7[276]

"And all this freedom of the gaze[142] is good for nothing?"[143] What? Is a telescope good for nothing?

7[277]

The great monsters of vanity, which have the power to attract us but not to *hold* us.

7[278][144]

Pascal against the Jesuits: that is Demosthenes against Philip: there one sees the aberrance from the general interest of humankind!

7[279]

I cannot stand it in Germany, the spirit of pettiness and servitude penetrates everything, down to the smallest city- and village-papers and likewise up to the most honorable artists and scholars — along with a thought-impoverished impertinence toward all independent humans and peoples. Moreover, one is hurried and anxious about the present, suspicious of what is coming, and so reproachful toward each other, and with a pompous pseudo-enjoyment seemingly puts the worries out of one's mind.

7[280]

There are really people who believe they have honored a matter by calling it *German*. It is the pinnacle of national stultification and impudence.

7[281]

Our disadvantage *after* Christianity: after that outrageous relaxation of all muscles and forces under the highest pride we are all sentenced to represent the weaker, weakened: unless we gained an outrageous kind of *masculinity* that would know how to bear this condition of human humiliation even more proudly than Christianity did. Can science not serve us to this end? We must counter the fantasy-effect of Christianity for magnanimous natures with something that surpasses it — a renunciation and rigor!

7[282][145]

The desire for repose not to be interpreted wrongly with Pascal! and that for movement!

7[283]

Felicitous age of the *Russians*! Energy of the will and transition to the arts!

7[284]

When I no longer bear the sight of another's *state of distress* or *state of fortune* and act to remedy it, be it by distancing myself, be it by amending the other's fate (even if already the thought of it torments me): for there is a *similar* process. That another's happiness *hurts* me, whereas its sight does someone else good: this would make a difference (likewise the sight of another's independence). To injure: a way to express that we feel our development inhibited. We feel robbed of a force: likewise other humans at the sight of another's misfortune. Compassion makes us suffer, likewise envy: both are *disadvantageous* for us. Pleasure in another's misfortune and another's fortune is *advantageous* for us, a source of *stronger development* (N⟨apoleon⟩ became cheerful when he found[146] his court embarrassed by a new ceremonial) The suffering other becomes embittered over our pleasure in his suffering and *disparages* such a one: he as the source of judgment, of the blaming and praising, he *demands equanimity*, but he himself **does not practice it**; otherwise he would not blame the one pleased at his suffering, but *be pleased* along with him (like those who laugh *along* about themselves); i.e., he admits through his practice that the other has a right to be as he is, just as he has a right to be annoyed at him. It is *unpleasant* for the others "but in itself not objectionable"! like everything bitter and painful in nature.

Someone who feels himself fortunate and sees that the other suffers from this (as an envious person) does not demand that this change; he enjoys it, *but* he enjoys it too when the other is pleased along with him, i.e., his fortune makes him willing to interpret the other's conduct as an increase of his fortune. His misfortune, to seek in the other's conduct a relief: in that one gives it to him to *help bear* it or in that one elevates oneself above him through blame. *The hatred of the not-compassionate is essentially vengeance: likewise, therefore, the demand for compassion*; it is the necessarily invoked emotional contradiction to that hatred.

7[285][147]

On the Deduction of Compassion.

As soon as compassion is *demanded* and *praised*, it receives a moral character as *good*. One submits to it, one does not shy away from declaring it — under different circumstances it is considered a weakness. The philosophers see in compassion, as in any *loss of self to a harmful affect*, a weakness. It *increases* the suffering in the world: even if ⟨it⟩ indirectly lessens the suffering, *this outcome may* **not** *justify it in the essence*! Assuming that it **ruled**: then humankind would *immediately* perish.

By contrast shared pleasure[148] *increases* the force of the world. The pleasure in the individual, who himself, *whatever may happen to him*, retains preference for the pleasure in himself, is a very high thought! One must help in order to be able to share pleasure again — but reining in one's soul long enough and keeping it cold so that it is not infected by misery: like the proper physician.

There is a distinguishing compassion which grasps extraordinarily far-flung kinds of suffering: it is to be honored as sign of a high *intellect*, not as such!

That we are well disposed toward the person who shows us compassion is a wretchedness: we should say: be brave, so that my suffering does not deprive you of your joyful temperament: we should *wish* not to lose the view onto the joyful element around us! But we are *tyrants*!

7[286]

To *enjoy along with them* our enemies' pleasure in our misfortune is possible.

7[287]

From many insights humans do not know how to gain something fortifying, they are *forbidden* fare e.g., my book.

7[288]

It is a refinement to choose one's examples from history and the sciences according to the general ignorance and deficiency of knowledge — otherwise we do not prove anything and evoke hatred because we embarrass. We need to descend to the poor in spirit, not in thoughts and goals, but in the material. To argue with nothing but tremendously well-known things: it is moreover pride, for the great truths shall not be proven with facts from a remote corner and learned brooding.

7[289]

I hear your Siren song, you wise men! Alas, nothing moves me so! But I say to you: you yourselves have sung it to yourselves, you were like me! You were fools of these beautiful paradises "justice, temperance": in truth they are *utopias*.

7[290]

In order to see in art a *means of power*: how one must distort things *or* strive for the overthrow of the existing! How much disappointment!

7[291]

to see one's inner suffering as in a drama is a higher level than merely suffering.

7[292][149]

Compensation of the poet, his sufferings and the *pleasure* in expressing the same

7[293]

The collapse of an old man's calculations is worthier of compassion than —

to lose the pretext of one's life and work, e.g., one's children

7[294]

1) Woe over the *feeling of sinfulness*! How it has increased suffering! 2) how it has turned the eye away from the natur⟨al⟩ consequences of guilt, thus arrested reason in the application to life! 3) how it has made egoistical and commanded putting the consequences *for others* (through inheritance as well) out of mind!

7[295]

You believe you can no longer feel passion for something, because it is only short-lived or because it is relatively valuable! But think of love for a woman! For money! For positions of honor! Even though there is no eternal taste, no eternal beauty and virtue, the *brief* phenomenon can *all the more* cause delight, so as ⟨to⟩ embrace it, as far as possible to *tear* it from the stream! *From now on tenderness for the transient* mixes into it!! NB.

7[296][150]

We easily become *dry* because we only have an eye for the subtleties of the psychic movements. The great train!

7[297]

Why want to dictate laws for things that we only know second-hand! "Do you want to be completely *universal*? Rather leave this bizarre pretense to the poor devils who themselves are nothing on their own."[151] Stendhal

7[298][152]

When humans *blush* over the vehemence of their undisguised drives, then art changes. The declaration of deep feelings counts as clumsy and coarse. *First* ceremonious manners. *Then serene* manners, still *freer* from any feeling (Louis XV): all *enthusiasme* and all energy disappear!

7[299][153]

To lend the humans of the Middle Ages *our* sensibility and sympathy.

7[300]

The feeling of power that lifts someone from the dust, makes orphans into heirs etc. is entirely equal to cruelty "I can do what I want," namely in regard to the one whom it *annoys*.

7[301][154]

The G⟨ermans⟩ have admiration for the foreign — from boredom; the French vanity — from boredom — the Italians love hatred etc. — from boredom.

The Frenchman scorns the foreign, object of ridicule.

7[302][155]

The passion for knowledge can come to a *tragic end*: are you afraid? As with any passion! — Ordinarily though, you scholars have no passion at all but a *habit countering your boredom*! — The attitude of the *different* peoples toward that! —

7[303]

Science can neither *prove* that all h⟨umans⟩ are equal, nor that proceeding according to this principle is in the long run useful.

7[304]

"Science"! What is it! *All* forces in its service! The experience of humanity from its drives, and a drive to know about the drives.

7[305][156]

Customs reflect the events of 100 years — not those of the present.

7[306][157]

(Northern) German culture does not stem from an aristocracy like the French, but from teachers (professors organists etc.) and preachers. *Entirely different* submission, always with the hidden thought that there is something *higher* than princes (Luther). Admiration *for the strangeness* of a prince, a state leadership, an army: naïve. One lets oneself be *oppressed*, but takes revenge in thoughts *about* things. — How *un*productive is the aristocracy! the **German** *race*-element

7[307]

The fast tempo in music and in life smooths out many characters and actions: if they are not to become unbearable: namely, the *change of affects* — the fast tempo is the thing of lasting moods, of ἦθος.[158]

7[308][159]

German aristocracy: even in luxury, in pomp, horticulture architecture manners unproductive

7[309]

And even if we did not trust ourselves with respect to the most difficult cases of moral calculation and reckoning, we still *all* believed we knew the moral multiplication tables and considered ourselves sure in this

7[310]

My thoughts have become my events: the rest is the medical history of every day.

7[311]

A storm: I feel it about 4 hours in advance, under the clearest sky. Once it is there, then my condition improves.

7[312]

The momentary political predominance of Germany cannot be sustained: it owes itself to the will power of a single person who, moreover, was so convinced of the weak character of all Germans that he feared neither parties nor princes. They may have the best organization and the most excellent obedience — but the commanders are born so seldom in this country and even more rarely those who command and have spirit. — Therefore, the superiority is a great danger — it cultivates arrogance and ambitions. — With parties one can do as one will, namely if one *wills*: but *velle non discitur*.[160] And indeed, it does not even take the will of a Richelieu, but that of a Bismarck, which is to say, a much more moody and passionate thing.

7[313][161]

The *peace-loving* German, one can count on his submission to the regiment and religion — because he hates the true *unrest* and *danger*: all the more he requires easy seemingly dangerous enthusiasms in order to feel like a hero. He vacillates very often because he does *not* want the deed!

[8 = N V 5. Winter 1880–1881]

8[1]

Religion of Courage

1. The passion of honesty.
2. The greatest question.
3. Courage and nothing more.

8[2]

1) the differing *growth* of the drives in the climate of different moral principles
2) Reasons for the disparity of moral judgment
3) Erroneousness and delusion of all moral judgments
4) Can science provide goals? No
5) Individual morality: our drives formed according to *our* ideal and with the aid of science. (As artists to *create* our ideal.
6) the favorable political and social conditions for these hermits!

8[3]

compassion cruelty.
love lust
envy ambition competition.
vengeance justice.
ridiculous original
cowardice humility
dissimulation actor.

murder war
robbery deception merchant
slave soldier civil servant.
insane poet saint
wisdom "prudence"

8[4]

Growth *against* the dismissive judgment can be guided:

a) by fear (its effects in Darwin, NB.)

b) by pride and defiance (vengeance and cruelty)

accordingly different: it is a matter of temperament.

8[5][1]

Enumeration of moral *presumptions*.

8[6]

NB, Introduction: All believe the current moral feelings are the moral feelings as such. But they are the Jewish ones.

8[7]

NB: if the current morality further evolves, *mankind will perish from it*. But the opposite is the assertion, yes, the *occasion*, to develop it further. Here I place the big question mark! Is civilization the path to happiness, to the highest passion and productivity?

8[8]

We need a heroic insight! in order to prepare the great *practical* question: **whether** to plant even *more* equality!

8[9]

Whether one happens to believe in compassion as miracle and source of knowledge or in the blood of Saint Januarius: then I think I am living still in a half-insane age.

8[10]

Out of compassion with others to dissimulate as religious? Phooey! We must *raise* them to our *courage*! And this is possible! Be it even through fatalism!

8[11]

Gradually insight increases and one *leaves one's hand off* the advancement and government of human culture: *one would have to do too much evil*! NB. NB.

8[12]

Happiness is reached on opposing paths; *from there*, no ethics is determinable (against Spencer)

8[13]

The feelings we have for certain customs and morals, the reasons for which are in circulation, have nothing to do with the origin, with the reasons for their emergence. NB.

8[14][2]

classicism and the advancement of equality, the desire for submission to an *absolute* norm: in the time of Augustus: return to the Greek ancient models. (Moral classicism: return to Socrates and the Stoa. Christ as *absolute* norm. The court. Everything founded upon eternity. Vergil — Homer. All equal under one lord. The new *ridiculum*:[3] "To be different from all others!" Ultimate reason: the individuals have exhausted themselves and pride turns against itself inwardly. (Pascal) (also Goethe)

8[15]

I am fortunate not to have had a moral education (except that by role models)

8[16][4]

No education, real needs preserve energy. What is to become of the civilized world! *Sand* and *slime*!

8[17]

"to treat all great interests with irony"[5] because one has no time to take them profoundly — now *European*

8[18]

as childish as Pascal and our theologians who with respect to knowledge and faith automatically believe that with faith it is always and only a matter of the Christian faith

8[19]

Only to speak about morality to such persons as have familiarized themselves with many animals' way of life.

8[20]

We steer clear of ugly painful scenes, we do not want to be *com*passionate. Those are the more refined natures. The coarser nature follows everything that excites and drives away boredom; around every quarrel, every brawl a crowd gathers. — Where there is the drive to help, the unpleasant feeling of compassion is overcome: and since thereby the pleasant feeling of being able to satisfy one's drive regularly emerges, one believes oneself that compassion is pleasant. Helping can also just be a consoling. The glazier in a hail!

8[21][6]

For those screaming and imploring for help one felt contempt (Aeschylus *Septem*[7])

But Prometheus!

8[22]

Manfred: give no one the *right* to punish him, to pardon, to *pity* him ("it ⟨is⟩ not so difficult to die, old man").[8]

8[23][9]

Clever and cheerful, like a lizard in the sun

8[24]

Z⟨acharias⟩ Werner and Kleist and Brentano

8[25]

to follow custom and finally get used to it[10] — that means though being *dishonest*! NB being *cowardly*! being *lazy*! Source of morality!!!

8[26]

Natural — unnatural — is nothing! The Greeks elevated love within the same sex to the highest degree of ideality: they just considered pederasty *good*.

8[27][11]

What meanness! God wants love from humans — and has hell at the ready for those who withhold it! Like Tiberius and Nero! Is it not respectable to resist such a tyrant?

God as the just and judge is *no* object of *love*! It is indelicate! He should have **to have renounced** judging! Christ did not feel subtly enough! In these things we are more mature! If God wanted to be the object of love, then — — —

8[28]

How is it that the Germans have no spirit! They feel slowly and do not let their feeling ripen, they thwart it through job or everyday things: that way they make themselves mediocre, they always remain like unripe fruits.

1) they do not understand how to have leisure
2) they do not take their experiences seriously, as significant enough for general reflection
3) they read too much and are eagerly servile to a ruling party or court
4) they make music not in order to bear a passion and to find relief, but in order to *excite* themselves!!! Hence, they need the most passionate music.

8[29][12]

The Germans *would like* all too gladly to have great passions — now, it does not matter that they do not know how to represent them without grimacing, in the long run they will have them! Then they will also recognize that although force comes first, there are kinds of force that come without grimaces.

8[30]

The less they have thought something through and brought themselves to clarity, the more insolently they paste the paints of feeling on, confident that ultimately the German always *believes* in a god because he sees someone comport himself incomprehensibly and sublimely.

8[31]

Pascal advised getting used to Christianity; one would sense that the passions diminish.[13] This means: to make one's *dishonesty* worthwhile and be delighted by it.

8[32][14]

To preach compassion — that would be something for artists to do before a hard, strictly private human ruled by the dark seriousness of passion! that is how music in Naples once worked! — But upon all these all too movable souls! Phooey!

8[33]

My earlier *style*: broad perspectives, much that is veiled, mysterious wonderful. The facts sparkling, like seeming illuminations of these mysteries. Basic belief: the essence not communicable; a sublime, presentient mood *makes* revelations. Sobriety *harms* **this** understanding. Contemplative repose and the memory of something terrible and longing alternate.

8[34][15]

My doubt in civilization: it removes the dangers, the great passions, the necessity of great humans — one should have only ramparts and cities built on Vesuvius: that way the productivity *and* the *enjoyment* is greatest!

8[35]

The value of altruism is *not* the result of science; but people of science let themselves be misled by the *now dominant drive* to believe that science confirms their drive's desire. (cf. Spencer).

8[36]

Assuming that science strengthens its reputation and governs: you shall experience an *appreciation* of the lie and of the capacity for fabricating as never before! Just as Christianity perhaps *counts for more* now than ever! Even among its adversaries!

8[37]

Perhaps the whole world knows that already: but I have known it only since yesterday, then it occurred to me! And now I live on this way, everyday only yesterday's discovery on my soul and ready to write it on the wall so that all the world may rejoice in it with me. — What folly!

8[38]

One day I found music poor and impertinent; it wanted to rob me of my thoughts and pretend to me that it is — — —

8[39]

The change in the meaning of words in Corcyra always occurs on a large scale! The civil peace cultivates quite different tastes, something else is convenient there and useful and *consequently* **praised**.[16]

8[40]

But if we let our passions grow, then along with this, as we know, the "crystallization":[17] I mean, we become *dishonest* and enter voluntarily into error?

8[41]

When we no longer want morally to praise or blame, do the drives then stop being developed?

8[42]

ever[18] melancholic — but a principle of valor since childhood makes for my having many small victories and consequently being more cheerful than befits my m⟨elancholy⟩.

8[43]

I have my goal and my passion: I want from art nothing but that it show me the former *transfigured* or delight me, encourage me and temporarily remove me. The *first* is my kind of religion: I see my ideal loved by others and transfigured and carried up into the clouds: I pray *with* them!

Art shall *not* abduct me from myself, *nor* save me from nausea.

8[44]

Love depicted vampire-like in R⟨ichard⟩ W⟨agner⟩, with the trump card to outrival the whole world in fortune — and as it were to make it poor, to appropriate all *possible* fortune for oneself and to avenge oneself as it were on everything that exists (what for? because it does not love us quite like this Senta Brünnhilde etc.)

8[45][19]

The cursed inclinations to the comfortable and cozy condemn the Germans to mediocrity of spirit and make them incapable of having a say in all great matters: e.g., on the question of happiness. If one unsettles them, then they are the most disgruntled and petty people, with that short-winded thirst for revenge of the mediocre that in every moment they must do harm.

8[46][20]

The "love of humanity" with the aid of a reasonable education — Stuart Mill, hilarious!

8[47][21]

They call *for* civilization who are very much in fear. Content *in* civilization are the weak, cowardly, lazy, despised, ordinary: equality as goal, finally as state. The *sand.* Morality (Christian-Jewish) is now that of civilization. Napoleon and the French people after the Revolution. Who was satisfied with the organization?

8[48][22]

Where there is heroism there is no *crime* anymore. For the belief that something is *good* is with heroism.

8[49]

with that firmness which he who stands in his place has, and the affability he feels toward all

8[50][23]

The Germans have a suspicion that one thinks them capable of passions — therefore they immediately make grimaces and excesses, *not* from the force of the affect, but in order to make themselves credible. Of this kind are even the passions in R⟨ichard⟩ W⟨agner⟩: such that in life one would have to think anyone crazy who runs after his feelings in such a way (nausea suffices to kill someone). Completely missing is the pleasure that used to be called moral: that someone know how to ride his horse, that it be beautiful daring and passionate like its rider; the latter though lets beauty daring and passion shine *through* his reason, which tempers everything and makes it tolerable for sight. From the insane pursuit of those horses one becomes dizzy and exhausted.

8[51][24]

Classicism: the pleasure of seeing so many others submit themselves, and of imagining the interior *struggle* makes submission easy, one takes it seemingly frivolously, in order to have the pleasure of seeing the most serious and the most arrogant groveling! *namely, renouncing their individuality*!

8[52]

The appeal for all penance preachers of despising the *great* **power** publicly! The appeal for the high-powered of the deepest humiliation and submission and abstinence — demonic magic!

8[53]

New valor: to hold in contempt honor! glory! name! — we *remunerate ourselves* and despise what glory others could give us!

8[54][25]

the complete incapacity of song has destroyed the sense for melody — now the dramatic and the sound of nature!

8[55]

Thinking makes mistakes. It is, namely, the inverse path of adaptation, from the weakest upward. The change of morality quite possible, like that of taste: just practice!

8[56]

Naïveté of the moral got lost through Christianity (and previously through Socrates), like the French naïveté under L⟨ouis⟩ XIV — for the same reasons.

8[57][26]

The cruelty and its pleasure in the strong person who breaks himself and submits to a law (Prince Christianity). Previously he took it out on others by shaping their fate (good or bad — it is cruelty, pleasure in *kneading* the clay.)

8[58][27]

Holiness: it is possible to accustom consciousness to *no longer noticing* that which goes on in the entrails, in the blood, or to *interpreting* it differently (in a heavenly sense).

8[59][28]

An action is blamed because it appears to us (or to the whole to which we reckon ourselves) shameful or dishonorable: in the inverse case one lauds it. Consequently, it is not in itself good or evil.

8[60]

For my part I have no concept of a h⟨uman⟩ who wants to be as *proper form demands* and who does not dare to love to hate to judge, unless he knows how proper form commands here. I certainly have no proper form! Yes, I despise everyone who wants to be like another! who glances over to see what the others say about his actions! who always thinks of the others, not to be useful to them, but in order not to be ridiculous in their eyes — were he ridiculous, he would give them a diversion! terrible! — But why should we not provide something to *laugh* about! We ourselves have the advantage from it when our fellow humans are in a good mood! — "But they no longer respect when they laugh!" — But why should they *fear* me? And woe to me when something ridiculous about me suffices to rob me of my self-respect! But this happens with the vain who want to *annihilate* themselves after a mistake in etiquette.

8[61]

NB An age of barbarism is beginning; the sciences will serve it! — Let us figure out how we will preserve *after all* the higher, the extract of our present knowledge: through a community of free individuals who say

1) there is no God
2) no reward or punishment for good and evil (ethical world)
3) good and evil are valid according to the ideal and the direction in which we live: the best part of it is bequeathed to us, moreover it is possible that these judgments themselves can be *wrong* with regard to the advancement of the respective ideal. The ideal

is the anticipation of the hopes of our drives (the dominant drives)

in order to *preserve* oneself nevertheless in the barbarism, this community will have to be rough and brave — ascetic preparation

8[62]

"*Health*" not to be defined as fixed. An ideal of the condition in which everyone can do best what he most likes to do: but the savage a society man and the scholar will wish a *completely different* condition! — We still suffer from the "classical" concepts that we have barely left behind for poetry. They say the Apollo is "*more beautiful*" than a fresco in Athens!

8[63]

The condition of humanity is still a very early one, and some of the most important questions for it have not even been raised. — Our present science works with some prejudices, as if humanity will always agree about them: e.g., about the value of the sympathetic action, about earthly welfare regarding health, etc. But when another ideal emerges, another drive comes to power, then science must subordinate itself again to *this one*! *I am trying to guess* the *principal prejudices* of the *present* science! It is *Europeanism*!

8[64]

They call it my courage, others will call it my shamelessness. The praising and blaming does not concern the matter but the relation of the praising or blaming person to this matter.

8[65][29]

With the beautiful voices and their training and enjoyment the enjoyment of the melody was lost: and the latter itself! The piano virtuosos came and introduced harmony. Now the orchestra imitates *their* achievements: and the *barbarism of the theatrical* effect on the passions places itself alongside and *inspires* the composers. This is cruder than the magic of the virtuosos.

8[66]

The same characteristics of the passions can be turned *in their favor* or *against* them, according to our general inclination, e.g., their deep seriousness, their enchantment with reality, their absolute demand of trust, etc.

8[67]

I have often believed that I could teach humans — and have had a mixed feeling of pride and love toward them. Now, at the end, I concede that I have nothing to teach, but that I ask from the heart that there may be such who would dignify me to learn from them: for the questions that I have raised for myself are powerful and — — —

8[68][30]

Haeckel: the disposition to accept the theory of descent and the unitarian philosophy would provide the best standard for the degree of mental superiority among humans: he mentions the English and the Germans: he omits the French (Lamarck and Comte!

8[69][31]

The life of women has a very provocative paradox: it amounts to an act that is the exact opposite of all modesty and the entire way of thinking they strive for through education. No wonder that for them everything becomes a miracle that is connected with this paradox!

8[70]

Languages as the work of individuals or priesthoods — like religions.

8[71][32]

How is the extraordinary pleasure to be explained that Comte took in altruistic feelings? *Amour*?

8[72]

The pleasure in ceremonies and formalities *great* in young civilizations: to be noted for the arts!

8[73]

Said about humans who have not thought: one yields to compassion not **so that** it arouse pleasant feelings (this would not be true, except with very singular humans), but *because* it has always aroused pleasant feelings: just as the animal loves the brood, etc., one affirms it when it is already there!

8[74]

"*Le long espoir et les vastes pensées*"[33] Lafontaine.[34]

8[75]

What do I care about those who demonstrate a *silly excitement*, when in general compassion is not readily adored!

8[76]

To cast off all human social moral fetters until we can dance and jump like the children

8[77]

I have taken the spirit of Europe into myself — now I want to make the counterstrike!

8[78]

The noble ἐσθλοί[35] the truthful, who do *not need to dissimulate*! As the powerful and individuals!

8[79][36]

the existence of the Church still gives the freethinkers freedom *before science*. NB even now!

8[80]

In Germany they have almost lost the desire and therefore also the sense for innocent music; one remembers the times when the good women, too, believed they were insufficiently prepared for the night if they did not have a nightcap, a heavy hot overly spiced wine, standing before them.

8[81]

Against Schopenhauer: he has the mien of a h⟨uman⟩ who is satisfied with himself for speaking as well as the characters in Racine and Schiller (according to Stendhal). Fine, he is full of passion, but first of all he is satisfied with speaking beautifully.[37]

8[82]

How does one arrive at *honoring* someone *because* he is capable of a deep and manifold compassion and is easily aroused to it? He must be unhappier than the others and always intent on consoling, helping the others up, etc. — thus, his unhappiness is *pleasant* 1) because it demonstrates an effect of *our* suffering 2) because it demonstrates the prospect of suffering's relief, of alleviation. We honor him because he is different from what we expect? — But why do we not despise him? Because if we do *not feel* him to be *honorable*, our effect upon him has nothing pleasurable for us. It nauseates us to make an impression on wretched souls. We are therefore secretly inclined to think of him as a capable good honorable human. Besides, we do not want to be pitied by bad fellows; it demeans us in our own eyes! Thus: when does being pitied not humiliate? When it elevates! This it does when a highly reputable human (through heart spirit position, etc.) or a god sympathizes with us — thus when an equation takes place that does us honor (through which we feel ourselves elevated higher!!) Thus: we like to honor the compassionate *so that* we can take pleasure in our own elevation! or *because*!

8[83]

The enthusiasm which in Germany immediately leads to stultification and to servility

8[84][38]

The result of all absolute morality would be the most extreme stunting of the human, indeed, annihilation. It is *not* proven by happiness!

8[85]

About our greatest men one still must say: might they have a bit more genius and be somewhat less actors!

8[86]

How German painters now paint, German musicians compose, German poets write poetry: one hears in it the presumption, the playacting of greatness.

8[87]

What does "willing" mean? women can cry at will. Men can also *will* to cry, but the effect fails to appear. What makes the difference? The practice of the mechanism is missing. — We can *will* to speak clearly, but nobody understands us. — Thus, success or non-success does *not* belong to the concept "will" — so it remains: to *desire*, i.e., to have representation and valuation.

8[88]

Very good time for the freethinkers — and not used!

8[89]

age of imitated *originality*. (as stimulant)

8[90]

Advantage of solitude: we let loose our entire nature, even its bad moods, *against our main object* and not upon other things and humans: in this way we live it *through*!

8[91][39]

Why do I interrupt passion?

I could put forth my case full-throatedly and vehemently and thrillingly, as I feel it — but afterwards I am half-dead and suffering, also full of chagrin, about exaggerations omissions, etc. Others have their spirit *completely* only in passion: I have mine in *suppressed* and combated passion. Everything does me *good* that reminds me of *this my condition*!!

8[92][40]

the belief in the reprehensibility of egoism has *weakened* humans. The Greek philosophers taught belief in the stupidity of non-philosophers *as cause of their misfortune*.

8[93]

All that is missing are the great convincing humans — otherwise everything is prepared for a complete change; principles, suspicion, dissolution of all contracts, indeed, the need for shock, the dissatisfaction.

8[94]

Religion nouvelle[41]

1) saved for rare moments
2) devotion to pleasure in self-sacrifice
3) no God, no beyond, no reward and punishment
4) no more accusing, no pangs of conscience, but *pangs of reason*
5) the I restored.
6) the beautiful felt as the self-sacrificing I
7) no general love of humans, instead rule of the drives

8) the highest prudence taken as norm, as *common* and not venerated therefore, because ordinary
9) the foolishness of magnanimity admired. Being compassionate always weakness and respite — conceded
10) not honored as sacrifice *for others*, instead as complete victory of the one affect over the others, so that we dedicate life, honor, etc. to it: thus, the fullness of passion is the essential.

8[95]

When I analyzed myself looking for the foundations of religious feeling, I found valor to be the most elevating feeling.

8[96]

W⟨agner⟩, whose flaw is not to be proud enough to despise the flatterers.

8[97][42]

Never has wrath unfolded into such gloomy majesty and such wealth of sublime nuances as with the Jews. What is an angry Zeus against an angry Jehovah! They have transferred it from their prophets to him. Wrath became holy and good thereby. And occasionally a beam of paternal goodness broke through these thunder clouds — in such a landscape Christ dreamed his rainbow, his heavenly ladder from God to the human: *nowhere else* could this have been done than among the people of the prophets!

8[98]

Science has brought much benefit; now one wants, suspicious of the religions and related matter, to submit ⟨oneself⟩ completely to *it*. But mistake! It can*not command*, show the way! rather only when one knows where to? *can* it benefit. Generally, it is mythology to believe that knowledge will always recognize that which is most beneficial and most indispensable to mankind — it will be just as able to harm as to benefit

— the highest forms of morality are perhaps impossible in the full light of day.

8[99][43]

To feel compassion and *not* be able to help is extremely bitter. *Sublimation of cruelty*: to arouse compassion. To *make* God suffer, the Christian's endeavor

8[100]

Beautiful: everyone calls beautiful that which is either the visible expression of what is pleasant (beneficial) to him or awakens the memory of it or ordinarily appears connected with it.

8[101][44]

The same drive develops as *cowardice*, under the impression of the blame that follows this action: and as *humility* under the impression of praise. NB. Perhaps I should not speak of sublimation; there are two kinds of development, one stunting, proceeding with contradictions of feeling, and one flourishing, itself conscious of the good. (Evil as melancholia

8[102]

fire in the body, snow on the head and the mouth full of black steam like Mount Etna — Savonarola

8[103][45]

The long after-shadows of Christianity (the philosophers too, such as Socrates, have contributed): they have *persuaded* humans of altruism as the source of happiness and made their *springs* weak (the personal passion) by adding to it good faith. *All* morality since then has been eager for sympathy: to *overbid* Christianity with universal love of humanity — that generates sand and mush! To *demolish* its foundation — task of science! I.e., of course, according to the current understanding: to make humans evil, egoistical etc.

8[104][46]

Astonished at the drive that seemed to want to rule him, he was annoyed, rebuffed his drive as much as possible, and, immediately distracted upon vanquishing it, he liberated himself from it by publishing the confession of his success.

8[105]

One single idea generates 1000 others with him; the slightest word drove his conversations into high regions where healthy logic did not always follow him, but the spirit incessantly made itself noticed.[47] He did *not* have *the need of* another *in order to become excited.* He immediately went very far, but watchful whether one had followed him.[48]

8[106][49]

cette civilisation[50] that always was a bit "his personal enemy," according to Talleyrand.

8[107][51]

"There is nothing noble and nothing low in the world." *Je suis lâche, moi, essentiellement lâche.*[52] Napoleon was **above** *honneur*![53]

8[108]

"I give my word, it gives me no qualms to do something that the world calls a degrading action."[54]

8[109]

My secret inclinations, *après tout*[55] those of nature, in contrast to certain affectations of greatness with which I must decorate myself, give me infinite resources to play a game with the credulity of the whole world (to deceive those who pretend to know me)[56]

8[110]

Music has not yet represented a wrathful god. W⟨agner⟩'s Wotan suffers from the weakness of the German character, he wants too many things and nothing with complete certainty. His wrath is not worthy of mention next to that of Michelangelo's God — though the latter too had only this one thought in his head.

8[111]

"Soldiers, wholly excited by victory, place themselves in such a proud region, from where with great effort one can make them descend."[57]

8[112][58]

The fear around all despots is to receive a reproach when one makes only the slightest mistake: one generates neither feelings nor spirit anymore, for one does not find the opportunity anymore to exchange a feeling or the slightest reflection. In this way the most different persons were put on the same level and finally became *identical*. The despot with external plans disdains the small successes that he could have scored with his environment; even when he has taken great pains with the art of seduction to subjugate it to himself: once this has *happened*, then he is far from making his yoke and himself agreeable.

8[113][59]

that the rule of women has weakened the kings of France: at Napoleon's court they were supposed to be only ornament.

8[114][60]

Napoleon was convinced that in France the women had more spirit than the men — he said it often. That the education they are given disposes them to a certain skillfulness against which one has to defend oneself.

8[115][61]

Napoleon called *dévouement*:[62] the one who would surrender his whole person, all his feelings, all his opinions: he repeated that it was necessary to devote ourselves, down to the smallest of our old habits, in order to have no more than one thought: that of his interest and his will.

8[116][63]

"I have the right to answer all your complaints with an immortal *Moi*.[64] I am apart from the whole world, I accept conditions from no one." "You must submit to all my fantasies and find it quite simple when I indulge in similar diversions"

8[117][65]

"the métier of war makes for an honesty among the generals such that they display even their most jealous affections: the habit of openly combating the enemy gives them the habit of not veiling anything; they see in all oppositions a field battle"

8[118][66]

A gigantic plan: ready to design it, ready to execute it; from time to time laying the foundations for it. Moved by this single thought: detached from all impressions of secondary rank that could have delayed his project. Through the scope of his *penetrating astuteness* and the *toughness of his will* the ⟨most⟩ extraordinary human. Had his goal been the well-being of mankind, the greatest human.

8[119][67]

consumed by suspicion and mistrust, slave of his inner passions, fearing all power, even that which he had created.

8[120]

The Great Question.

[9 = M II 2. Winter 1880–1881]

The Plowshare.

Thoughts

on the Presumptions of Morality.

By

Friedrich Nietzsche.

9[1][1]

Let the foreigner look no more for naïveté, not to speak of originality, among the Germans! In France naïveté was smothered by the court, in Germany by the "geniuses" — for far too long they used it for playacting and conducting war. That was the achievement of the cursed, envious darkness in all of those geniuses, who could not forgive the French their spirit and their graceful suppleness and the Greeks their originality and put forward against these "German naïveté." But it is not only ghosts that disappear when one speaks of them, but also real qualities among peoples and individuals.

9[2][2]

Not wanting to endure any discontent with oneself is often the sign of a revolting softness — and yet it is extolled as moral! We must know how to endure many pains for the sake of a goal, yes seek out and freely elect pains if the goal requires such hardship. Do we have a covenant with fate that our ship should suffer no shipwreck? That our journey pass through no desert?

9[3][3]

"May humans preserve us while we care and think for them: otherwise the birds and the bees will do it. — But we are too proud to be able to be 'rewarded': and too earnestly engaged to have time and favor for fame." — So the philosophical Muses once sang.

9[4]

About the weather, about diseases and about good and evil everyone thinks he can have his say. This is the sign of intellectual commonness.

9[5]

All moral systems which dictate how one *ought to act* lacked the knowledge of *how one acts* — but all believed they had it, as every human believes he does.

9[6][4]

With a great goal is one not only above his slander but also his wrong? His crime? — So it seems to me. Not that one *hallowed* it through his goal: but one made it great.

9[7][5]

What *could* the Germans owe to their Schopenhauer? That he annihilated the glassy and glittering idealism of general noble words and proud feelings which in particular Schiller and his circle circulated and comes to know best through Wilhelm von Humbold⟨t⟩'s correspondence with Schiller — that false "classicism" which had an inner hatred for the natural nakedness and terrible beauty of things and which with nobly feigned gestures and nobly feigned voices automatically demanded a disguised and merely ostensible nakedness and gracefulness, a sort of Canova-style, in regard to everything (characters passions times, customs): all of which — it is a whole collection of noble half-measures — at close range greatly pained Goethe, without his proceeding differently against it than was his way, mildly demurring, silent, looking away, resolved on his better and own course. Schopenhauer the Crude caused the devilry of the world to become visible again — he did not get quite so far as to discover and expose the devilry of the good and the beauty and goodness of devilry. — In any case one would now be very backward if after Schopenhauer one were still to feel as Schiller would: but *therewith* of course still a hundred times superior to what the present-day German has truly become since that time!

9[8]

How often is marriage crudely and sensationally broken up, merely in order to bring about a moral or legal condition in which a marriage that has become intolerable can be dissolved!

9[9][6]

To reflect on the possible motives of your friends and enemies ought to be as much a point of honor for you as to judge these persons publicly.

9[10][7]

You know quite well it is a point of honor to speak publicly about a person's character and motives. Friend! It is also a point of honor to *reflect* upon them for yourself!

9[11][8]

[. . .] It now hardly sounds credible that *something opposite* also wants to count and has counted as *good* — to say "I" more often and more strongly than ordinary humans, to assert oneself against them, to brace oneself against every attempt to turn us into a tool and member, to make oneself independent, at the risk of subjecting or sacrificing others to oneself if independence is not otherwise achievable; to prefer society in a state of emergency to those fair safe uniform economies, and to consider the expensive wasteful thoroughly personal manner of living as the condition for "the human being" to become higher more powerful more fruitful bolder more unusual and rarer — so that humanity *decrease in number and grow in worth.*

9[12][9]

In customs our events and thoughts outlive us: provided that they were strong enough to shape customs: but who could look into the customs of the present as into a mirror of the present: we must seek then in the customs of the present the persons and things from one hundred years ago and more, not *us and our experiences*: our grandchildren will perhaps have to bear the burden of *these*!

9[13][10]

[. . .] then one must also take into the bargain the German boring women: who are at once of a dull, complacent mind and lively, sensitive and vindictive. But it is said of them as well that in extraordinary circumstances they are as strong as lionesses and fine enough to crawl through the eye of a needle.[11]

9[14][12]

The monk who through poverty, chastity, obedience turns away from the world, who particularly with the last virtue, but really with all three, renounces the will to power: he does not so much withdraw from the "world" as rather from a certain culture, which has its happiness in the feeling of power. He retreats into an earlier stage of culture that sought with spiritual raptures and hopes to keep harmless the deprived impotent lonely unwed childless one.

9[15][13]

[. . .] perfect knowledge would presumably let us circle around things coldly and luminously like a star — for a short while still! And then *our* end would be there as the end of beings craving for knowledge, who from the spinning of ever finer threads of interest, enjoy a spider-existence and spider-happiness — and who in the end perhaps voluntarily cut off the thinnest and most delicate thread because no even finer thread will let itself be spun from it. —

9[16]

The genius is misjudged and misjudges himself, and that is his good fortune! Woe, if he recognizes himself! If he falls into self-admiration, the most ridiculous and dangerous of all conditions! There is nothing left of the richest and most productive human anymore when he admires himself; with that he has descended lower, become less than he was — formerly, when he could still rejoice *in himself*! When he still suffered from himself! Then he still maintained the stance toward himself as to an *equal*! Then there was still blame and admonition and shame! But when he looks *up to* himself, then he has become his servant and devotee and may do nothing else but obey, that is: *imitate himself*! In the end he beats himself to death with his own wreaths; or he is left standing before himself like a statue, that is, as stone and petrifaction!

9[17]

"There are so many dawns that have not yet broken."[14]

Rig Veda.

[10 = Mp XV 1b. Spring 1880–Spring 1881]

10[A1]

Yes, we want humans to live moderately and properly and justly — but everyone? That I do not dare to decide. Mankind ⟨would⟩ come to an end too quickly!

10[A2]

Our genius and our virtue grow with our hatred.

10[A3][1]

When very dissolute h⟨umans⟩ are finally sated and become preachers of chastity, then this is quite *honest* — they know *only* the horrible side of the matter (as Sophocles once instructed Pericles:) or remember what is disgusting and self-despising in it. — Then there truly are p⟨eople⟩ who know sensuality from hearsay and *fear* it terribly — these too preach chastity, following the Bible.

10[A4]

grand opera, of French-Italian-Jewish descent

10[A5][2]

Accidents and profound sufferings cannot be precluded. Should we arrange our entire life and thought *accordingly*? ἀταραξία.[3] Possible it is. But brave it is not! (Semitic.) — But no! We do not want to spoil the good for ourselves, and after all we have one means — — — —.

10 [A6][4]

Phooey, such cheap virtues! Write a few pamphlets against animal cruelty!

10[A7]

The pathos of the dramatic artist is an object of scorn when it shows itself elsewhere than on the stage — he is above all simply an actor.

10[A8]

One must put to the test, who among friends and those "for whom our well-being lies close to their hearts" stands firm: treat them roughly once.

10[A9]

Memory: we notice that we approach the thing, we arrive at a sensation which we occasionally also had when we thought of the thing.

10[A10]

We see things *frivolously* when we submit to such one-sided observations and act fanatically — it is our kind of frivolity. We know very well that it is imprecise. An artist though, *if* he were to come this far, would wonder at *how rigorous* and *serious* he had become.

10[A11]

There is, with respect to *things*, dedication (from its perspective, deduction) and pride (induction)

10[A12]

The strangest book? NB

10[A13][5]

Napoleon often said he alone had stopped the course of the Revolution; after him it would continue. — "He knew his time quite well and fought it continuously." "He has changed the meaning of all words and caused all parties to degenerate." R⟨émusat⟩

10[A14][6]

Often it is necessary to ally oneself with someone in order to suppress him. *When* we count as the best connoisseur of someone, then our disloyalty weighs terribly heavy.

10[A15][7]

To pay for services so that they are no longer spoken about. — Exaggerated rewards generate pretensions, but no gratitude. R⟨émusat⟩

10[A16][8]

To *raise up* the souls in one's surroundings by sharing one's splendor with them! Napoleon shared nothing, he was jealous, he wanted to *have* all the splendor — that way he belittled the people around him and put them out of sorts.

10[B17][9]

The immediate imitation of a feeling and subsequent *imputation* of an occasion

Music twi⟨light⟩

Whence this practice? Fear has coerced the imitation of all gestures in order to draw conclusions about the feeling (with respect to the enemy)

Innervation of the faces of fearful and coquettish women

This capacity *de*creases among proud, self-important humans — it increases in *anxious* ages (the understanding of the imitative arts grows then)

10[B18]

How is it that I always **thirst** for humans who do *not* become small in the face of nature, on a walk on the fortified heights above Genoa! Do I not know how to find them?

10[B19][10]

The excitement, the nervousness — is a perpetual anxiety.

10[B20][11]

We are no longer getting to know things, because no danger forces us to *have to* know them. It's turning into a hobby: and in its stead a laziness as well.

10[B21]

Everything to be compiled in which I *forgive*. To stand above sins, to admit them.

10[B22]

The Epicureans melancholics with a weak stomach — hence their "belly lust"[12]

10[B23][13]

Horace and Catullus translated from the Greek and made everything foreign contemporary and Rome-accordant, at least Rome-familiar. Thus, no Romanticism!

10[B24]

the matter is *worth neither robbery nor robber* ego

10[B25]

Our first joy in a poet is to encounter a thought, a feeling that we *too* have;[14] e.g., Horace when he speaks of his villa.[15] Moreover, that he states *our* thoughts so *nicely*! — he honors us thereby!

10[B26]

Dreams: eating the toad. — "Alpa, Alpa, who carries his ashes to the mountain?"[16] — the blood moon.

10[B27]

I am often ashamed by how good I have it now, and it spurs me mightily to think what someone could do with this repose — and I!

10[B28]

The soul's state of war is only *beginning*! Let it become what it will: forward! To despise falseness, to bear all suffering cheerfully, whatever strikes us thereby, to walk naked in the hail — to despise and bear the injustice we do to ourselves — he scorns "health," "well-being," etc.

10[B29]

Even the slightest thing we do *intentionally*, e.g., chewing, is for the most part unintentional. The *intention* relates to an immense realm of possibilities.

10[B30][17]

To figure out humans more instinctively. Carnot revealed Jourdan, Hoche, Bonaparte.

10[B31]

When I celebrated Schopenhauer as my educator, I had forgotten that for a long time already none of his dogmas had withstood my distrust; but it did not matter to me how often I had written "badly proven" or "unprovable" or "exaggerated" under his sentences because I gratefully enjoyed the mighty impression that Schopenhauer himself, freely and boldly positioned before things, against things, had made on me for a decade. When I later offered Richard Wagner my veneration on a festive occasion, I had in turn forgotten that his whole music had shrunken for me to some one hundred measures, taken from here and there, that lay close to my heart, and to whose heart I lay close — it will still be the case now — and no less had I forgotten over the picture of this life — this mighty life coursing as its own stream and as it were uphill — to say what I thought of Richard Wagner with regard to truth. Who would not want to be of a different opinion than Schopenhauer, I have always thought — by and large: and who *could* be of one o⟨pinion⟩ with Richard Wagner, in large part and in small!

10[B32][18]

Ce qui importe, ce ne sont point les personnes: mais les choses.[19] Carnot.

When (according to Victor Hugo) *Napoleon perça sous Bonaparte,*[20] Carnot took sides against him; he voted against the lifelong Consulate, he advocated for the preservation of the Republic. In 1814 he forgot the empire in order to remember that the fatherland was in danger. Napoleon says, "Carnot, I have come to know you too late." "No one has given me the impression of true greatness so much as Carnot" Niebuhr

10[B33]

Encouragement of a friend. It is not yet too late for you to attain greatness of character.

10[B34]

conciliatory natures, who replace in themselves the hatred for Germans among the French and Americans, the hatred for the Jews among the Germans, with an intentional benevolence — not out of contradiction, but out of a need for justice. Thus disposed against entire historical periods!

10[B35]

Ten years teacher and never punished.

10[B36][21]

Hot water, working mentally outdoors and while walking, clean and *thrifty* habits, the morning in fresh air and schedule of military rigor. Nighttime accounting in the spirit of the ancient philosophers.

10[B37][22]

We do not believe fate with regard to weak persons and mutable things.

Our views on fate are fate.

The world of purposiveness is in its *entirety* a **piece** of the *purposeless irrational world.*

1. If we wanted to estimate real existence intellectually or, 2. morally: then it appears intellectually *low* and morally *base.* And it would be *nausea* to live! Let us therefore remove these predicates *from* the world! Also the individual in his *entirety* is as stupid and as immoral as the *rest of the world* and even the *best* individual in it!

Thus, *either* to want to perish! *or* to unlearn praising and blaming. **Indifference**

Cost of the *dead* world. The drives and their development show **in the end** their *irrationality*; they *contradict each other* (in the form of the intellect that does not like existence) as the pain displays the same.

Our prudence can *cope* with existence

10[B38]

To *seek out* humans around oneself among whom one can preserve and show one's ideal humanity. At first make the task easier for oneself and then gradually draw *stranger* humans into one's circle. — But at first build one's circle, chase others away.

Perhaps in this way we bring about conditions which the expediency of selection only offers over millennia and to a much more weakened humankind! (as its degree of intellect is, for better or worse! = the sun's waste of light,[23] etc.)

10[B39]

I am painfully *just*, because it preserves *distance.*

10[B40]

I cannot bear being near a human being who spits

10[B41]

Which traits of the human are unfavorable for selection, thus are not preferred by women? Books[24] are means to propagate them *after all.*

10[B42]

Even with humans *experiments* necessary, as in Darwinism!

10[B43][25]

Insanity without delusions (Affective Insanity)[26]

a) Impulsive insanity when one must follow without will of one's own.

Manie sans délire[27]

(perhaps as abortive or masked epilepsy?)

10[B44][28]

The negro hides the fetish, when it is not supposed to see something, under his garment.

10[B45][29]

With the Pacific Islanders the aristocracy is immortal, the bourgeoisie not.

10[B46]

1) My *success* with the enthusiasts: I soon became tired of it and distrustful

2) I have never complained of lack of attention and do not know the feeling.

3) I hope *step by step* to approach the higher natures, but hardly know *where* they are and *whether* they are there! Thus far I have always overcome my eulogists and critics when I went a step further (and overcame *myself*)

10[B47]

the sublime seek to *lift* themselves a bit more, up to where their fantasy stopped — they so much wish to go *beyond themselves.*

10[B48]

Spencer thinks mankind has *unwittingly* arrived at everything appropriate to its needs — at judgments that accord with *truth*!! Nonsense! The opposite!

10[B49]

Bismarck, whose merit it is to spoil for the Germans the pleasure in the European party templates.

10[B50]

what cheerfulness is now possible! We have chased away the specters and acquired for ourselves the right to *irrationality*: we *no longer want* to be more prudent than the world is!

10[B51][30]

The individual can now really achieve a happiness that is impossible for mankind. Formerly nobility: now it just requires that one *feels* others as slaves, as our *fertilizer*

10[B52]

I wish to deprive science a bit of its *solemnity* — it has now become a diversion, since no *cares* are behind it. I believe soon there will be a *surplus* of *spirit* that must be wasted!

10[B53]

So far we have still been making things *difficult* for ourselves (e.g., with regard to overpopulation), because we do not dare execute our new valuations. One will soon have to *note* of life that it is *lived* with a surplus of spirit!

10[C54]

1. § Knowledgeable human being, its becoming, its prospects.
2. § Primal morality
3. § Christianity
4. § Time-morality (compassion).

5. § Orientation about the immediate surroundings, estates peoples etc.

6. § Aphorisms on the affects.

10[D55]

At first one has good faith in one's intellectual passions: when the better insight stirs, *defiance* appears, we do not want to give in. *Pride* says that we have enough spirit to advance our objective. *Arrogance* despises objections as a base dry-hearted point of view. *Lasciviousness* still counts up its pleasures *during* their enjoyment and very much doubts that better judgment can achieve such a thing. *Compassion* with the idol and its difficult fate is added, it forbids looking so closely at its imperfections: *gratitude* does the same and still more. Most of all the *intimate closeness*, the *loyalty* in the air around the celebrated person, the commonality of happiness and danger. Alas, and his trust in us, his self-indulgence in front of us, it chases away from us the thought that he may be wrong, like a betrayal, an indiscretion.

10[D56]

If the good as such were good, then it would be a limitation of God's omnipotence: he creates everything, this he commands and that he forbids the creation, the strength for *both* he has given to it. If it were good and evil as such, then God's commandment and prohibition would not be necessary. If the as-such were knowable, then the human would not need God *and priests*. Consequently, the latter decree: morality is comprehensible only from the angle of God's commandment, *not* from the angle of the advantages and disadvantages for the acting person. They rebuff this view on the critique of actions.

10[D57]

"breakfast-beauty"

10[D58]

So is the morality of a priest a *greater* one because he continuously has the Church's interest as his guideline and rather defers by contrast his own? Is not this feeling as a large complex merely a *prouder* kind of egoism? And similarly with the mother with respect to her child? Citizens with respect to the state? This "self-renunciation" is quite specious: one lives for **one's** *passion*! and sacrifices something slighter of oneself.

10[D59][31]

To consider the human of sympathetic and disinterested actions as the *moral* one is a fashion for which Christianity may be blamed with respect to Europe. Otherwise the one feeling strongly responsible for his well-being and his highest interest counts as moral, who says "I" even more than all others: even when he sacrifices the others thereby to himself, like the great conquerors. To harm nobody and to benefit him as much as possible, but oneself the most — that has not counted as moral, because it was considered impossible. And rightly so! Such is not the nature of things that one could bring two opposite passions in accord. Because we are here and because we assert and develop ourselves to the maximum we must consider our interests to be higher than others and take our strength from this: *one cannot take a step forward without somehow violating another's interest.* Just because we *cannot know it sufficiently*, a guideline according to the interest of *each* individual and *all* others is impossible. Indeed, with ourselves it is just so: what we decree to be our main interest lives *at the cost* of *our* other interests. That impossibility is already proven in ourselves. The "legality" the sparing of other rights is possible only in a very crude sense. Its source is a subtler injustice; it is the existential condition for a *very crude* concept of "existence"! But *willing to exist* is already unjust.

10[D60][32]

Such an adaptation as Spencer envisions is imaginable, but so that each individual becomes a useful instrument and also perceives himself only as such: thus, as *means*, as *part* — hence *with annulment of the individualism* according to which one wants to be *purpose* and *a completeness*, and indeed in both a *uniqueness*! This transformation is possible, indeed perhaps history is taking its course toward that! But then the individuals will become **ever weaker** — it is the history of the *demise of mankind*, where the principle of disinterestedness, the *vivre pour autrui*,[33] sociality rule! If the individuals are to become stronger, then society must remain a *state of emergency* and always have to expect changes: to lead a *provisional existence perpetually*.

10[D61]

One step further in the sense for reality and it suppresses the adventurous sense, the flight into the open, it seems unpermitted to make claims on the basis of so little knowledge, of such weak analogies, and then to speculate on the basis of these claims. The spontaneous superior force moves under the yoke of precautions, gathering of material, skepticism in the evaluation of the individual pieces of material. Thus — intellectual immorality is *necessary* up to some undefinable degree.

10[D62]

In Milton and Luther, where music belongs to life, the flawed fanatical development of the intellect and the lack of restraint in the hating and shouting is perhaps also brought about by the lack of discipline in music.

10[D63]

To what extent the acting person is *reckless* with himself? —

The intellect that ponders in advance the third fourth fifth consequence of a deed must nevertheless stop somewhere and act on the basis of uncertainties i.e., with the feeling of incomplete insight into the consequences still to act as though he were certain with respect to the consequences: to risk with the mien of resolve and absolute insight, i.e., to play-act or to deceive oneself, to silence one's intellectual conscience.

10[D64]

The *unjust* ground in the most noble, e.g., in Christ

10[65]

The *collected* moral qualities in every human in varying proportions: they are names for *unknown constitutive* proportions of *physical factors*.

10[D66][34]

Necessity to release a growing, *inflating* state of excitation through an *emptying* state of excitation (taking out one's rage, thoughts of vengeance etc.). Example: The person with a headache who has a loud party nearby and, finally, because the pain is so great, focuses his thoughts on an enemy and in his mind does him harm: or even strikes himself with his fists. Here something *immoral* is the *physically necessary* remedy against insanity: an example of how *immoral* actions have the value of *health factors*.

10[D67]

Object and subject — flawed opposition — no point of departure for thinking! We let ourselves be seduced by language.

10[D68][35]

Jean Gerson: "God does not want certain actions because they are good, rather they are good because he wants them, just as others are evil because he forbids them." The Jesuit⟨s⟩

10[D69][36]

The purpose of the action and the purpose of the acting person are to be distinguished.

10[D70]

Escobar:[37] "In truth, when I think about the disparity of the moral feeling, then I think it is a fortunate effect (*effet*) of providence, for the disparity of opinion helps us to *bear* the yoke of the Lord *more agreeably*."

10[D71]

The best and most spiritual human has removed the *crude* insulting *sight* of the deceiving and willfully self-affirming human (at the expense of others) from his eyes; he has retreated into such fine and nebulous spheres where that element *appears* angel-like. He is the subtlest of the unjust, he has understood how to maintain an *appearance contrary to his injustice.*

10[D72]

99 parts of all "creating" is imitation, in sounds or thoughts. Theft, more or less consciously.

10[D73]

Be ten times cold and unfriendly toward someone, finally it is your law, your daily quantum.

10[D74][38]

The excessive use of music and liquor, through which the intellectual powers of a people suffer, whereas its[39] affects increase — so that, according to most reliable tables, the Germans exceed all p⟨eoples⟩ in suicides, namely in proportion to the cleansing of the race.

10[D75]

We have entered the age of *diplomatic artistry*. Nobody believes anymore in a promise, in a thorough investigation of crises, in a lasting, unchanged state of power relations; one improvises and works with dissimulated preference for now this, now that opinion or party. The end no longer hallows the unholy means, but one forgets very quickly.

10[D76]

We can perceive our "mental activity" altogether as the *effect* objects *have upon us*. Cognition is *not* the activity of the subject, but only seems to be; it is a change of the nerves, brought about by *other things*. Only by bringing along the deception of the *will* and saying "I know" in the sense of "I want to know and consequently I do it," do we turn the matter around and see in the *passivum* the *activum*. But even the expression passive-active is dangerous!

10[D77]

Those forms of cognition are products of the effects of other things upon us. We furnish all things with them, because all things have furnished us with them. Our activity is seemingly productive.

10[D78]

How small the sphere of idealism is among young men! They think so slightly of company honor promotion influence. Indeed, they are more banal in *everything* because their energy and their drive is *used up* for any little domain. And how they disappoint when the gaze of the other falls *upon it*!

10[D79]

The supplementation (e.g., when we believe we see the movement of a bird as movement), the immediate *poetic completion* already begins with sensory perception. We always formulate *complete* humans from that which we see and know of them. We do not tolerate the *void* — this is the impertinence of our imagination: how little is it bound and accustomed to truth! We do *not* content ourselves for a moment with the known (or knowable!). The *playful processing of the material* is our ceaseless basic activity, thus exercise of the imagination. One may consider as proof for how powerful this activity is the play of the optic nerve when the eye is closed. We read and listen in the same way. *Precise* listening and seeing is a very high level of culture — we are still far from it. As yet we do not feel the *lying* in it at all! This spontaneous play of fantasizing force is the basic life of our mind: the thoughts *appear* to us; whereas *becoming aware*, the reflection of the process in the process is only the relative *exception* — perhaps a refraction at the contrast.

10[D80][40]

Zechariah 9, 9. J⟨esus⟩ shall enter on the pack ass and the foal of an ass.[41] The former — they are the Jews who believe in him; they have borne the yoke of the law. The foal are the heathens who lived lawlessly: but Christ put upon them the harness of his words; then they lay down willingly and let themselves be laden with everything he wanted.

The Last Supper (eucharistic meal). The sacrifice of the wheat flour cake was ordered for those who wanted to cleanse themselves of leprosy.

10[D81][42]

The struggle for the interpretation of the Old Testament: according to the Alexandrian method it was interpreted entirely as *a book of Christian doctrine*.

In conflict with the Jews who interpreted the messianic passages differently. Justin mocks their exegetical acrobatics.

10[D82]

A world without subject — is it thinkable? But let us imagine[43] now all life suddenly annihilated, why could everything else not continue to move calmly and be exactly as we see it now? I do not mean that it would be that way, but I do not see why one could not imagine it. Supposing colors are subjective — *nothing* tells us that they could *be thought objective*. The possibility that the world resembles the one that appears to us is not eliminated by recognizing the subjective factors.

To think the subject away — that means wanting to represent the world without subject: it is a contradiction: to represent without representation! Perhaps there are one hundred thousand subjective representations. To think our human representations away — then that of the ant remains. And if one thought all life away and only the ant left over: would existence really depend upon it? Yes, *the value of existence* depends on sentient beings. And for human beings existence and valuable existence is often one and the same.

10[D83]

The human ultimately discovers *not* the world but his organs of touch and feelers and their laws — but is their existence not already sufficient proof of reality? I think the mirror *proves* the things.

10[D84]

They take the easy way out and seek to understand me from the transition to the other extreme — they do not notice anything of the continuous struggle and the occasional blissful pauses in the struggle, do not realize that these earlier writings originated from such rapturous silences where the struggle seemed finished and where one already began to reflect about it and to calm down. It was a delusion. The struggle continued. The extreme language betrays the commotion that raged just before and the violence with which one sought to hold onto the delusion.

10[D85]

The *highest* value of fantasizing thought (which some apparently call right away productive thought) is to think up possibilities and to practice their mechanisms of feeling which later can be used as tools for the exploration of real being. This latter must first be fathomed, as it were, through all kinds of experiments and be discovered as the quarry of accident. All *mechanisms* in the great task of rigorous research have at first been posited and practiced as "the truth" itself. In this respect poets and metaphysicians are still always highly desirable; they search for the *possible* world and find here and there something usable. They are also test stations. Blind animals that continuously grope around and try to forage, *discover* foods (but also perish more easily or degenerate). Other animals live off the *accepted* foods.

10[D86][44]

On the part of the heathen-Christians one had absolutely no understanding for Israel's privileges and for Old Testament institutions.

10[D87]

NB Continuation of the freest cognition and life with *provisional* character!

10[D88][45]

19th century, Reaction: one sought the *fundamental principles* of all that had *persisted* and sought to prove it as *true*. Persistence, fertility, and good conscience counted as *indicium*[46] of truth! This the conservative attitude: it collected everything that was not yet shattered, it had the egoism of the property-owning class as the strongest objection to the philosophy of the 18th century: for those without property and the discontented one *still* had the Church, probably also the arts (for the few very gifted also the veneration of genius as thanks when they worked for conservative interests). With *history* (new!!!) they *proved*, they *enthused* for the great productive complexes (*nations*!!!) called cultures. They cast an immense *part* of the *enthusiasm for research* and likewise of the *sense for veneration* onto the past: the newer philosophy and natural science *forfeited* this *part*! — — Now a new **backlash**! History *in the end* proved something else than they wanted: it proved to be the *safest* means of annihilation of those principles. Darwin. On the other hand, skeptical historicism as aftereffect, the aftertaste. One came to know *better* the *motive* forces in history, not just "beautiful" ideas! Socialism grounds itself *historically*, likewise the national wars from history!

10[E89]

To act and think like many, all, gives a feeling of power. "Like no one else" — is a sign of the f⟨eeling⟩ o⟨f⟩ p⟨ower⟩. — Moral prescriptions are stopgaps for the indiv⟨iduals⟩ who cannot recognize themselves as strictly individual and must have a norm external to themselves.

10[E90]

Duty a constraint where our ind⟨ividuality⟩ *partly* comes up *short*, *partly* approves.

10[E91]

It is not necessary to love animals *in order* to hate humans. Like Schopenhauer. One may think of Voltaire, the first to —

10[E92]

W⟨agner⟩ the first in our times who aspires to high goals out of the *unification* of the arts. He began the experimentation in this domain.

10[E93]

Our sensory world does not truly exist; it contradicts itself: it is a delusion of the senses. But what then are the senses? The causes of the deception must be real. But we know of the senses only through the senses, and this would belong therefore within the world of delusion. Thus, something *deludes that we do not know*, and its first delusion is the senses. Our multiplicity is part of this: but how could we, delusive images, arrive at knowledge about the delusion? How could a dream image know that it belongs to the dream? — Consequently, we also must be *that which deludes*: i.e., *we* must also be real, not as individuals, but as unity behind the many, and so our consciousness must stem from the fact that the world is a delusion, purely logically thought: *we ourselves are* this somehow. But how can the true, the truthful be the cause of a delusive world? — It must *need* it: perhaps the true is anguished like an artist and seeks redemption in pleasurable representations and images,[47] a subtraction — truth is perhaps the *pain* and semblance is a solace, change is the turning from one side to the other of the gravely suffering being who seeks a better position. Perhaps though the true is *full of desire* and overflows in fantasies like an artist (*Birth of Tragedy*). The world an aesthetic phenomenon,[48] a series of states in the cognizant subject: a phantasmagoria according to the law of causality. That the intellectual process first emerges in the animal realm and without animals no world could exist also belongs in that drama that the subject plays for itself: it is a delusion. History is a supposition — nothing more; causality the means to dream *deeply*, the trick to deceive oneself about the illusion, the finest apparatus of the artistic deception.

10[E94]

The topsy-turvy world: breeding ground of fanaticism.

To live and act as a matter of habit in unbelief, like the Christian — but in single moments to condemn one's life and oneself — this curse-worthy state, in which life is not allowed to be good, so that the fantasy of a few strange minutes may *seem* to disclose the meaning of existence! We want no longer to tolerate in philosophy this way of thinking that recognizes the judge and prosecutor of existence in the little or great madness, and to balk against its[49] living on sheltered under the veil of art. — Are we here without tolerance? Newly fanatical? — One should first see what we want to do: nothing more and nothing further than to *bother* no more with the *topsy-turvy world*.[50]

10[E95]

The *world* as far as we can recognize it is our own nerve activity, nothing more.

10[E96]

The other religions are against the real evils, Christianity against the moral evils (in part imaginary ones)

10[F97]

Fatigue has an advantage for the thinker: it allows to run ahead even those thoughts that otherwise, with more composure and hence more dissimulation, we would not admit. We become careless about deceiving ourselves, and lo! here the truth comes over us.

10[F98]

Amor and Psyche.[51] — When the eye looks all too impertinently into the pleasure of the senses, then the pleasure is very quickly something disgusting. One must understand, like the Greeks, how to mix in gods and fantasies and to veil the coarse eyes; one must be able to forget or at least never to mention much directly by name; the pleasure must steal up on the intellect when it is sleeping or dreaming.

10[F99]

"You are happy! Every time your character reaches its high tide, your intellect also reaches its." B: You are forgetting something!

10[F100]

The properties of a thing stimulate our *sensations* e.g., that it is gray, and the shape, the kind of movement, above all its existence as body and substance — everything is tied up with feelings of pleasure and displeasure and consequently with trust, affinity, desire to approach or fear, etc. The same thing can, by virtue of its various properties, attract and instill fear in us. — *That* its properties excite such feelings though, that is judgment — and this *judgment* presupposes experiences and belief in identity in the experiences. In the end, though, even the oldest experience again presupposes judgment, in other words *interpretation of a stimulus*, so that it is either pleasurable or painful. "Does this stimulus increase our strength or decrease it?" In short, a judgment is the source by which the feeling of strength emerges or decreases. — Thus, the effects of things are in the end pleasant or unpleasant, according to whether we believe they promote our strength or not. This *belief* though cannot in turn stem from experience, but would have to take — its origin from the emerging feeling of strength. One believes in strength *where one has the feeling of strength. Feeling of strength counts as proof of strength.* After this proof the sensation of stimulation changes into pleasure: — thus: All properties of a thing are in truth stimuli within us which partly increase the feeling of strength, partly decrease it: each thing is a sum of judgments (fears, hopes, some of it instills trust, something else not). The more we now know physics, the *less fantastic* this sum of judgments becomes (the false subsumptions fall away, e.g., everything that is black is dangerous.) — In the end we grasp: a thing is a sum of stimulations in us: *but since we are nothing solid, a thing is also not a solid sum.* And the more we know how to impute solidity to things, — — —

10[F101]

As proof that a skeptic occasionally needs exuberant enthusiasms in order then to return again to the land of the "maybe-and-also-maybe-not": I want to relate what sentences my swarming[52] doves brought home to me from the clouds. First: the most common form of knowledge is that without awareness. Awareness is knowledge of a knowing. Feeling and awareness have everything essential in common and may be identical. The first emergence of a feeling is the emergence of knowledge about a knowing: a process that contains nothing difficult and mysterious, as it gives to knowledge only a change of direction — and for this, accidental occasions suffice that one perhaps can guess. Before there was a feeling, there was for a long time — namely always — knowledge: recognizing and inferring as its functions. Knowledge is the property of all driving forces — it amounts to the same to say it is the property of matter, provided one knows what matter is: the driving force thought of as a prejudice of our senses: so that force and matter are one, either defined as an "as such" or, in keeping with the relation to our senses, defined as the limit of our feeling for force. The driving forces are nothing final and resistant to analysis in principle, as Schopenhauer believed, who understood them as the "will": within them we can still distinguish knowledge conceptually as their property: without recognition and inference there is no drive, no driving and willing. The intellect (and not the feeling) is innate to "the essence of things;" feeling is an accident in the history of its orientations and in itself nothing new. In order to understand the first laws of mechanics, one must attribute recognition and inference to the driving forces — but no awareness of them, no feeling. But recognition and inference presuppose multiplicity yet identity of forces, or at least duality. Error in recognizing and inferring has only been possible since there has been feeling. — So! Now fly back, you doves, and give to your clouds what is theirs!

Reference Matter

Notes

The following symbols are used throughout the text and notes:

[ ]	Deletion by Nietzsche
| |	Addition by Nietzsche
{ }	Addition by the translator or editors
⟨ ⟩	Addition by the editors (Colli and Montinari)
[?]	Unsure reading
[+++]	Gap in the manuscript
— — —	Unfinished or incomplete sentence or thought
Italics	Underlined once by Nietzsche
Bold	Underlined twice or more by Nietzsche
NL	Books in Nietzsche's personal library

Variants and editions of Nietzsche's works are referred to by the following abbreviations:

CW	*The Complete Works of Friedrich Nietzsche*
KGB	*Briefwechsel: Kritische Gesamtausgabe*
KGW	*Kritische Gesamtausgabe*
KSA	*Kritische Studienausgabe*
Cp	Correction in the proofs
Fe	First edition
Fe[2]	First printing of the 1887 second edition of *JS*

Le	Twenty-volume 1894 Leipzig edition of Nietzsche's works (*Großoktav-Ausgabe*)
Le[2]	*Großoktav-Ausgabe*, second edition (1897, edited by Fritz Koegel)
Ms	Manuscript
Pd	Preliminary draft
Pm	Printer's manuscript (clean final copy of handwritten MS)
PmG	Change made by Gast in the printer's manuscript
PmN	Change made by Nietzsche in the printer's manuscript
Pp	Page proofs
Sd	Second draft
Se	Subsequent emendation
Up	Uncorrected proofs

Titles of Nietzsche's works are referred to by the following abbreviations:

AC	*The Antichrist*
BGE	*Beyond Good and Evil*
BT	*The Birth of Tragedy*
D	*Dawn*
DD	*Dionysus Dithyrambs*
DS	*David Strauss the Confessor and the Writer*
EH	*Ecce Homo*
GM	*On the Genealogy of Morality*
HAH	*Human, All Too Human*
HL	*On the Utility and Liability of History for Life*
IM	*Idylls from Messina*
JS	*The Joyful Science*
JSA	*The Joyful Science, Appendix: Songs of Prince Vogelfrei*
JSP	*The Joyful Science, Prelude in German Rhymes*
MM	*Mixed Opinions and Maxims*

NCW	*Nietzsche Contra Wagner*
SE	*Schopenhauer as Educator*
TI	*Twilight of the Idols*
UO	*Unfashionable Observations*
WA	*The Case of Wagner*
WB	*Richard Wagner in Bayreuth*
WP	*The Will to Power*
WS	*The Wanderer and His Shadow*
Z	*Thus Spoke Zarathustra*

The editorial apparatus from *KSA* 14 has been supplemented with information drawn from *Kritische Gesamtausgabe*, Abteilung 5, Band 3: *Nachbericht zum ersten Band der fünften Abteilung. Morgenröthe*. Edited by Marie-Luise Haase. Compiled by Marie-Luise Haase and Michael Kohlenbach, in collaboration with Marco Brusotti, et al. De Gruyter, 2003.

In order to distinguish the Colli-Montinari editorial apparatus in *KSA* 14 from Nietzsche's variants and letters and from the translators' and editors' notes, when the source of the note is not clear, this volume follows the *KSA* convention of italicizing Colli's and Montinari's editors' notes.

[1 = N V 1. Beginning of 1880]

1. *How . . . preserved?]* Cf. 3[171].

2. *nature peoples] Naturvölker* {This term, in contradistinction to *Kulturvölker* ("culture peoples"), was used by Johann Gottfried Herder, *Älteste Urkunde des Menschengeschlechts* ("The oldest original source of humanity") (Tübingen: Cotta, 1806), 1, 83.}

3. Reference is to Herbert Spencer, *Die Thatsachen der Ethik*, trans. Benjamin Vetter (Stuttgart{: Schweitbart,} 1879). *NL*. {Cf. *The Data of Ethics* (London: Williams and Norgate, 1879), 29: "The satisfactions which ferocious gods were supposed to feel in contemplating tortures, has been, in large measure, transformed into the satisfaction felt by a deity in contemplating that self-infliction of pain which is held to further eventual happiness. . . . [S]upposing

that from the savage who immolates victims to a cannibal god, there are descendants among the civilized, who hold that mankind were made for suffering, and that it is their duty to continue living in misery for the delight of their maker, we can only recognize the fact that devil-worshippers are not yet extinct."} Cf. 1[17, 105].

4. Cf. *D* 397.

5. Cf. 1[58, 109].

6. Cf. 1[11, 105].

7. {Cf. Spencer, *The Data of Ethics*, p. 40: "It is curious to see how the devil-worship of the savage, surviving in various disguises among the civilized, and leaving as one of its products that asceticism which in many forms and degrees still prevails widely, is to be found influencing in marked ways, men who have apparently emancipated themselves, not only from primitive superstitions but from more developed superstitions."}

8. Not finished.

9. Cf. 2[35, 39]; 4[128].

10. Allusion to Richard Wagner.

11. *saplings] Trieben* {N plays here on the multiple meanings of *Trieb*: "drive," "sapling," "shoot."}

12. {Cf. Johann Julius Baumann, *Handbuch der Moral nebst Abriss der Rechtsphilosophie* ("Manual of moral philosophy together with a summary of the philosophy of law") (Leipzig: S. Hirzel, 1879), 40. *NL*. N drew frequently from Baumann's *Handbuch* in this notebook's entries. Subsequent references will be cited as "Baumann" followed by the page number.}

13. {Cf. e.g., Baumann, 5–6.}

14. *yet it . . . motion]* {Cf. Baumann, 7: "*gerade wie bei den Thieren; nach dem Schlaf, nach der Ruhe, nach dem Essen wollen sie sich tummeln und das, womit sie es thun, ist nur die accessorische Determination*" ("just as with animals; after sleep, after rest, after eating they want to move about, and what prompts them to do it is only the accessory determination").}

15. Cf. 3[85].

16. Cf. 3[17].

17. Cf. 1[13, 109].

18. Cf. 1[80, 43].

19. *Strictly speaking, . . . effect.]* {Cf. Baumann, 9–10.}

20. *education and lack of education] Bildung und Unbildung* {German has three distinct words for education: *Ausbildung, Erziehung*, and *Bildung*, which correspond, approximately, to formal education, upbringing, and education in the comprehensive sense of formation.}

21. Cf. 3[38].

22. Cf. 3[63].

23. *"In the eyes lies the soul"] "In den Augen liegt die Seele"* {N's twist on the proverbial: "*Die Augen sind die Fenster der Seele*" ("The eyes are the windows of the soul"); also "*Die Augen sind die Spiegel der Seele*" ("The eyes are the mirrors of the soul").}

24. Cf. 1[61].

25. {Cf. *JS* 89.}

26. Cf. 3[121].

27. Cf. 1[103].

28. *bespoken by such narrow minds] Köpfe wahrlich nicht im Munde führen* {N's German is a variant of the idiom *Worte im Munde führen*, or "to speak publicly of a matter close to one's heart, mind, or purpose."}

29. Cf. 3[123].

30. *e.g., . . . bracelet]* {Cf. Stendhal, *Le Juif (Filippo Ebreo)*, in *Nouvelles inédites* (Paris: Michel Lévy Frères, 1855), 244: "*'Elle m'aura vu passer avec ma cassette remplie de bijoux d'or, pensai-je; elle veut que je lui fasse cadeau d'un de mes colliers, et, parbleu! c'est ce que je ne ferai pas.' Je m'imposai de ne plus passer dans cette rue; mais, malgré moi et presque sans me l'avouer, je me mis à ne plus boire de vin, et chaque jour je faisais* bourse à part *de cette économie. . . . Quand j'eus économisé douze francs, c'était le prix de mes colliers d'or les plus communs, je passai plusieurs fois dans la rue de Stella. Enfin, je la rencontrai; . . . Dans la conversation, je lui dis que depuis trois mois je me privais de vin pour économiser la valeur d'un de mes colliers, et pouvoir le lui offrir.*" ("'She will have seen me pass by with my coffer full of gold jewelry, I thought; she wants me to make her a gift of one of my necklaces and, by God!, that's what I shall not do.' I made a point to myself of no longer passing through this street; but in spite of myself and almost without admitting

it I began drinking no more wine and every day put *something aside* from these savings. . . . When I had saved up twelve francs, which was the price of my most common gold necklaces, I passed several times through Stella's street. I finally met up with her; . . . In the conversation I told her that I had gone without wine for three months in order to save up the cost of one of my necklaces and be able to offer it to her.")}

31. *diplomat] Written over*: liar

32. Cf. 1[16, 96].

33. {Cf. Baumann's remarks on *Übung* ("practice"), 17–18, 27ff.}

34. Cf. 1[84].

35. *Spencer p. 52]* Spencer, *Die Thatsachen der Ethik* {*The Data of Ethics*, 48: "We hear with surprise of the savage who, falling down a precipice, ascribes the failure of his foothold to a malicious demon; and we smile at the kindred notion of the ancient Greek, that his death was prevented by a goddess who unfastened for him the thong of the helmet by which his enemy was dragging him. But daily, without surprise, we hear men who describe themselves as saved from shipwreck by 'divine interposition,' who speak of having 'providentially' missed a train which met with a fatal disaster, and who call it a 'mercy' to have escaped injury from a falling chimney-pot — men who, in such cases, recognize physical causation no more than do the uncivilized or semi-civilized. The Veddah who thinks that failure to hit an animal with his arrow resulted from inadequate invocation of an ancestral spirit, and the Christian priest who says prayers over a sick man in the expectation that the course of his disease will so be stayed, differ only in respect of the agent from whom they expect supernatural aid and the phenomena to be altered by him: the necessary relations among causes and effects are tacitly ignored by the last as much as by the first."}; cf. 1[11].

36. {Georg Gustav Roskoff, *Das Religionswesen der rohesten Naturvölker* ("The essence of religion among the primitive nature peoples") (Leipzig: Brockhaus, 1880.)}

37. *Spencer]* Spencer, *Die Thatsachen der Ethik*, 53. {*The Data of Ethics*, 49: "Why do I here make these reflections on what seems an irrelevant subject? I do it because on studying the various ethical theories, I am struck with the fact that they are all characterized

either by entire absence of the idea of causation, or by inadequate presence of it. Whether theological, political, intuitional, or utilitarian, they all display, if not in the same degree, still, each in a large degree, the defects which result from this lack."}

38. Cf. 1[13, 58].

39. *species-being] Gattungswesen* {*Gattungswesen* is a concept treated at length by Ludwig Feuerbach in *The Essence of Christianity*, where he develops the contrast between individuality and species-being. It was later adopted by Marx.}

40. Cf. 3[85].

41. {Cf. Baumann, 172: "*Eine Haupthülfe für das Gedächtniss ist die Stimmung in sich zu erzeugen, welche gewöhnlich mit der Sache, um die es sich handelt, verbunden war . . .*" ("A principal aid for memory is to engender in oneself the mood usually linked with the matter in question . . .").}

42. *Whoever acts . . . superstitious]* {N's German phrase in the first two statements is identical: *Wer so thut*, translated as "Whoever acts so" and "Whoever pretends." The phrase has, according to use, either the meaning of "to act in a certain way" or "to act as if." N's repetition exploits the phrase's double meaning.}

43. {Cf. Baumann's theory of will and action, 38–43.}

44. *We always . . . us.]* {Cf. Baumann, 12: "*es hat zunächst ein mannichfaches Tasten und Tappen statt, aus dem sich allmälich eine Art als die werthvollste oder als die in diesem Individuum bleibende absetzt*" ("at first a manifold groping and feeling takes place, out of which one kind gradually sets itself off as the most valuable or in this individual as the most lasting").}

[2 = N V 2. Spring 1880]

1. Cf. 2[54].

2. Cf. 2[52]; 3[14].

3. *St{uart} Mill (Comte)]* Cf. John Stuart Mill, *Auguste Comte und der Positivismus* {trans. Elise Gomperz,} Vol. IX in *John Stuart Mill's Gesammelte Werke in 12 Bänden* {*Collected Works in 12 volumes*}, ed. Theodor Gomperz (Leipzig{: Fues,} 1874){, 64–65}. *NL.* {English original: *Auguste Comte and Positivism* (London: Trübner & Co., 1865), 91–92.}

4. Cf. 3[131].
5. Cf. *D* 141.
6. {Allusion to Richard Wagner.}
7. *barcarole]* {A song traditionally sung by Venetian gondoliers.}
8. Cf. 1[24]; 2[39]; 3[16]; 4[128].
9. Cf. 3[153].
10. Cf. 1[24]; 2[35]; 3[16]; 4[128].
11. *the gods . . . ascetics]* {Cf. N to Paul Rée, 28 May 1880, *KGB* III:1, 21.}
12. Cf. 2[6]; 3[14].
13. Cf. 3[8].
14. *want . . . devil] From*: are presumptuous because they were long depressed (secretaries of eminent gentlemen).
15. Cf. *D* 159.
16. *organized onto] anorganisirt* {A literal translation of N's neologism.}
17. Cf. 3[17].
18. *faut⟨e⟩-de-mieux-man]* "for lack-of-better-man"

[3 = M II 1. Spring 1880]

1. *L'Ombra]* "shadow" in Italian; but in Venice also "a glass of wine."
2. *these . . . treatment] Pd*: would have with difficulty read said writings through to the end, had acquaintance with the author not led me this far. They likewise have that cult of the inverted world, which is not less an emblem of fanaticism and that I would so describe. The fanat⟨ic⟩ ordinarily lives in a completely different belief and with completely different strivings, often the most honorable: but then come minutes breathing enchantment and fright, where he — — — Cf. 10[E94].
3. *a greater . . . qualities] Pd*: artistically more favorable
4. Cf. 2[59]; *D* 291.
5. *presumptuousness . . . confused] Pd*: the hypocrisy of the absence of pretense very interesting
6. Cf. *D* 550.
7. *To this extent . . . for]* {Cf. Herbert Spencer, *Die Thatsachen der Ethik*, trans. Benjamin Vetter (Stuttgart: Schweitbart, 1879),

179. *NL*. English original: *The Data of Ethics* (London: Williams and Norgate, 1879), 163: "And Aristotle, like Plato, comes to the remarkable conclusion that the pleasures of the intellect . . ."}

8. *humans] From*: we

9. Cf. *D* 312.

10. Cf. 2[6, 52].

11. Cf. 1[24, 35, 39], 4[128].

12. Cf. 1[57], 2[73].

13. Cf. *D* 145.

14. *or of an emptiness . . . word] Pd*: . We always remain *in ourselves*. (As with pollu⟨tion⟩)

15. *Pd at the end*: we are on the open sea

16. *witty . . . rich-in-spirit . . . poor-in-spirit] Geistreichen . . . Reichen des Geistes . . . Geistig-Armen* {N's word play refers to the first of the Beatitudes from the Sermon on the Mount, Matthew 5:3: "Blessed are the poor in spirit for theirs is the kingdom." In Luther's translation: "*Selig sind, die da geistlich arm sind, denn das Himmelreich ist ihr.*"}

17. *phrase] Pd*: joke

18. *But would . . . breached?]* {Cf. Arthur Schopenhauer, *Die Welt als Wille und Vorstellung*, Vol. 1, ed. Julius Frauenstädt (Leipzig: F. A. Brockhaus, 1873), 442–43. *NL*; *The World as Will and Representation, Volume 1*, trans. Judith Norman, Alistair Welchman, and Christopher Janaway (Cambridge: Cambridge University Press, 2010), 401–2.}

19. Cf. *D* 104.

20. {Allusion to Richard Wagner.}

21. *musician] Musiker* {N uses the word in its older comprehensive meaning, which includes both musician and composer.}

22. *namely . . . cognition] Pd*: (e.g., like the art enthusiasts)

23. Cf. *D* 133.

24. {Cf. N to Heinrich Köselitz, 20 August 1880, *KGB* III:1, 36–37.}

25. *Perhaps human compassion . . . mimicking.]* {Cf. Baumann, *Handbuch der Moral*, 124: "*Mitleid heisst das Wehe Anderer nachfühlen, es fällt also unter den Begriff, Anderer Zustände nachbilden, dieses ist aber eine Art der Nachahmung, welche ein ganz allgemeiner menschlicher Zug ist.*" ("Compassion means feeling the woe of

others, so it falls under the concept of imitating the conditions of others, but this is a kind of imitation, which is a very common human trait.")}

26. {Cf. *TI* "Sayings" 25.}

27. *fashion] Pd*: fashion of the court

28. Cf. 1[75], 3[70].

29. *that marriage . . . other.]* {Cf. Hans Martensen, *Die Christliche Ethik* ("Christian ethics"), Vol. 1 (Gotha: Besser, 1873), 506–7.}

30. *once . . . never]* {N is playing on the German phrase "*einmal ist keinmal*," "once is never."}

31. *One should . . . genius] Pd*: People almost always ruin their character in the company of a genius and acquire fantasized slave souls

32. Cf. *D* 141.

33. *affords . . . muscles] Pd*: promotes the calming of nerves and muscles, which entails reasonableness in contrast to affect

34. *quia absurdus est]* "because he is absurd" {Ordinarily "*credo quia absurdum est*," "I believe because it is absurd." Voltaire's modification of Tertullian.}

35. *Pd at the end*: if a saint of the old stamp were to appear today, he would appear very indifferent or comical to everyone, and especially to the jealous worshipers of holiness

36. *have a clear . . . ahead] Pd*: to come to insight into the essence

37. *concealed, . . . strict] Pd*: to subdue, to exhibit much goodwill — this way of life would be too strict for our comfortable humans: they are the wives and children of a capable soldiery — and austere country gentry

38. Cf. *BGE* 149.

39. Cf. *D* 210.

40. *it is . . . sin.]* {Cf. Alexandre Rodolphe Vinet, *Études sur Blaise Pascal* ("Studies on Blaise Pascal") (Paris: Ducloux, 1848), 252; cited by Martensen, *Die Christliche Ethik*, 236.}

41. *enduringly . . . it] Pd*: founded to endure, so that only middling minds are required to maintain it

42. Cf. *BGE* 219.

43. Cf. *D* 11.

44. *Pd at the end*: (e.g., honor father and mother that you prosper and live a long life on earth — the latter as divine consequence)

45. *teaching, perhaps] Pd*: become. — Through what assumption could he be praised more than happened here? — Perhaps.

46. *perhaps then . . . often.]* Cf. *Z* IV "On Superior Humans," 16. {Cf. William Edward Hartpole Lecky, *Geschichte des Ursprungs und Einflusses der Aufklärung Europa*, trans. H. Jolowicz, 2nd ed., Vol. 1 (Leipzig and Heidelberg: C. F. Winter, 1873), 183 note. *NL*: "*Niemand hat ihn ⟨Jesus⟩ je lachen sehen, sondern vielmehr weinen.*" English original: *History of the Rise and Influence of the Spirit of Rationalism in Europe*, 2nd ed. (London: Longmans, Green, and Co., 1865), 258 note: "No one had ever seen Him laugh, but rather weeping." Cf. also Martensen, *Die Christliche Ethik*, 236 note: "*Woher kommt's, daß wir in unsern evangelischen Berichten nirgends finden, daß der Erlöser der Welt gelacht habe, während mehr als einmal von ihm berichtet wird: Jesus weinte?*" ("How is it that we nowhere find in our gospel accounts that the Redeemer of the world laughed, while more than once it is reported of him that Jesus wept?")}

47. Cf. *D* 42.

48. *pessimism . . . be] Pd*: discontent with existence. Christianity and pessimism.

49. *The truth . . . simple?]* {An allusion to the Latin proverb *simplex sigillum veri*, "simplicity is the seal of truth."}

50. Cf. *D* 5.

51. *Pd*: The spirit which h⟨umans⟩ apply for combating ills, they lack for the *discovery* of pleasure. Up to now humanity has managed every kind of means of consolation — at last science closes in on the monsters — and now we too must defend ourselves against the means of consolation, which have become a power in their own right: having needs and demanding satisfaction.

52. Cf. 1[54]. *Pd*: Love for property is [—] love for what we have produced. The *species-preserving drive of all hereditary properties the most securely transmitted* — which is the point of departure? The deception, by virtue ⟨of which⟩ some fish keep watch over their eggs — they see it as *food*, which they *keep* and *protect*. When things finally alter, the food is not to their taste — but the *habit* is planted, with the next eggs they take up the watch again. (S⟨ee⟩ previous.)

53. *that some . . . enemy.]* {Cf. Spencer, *Die Thatsachen der Ethik*, 16; *The Data of Ethics*, 16: "Where, as among certain fish, the male keeps guard over the eggs, driving away intruders, . . ."}

54. {Cf. Spencer, *Die Thatsachen der Ethik*, 264–65; *The Data of Ethics*, 245–46.}

55. *Pd at the end*: That is evident in the old *history* of humanity.

56. *"Struggle for existence"]* {In English in the text.}

57. *ius talionis]* "right of retaliation"

58. *slanderer] Ehrenräuber* {N uses the archaic word *Ehrenräuber*, lit. "honor-robber."}

59. *executed; . . . wars.] Pd*: become. But how does it happen that those who start a war are canonized?

60. *label] Pd*: mask

61. Cf. *D* 174.

62. *spread . . . an] Pd*: spread uniformly over everyone, a quiet little cloud over a silent enormous steppe, an

63. *correspond . . . humans] Pd*: correspond to humans and indeed with respect to the whole

64. *Pd at the end*: Their ethic sifted Christ one more time.

65. *superstition . . . belief]* {N plays here on the closeness of the German words for superstition, *Aberglaube*, and belief, *Glaube*.}

66. *Credat Judaeus Apella]* "Let the Jew Apella believe it" {Horace, *Satires*, 1.5.}

67. *com-passion] Mit-leid* {N hyphenates the word for emphasis.}

68. *Pd at the end*: among southern Italians a human life is considered frivolously.

69. *Pd*: In avoiding pain, one also avoids dangers: in this way much pleasure and excitement that earlier humans had goes out of mod⟨ern⟩ life. [Substitution:] Revolutions and wars are crude remedies.

70. *Excess of force . . . discharge)]* {Cf. Baumann, *Handbuch der Moral*, 6: "*der blosse Ueberschuss an Muskelkraft drängt zu irgendwelcher Entladung*" ("the sheer excess of muscle power urges any kind of discharge")}

71. *custom] Sitte* {The meaning of *Sitte* shifts and at times oscillates between "custom" and "morality" up to 3[132], where it stabilizes in the sense of "morality."}

72. *Deleted at the end*: Or rather, so perhaps one day it will be.

73. Cf. 1[83].

74. *Ideas by] Pd*: Ideas, the choice crown jewel of his inventions, by

75. *would be] Pd*: would be: he would perhaps have choked on it

76. *between heaven and earth]* After Shakespeare, *Hamlet* 1: 5{, 174}.

77. *many generations] Pd*: one human

78. Cf. 1[90].

79. *impossible. They] Pd*: impossible. The Jews have not taken the part of princes, rather of their God, and with savage heroism. They

80. Cf. 2[13].

81. *of Christianity] Pd*: of Jews and Christians (on this account the new Europe is darker than Greece)

82. *responsibility] Pd*: responsibility (developed with respect to a future *judgment*)

83. Cf. *D* 231, *GM* I 4.

84. *simple . . . bad]* {N plays here on the near homonymy of the German words for simple and bad, *schlicht* and *schlecht*.}

85. *Pd*: Our freethinking [—] to be viewed as an exaggerated one-sided *action*, no balance. Likewise artistic creativity, it throws artists out of their center. To conceal oneself — The solitaries' danger. To deny oneself — to forget oneself — all defects!

86. *followers latch as] Pd*: followers [dictate to him through their numbers the law of his further behavior and without him noticing it] latch as

87. *Pd at the end*: As we are sad, we do not want to do without the general sorrow of the world (Christians' pessimism).

88. Cf. *BGE* 41.

89. *Nature] Pd*: The lower body projects onto the brain, and the brain-image in turn onto the lower body. Nature

90. *Pd*: [will to life] The drive for self-preservation is a piece of mythology. There is no immediate instinctive fear of death. Derived first. We flee before pain, the unknown, etc. One still wants to *enjoy oneself* often, hence one wants to live. Will to life nothing immediate.

91. *forever] immerdar*

92. *così fan tutti]* "the way everyone does" {N is playing on the title of Mozart's opera, which uses the feminine *tutte* and refers specifically to the way every woman does.}

93. *education to originality . . . another's originality]* {The connection of education, imitation, and originality is an echo of Johann Joachim Winckelmann, *Reflections on the Imitation of Greek Works in Painting and Sculpture* (1755).}

94. Cf. 2[36].

95. *painted . . . wall]* {Cf. Daniel 5:1–31.}

96. *forbidding the silkworm]* Cf. Goethe, *Torquato Tasso* V: 2{, 3081–84}.

97. *feel humiliated. This] Pd*: feel humiliated: in this humility lies the distinguishing mark of Jewish morality (Christ understood this better than the Pharisees of his time). This

98. *life, the] Pd*: life: and the Jews, who created this idealism (and the models for its elucidation) are certainly not the idealists of life. The

99. *Pd*: What voluptuary philosophers have not fantasized about the happiness that is supposed to commence with the cessation of the sex drive!

100. Cf. *D* 388.

101. *a potiori and not a nihilo]* "according to potency and not according to nothing"

102. Cf. 1[4].

[4 = N V 3. Summer 1880]

1. Cf. *D* 150.

2. Cf. *D* 424.

3. *Lord Byron]* Cf. Lord Byron, *Vermischte Schriften, Briefwechsel und Lebensgeschichte* ("Miscellaneous works, correspondence and biography"), ed. Ernst Ortlepp (Stuttgart{: J. Scheible,} no date), 3:248. *NL*.

4. Cf. *D* 107.

5. Cf. *D* 107.

6. Cf. *D* 33.

7. Cf. 9[1].

8. Cf. 4[146].

9. Cf. *D* 235.

10. *Adam Bede]* {Reference to the novel *Adam Bede* by George Eliot (1859), in which the title character's fiancée, Hetty Sorrel, murders the child she had conceived by another lover.}

11. *many-sided . . . one-sided] vielartig . . . einartig* {A complex and untranslatable word-play on the noun *Art* ("kind," "species," "sort," but also "nature," "manner," "method") and the adjective *artig* ("well-behaved," "polite," "civil," "courteous").}

12. *Goethe bows . . . him.]* {Reference to Goethe's 1771 eulogy "Zum Schäkespears Tag" ("On Shakespeare's Day"), which contains the celebrated exclamation "*Natur, Natur! nichts so Natur als Schäkespears Menschen!*" ("nature, nature! nothing so much like nature as Shakespeare's people!").}

13. *Eroica]* {Ludwig van Beethoven's Symphony no. 3 in E flat major, Op. 55, 1803.}

14. Cf. Karl Semper, *Die natürlichen Existenzbedingungen der Thiere*, 2 vols. (Leipzig{: F. A. Brockhaus}, 1880), 1:97–98. *NL*. {English translation: *Animal Life as Affected by the Natural Conditions of Existence* (New York: Appleton & Co., 1881).}

15. Cf. *D* 197.

16. *Goethe . . . nature.]* {Cf. Johann Peter Eckermann, *Gespräche mit Goethe in den letzten Jahren seines Lebens* ("Conversations with Goethe in the final years of his life"), 3 January 1830 (Leipzig: F. A. Brockhaus, 1868), II:115.}

17. Cf. *D* 42.

18. Cf. *D* 550, 474.

19. Cf. *D* 440.

20. *vita contemplative . . . vita practica]* "contemplative life" . . . "practical life" {N contrasts the contemplative life with the practical life. The more familiar contrast is that between the contemplative and active lives (*vita contemplativa, vita activa*), a contrast N himself draws in *D* 41.}

21. Cf. *Z* IV "The Sorcerer" 1.

22. Cf. *D* 226.

23. *the . . . politeness]* Cf. J. J. Baumann, *Handbuch der Moral nebst Abriss der Rechtsphilosophie* ("Manual of moral philosophy together with a summary of the philosophy of law") (Leipzig{:

S. Hirzel}, 1879), 177–78. *NL.* {: "*Die chinesischen Cardinaltugenden sind: Weisheit, Gerechtigkeit, Humanität (Wohlwollen), Anstand (die gebührende Ehre erweisen). Der Anstand ist eine besondere Tugend, da die Chinesen sehr reizbar gegen Verletzungen oder Vernachlässigungen sind; daher ebenso wie die Japanesen sehr höflich* . . ." ["The Chinese cardinal virtues are: wisdom, justice, humanity (benevolence), propriety (to give due honor). Propriety is a special virtue, with respect to which the Chinese are very sensitive to its violation or neglect; wherefore just like the Japanese very polite . . ."].}

24. *The . . . parents]* Cf. Baumann, 161–62{: "*ist die chinesische Moral ganz auf die Liebe der Kinder zu den Eltern erbaut*" ["the Chinese morality is founded completely upon children's love for their parents"].}

25. *κρεῖττον τ᾽ἀγαθὸν ἀληθείας] kreitton t'agathon aletheias*; "the good [is] greater than the truth" {The Greek text may be an abbreviated quotation of these words from the Neoplatonic philosopher Proclus's commentary on Plato's *Republic*: τὸ γὰρ αὖ ἀγαθὸν κρεῖττόν ἐστιν τῆς ἀληθείας. Proclus, *In Platonis rem publicam commentarii.* I.115.26–116.24. N's glossing of "the good" ("*agathon*") as "the useful" is an interpretive translation.}

26. *κρεῖττον . . . the neo-Platonists]* {Cf. Baumann, 135.}

27. Cf. *D* 427.

28. Cf. *D* 88.

29. Cf. *D* 90.

30. *(Baum⟨ann⟩ . . . God.]* Cf. Baumann, 243; 4[52].

31. Cf. *D* 41.

32. Cf. *D* 88. {Cf. Johannes Janssen, *Geschichte des deutschen Volkes seit dem Ausgang des Mittelalters. II. Vom Beginn der politisch-kirchlichen Revolution zum Ausgang der socialen Revolution von 1525* ("History of the German people since the end of the Middle Ages, II. From the beginning of the political-ecclesiastical revolution to the end of the social revolution of 1525") (Freiburg: Herder, 1879), 70–71, 73–74.}

33. *he went . . . blacksmiths.]* {Cf. Baumann, 379, quoting Philipp Melanchthon in the "Apology of the Augsburg Confession": "*Das Mönchsleben ist um nichts mehr ein Stand der Vollkommenheit, als*

das Leben des Ackerbauers oder Schmiedes." ("The monk's life is no more a state of perfection than the life of the farmer or the smith.")}

34. *Just so . . . prophet!]* {Cf. Friedrich Schlegel, Athenäum Fragment 80: "*Der Historiker ist ein rückwärts gekehrter Prophet*" ("The historian is a backwards-facing prophet"). *Kritische Friedrich Schlegel Ausgabe*, ed. Ernst Behler with Jean-Jacques Anstett and Hans Eichner. (Munich and Paderborn: Verlag Ferdinand Schöning, 1967ff.), II:176.}

35. *Napoleon . . . Cabanis]* {Cf. Stendhal, *Correspondance inédite* (Paris: Michel Lévy Frères, 1855), I:236. *NL*.}

36. Cf. *D* 207.

37. *"I cannot do otherwise."]* {Allusion to the words traditionally ascribed to Martin Luther in his own defense to Emperor Charles V on April 17, 1521 at the Diet of Worms where he had been summoned to renounce his writings, teaching, and actions: "Here I stand and cannot do otherwise. So help me God. Amen."}

38. Cf. 10[A3]; *JS* 14.

39. Cf. 4[90].

40. *amour-passion . . . amour-physique]* "passionate love . . . physical love" Cf. Stendhal, *De l'amour* (*On Love*), Book One, Chapter One.

41. Cf. *D* 211.

42. Cf. *D* 197.

43. Cf. John Stuart Mill, *Gesammelte Werke*, Vol. X, ed. Theodor Gomperz {(Leipzig: Fues, 1874)}, 195; cf. also 212–16. *NL* {"Coleridge," in *The Collected Works of John Stuart Mill*, Vol. X, ed. J. M. Robson (Toronto: University of Toronto Press, 1969), 125: "Now the Germano-Coleridgean doctrine is, in our view of the matter, the result of such a reaction. It expresses the revolt of the human mind against the philosophy of the eighteenth century." Cf, also 138–41.}

44. Cf. 4[303].

45. Cf. 4[80].

46. Cf. *D* 122.

47. *"The eye . . . Semper]* {Cf. Semper, *Die natürlichen Existenzbedingungen der Thiere*, 1:122; *Animal Life*, 99.}

48. *"A color . . . Semper]* Cf. Semper, *Die natürlichen Existenzbedingungen der Thiere*, 2:229–32. {*Animal Life*, 385–88.}

49. Cf. Semper, *Die natürlichen Existenzbedingungen der Thiere*, 1:35. {*Animal Life*, 31.}

50. *Desensualization] Entsinnlichung* {The word echoes its near homonym *Entsittlichung*, or moral depravity.}

51. Cf. *D* 304.

52. *All extremely . . . Wotan)]* {Cf. Richard Wagner, *Gesammelte Schriften und Dichtungen* ("Collected writings and poetry"), Vol. 6 (Leipzig: E. W. Fritzsch, 1872), *Siegfried* III 1, 156–57.}

53. Cf. *D* 20.

54. *free-perpetrators] Freithäter* {A coinage N makes to parallel "freethinkers" [*Freidenker*].}

55. Cf. *D* 20.

56. *According to Aristotle]* {Cf. Aristotle, *Poetics*, 1449b24–28.}

57. *post hoc]* {Reference to the logical fallacy *post hoc, ergo propter hoc* ("after this, therefore because of this").}

58. {Cf. William Edward Hartpole Lecky, *Sittengeschichte Europas von Augustus bis auf Karl den Grossen*, trans. H. Jolowicz (Leipzig & Heidelberg: C. F. Winter, 1879), 1:141. *NL*. English original: *History of European Morals from Augustus to Charlemagne* (London: Longmans, Green, and Co., 1869), 1:164.}

59. *Καλόν] kalon*, "good," "beautiful"

60. *honestum]* "honorable"

61. *To revere . . . godhead]* {Cf. Baumann, 88–89, 254.}

62. {Cf. Prosper Mérimée's short story *Les âmes du Purgatoire* ("The souls of purgatory"), first published in the *Revue des Deux Mondes* 15 August 1834.}

63. Cf. 1[24], 2[35, 39].

64. {Cf. Baumann, 99: "*In Indien war das Ideal Contemplation, aber Vorstufe zu ihr ist die Bethätigung des Einzelnen nach den Vorschriften seiner Kaste*" ("In India the ideal was contemplation, but preparation for it is the individual's occupation according to the rules of his caste").}

65. {Cf. Baumann, 98: "*die Stoiker vollends kehrten gänzlich zu der Ansicht des Sokrates zurück: die Tugenden definirten sie als Wissenschaften, die Leidenschaften waren ihnen falsche Urtheile ganz*

und gar." ("the Stoics returned entirely to the view of Socrates: they defined the virtues as sciences, to them the passions were through and through false judgments.").}

66. Cf. Baumann, 99–101.

67. Cf. *D* 209. {Cf. Baumann, 103.}

68. Cf. *D* 125.

69. {Cf. Baumann, the chapter "*Das Geschlechtsleben*" ("Sex life"), esp. 270–71.}

70. *"That wants . . . opinions]* N is referring to the following passage from Stendhal, "*Lord Byron en Italie,*" in *Racine et Shakspeare* {[sic]. *Études sur le romantisme* ("Racine and Shakespeare: Studies of romanticism")} (Paris{: Michel Lévy Frères,} 1854), 267–68, *NL*: "*Monsignor de Brême rappela l'anecdote si connue de M. le général de Castries, qui, choqué de la considération avec laquelle on écoutait d'Alembert, s'écrie: Cela veut raisonner, et cela n'a pas mille écus de rente!*" {"Monsignor de Brême recalled the well-known anecdote of General de Castries, who, taken aback by the deference with which people listened to d'Alembert, exclaimed: It wants to reason but it doesn't have assets amounting to a thousand crowns!"}

71. Cf. *D* 33.

72. Cf. *D* 35.

73. *has become second nature] ins Blut übergehen* {N is using an idiomatic German expression (more commonly, "*in Fleisch und Blut übergehen*"), literally: "to pass over into flesh and blood," like a transfusion.}

74. Cf. 4[23].

75. Cf. *D* 483.

76. Cf. *D* 59.

77. {Cf. I John 1:1.}

78. Cf. *D* 114.

79. Cf. Hermann Lüdemann, *Die Anthropologie des Apostels Paulus und ihre Stellung innerhalb seiner Heilslehre: Nach den vier Hauptbriefen dargestellt* ("The anthropology of the Apostle Paul and its place in his doctrine of salvation: As represented in the four major letters") (Kiel{: Universitäts-Buchhandlung}, 1872){, 25}. (Hereafter Lüdemann.) As fruits of N's reading of this work, see in addition 4[158–64, 167, 170–72]. On N's reading of this

text, cf. the Chronicle of N's Life in *CW* 19 and Jörg Salaquarda, "*Dionysos gegen den Gekreuzigten. Nietzsches Verständnis des Apostels Paulus,*" in *Zeitschrift für Religions- und Geistesgeschichte* XXVI (1974): 97–124, esp. 101–2; {English translation: "Dionysus versus the Crucified One: Nietzsche's Understanding of the Apostle Paul," trans. Timothy F. Sellner, in *Studies in Nietzsche and the Judaeo-Christian Tradition*, ed. James C. O'Flaherty, Timothy F. Sellner, and Robert M. Helm (Chapel Hill: University of North Carolina Press, 1985), 100–29.} Cf. in addition *Nietzsche: Wege der Forschung*, Vol. 521 (Darmstadt{: Wissenschaftliche Buchgesellschaft,} 1980), 321–22, where the editor, Salaquarda, cites the as yet unpublished graduate study by Michael Jacob ("*Gott am Kreuz. Studien, Thesen und Texte zur Relation von metaphysischer Gottesrede und Leben Jesu bei Fr. Nietzsche*" ["God on the Cross: Studies, theses, and texts on the relation of metaphysical speaking of God and the life of Jesus in Nietzsche"], East Berlin, 1978) and reproduces Jacob's complete concordance, which has been used in the following for the completion of bibliographical references.

80. Cf. Lüdemann, 26–27, 33, 35n1.

81. Cf. Lüdemann, 35n4.

82. Cf. Lüdemann, 37 and 36 end of n2.

83. Cf. *D* 72; Lüdemann, 36–38 and 37n1.

84. Cf. Galatians 5:17, Romans 7:17–18; Lüdemann, 52, 69, {71–72,} 87.

85. *πν⟨εῦμα⟩] pneuma*, "spirit"

86. Cf. Lüdemann, 92–93.

87. Cf. Lüdemann, 106–48; the Pauline concepts mentioned here are mainly from the Letter to the Romans; cf. *D* 68.

88. *νοῦς] nous*, "mind"

89. *"The flesh . . . eliminated"]* {Cf. Lüdemann, 99.}

90. *Paul]* {Cf. Romans, 8:3: "he condemned sin in the flesh"}

91. *ἁμαρτία] hamartia*, "sin"

92. *πνεῦμα ἀν⟨θρώπου⟩] pneuma anthropou*, "spirit of the human being"

93. *παράβασις] parabasis*, "transgression"

94. *πνεῦμα Θεοῦ] pneuma theou*, "spirit of God"

95. *σάρξ] sarx*, "flesh"

96. *Therapeuts]* {Ancient monastic group of Egyptian Jews in Alexandria, described by Philo in *De vita contemplativa* ("On the Contemplative Life").}

97. *Essenes]* {Ascetic, pacifist Jewish mystical sect that flourished in Palestine from the second century BCE to the first century CE.}

98. *Ebionites]* {Ascetic sect of first centuries CE Jewish Christians.}

99. Cf. *D* 87.

100. Cf. *D* 66.

101. Cf. *D* 68; Lüdemann, 147.

102. *Sarx]* "flesh"

103. Cf. *D* 68. {Cf. Lüdemann, 73.}

104. *σάρξ]* {Cf. note 95.}

105. Cf. *D* 68.

106. *If through . . . it.]* {Cf. Lüdemann, 215.}

107. *The anti-divine . . . perishes]* {Cf. Lüdemann, 214.}

108. Cf. Lüdemann, 217.

109. *four main letters]* {Refers to the four main Pauline letters: Galatians, I and II Corinthians, and Romans.}

110. {Written in connection with N's reading of Jacob Wackernagel, *Über den Ursprung des Brahmanismus* ("On the origin of Brahmanism") (Basel: Schweighauserische Verlagsbuchhandlung, 1877). *NL.*}

111. {Written in connection with N's reading of Wackernagel.}

112. {Written in connection with N's reading of Wackernagel.}

113. *Dulce . . . locus.]* Cf. Horace, *Carmina* Book IV, Ode 12, v.28. {The complete sentence is, "*Misce stultitiam consiliis brevem: / Dulce est desipere in loco.*" ["Mix a little foolishness with your prudence: / It's good to be silly at the right time."] The phrase following the dash, "*Sed non hic locus*" ["But not this time"] is N's gloss. *Locus* in both has the temporal meaning of season, or time. Horace himself was adapting a piece of proverbial wisdom. Horace, *Odes and Epodes*, ed. and trans. Niall Rudd (Cambridge, MA: Harvard University Press, 2004), 252–53.}

114. {Written in connection with N's reading of Wackernagel.}

115. Cf. *D* 96.

116. Quotation from J. Wackernagel, *Über den Ursprung des Brahmanismus*, 28–29. {N changes the beginning of the

sentence. It reads: "*Nicht die Götter gelten als Geber der Gaben.*" ("The gods do not count as givers of gifts.")}

117. {N uses the word "order" here in the specific sense of a religious order, e.g., the Jesuit Order.}

118. {Cf. Moritz von Engelhardt, *Das Christenthum Justins des Märtyrers: Eine Untersuchung über die Anfänge der katholischen Glaubenslehre* ("Justin the Martyr's Christianity: An examination of the beginnings of Catholic doctrine") (Erlangen: Deichert, 1878), 136–37.}

119. {The quotations can be found in Engelhardt, *Das Christenthum Justins des Märtyrers*, 456 and 457n. The Cyprian quote can also be found in Lecky, *Sittengeschichte Europas von Augustus bis auf Karl den Grossen*, 1:370; *History of European Morals from Augustus to Charlemagne*, 1:452.}

120. *Cyprian]* {Cyprian authored the famous phrase "*extra ecclesiam nulla salus*," "outside the church there is no salvation."}

121. {Cf. Wackernagel, 14.}

122. Cf. *D* 188.

123. Cf. Alfred Espinas, *Die thierischen Gesellschaften* ("Animal societies"), trans. from the French {*Des sociétés animales* (Paris: Baillière, 1877)} by W. Schloesser (Braunschweig{: F. Vieweg und Sohn,} 1879), 150ff. *NL*.

124. *commensals] Commensalisten* {Unlike parasites, commensals live off but do not harm their hosts. The term was first introduced in 1876; cf. Pierre-Joseph van Beneden, *Les commensaux et les parasites dans le règne animal* ("Commensals and parasites in the animal kingdom") (Paris: Librairie Germer Baillière, 1875).}

125. *The so-called . . . nourishment.]* {Cf. Semper, II:161–62/*Animal Life*, 331.}

126. *Formerly free . . . organs.]* {Cf. Semper, II:181–82/*Animal Life*, 347.}

127. {Cf. Baumann, 127.}

128. {Written in connection with N's reading of Wackernagel.}

129. Cf. *D* 405.

130. Cf. *D* 6.

131. Cf. *D* 147.

132. *boastful posturing] in Schaum zerschlugen* {"empty boasting, posturing"; literally, "beaten into foam."}

133. Cf. Lüdemann, 13; Acts of the Apostles 2:4.

134. Cf. Lüdemann, 16–19; 4[293].

135. *νοῦς] nous*, "mind"

136. Cf. Lüdemann, 8, 9, 110, 168–69, 172, 183, 192, 190–91, 191; *D* 68.

137. Cf. I Corinthians 15:35–55.

138. Cf. I Corinthians 2:3–6.

139. *σάρξ]* {Cf. note 95.}

140. *πνεῦμα] pneuma*, "spirit"

141. *spiritual union] Einvergeistung* {N's coinage plays on "Einverleibung" ("incorporation," "annexation"), substituting "*Geist*" ("spirit") for "*Leib*" ("body").}

142. *"If justification . . . purpose."]* Galatians 2:21.

143. *ἁμαρτία] hamartia*, "sin"

144. Written in connection with N's reading of Lüdemann; cf. *D* 68.

145. *le . . . crime]* "bad taste leads to crime." {Cf. Prosper Mérimée, "*Notes et souvenirs*," in Stendhal, *Correspondance inédite. Précédée d'une introduction par Prosper Mérimée* (Paris: M. Lévy Frères, 1855), XXIII. *NL*: "*Il admirait beaucoup ce mot de M. de M . . . 'que le mauvais goût mène au crime.'*" ("He [Stendhal] greatly admired this word of Mr. de M [Baron Louis Adolphe de Mareste, a close friend of both Stendhal and Mérimée] 'that bad taste leads to crime.'")}

146. {Cf. Wackernagel, 26–27.}

147. {Ninon de Lenclos, a 17th-century woman of letters, was celebrated for her perfumed baths comprised of a liter of milk, two teaspoons of honey, and five handfuls of salt.}

148. *"field of calamity"]* Cf. *D* 77, notes 174 and 175, *CW* 5, 307. {The citation is from Empedocles; cf. *Empedocles: The Extant Fragments*, ed. M. R. Wright (New Haven: Yale University Press, 1981), 278.}

149. {A paraphrase of, rather than a verbatim quotation from, Ecclesiastes, or The Book of Qoheleth.}

150. Written in connection with N's reading of Lüdemann; cf. *D* 68.

151. *σάρξ]* {Cf. note 95.}

152. *it is as . . . me.]* {Cf. Baumann, 156.}

153. Cf. *D* 84.

154. {Written in connection with N's reading of Wackernagel.}

155. Cf. *D* 188.

156. Cf. *D* 366.

157. *Rakóczy March]* {A Hungarian march and unofficial state anthem used by Franz Liszt in his Hungarian Rhapsody No. 15, S. 244/15, in A minor (1853), and by Hector Berlioz in his *La damnation de Faust*, op. 24 (1846).}

158. Cf. *D* 176.

159. Cf. *D* 189.

160. Cf. *D* 189.

161. Cf. *JS* 236; *CW* 6, 12[112].

162. Cf. *D* 189.

163. Cf. *D* 188.

164. Cf. *D* 188.

165. Written in connection with N's reading of Lüdemann; cf. *D* 68.

166. *σάϱξ]* {Cf. note 95.}

167. Written in connection with N's reading of Lüdemann.

168. Written in connection with N's reading of Lüdemann; cf. *D* 68.

169. Written in connection with N's reading of Lüdemann; cf. *D* 68.

170. Written in connection with N's reading of Lüdemann; cf. *D* 68.

171. Cf. *D* 88.

172. *unvarnished truths] blutige Wahrheiten* {Literally: "bloody truths."}

173. {Cf. Baumann, 254.}

174. *ἀναγκαῖα] anankaia*, "necessities"

175. *bare necessities] Nothdurft* {Literally: "nature's call." N is using the word figuratively.}

176. *The work of art . . . life.]* {Cf. Stendhal, *Rome, Naples et Florence* (Paris: Michel Lévy Frères, 1854), 271, 300. *NL*.}

177. *as . . . said]* Cf. *WB* 4.

178. Cf. *D* 26.

179. Cf. *D* 309.

180. *At the end of the Ms following a long dash the crossed out word*: Yes

181. Cf. *D* 496, 542.

182. Cf. *D* 130.

183. *ἀνάγκη] ananke*, "necessity"

184. Cf. 4[218].

185. Cf. 4[316, 317], 6[3].

186. *The animals . . . like]* {Cf. Semper II; 228–29/*Animal Life*, 384–85.}

187. Cf. *D* 360.

188. Cf. *D* 360, 199.

189. *All Greeks . . . presupposed.]* {Cf. Plato, *Gorgias*, 492b–c.}

190. *All were . . . him.]* {Cf. Plato, *Gorgias*, 483a–484c.}

191. *ring of Gyges]* {Mythical, magical ring that allowed its wearer to become invisible. The source is Plato's *Republic* 359a–360d, which stands behind N's entire discussion in this entry.}

192. {Reference to *Hiero*, a dialogue by Xenophon (428–354 BCE) between Hiero I, tyrant of Syracuse, and Simonides in which the lots of the tyrant and the common citizen are compared. Hiero points to the difficulties the tyrant endures while Simonides argues that a tyrant, by ruling well, may make himself popular and enjoy happiness.}

193. Cf. John Stuart Mill, *Gesammelte Werke*, ed. Theodor Gomperz, vol XII, trans. Sigmund Freud. *NL*.

194. *The order . . . created.]* {Cf. N to Heinrich Köselitz, 30 March 1881, *KGB* III:1, 79.}

195. *lips] Ms*: love

196. Cf. *JS* 99.

197. *be a man . . . me]* Cf. Goethe's prefatory remarks to the second edition (1775) of *Werther*.

198. Cf. 5[5].

199. *Vademecum Vadetecum]* {*Vademecum*, "go with me," is a guide or manual, i.e., a book one always has at hand. *Vadetecum*, "go with you," is N's playful adaptation.}

200. Cf. 4[295, 317]; 6[3].

201. Cf. 4[295, 316]; 6[3].

202. Cf. *D* 52.

203. *dreams . . . rakes]* {Tannhäuser in Wagner's opera.}

204. *faithfulness . . . water]* {Senta in Wagner's *The Flying Dutchman.*}

205. *and the beloved . . . prince]* {Cf. Wagner's *Lohengrin* and *The Flying Dutchman.*}

206. *Hungarian Rhapsody II]* {Composition by Franz Liszt, S244/2, in C-sharp minor (1847), versions for piano as well as for orchestra, the second and best known of Liszt's set of 19 rhapsodies.}

[5 = Mp XV 1a. Summer 1880]

1. *He]* {Richard Wagner}

2. *he]* {Richard Wagner}

3. Cf. 4[309]. *Ms at bottom of page*: yes, good! good!

4. Cf. *D* 543.

5. {Allusion to Richard Wagner.}

6. *sacrificium . . . amorem]* "sacrifice of the mind out of love"

7. Cf. *D* 205.

8. *be right side up] gerade sein lassen* {N plays here on the colloquial expression *fünf gerade sein lassen*; literally, "to let five be even." In everyday language, its sense is "not to be too particular," or "to let a point be stretched."}

9. Cf. N to Heinrich Köselitz (= Peter Gast), 2 August 1880 {*KGB* III:1, 32–33}.

10. *correct feeling]* Cf. *WB* 5 {*CW* 2, 282}.

11. *mass]* Uncertain reading.

12. Cf. *D* 73.

13. *say] Ms*: something

14. Cf. *D* 192. {Cf. Hans Martensen, *Die Christliche Ethik* ("Christian ethics"), Vol. 1 (Gotha: Besser, 1873), §§108 and 109 for N's sources on Francis de Sales and Fénelon, respectively.}

15. *The "completion" . . . being]* {Cf. Plato, *Symposium*, 192e–93a.}

16. *At the end marks indicating a continuation; no continuation extant.*

17. Cf. *D* 449.

18. Cf. *D* 124; 5[47], 6[119].

19. *it is faith . . . happy and unhappy] es ist Glaube der selig und unselig macht* {N plays on the colloquial expression *wer's glaubt*

wird selig; literally, "whoever believes becomes blessed." In standard German the phrase's meaning is unequivocally ironic: "whoever believes this is naïve." The expression goes back to a Gospel verse: "The one who believes and is baptized will be saved" ("*Wer da glaubet und getauft wird, der wird selig*") (Mark 16:16).}

20. Cf. *D* 124; 5[43], 6[119].

[6 = N V 4. Autumn 1880]

1. {Written in connection with N's reading of Jacob Wackernagel, *Über den Ursprung des Brahmanismus* ("On the origin of Brahmanism") (Basel: Schweighauserische Verlagsbuchhandlung, 1877). *NL*.}

2. Cf. *D* 109.

3. *Lord Byron]* Lord Byron, *Vermischte Schriften, Briefwechsel und Lebensgeschichte* {"Miscellaneous works, correspondence and biography"}, ed. Ernst Ortlepp (Stuttgart{: J. Scheible,} no date), 2:31. *NL*.

4. Cf. 4[295, 316, 317].

5. Cf. Madame de Rémusat, *Mémoires 1802–1808*, 3 vols., ed. Paul de Rémusat (Paris{: Calmann Lévy,} 1880), II:246 {about General Anne-Jean-Marie-René Savary (1774–1833)}. *NL*. (Henceforth "Rémusat" followed by volume and page number.)

6. Cf. *D* 46.

7. *What a nice . . . head]* {An allusion to Montaigne's *Essais* ("Essays") (Paris: Chez Firmin Didot Frères, Fils et Cie., 1864), 562. *NL*: "*Oh! que c'est un doux et mol chevet, et sain, que l'ignorance et l'incuriosité, à reposer une teste bien faicte!*" ("Oh, what a sweet and soft and healthy pillow is ignorance and incuriosity, to rest a well-made head." *The Complete Essays of Montaigne*, trans. Donald M. Frame [Stanford: Stanford University Press, 1958], 822.) N also owned the 3-volume German translation of Montaigne's work: *Versuche, nebst des Verfassers Leben, nach der neuesten Ausgabe des Herrn Peter Coste, ins Deutsche übers* ("Essays, together with a biography of the author, based on the latest edition by Mr. Peter Coste, trans. into German") (Leipzig: Friedrich Lankischens Erben, 1753–54). Cf. *D* 46, n105, *CW* 5, 300.}

8. Cf. *D* 308.

9. Rémusat I:267.
10. Rémusat I:267–68.
11. *raisonnement]* "reasoning"
12. Rémusat I:268.
13. Rémusat II:247{about General Savary}.
14. Rémusat II:245, 242–43.
15. *he trusted . . . hand.]* {About Duroc, not about Savary.}
16. Rémusat I:271.
17. Rémusat II:241.
18. *market crying] Marktschreierei*
19. Rémusat I:273.
20. *"In France . . . an interest in persons."]* {A mistranslation of Rémusat's "*A Paris, et Paris c'est la France, l'on ne sait jamais prendre intérêt aux choses, si l'on n'en prend aux personnes,*" i.e., "In Paris, and Paris is France, you never know how to take an interest in things, if you don't take an interest in people."}
21. Rémusat I:274.
22. Rémusat I:392.
23. Rémusat I:393.
24. *bonhomme]* "good-natured fellow"
25. Rémusat I:384–85.
26. *Je réussirai!]* "I shall succeed"
27. Rémusat I:385.
28. Rémusat I:385–86.
29. Rémusat I:387.
30. Rémusat I:389.
31. *noblesse]* "nobility"
32. *modern] Le, Le^2*: tired
33. Rémusat I:395. Cf. *D* 251; 7[67, 284].
34. Rémusat I:402–3.
35. *least] Ms*: at the least
36. Rémusat I:407.
37. Rémusat I:408, 407.
38. Rémusat I:409; cf. Montaigne, *Essais* Book III, Chapter VII {476}.
39. *Vengeons . . . médire]* "We avenge ourselves by slandering it"
40. Rémusat I:409–10.

41. *I loved the man]* {Allusion to Richard Wagner.}

42. *how he shut . . . hatred]* {Cf. Goethe, *An den Mond* ("To the moon"): "*Selig, wer sich vor der Welt / Ohne Haß verschließt*" ("Blessed is he who shuts himself off from the world / Without hatred"). *Goethes Gedichte in zeitlicher Folge*, 2 vols., ed. Heinz Nicolai (Wiesbaden: Insel Verlag, 1958), I:217.}

43. *peoples] From*: Germans

44. *Ms at the end*: Better to turn! NB. I will love any artist who — — — and who now does not — — —

45. {Cf. Rémusat I:321.}

46. {Cf. Rémusat I:333–34.}

47. *"Pour être . . . causé"]* "To be a truly great man, one must really have improvised a portion of one's glory, displaying oneself above the event one has brought about." {Cf. Rémusat I:334.}

48. {Cf. Rémusat I:334.}

49. {Cf. Rémusat I:336.}

50. {Cf. Rémusat I:335.}

51. *odium generis humani]* "hatred for the human race"

52. {Cf. Rémusat I:271.}

53. {Cf. Rémusat I:273.}

54. Cf. *JS* 14.

55. Cf. 6[141, 145].

56. *The . . . semen]* Cf. J. J. Baumann, *Handbuch der Moral nebst Abriss der Rechtsphilosophie* ("Manual of moral philosophy together with a summary of the philosophy of law") (Leipzig{: S. Hirzel,} 1879), 270, 273–74.

57. *Up to now . . . Brahmins).]* {Written in connection with N's reading of Wackernagel.}

58. Cf. *D* 77.

59. {Cf. Rémusat II:378.}

60. Rémusat II:400.

61. *une privation . . . le talent]* "for happiness and even for talent an irremediable lack"

62. *tu]* "you"

63. *you] Du*; *from*: *tu*

64. *continuous production] Fortzeugung* {N's coinage, a play on *Fortsetzung*, or "continuation."}

65. *contradictio in adjecto]* "contradiction in terms"

66. Cf. *JS* 22.

67. {Cf. Jules Gabriel Janin, *Les petits bonheurs* ("Little pleasures") (Paris: Morizot, 1862), 231.}

68. Rémusat II:323.

69. After Emerson?

70. *attitude] Attitüde* {The "*attitüde*" emerged in France alongside the *tableau vivant* as a social diversion of the educated classes in the eighteenth century. The attitude is a lay actor's monodramatic pose, struck to resemble a famous classical sculpture, e.g., Niobe, or to invoke a tragic figure, e.g., Medea.}

71. Rémusat I:140–41 (on Joséphine Beauharnais).

72. *l'entraînement de ma destinée]* "training my destiny"

73. Rémusat I:141 {*KSA* 14 has I:41}.

74. Rémusat I:153.

75. Rémusat I:154 (on Hortense Beauharnais).

76. *je crois . . . penser.]* "I believe the external world has been created quite simply to be for us an occasion for thought." Quoted from Ximénès Doudan, *Mélanges et lettres* {"Compositions and letters"}, 2 vols. (Paris{: Calmann Lévy,} 1878), II:350–51. *NL.*

77. Rémusat I:142, 144.

78. Rémusat, I:151–52 (on Eugène Beauharnais).

79. Rémusat, I:157 (on Hortense Beauharnais).

80. N's translation of Ximénès Doudan, *Mélanges et lettres,* II:566: "*Les volontés sont si faibles, qu'on dirait que c'est le hasard qui les pousse. Non consilia a casu differo.*" {"Their wills are so weak, one would say they are driven by chance. I cannot tell plans and chance apart."}

81. *Napoleon knew . . . him.]* {Rémusat I:118.}

82. *"My anger . . . (cou).]* Rémusat I:120, n1.

83. *"He finds . . . Talleyrand."]* {Rémusat I:117–18.}

84. Rémusat I:124.

85. *intraitable]* "intractable"

86. Rémusat I:124–25.

87. *une petite . . . détail]* "dread about a small detail"

88. Rémusat I:125.

89. Rémusat I:125.

90. Rémusat I:125 {Quoting Napoleon}.

91. Rémusat I:126.

92. Rémusat I:128.

93. Rémusat I:136.

94. Rémusat I:139. The text in Lafontaine's *Adonis* is: "*Ni la grâce plus belle encore que la beauté*" {"Nor grace more beautiful still than beauty."}

95. *I propose . . . model] Ich schlage das Bild vor* {The sentence reads, literally, "I propose the image." N resorts to an untranslatable wordplay on the verb *vorschlagen*, "to propose," and the nouns *Bild*, "image," and *Vorbild*, "model."}

96. Cf. *JS* 152.

97. Cf. *D* 207; *JS* 5; 4[57].

98. Cf. *D* 339.

99. *The Quietists . . . behalf.]* {Cf. Martensen, 1:418.}

100. Cf. *D* 124; 5[43, 47].

101. *Not to be . . . than to be] Das Nichtsein könnte uns* werthvoller *scheinen als das Sein.* {Allusion to *Hamlet* III, 1, 57.}

102. *with a bribed servant].* Cf. 6[16].

103. Cf. Goethe, *Faust* I, 465; cf. *D* 545.

104. *Vacherot]* Étienne Vacherot, French philosopher and student of Victor Cousin. {Cf. Alfred Fouillée's comments on Vacherot in "La morale contemporaine. II. Le positivisme français et la morale indépendante," in *Revue des Deux Mondes* (September 15, 1880): 273–306, 299–300.}

105. *true nature]* Cf. 6[150].

106. {Cf. Fouillée's comments on Spencer and Littré in "La morale contemporaine. II. Le positivisme français et la morale indépendante," 283–84. N's comments on Littré in the following fragments are drawn from his reading of Fouillée's essay, which reviews Littré's *La science au point de vue philosophique.*}

107. Cf. 6[55, 145].

108. *odium generis humani]* "hatred for the human race"

109. *concordia]* "harmony"

110. Cf. 6[55, 141].

111. *Spencer and Littré]* {Cf. Spencer, *Die Thatsachen der Ethik*, 17–18; Emile Littré, *La science au point de vue philosophique*

{"Science from the philosophical point of view"} (Paris: Didier, 1876), 297. *NL.*}.

112. Cf. 6[136].

113. Cf. *D* 122.

114. Cf. *JS* 26.

115. *"Thou shalt not kill"]* {Cf. Exodus 20:13; Deuteronomy 5:17.}

116. {Cf. Fouillée, "La morale contemporaine. II. Le positivisme français et la morale indépendante," 282.}

117. Cf. Littré, *La science au point de vue philosophique*{, 346–47}.

118. {Cf. Littré, 346–47.}

119. {Cf. Littré, 339–40, 346.}

120. Cf. *D* 132, 174.

121. Cf. *JS* 14.

122. *"Thou shalt not steal"]* {Cf. Exodus 20:15; Deuteronomy 5:19.}

123. Cf. *JS* 3, 55.

124. Rémusat I:113.

125. Cf. *JS* 55.

126. Cf. *D* 67.

127. {Rémusat II:271–72: "*ce besoin de conserver des illusions sur son maître, besoin inspiré par la vanité humaine qui n'aime point à rougir de celui auquel elle s'est soumise*"}

128. *drives and drivelets] Trieben und Triebchen*

129. Rémusat II:274.

130. Cf. 6[220].

131. Cf. Goethe, *Italienische Reise* (*Italian Journey*), Sicily 1787, Alcamo 19. April {*Sämmtliche Werke in vierzig Bänden* ("Collected works in forty volumes"), Vol. 23 (Stuttgart und Tübingen: J. G. Cotta, 1856), 338. *NL*}.

132. Cf. Goethe, *Italienische Reise*, Sicily 1787, Palermo 9. April {*Sämmtliche Werke* 23:304}.

133. Cf. 6[221].

134. Cf. *D* 267.

135. *Many . . . extraordinary!]* Cf. *JS* 186.

136. Cf. *D* 38.

137. *hanging garden]* {A reference to the legendary Hanging Gardens of Babylon, one of the seven wonders of the ancient world,

built by King Nebuchadnezzar II (reigned 605–562 BCE). According to legend, abundant — and, presumably, labor-intensive — terrace gardens overhanging the facades of the desert palace to console Queen Amytis over the loss of her lush homeland.}

138. Cf. *D* 364, 473.

139. Cf. 7[236].

140. Rémusat II:274.

141. Jacob Burckhardt, *Der Cicerone* (Leipzig{: Seemann,} 1869), 396. *NL*.

142. Cf. 6[192].

143. Cf. 6[200].

144. Burckhardt, *Der Cicerone*, 399.

145. Cf. *D* 335.

146. Cf. 11[283].

147. Cf. *D* 84.

148. {Cf. George Eliot, *Middlemarch: Aus dem Leben der Provinz*, trans. Emil Lehmann. Vol. 4 (Berlin: Duncker, 1873), 290–93, 313. *NL*. Rather than translating back from Lehmann's German, we have used the language of Eliot's English text: *Middlemarch: A Study of Provincial Life* (New York: Penguin Books, 2015).}

149. *To beseech . . . weariness"]* {N paraphrasing George Eliot, *Middlemarch*, 739: "she besought hardness and coldness and aching weariness."}

150. *"Sublime . . . reproaches"]* {N paraphrasing *Middlemarch*, 739: "The fire of Dorothea's anger was not easily spent, and it flamed out in fitful returns of spurning reproach."}

151. *to fall . . . awakening]* {N paraphrasing *Middlemarch*, 740: "on the cold floor she sobbed herself to sleep. In the chill hours of the morning twilight, when all was dim around her, she awoke."}

152. *"narrow . . . calamity"]* {Cf. *Middlemarch*, 740.}

153. *"All the . . . power."]* {N paraphrasing *Middlemarch*, 740–41: "all this vivid sympathetic experience returned to her now as a power."}

154. {Cf. Baumann, 110: *die Moral* "*muss Ideale geben, aber auf Grund der festen Gesetze menschlichen Wesens, nicht Phantome einer blos geträumten Menschheit.*" ("morality 'must provide ideals,

but based on the fixed laws of human nature, not phantoms of a merely dreamed humanity.'")}

155. {Cf. Ralph Waldo Emerson, *Versuche (Essays)*, trans. from the English by G. Fabricius (Hannover: Meyer, 1858), 225. *NL*: "*Für jeden Freund, den er im Dienste der Wahrheit verliert, wird ihm ein besserer wieder zu Theil*"; *The Collected Works of Ralph Waldo Emerson, Volume 2: Essays: First Series* (Cambridge, MA: Harvard University Press, 1971), "Circles," 182: "For every friend whom he loses for truth, he gains a better."}

156. Cf. *D* 270.

157. *Middle Kingdom] Reich der Mitte* {In German, *Reich der Mitte* translates "Zhongguo," imperial China's self-description, dating from ca. 1000 BCE, as the center of the world. In English, the Middle Kingdom (also called the Middle Empire) refers primarily to the period in the history of ancient Egypt from the 11th to the 13th dynasties (ca. 2030–1650 BCE); in German, Egypt's Middle Kingdom is called "*Mittleres Reich*."}

158. {Written in connection with N's reading of Stendhal, *Histoire de la peinture en Italie* ("History of painting in Italy") (Paris: Michel Lévy Frères, 1868). *NL*.}

159. Cf. 9[6].

160. *molded] angebildet* {N's coinage: literally, "formed onto."}

161. Cf. *D* 45.

162. Cf. Tacitus, *History* V, 5, 9.

163. Cf. Tacitus, *History* V, 5.

164. Cf. Tacitus, *History* V, 4, 5, 13.

165. *impotentia]* "weakness," "lack of self-control"

166. A quotation?

167. Cf. *JS* 205.

168. Cf. 6[438].

169. {Cf. Baumann, 10–11.}

170. Cf. Tacitus, *Annals* XV, 44. {Quoted by William Edward Hartpole Lecky, *Sittengeschichte Europas von Augustus bis auf Karl den Grossen*, trans. H. Jolowicz (Leipzig & Heidelberg: C. F. Winter, 1879), 1:373n2. *NL*. *History of European Morals from Augustus to Charlemagne* (London: Longmans, Green, and Co., 1869), 1:456–57n4.}

171. *flagitia]* "atrocities"

172. Cf. *D* 367.

173. *(Pique-bonheur)]* "pique-happiness" Cf. Stendhal, *De l'amour*, XXXVIII.

174. Cf. Tacitus, *History* V, 4, 5.

175. Cf. *D* 447.

176. {In connection with N's reading of Lüdemann. Cf. note to 4[157] above.}

177. Cf. *JS* 235.

178. Stendhal, *Rome, Naples et Florence* (Paris{: Michel Lévy Frères,} 1854), 255. *NL*.

179. Stendhal, *Rome, Naples et Florence*, 255.

180. *la saillie . . . l'utile]* "the projecting out of the useful"

181. Stendhal? {Cf. *Rome, Naples, et Florence*, 247–48.}

182. Cf. Stendhal, *Rome, Naples et Florence*, 387–88.

183. Cf. Stendhal, *Correspondance inédite. Précédée d'une introduction par Prosper Mérimée* ("Unpublished Letters. Preceded with an introduction by Prosper Mérimée") (Paris{: Michel Lévy Frères}, 1855), 77. *NL*: ". . . *son livre* [*Considérations sur les principaux événements de la Révolution française von Mme. de Staël*]*; mais combien ce style* tendu *et* visant *à l'*effet *est au-dessous de sa charmante et entraînante conversation*" (". . . her book ["Considerations on the main events of the French Revolution by Madame de Stael"]; but how far beneath her charming and entrancing conversation is this *strained* style *intent* on *effect*.") {Cf. also Stendhal, *Rome, Naples et Florence*, 349: "*Je revois avec plaisir que ce grand homme* [*Mozart*] *n'a pas toujours eu un style tendu, comme nos tragiques ennuyeux.*" ("I see again with pleasure that this great man [Mozart] did not always have a strained style, like our boring tragedies.")}

184. {Cf. Karl Baedeker, *Italien: Handbuch für Reisende. Erster Theil: Ober-Italien bis Livorno, Florenz und Ravenna, nebst der Insel Corsica und den Reise-Routen durch Frankreich, die Schweiz und Oesterreich* ("Italy: Handbook for travelers. First part: Upper Italy to Leghorn, Florence and Ravenna, together with the island of Corsica and the travel routes through France, Switzerland and Austria") (Leipzig: Karl Baedeker, 1879), 285: "*Merkwürdig ist, dass auch Frauen an der Universität Bologna gelehrt haben. So im*

XIV. Jahrh. Novella d'Andrea, ihrer Schönheit wegen jedoch hinter einem Vorhange." ("It is noteworthy that women also taught at the University of Bologna. For example in the fourteenth century Novella d'Andrea, on account of her beauty however from behind a screen.").}

185. *The luxurious . . . Athens).]* {Written in connection with N's reading of Stendhal, *Histoire de la peinture en Italie.*}

186. *temperament] Gemüth* {"nature," "disposition," "temperament"; N is using the word here in a special sense referring to a proverbially German temperament marked by a cozy, self-complacent kind of sociability.}

187. Stendhal, *Rome, Naples et Florence*, 387: "*Je remarque que, dans tout ce que font les Allemands, ils sont beaucoup plus influencés par un vain désir de* faire effet *que par aucun transport d'imagination ou par la conscience d'une âme extraordinaire.*" {"I notice that in everything the Germans do, they are far more influenced by a vain desire *to create an effect* than by any transport of the imagination or by the consciousness of an extraordinary soul."}

188. Cf. *D* 193.

189. After Stendhal?

190. *Crossed out at the end*: "Passion is much too rare." After Stendhal?

191. *white linen] weißer Wäsche* {Literally, "white laundry"; Lassalle was known to be very vain, to have paid a lot of attention to what he wore, and to have preferred to circulate in upper-class society.}

192. *"object . . . experience,"]* N refers here to J. J. Baumann's theory on "the nature of the will and the laws of the will's formation" in *Handbuch der Moral nebst Abriss der Rechtsphilosophie* {cf. note 56 above}, 1ff., 17–18, 59.

193. {In connection with N's reading of Baumann.}

194. {In connection with N's reading of Baumann.}

195. *implanted in ourselves] uns angelehrt* {*angelehrt* is N's coinage. The phrase's literal meaning is "taught onto us."}

196. {Cf. Epictetus, *Enchiridion* 22. *Epiktets Handbuch*, from the Greek. With explanatory notes by Gottlieb Christian Karl Link (Nürnberg: Johann Eberhard Zeh, 1783), 32–33. *NL.*}

197. Cf. *D* 130.

198. *agons]* "contests"

199. *Arcadia or Campan]* {Arcadia is the name of an ancient Greek province which in the poetic tradition came to stand for a state of lasting pastoral harmony. N is presumably referring to Goethe's use of the topos as the epigraph to his *Italienische Reise*: "Auch ich in Arkadien!" ("I, too, am in Arcadia"). The Campan, a valley in the French Pyrenees, is the scene for a fictional dialogue text by Jean Paul from 1797, *Das Kampaner Tal, oder über die Unsterblichkeit der Seele* ("The Campanerthal, or discourses on the immortality of the soul"), in *Werke in drei Bänden*, ed. Norbert Miller (Munich: Carl Hanser Verlag, 1969), II:7–52.}

200. *émeute]* "riot"

201. Cf. Giacomo Leopardi, *Canti* "*L'infinito*" ("The Infinite") (1821). {N quotes from the poem's final verse. Cf. *Giacomo Leopardi*, German trans. by Paul Heyse, Part 1: *Nerina – Gedichte* (Berlin: W. Hertz, 1878), 32. *NL*.} Cf. *D* 575.

202. *he]* Richard Wagner

203. {Cf. N to Heinrich Köselitz, 20 August 1880, *KGB* III:1, 36-37.}

204. *and against . . . believe] From*: yes, against whose articles of faith and projects I have so often battled, have on their side as well occasion for a small act of revenge. Also hope

205. *thought-drives]* {Cf. Georg Heinrich Schneider, *Der thierische Wille. Systematische Darstellung und Erklärung der thierischen Triebe und deren Entstehung, Entwickelung und Verbreitung im Thierreiche als Grundlage zu einer vergleichenden Willenslehre* ("The animal will. Systematic presentation and explanation of animal instincts and their origin, development and spread in the animal kingdom as a basis for a comparative theory of will") (Leipzig: Ambr. Abel, 1880), 147–49, 292–94, 412–15. *NL*.}

206. Cf. *D* 129.

207. Cf. 9[9, 10].

208. Cf. *D* 514.

209. *worry-free state] Sorgenstuhl Staat* {"*Sorgenstuhl*" is literally "care-chair," i.e., a retirement chair, or a chair where one rested from one's cares and left them to others. In contemporary German, the word is antiquated.}

210. *I have . . . proceeds] ich habe so viele Aus- und Einnahmen* {N makes a dubious word-play here on the words *Ausnahme* and *Einnahme*, employing them as if they meant, translating literally, "out-take" and "intake," in the material sense of expenses and receipts. "Receipt," or "proceed," is indeed the meaning of *Einnahme*, but *Ausnahme* has no other meaning but "exception."}

211. Cf. *D* 467.

212. *necessary!] The following crossed out*: Can I conceal from myself, all the silence and loneliness notwithstanding, that what I think must hurt many people?

213. *Netherlandish eyes]* {N refers to a polemical trope in classicist art theory regarding a nationalized aesthetic of the ugly said to presuppose Dutch or Netherlandish eyes and bodies. See Johann Joachim Winckelmann, *Reflections on the Imitation of Greek Works in Painting and Sculpture*, complete German text with facing English translation by Elfriede Heyer and Roger C. Norton (La Salle, Illinois: Open Court, 1987), 20–21.}

214. Cf. *D* 168.

215. *otium]* "leisure"

216. Cf. *D* 366; 4[240].

217. Cf. *JS* 277.

218. {Cf. Epictetus, *Enchiridion* 5; *Epiktets Handbuch*, 14.}

219. {Cf. Epictetus, *Enchiridion* 48; *Epiktets Handbuch*, 82.}

220. Perhaps related to 6[379].

221. Ch. *D* 118, 6[418, 419].

222. Cf. *D* 536.

223. *carry on . . . hothouse]* {N exploits here the semantic range of *Trieb* ("drive") and *treiben* ("to drive") which the translation cannot duplicate: "carry on humanely" is *menschlich treiben*; "drive it too far" is *übertreiben*; "hothouse" is *Treibhaus*.}

224. {In connection with N's reading of Alfons Bilharz, *Der heliocentrische Standpunct der Weltbetrachtung: Grundlegungen zu einer wirklichen Naturphilosophie* ("The heliocentric point of view of the world: Groundwork for a real philosophy of nature") (Stuttgart: J. G. Cotta, 1879). *NL*.}

225. {Cf. *Bilharz, Der heliocentrische Standpunct*, 128–31.}

226. Cf. *JS* 225.

227. Cf. 6[410]. {Cf. Bilharz, *Der heliocentrische Standpunct*, 114.}

228. Cf. 6[410]. {Cf. Bilharz, *Der heliocentrische Standpunct*, 114.}

229. {In connection with N's reading of Karl Semper, *Die natürlichen Existenzbedingungen der Thiere*, 2 vols. (Leipzig: F. A. Brockhaus, 1880). *NL. Animal Life as Affected by the Natural Conditions of Existence* (New York: D. Applegate, 1881).}

230. Cf. Semper, *Die natürlichen Existenzbedingungen der Thiere*, 1:93{/*Animal Life*, 76}.

231. Cf. Semper, *Die natürlichen Existenzbedingungen der Thiere*, 1:93–94{/*Animal Life*, 76–77}.

232. {N quotes here Hippolyte Taine, *Die Entstehung des modernen Frankreich*, Vol. 1: *Das vorrevolutionäre Frankreich* ("The emergence of modern France, Vol. 1: Prerevolutionary France"), trans. L. Katscher (Leipzig: Ernst Julius Günther, 1877), 161. *NL*.}

233. Cf. *D* 197. {In connection with N's reading of John Stuart Mill, *Gesammelte Werke*, Vol. X, on "Coleridge."}

234. Cf. *D* 121, 243; 6[431, 433, 435, 441].

235. Cf. *D* 444.

236. Cf. *D* 121, 243; 6[429. 433, 435, 441].

237. Cf. *D* 438.

238. Cf. *D* 121, 243; 6[429, 431, 435, 441].

239. {Cf. D 117; 6[362, 412, 413, 433].}

240. Cf. *D* 121, 243; 6[429, 431, 433, 441].

241. Cf. *D* 549.

242. Crossed out by N.

243. Cf. *JS* 1; 6[291].

244. Crossed out by N.

245. Cf. *D* 121, 243; 6[429, 431, 433, 435]. {In connection with N's reading of Bilharz.}

246. *see . . . into the world] sehen unsere Gesetze in die Welt hinein* {N gives an intransitive verb, "*hineinsehen*," a transitive meaning here. Our translation preserves its literal sense.}

247. *Our knowing . . . images.]* Crossed out by N.

248. Cf. *JS* 14.

249. Cf. *D* 468.

250. Cf. Emerson, *Essays*, 149. On the same page N noted to himself: "*This is the thing* and not just the allegory. My suspicion

that we have a language for chemical facts." This gloss refers to the following passage in Emerson: "*ich befinde mich endlich einem so wahren und mir gleichgesinnten Menschen gegenüber, daß ich . . . mich so einfach in solcher Ungetheiltheit zu ihm stellen kann, wie ein chemisches Atom sich zum andern stellt.*" (underlined by N). {*The Collected Works of Ralph Waldo Emerson, Volume 2: Essays: First Series* (Cambridge, MA: Harvard University Press, 1971), "Friendship," 119: "I am arrived at last in the presence of a man so real and equal, that I . . . may deal with him with the simplicity and wholeness with which one chemical atom meets another."}

251. Cf. *JS* 14.

[7 = N V 6. End of 1880]

1. Cf. *D* 169; *JS* 122.

2. {Cf. Balthazar Gracian, *Hand-Orakel und Kunst der Weltklugheit* ("Hand-Oracle and art of sophistication"), drawn from his works by Don Vincencio Juan de Lastanosa, and trans. from the Spanish by Arthur Schopenhauer, 3rd ed. (Leipzig: F. A. Brockhaus, 1877), § 276, p. 177. *NL*: "*Mit zwanzig Jahren ist der Mensch ein Pfau; mit dreißig, ein Löwe; mit vierzig, ein Kameel; mit funfzig, eine Schlange; mit sechszig, ein Hund; mit siebenzig, ein Affe; mit achtzig, — nichts.*" ("At twenty, a human being is a peacock; at thirty, a lion; at forty, a camel; at fifty, a snake; at sixty, a dog; at seventy, an ape; at eighty, — nothing.")}

3. Cf. Stendhal, *Histoire de la peinture en Italie* ("History of painting in Italy") (Paris{: Michel Lévy Frères,} 1868), 179. *NL*. Hereafter, "Stendhal, *Peinture*," followed by the page number.

4. {Cf. Stendhal, *Peinture*, 332.}

5. {Cf. Stendhal, *Peinture*, 335.}

6. Cf. *D* 242.

7. Cf. *D* 553, crossed out by N.

8. Stendhal, *Peinture*, 208.

9. *but proof . . . M⟨ichel⟩angelo!]* {In connection with Stendhal's remarks on Michelangelo in *Peinture*, 294ff.}

10. Allusion to Richard Wagner.

11. *seriousness is that there!] From*: seriousness, to curse where one is stupid!

12. {Cf. Stendhal, *Racine et Shakspeare* [*sic*]. *Études sur le romantisme* ("Racine and Shakespeare: Studies of romanticism") (Paris: Michel Lévy Frères, 1854), "*De la moralité de Molière*," 68–71, esp. 71. *NL*. Hereafter "Stendhal, *Racine*" followed by chapter title and page number.}

13. {Cf. Friedrich Schiller, "*Über Anmuth und Würde*" ("On Grace and Dignity"), *Neue Thalia*, 1793.}

14. Cf. Blaise Pascal, *Gedanken, Fragmente und Briefe* II, 244–47; in the French edition II: 340–43.

15. Cf. 7[96, 211].

16. Cf. *D* 172.

17. Cf. *D* 238.

18. Cf. 15[60].

19. {An allusion to a saying attributed to King Frederick the Great and indirectly quoted by Kant in 1784: "Only one ruler in the world says: *Argue* as much as you will and about whatever you will, *but obey*!" Immanuel Kant, "An Answer to the question: What is enlightenment?," in *Practical Philosophy*, trans. Mary J. Gregor, ed. Allen W. Wood (Cambridge: Cambridge University Press, 1996), 11–22; at p. 18.}

20. Cf. Stendhal, *Peinture*, 255, 258.

21. Cf. *D* 357.

22. Cf. 7[102, 126, 181].

23. *"How do I matter?"]* {Cf. N to Franz Overbeck, 31 October 1880, *KGB* III:1, 43; N to Heinrich Köselitz, 7 November 1880, *KGB* III:1, 44.}

24. *change the feeling] umempfinden* {N's coinage, literally, "to re-sense" or "to re-feel."}

25. {Perhaps in connection with N's reading of Stendhal, *Peinture*.}

26. Cf. 7[62, 65].

27. Cf. *D* 38.

28. *ἀγών] agon*, "contest"

29. Cf. 7[54, 65].

30. Cf. *D* 189.

31. Cf. 7[54, 62].

32. {Cf. N to Heinrich Köselitz, 24 November 1880, *KGB* III:1, 50.}

33. *humans]* {*Ms*: *M*; read by Colli and Montinari in *KSA* as "*M⟨uster⟩*" ("models") following 7[69]; later amended to "*M⟨enschen⟩*" ("humans").}

34. Quotation not located.

35. Cf. *JS* 46; 11[72].

36. Cf. 7[37].

37. Cf. *JS* 77.

38. Stendhal, *Peinture*, 118.

39. *passionner les détails]* "to be passionate about details"

40. Stendhal, *Racine*, "*De la moralité de Molière*," {67: "*Du temps de madame d'Épinay et de madame Campan, il y avait la manière approuvée et de bon goût de mourir, de se marier, de faire banqueroute, de tuer un rival, etc.*" "In the time of Madame d'Épinay and Madame Campan, there was the approved and tasteful manner of dying, of marrying, of going bankrupt, of killing a rival, etc."}

41. *"il faut . . . autre"]* "one must be like another" {Cf. Stendhal, *Racine "De la moralité de Molière,"* 74.}

42. {N to Heinrich Köselitz, 30 March 1881, *KGB* III:1, 77.}

43. Stendhal, *Peinture*, 278–79.

44. Cf. 7[30, 211]; *D* 131.

45. *D* 206.

46. {Cf. Stendhal, *Racine*, 27.}

47. Left out of *Le*; cf. however Elisabeth Förster-Nietzsche, "*Nietzsches Bibliothek*," in Arthur Berthold, *Bücher und Wege zu Büchern* (Berlin{: Spemann,} 1900), 452{: "*Einiges [Bücher] nahmen mein Mann und ich auf Wunsch meines Bruders mit nach Südamerika und es ist dort zurückgeblieben, z. B. Bret Hartes Novellen.*" ("Some things [books] my husband and I took to South America at my brother's request and they were left behind there, e.g., Bret Harte's novellas.")}

48. *Bret Harte]* {Cf. N to Franz Overbeck, 14 November 1879, *KGB* II:5, 464.}

49. *ἀγών]* {Cf. note 28.}

50. Cf. 7[45].

51. *heavy . . . matter] From*: I, to which I say, "how do I matter?" and which says to me in return "I am everything apart outside myself."

52. Cf. 7[196].
53. Cf. *D* 175.
54. Cf. 7[118].
55. *ravaler]* "to swallow"
56. Cf. Stendhal, *Peinture*, 184.
57. Added later, perhaps to 7[112].
58. Cf. Stendhal, *Peinture*, 183.
59. *to the previous page]* I.e., to 7[111].
60. Cf. Stendhal, *Racine*, 72: "*Eteindre le courage civil fut évidemment la grande affaire de Richelieu et de Louis XIV.*" {"To extinguish civic valor was manifestly the great enterprise of Richelieu and Louis XIV."}
61. Cf. Stendhal, *Racine*, 71–72: {"*L'on a horreur d'un péril qui peut être ridicule. L'homme le plus intrépide n'ose se livrer à la chaleur du sang qu'autant qu'il est sûr de marcher dans une route approuvée. Mais aussi quand la chaleur du sang, l'opposé de la vanité (passion dominante), produit ses effets, on voit les incroyables et sublimes folies des attaques de redoute, et ce qui est la terreur des soldats étrangers sous le nom de furia francese.*" ("One abhors a peril that may be ridiculous. The most intrepid man only dares yield himself to his blood's passion to the extent he is sure of walking an approved path. But even when the blood's passion, the opposite of vanity (ruling passion), produces its effects, one sees the incredible and sublime follies of redoubt attacks, which is the terror of foreign soldiers under the name of *furia francese* [French furor].")}
62. *Furia francese]* "French furor" {This phrase would seem to be an allusion to the taking of the Cheverino redoubt in 1812 by French Napoleonic troops, a battle widely known for its bloody ferocity and doubtless familiar to Stendhal. It was later the subject of a story by Prosper Mérimée, "L'enlèvement de la redoute" (1829).}
63. {Cf. August Siebenlist, *Schopenhauer's Philosophie der Tragödie* (Pressburg and Leipzig: Stampfel, 1880), 29–30. *NL*.}
64. Cf. 7[45].
65. Cf. *D* 64.
66. *πόλις]* "polis"
67. *Corcyrean soul]* Cf. Thucydides, III: 70–85; *WS* 31.
68. Cf. *CW* 4, 31[4], p. 365.

69. Cf. Stendhal, *Peinture*, 184.

70. Cf. 9[13].

71. *through . . . needle]* {Cf. Matthew 19:24.}

72. Cf. *D* 327.

73. Stendhal, *Peinture*, 205n2; cf. *D* 161; 7[150, 214].

74. Stendhal, *Peinture*, 205–6.

75. Stendhal, *Peinture*, 207.

76. *Et odoratus est deus suavitatem.]* "And the Lord smelled a sweet savor" Genesis 8:21 (KJV), cited by Pascal, *Gedanken, Fragmente und Briefe* I, 42.

77. Stendhal, *Peinture*, 185.

78. {Cf. Stendhal, *Peinture*, 250.}

79. {Stendhal, *Peinture*, 251.}

80. Stendhal, *Peinture*, 270.

81. Cf. *D* 170.

82. *As long . . . Apollo]* {In connection with N's reading of Stendhal's *Peinture*, where Stendhal frequently refers to the beauty of the *Apollo Belvedere*, a marble sculpture housed in the Vatican Palace that was long considered by Europeans to exemplify aesthetic perfection.}

83. *Lord Byron . . . sufferings."]* {Cf. Stendhal, *Racine*, "*Lord Byron en Italie*," 264.}

84. *"Always preoccupied . . . author."]* {Stendhal, *Racine*, "*Lord Byron en Italie*," 268.}

85. Cf. Stendhal, *Racine*, "*Lord Byron en Italie*," 274.

86. Cf. Stendhal, *Racine*, "*Walter Scott et la princesse de Clèves*," 297.

87. Cf. *D* 110.

88. *"Time . . . sorrow"]* {Cf. Pascal, *Gedanken, Fragmente und Briefe* I, 184.}

89. *the boar . . . son]* {Cf. Pascal, *Gedanken, Fragmente und Briefe* II, 31–32.}

90. In connection with N's reading of Stendhal.

91. *"de l'amour" symbolice!]* "'of love' symbolically!"

92. Reference to Stendhal not located.

93. {Cf. Stendhal, *Rome, Naples et Florence* (Paris: Michel Lévy Frères, 1854), 267. *NL*.}

94. *I cannot do otherwise]* {N here identifies with Martin Luther's declaration at the Diet of Worms where he had been summoned to renounce his writings, teaching, and actions. Cf. 4[68].}

95. Cf. 7[45].

96. *evil desires]* "evil desire" ("*böse Lust*") is the German translation for "concupiscence" by C. F. Schwartz in B. Pascal, *Gedanken, Fragmente und Briefe* I, 219, 241; II, 119, 127, 246. Some of these passages are marked by N.

97. *The . . . death]* Cf. Pascal, *Gedanken, Fragmente und Briefe* I, 40.

98. *Condemned to death]* Cf. Pascal, *Gedanken, Fragmente und Briefe* II, 22.

99. With shaky hand, probably written down while walking.

100. {Cf. Pascal's remarks on the "means to attain faith" in *Gedanken* II, 134–50, especially the "wager," which is marked several times in N's copy, 136–41.}

101. *Schopenhauer's curse]* {Cf. Arthur Schopenhauer, *Die Welt als Wille und Vorstellung*, Vol. 1, ed. Julius Frauenstädt (Leipzig: F. A. Brockhaus, 1873), 384–85. *NL*; *The World as Will and Representation, Volume 1*, trans. Judith Norman, Alistair Welchman, and Christopher Janaway (Cambridge: Cambridge University Press, 2010), 351–52.}

102. *Beethoven] From*: R. Wagner

103. Cf. 7[107].

104. *Age of . . . now!]* {Cf. Stendhal, *Racine*, 43.}

105. *What I . . . me.]* {Cf. Stendhal, *Rome, Naples et Florence*, 81: "*L'Allemand, au lieu de rapporter tout à soi, se rapporte tout aux autres.*" ("The German, instead of relating everything to himself, relates everything to others.")}

106. Cf. 7[59].

107. Cf. Pascal, *Gedanken, Fragmente und Briefe* I, 369; in the French text, I, 407: "*Je promets même de lui sacrifier toutes les vengeances*" {"I promise to sacrifice to him (i.e., God) even any vengeance." This promise dates from a religious awakening Pascal experienced on 23 November 1654 and that he recorded in the same night on a memorial sheet, the "secret paper." Upon his death on 18 August 1662, this sheet was found sewn into the lining of his clothes.}

108. Cf. *D* 560; 7[30, 96].

109. Cf. *D* 161; 7[140].

110. Cf. *D* 207.

111. Cf. 7[230].

112. *Quem in finem]* "In the end"

113. Cf. 1[54], 3[85].

114. *Port Royal]* Cf. note to 7[260].

115. Following Stendhal; cf. 7[217]; *JS* 29.

116. *3 unities]* {Reference to Aristotle's *Poetics*, the three unities — of time, space, and action — in drama.}

117. {Cf. Stendhal, *De l'amour*, §48 "*De l'amour allemand*," 151. *NL*.}

118. Written in connection with N's reading of Pascal's *Gedanken*.

119. See note to 7[233].

120. Cf. 6[207].

121. {Cf. Stendhal, *De l'amour*, 150.}

122. Cf. *D* 38.

123. N is probably thinking of passages like that in Aeschylus, *The Libation Bearers*, 596–601.

124. *ridiculum]* "ridiculous"

125. *deus absconditus]* "the hidden God"

126. *Young Germany]* "*Junges Deutschland*" {A group of young writers committed to a variety of progressive ideas. The group existed from roughly 1830 to 1850. Between 1834 and 1842, their works were forbidden throughout the German Confederation.}

127. N is referring to Pascal, *Gedanken, Fragmente und Briefe* I, 111–25.

128. Cf. *D* 347.

129. Cf. Pascal, *Les Provinciales* (Paris{: Firmin Didot Frères,} 1853), Sixteenth Letter. N probably knew the passage from Sainte-Beuve, *Port Royal* (Paris{: Hachette,} 1848), III, 84, which also contains the parallel Pascal-Demosthenes; cf. 7[261, 278].

130. *cette . . . l'eglise]* "this holy and terrible voice that astonishes nature and that consoles the church." {In January 1654 Marguerite Périer was consigned to the care of Port Royal Abbey. She suffered from a serious eye condition described as "*lacrimal fistula*." On 24 March 1656 she announced she had been cured by pressing her eye against a reliquary.}

131. Cf. Sainte-Beuve, *Port Royal*, III 83–84.

132. *Pascal]* N is thinking of passages like the following, marked by him in Pascal, *Gedanken, Fragmente und Briefe* II, 270: "*Sub te erit appetitus tuus.* {"Your desire will be subjugated."} For inclinations once dominated are virtues. We must make use of them like slaves . . ."

133. Written in connection with N's reading of Stendhal, *Racine*.

134. See note to 7[267]; cf. *D* 192.

135. Cf. Aristotle, *Rhetoric*, 1372a 4–6; citation is not literal. {N translates the quotation from the French cited in Eugène Auguste Ernest Havet, "*Des* Provinciales *de Pascal*," *Revue des deux mondes* (October 1, 1880):516–53, 526.}

136. *In Inquisition . . . there.]* {Cf. Abbé Claude Fleury, *Discours sur l'histoire ecclésiastique*, Eighth Discourse, no. xv, quoted in Havet, 527note.}

137. *If one . . . Church.]* {Cf. Havet, 527.}

138. {Cf. Havet, 529.}

139. {Cf. Pascal, *Les Provinciales*, Fifth Letter, 82: "*Mais, pour dégager l'âme de l'amour du monde, pour la retirer de ce qu'elle a de plus cher, pour la faire mourir à soi-même, pour la porter et l'attacher uniquement et invariablement à Dieu, ce n'est l'ouvrage que d'une main toute-puissante.*" ("But, to release the soul from the love of the world, to withdraw it from what it holds dearest, to make it die to itself, to carry it and attach it solely and invariably to God, this is the work of an all-powerful hand.") Quoted in Havet, 528.}

140. {Cf. Havet, 549 and note 5, where Havet quotes this list of names from La Bruyère's *Les caractères* (1688).}

141. Connection not developed.

142. *gaze] Written over*: spirit

143. Reference not located.

144. Cf. Sainte-Beuve, *Port Royal*, III 83ff.

145. Cf. Pascal, *Gedanken, Fragmente und Briefe* II, 29–30.

146. *N⟨apoleon⟩ . . . found]* Cf. Madame de Rémusat, *Mémoires 1802–1808*, 3 vols., ed. Paul de Rémusat (Paris{: Calmann Lévy,} 1880), I:395; 6[33]; 7[67]; *D* 251.

147. Cf. *D* 134.

148. *shared pleasure] Mitfreude* {N's coinage.}

149. Cf. Goethe, *Tasso*, V, 5, ll. 3432–33: "*Und wenn der Mensch in seiner Qual verstummt, / Gab mir ein Gott zu sagen, wie ich leide.*" {"And when the man fell silent in his anguish, / A god taught me to say how I suffer."}

150. After Stendhal?

151. *"Do you . . . own."]* {Cf. Stendhal, *Racine*, 104.}

152. {Cf. Stendhal, *Racine*, 246–47; *Peinture*, 402.}

153. {Cf. Stendhal, *Racine*, 252; *Peinture*, 405.}

154. {Perhaps in connection with N's reading of Stendhal, *De l'amour*, 173. Cf. 7[306].}

155. Cf. *D* 429.

156. Cf. 9[12]. {Cf. Stendhal, *Racine*, 82; *Rome, Naples et Florence*, 303.}

157. Cf. 7[301, 308].

158. *ἦθος]* "ethos"

159. Cf. 7[306].

160. *velle non discitur]* "willing is not learned"

161. Cf. *D* 207.

[8 = N V 5. Winter 1880–1881]

1. Cf. the subtitle of *Dawn*: "Thoughts on the Presumptions of Morality."

2. Written in connection with N's reading of Stendhal, *Racine*. *NL*.

3. *ridiculum]* "ridiculous"

4. Cf. *D* 174, 175.

5. {Stendhal, *De l'amour* (Paris: Michel Lévy Frères, 1868), 129.}

6. Cf. *D* 157.

7. *Septem]* "Seven" {An abbreviated reference to Aeschylus's *Seven against Thebes*.}

8. After Byron's *Manfred*, Act I, scene 1; cf. *D* 437.

9. Cf. N to Peter Gast (*KGB* III:1, 56), Franz Overbeck (*KGB* III:1, 57), his mother and sister (*KGB* III:1, 56), 8 January 1881.

10. *to follow . . . it]* {Cf. Pascal, *Gedanken* II, 144–45.}

11. Cf. *JS* 140.

12. Cf. 7[238]; 8[50].

13. *Pascal . . . diminish]* {Cf. Pascal, *Gedanken* II, 139.}

14. Cf. *D* 172.

15. Cf. *JS* 283.

16. Cf. Thucydides, III, 82. {Cf. *WS* 31, *CW* 4, 171–72, where N comments on this passage in Thucydides.}

17. *"crystallization"]* After Stendhal, *De l'amour*, I, VI-XII.

18. *ever] Le*: purely; *Le*[2]: I am purely

19. Cf. *D* 207.

20. {Cf. *John Stuart Mill's Gesammelte Werke*, ed. Theodor Gomperz. Vol. 1: *Die Freiheit. Das Nützlichkeitsprincip. Rectoratsrede* (Leipzig: Fues [R. Reisland], 1869), *NL*; "*Das Nützlichkeits-Princip*," trans. Adolph Wahrmund, 157; *Utilitarianism*, Ch. III, "Of the Ultimate Sanction of the Principle of Utility": "until, by the improvement of education, the feeling of unity with our fellow creatures shall be (what it cannot be denied that Christ intended it to be) as deeply rooted in our character, and to our own consciousness as completely a part of our nature, as the horror of crime is in an ordinarily well-brought up young person."}

21. Cf. *D* 174.

22. Cf. 9[6]; *JS* 267.

23. Cf. 8[29].

24. Written in connection with N's reading of Stendhal, *Racine*.

25. Cf. 8[65].

26. Cf. *CW* 6, 14[20].

27. Cf. *D* 86.

28. Cf. *D* 102.

29. Cf. 8[54].

30. {Cf. Émile Littré, *La science au point de vue philosophique* ("Science from the philosophical point of view") (Paris: Didier, 1876), 557–59. *NL*.}

31. Cf. *JS* 71; *CW* 6, 12[111].

32. {Cf. Mill, *Auguste Comte und der Positivismus, John Stuart Mill's Gesammelte Werke*, Vol. IX, 96ff.; *Auguste Comte and Positivism* (London: Trübner & Co., 1865), 135ff.}

33. *Le long . . . pensées]* "long hope and vast thoughts"

34. {Jean de La Fontaine, *Fables* XI, 8: "*Le Vieillard et les trois jeunes hommes*" ("The old man and the three young men") (1678), Verse 11; cited by Littré, *La science au point de vue philosophique*, 474.}

35. *ἐσθλοί]* "noble," "brave," "good"

36. Cf. *JS* 180.

37. *satisfied with . . . beautifully.]* Cf. Stendhal, *Racine*, {113: "*je trouve que les personnages de Racine, d'Alfieri, de Manzoni, de Schiller, ont toujours la mine de gens* contents de si bien parler. *Ils sont remplis de passion; soit, mais ils sont d'abord contents de bien parler.*" ("I find that the characters of Racine, Alfieri, Manzoni, Schiller always look like people *who are pleased to speak so well.* They are filled with passion, to be sure; but in the first place they are pleased to speak so well.")}

38. Cf. *JS* 1.

39. Cf. *JS* 96.

40. Cf. *JS* 328.

41. *Religion nouvelle]* "new religion" {Cf. Stendhal, *Rome, Naples et Florence* (Paris: Michel Lévy Frères, 1854), 297. *NL.*}

42. Cf. *JS* 137; *D* 38.

43. Cf. *D* 113.

44. Cf. *D* 38.

45. Cf. *D* 174.

46. {Cf. Madame de Rémusat, *Mémoires 1802–1808*, ed. Paul de Rémusat (Paris: Calmann-Lévy, 1880), I, 115–16. *NL.* Hereafter, "Rémusat" followed by volume and page number.}

47. *One single . . . noticed.]* Rémusat I, 115–16.

48. *He did . . . him.]* Rémusat I, 116–17.

49. Rémusat I, 112; cf. *JS* 362.

50. *cette civilisation]* "this civilization"

51. Rémusat I, 108.

52. *Je suis . . . lâche]* "Myself, I am a coward, essentially a coward."

53. *honneur]* "honor"

54. Rémusat I, 108.

55. *après tout]* "after all"

56. Rémusat I, 108.

57. Rémusat II, 280.

58. Rémusat II, 299–300.

59. Rémusat II, 303.

60. Rémusat II, 303.

61. Rémusat II, 167.

62. *dévouement]* "devotion"

63. Rémusat I, 114–15; cf. *JS* 23.
64. *Moi]* "Me"
65. Rémusat II, 280.
66. Rémusat II, 277–78.
67. Rémusat II, 278.

[9 = M II 2. Winter 1880–1881]
1. Cf. 8[56]; 7[268].
2. Cf. *D* 343.
3. Cf. *D* 482.
4. Cf. 8[48]; 6[271]; *JS* 267.
5. Cf. *D* 190.
6. Cf. 9[10]; 6[375].
7. Cf. 9[9]; 6[375]. *Crossed out at the end*: the point of honor before your own court of arbitration.
8. Originally a continuation of *D* 132.
9. Cf. 7[305]. {Cf. Stendhal, *Racine*, 82n1: "*Les changements politiques ne passent dans les mœurs qu'après cent ans.*" ("Political changes do not become customary until a hundred years have passed."); cf. Stendhal, *Rome, Naples et Florence*, 383: "*On peut dire que le gouvernement ne passe dans les mœurs qu'au bout de cent ans.*" ("It can be said that rule of government only becomes custom after a hundred years have passed.")}
10. Cf. 7[135]; originally a continuation of *D* 207.
11. *the eye of the needle]* {Cf. Matthew 19:24.}
12. *Pd*: Poverty chastity obedience (the last as negation of the will to power) renunciation of the world apparently. It leads in fact to another stage of culture, the poor slave without wife who compensates himself with spiritual hopes and intoxications: nerve power — — —
13. Originally a continuation of *D* 44.
14. Epigraph for *D*. Cf. N to Peter Gast, 9 February 1881 {*KGB* III:1, 61}.

[10 = Mp XV 1b. Spring 1880–Spring 1881]
1. Cf. *JS* 14; 4[72].
2. Cf. *JS* 306.

3. *ἀταραξία]* "calmness," "serenity"

4. Cf. Richard Wagner in *Bayreuther Blätter*, 1879. {In October 1879, Wagner published an open letter in the *Bayreuther Blätter*, translated as "Against Vivisection" in *Richard Wagner's Prose Works*, Vol. 6: *Religion and Art*, trans. William Ashton Ellis (London: Kegan Paul, Trench, Trübner & Co., 1897), 193–210.}

5. {Cf. Madame de Rémusat, *Mémoires 1802–1808*, ed. Paul de Rémusat (Paris: Calmann-Lévy, 1880), III, 224, 225. *NL*. Hereafter, "Rémusat" followed by volume and page number.}

6. Rémusat III, 225.

7. Rémusat III, 170.

8. Rémusat III, 170.

9. Cf. *D* 26.

10. Cf. *D* 471.

11. Cf. *D* 460.

12. *"belly lust"]* "*Baucheslust*" {Reference to Wilhelm Müller (1794–1827), "Die Arche Noäh," lines 7 and 8: "*Und als die Welt auf's Neue / In Bauches Lust versank, . . .* " ("And when the world once more / Sank into belly lust") from Vol. 2 (1824), in *Gedichte* (Berlin: Behr, 1906), 88–89.}

13. Cf. *JS* 83.

14. *too have]* Above the line, between "too" and "have," an illegible word scribbled in.

15. {Cf. *Satires* 2. 6.}

16. *"Alpa . . . mountain?"]* {Cf. *Z* II "The Soothsayer." Cf. also Reinhard von Seydlitz, *Wann, warum, was und wie ich schrieb* ("When, why, what and how I write") (Gotha: Verlag Friedrich Andreas Perthes, 1900), 36: "*Nietzsche erzählte lachend, er habe im Traum einen endlosen Bergpfad hinauf steigen müssen; ganz oben, unter der Spitze des Berges, habe er an einer Höhle vorbei gehen wollen, als aus der finstern Tiefe ihm eine Stimme zurief: 'Alpa, Alpa, — wer trägt seine Asche zu Berge?'* " ("Nietzsche laughingly related that in a dream he had to climb an endless mountain path; high up, under the mountain peak, he wanted to go past a cave when a voice called out to him from the dark depths: 'Alpa, Alpa, — who carries his ashes up to the mountain?'")}

17. Cf. *D* 167. {Cf. Jules Michelet, *Das Volk* ("The people") (Mannheim: Hoff, 1846), 397. *NL.*}

18. Cf. *D* 167.

19. *Ce qui importe . . . mais les choses.]* "What matters is not people but things."

20. *Napoleon perça sous Bonaparte]* "Napoleon showed through Bonaparte"

21. Number 4 in a series of addenda (for a postscript to *D*).

22. Cf. *D* 130.

23. *sun's . . . light]* {Cf. Richard A Proctor, *Unser Standpunkt im Weltall*, trans. Wilhelm Schur (Heilbronn: Henninger, 1877), 28–29. *NL.* Original: *Our Place Among Infinities* (New York: Appleton, 1876).}

24. *Books]* [?]

25. Cf. *D* 87. {Cf. Henry Maudsley, *Zurechnungsfähigkeit der Geisteskranken* (Leipzig: Brockhaus, 1875), 126–27, 135–37, 160, 224, 230. *NL.* Original: *Responsibility in Mental Disease* (London: Henry S. King & Co., 1874).}

26. *(Affective Insanity)]* {In English in N's text; the English appears as well in the German translation, parenthetically, after *Gefühlsirrsinn*; cf. Maudsley, 66, 127.}

27. *Manie sans délire]* "Insanity without delirium" {Maudsley credits Philippe Pinel (1745–1826) with first discovering this form of insanity; cf. 135, 137.}

28. Cf. John Lubbock, *Die Entstehung der Zivilisation und der Urzustand des Menschengeschlechtes, erläutert durch das innere und äußere Leben der Wilden*, trans. A. Passow, with an introductory preface by Rudolf Virchow (Jena{: Costenoble,} 1875), 189. *NL.* {Original: Sir John Lubbock, *The Origin of Civilization and Primitive Condition of Man: Mental and Social Condition of Savages* (London: Longmans, 1870), 134; "The negro in Guinea beats his Fetish if his wishes are frustrated, and hides it in his waist-cloth when he is about to do something of which he is ashamed, so that the Fetish may not be able to see what is going on."}

29. Cf. Lubbock, 312 {*The Origin of Civilization*, 245: "In the Tonga Islands the chiefs are regarded as immortal, the Tooas or common people as mortal;"}

30. Cf. *BGE* 9.

31. Cf. *D* 132.

32. Cf. *D* 132.

33. *vivre pour autrui]* "to live for others"; after Comte.

34. {Cf. Julius J. Baumann, *Handbuch der Moral nebst Abriss der Rechtsphilosophie* ("Manual of moral philosophy together with a summary of the philosophy of law") (Leipzig: S. Hirzel, 1879), 73, 67. *NL.*}

35. {Cf. Paul Bert, *La morale des Jésuites* ("Jesuit morality") (Paris: Charpentier, 1880), 8–9. *NL.*}

36. {Cf. Bert, 9.}

37. *Escobar]* Antonio Escobar y Mendoza, a Jesuit who was an object of Pascal's polemics. {Cf. Bert, 35n, where the entire sentence is italicized. Bert also quotes this line in his preface, xxi–xxii.}

38. Cf. *D* 207.

39. *its] Ms*: theirs

40. Cf. Moritz von Engelhardt, *Das Christenthum Justins des Märtyrers* ("The Christianity of Justin the Martyr") (Erlangen{: Deichert,} 1878), 312, 322. Cf. N to Franz Overbeck, 22 June 1880 {*KGB* III:1, 23} and Overbeck to N, 10 July 1880 {*KGB* III:2, 86}; cf. also the Chronicle of N's Life in *CW* 19.

41. *foal of an ass.]* {Zechariah 9.9: "Rejoice greatly, O daughter Zion! Shout aloud, O daughter Jerusalem! Lo, your King comes to you; triumphant and victorious is he, humble and riding on a donkey, on a colt, the foal of a donkey."}

42. Cf. Engelhardt, 439–40.

43. *let us imagine] Ms*: let it imagine

44. Cf. Engelhardt, 440.

45. Cf. *D* 197, 180.

46. *indicium]* "proof," "evidence"

47. *images] Written over*: in appearance

48. *The world . . . phenomenon]* {Cf. *BT* Preface 5, §§ 5, 24.}

49. *against its] Ms*: his

50. *Ms at the lower margin of the page*: not as individual but as unity behind multiplicity

51. *Amor and Psyche.]* {"Amor and Psyche," or "Cupid and Psyche" is a story about overcoming the obstacles to love in *The*

Golden Ass by Apuleius (second century CE). N makes use here of the central detail of Apuleius's plot, namely, that Psyche, not being permitted as a mortal to behold the face of the god Amor, could only be visited by her lover while asleep at night.}

52. *swarming] schwärmenden* {The German verb *schwärmen* has a double meaning: both "to swarm," like a flock of birds, or like a school of fish or a colony of bees, and "to enthuse," "to be enthusiastic."}

Translator's Afterword

J. M. Baker Jr.

The unpublished fragments from the period of *Dawn* (late 1879 to early 1881) display Nietzsche's continuing iteration of the themes and problems motivating the works of his middle period, *Human, All Too Human*, *Dawn*, and *The Joyful Science*.[1] Chief among these are the following: first, the conceptual triad of morals, customs, and ethics, which undergirds Nietzsche's critique of morality as the reification into law or dogma of ultimately unstable conceptions of good and evil; second, his assessment of Christianity's part in the determination of moral values as the highest values and of redemption as the representation of humanity's highest aspirations; third, the resulting polar tension between, on the one hand, Nietzsche's critique of modernity as an unrecognized aftereffect of the Christian world view and morality and, on the other hand, his contrasting view of modernity as the springboard to "the dawn" of a transformed humanity and culture; fourth, Nietzsche's continuous internal debate with exemplary figures in his own life and culture — Napoleon, Schopenhauer, and Wagner — who

1. We wish to express our thanks to Gary Handwerk for guiding us into the project, Denise Rochat for assistance in matters French, and Radcliffe Edmonds for assistance in a matter of ancient Greek. We owe thanks to Duncan Large for his review of the translation and his rigorous criticism and advice. We are most grateful to Alan Schrift for overseeing the progress of this volume with generous criticism, abundant patience, and unstinting support.

represented challenges to hitherto existing morals and culture, challenges that remained exemplary for Nietzsche precisely in their failure. As a whole, the unpublished fragments from the period of *Dawn* reveal how consequently Nietzsche's symptomatic, often polemical analyses of morality and culture aimed from the beginning at a radical probing of morality's and culture's unstated or unrecognized premises and motives.

The challenge for the translator of Nietzsche's notebooks is somewhat different from that facing the translator of his published works. Nietzsche's completed texts are landmarks of German prose style. They instance a penetrating directness of style that, while not without precedent, had not been in favor since Lichtenberg and the Enlightenment. At the same time, they instance a peculiar combination of urgency and irony that has precedents in the Romantic era. Their translation requires an ear for precise nuance along with an aptitude for variation in rhythm and tone. Nietzsche was fond of abrupt changes in register, or key.

While the notebooks are manifestly the work of the same hand as the published works, they also differ in that they are marked by an unusual, if not an excessive, rapidity of thought and expression. As Giorgio Colli remarked, Nietzsche was "an authentic *homo scribens*."[2] The result in the notebooks is a frequent brusqueness of diction and syntax that distinguishes them not only from the published works but also from other well-known notebook collections, say, those of Kierkegaard, Gide, and Kafka. Often enough, in familiar notebook fashion, Nietzsche simply writes enough to indicate a thought's direction without spelling it out. At other times, however, he abruptly breaks off thoughts or paratactically runs thoughts together without explicit indication of their inner connection. A striking characteristic of the notebooks is the limited range of action verbs employed. A symptom of the noted rapidity

2. Giorgio Colli, *Dopo Nietzsche* (Milan: Adelphi, 1974), 131. Colli makes this observation in a section headed "The Harvest's Impatience" ("*Impazienza della vendemmia*").

is Nietzsche's repeated use, as if by default, of the verbs "to make" (*machen*) and "to give" (*geben*), whereas his published texts employ to great effect a huge variety of action verbs, many of them compound verbs. Overall any temptation to smooth over the notebooks' brusque style has been resisted here. Only in exceptional instances, where readability was at risk, has Nietzsche's writing been "improved."

I.

It belongs to Nietzsche's directness of style that he shunned technical vocabulary, including the often Latinate terminology of formal philosophy most familiar to readers through the example of Kant. That said, some of his central concepts and terms do require comment. First among them is the word "morality." One German word for "morality" is the simple cognate *die Moral*, the word used in the title of *On the Genealogy of Morality* and used over and over in the notebooks. Nietzsche's use of the word would not bear comment, except that he often uses it in a way that makes its meaning indistinguishable from custom or convention. This befits Nietzsche's basic intention: morality is finally nothing more than the power of custom and convention. In general, the German word is rendered here as "morality," though on occasion context dictates its translation as custom. Nietzsche makes less frequent use of the word *Sitte*. This word is a more complex matter because it can mean with equal justice morality and custom, especially custom in the sense of long approved custom. The important precedent here is Kant's *The Metaphysics of Morals*, where the word translated as "morals" is *Sitten*.

A frequent topic in the notebooks of fundamental importance to *Dawn*'s critique of morality is dissimulation (*Verstellung*), a word with a wide semantic field. Nietzsche primarily uses it in the sense of dissimulation, hypocrisy, or pretense, but its meanings also include obstruction, rearrangement, and misplacement. In its verbal form, *verstellen*, it includes the meanings rearrange, reset, adjust, block, shift, misplace. As a reflexive verb, *sich verstellen*, its meaning is to simulate, or to hide one's feelings. Nietzsche's use of the word sometimes spans the field. The noun and verb are mainly translated here as "dissimulation" and "dissimulate," respectively, as that is the sense in which Nietzsche most often employs them. The Latinate English word "dissimulate" must serve to imply the secondary sense of blocking or misplacement that is embedded in the German word.

Companion to dissimulation is the pivotal theme of honesty, or *Redlichkeit*. German has two words for honesty, *Redlichkeit* and *Ehrlichkeit*. The latter is more commonly used and in spoken German is certainly the more familiar word. *Redlichkeit*, because it has the connotation of truthfulness and integrity, implies a higher level of virtue. Its nearest English equivalent would be "probity," which, like *Redlichkeit*, is less customary and includes the senses of truthfulness and integrity. But because Nietzsche himself does not explain his varying usage, it seemed better to use the same English word for both. In the text of *Dawn* Nietzsche uses *Ehrlichkeit* more often than *Redlichkeit*. Significant exceptions, however, are §91, with its ironical heading "God's honesty" (*Die Redlichkeit Gottes*), and §456. The latter is especially significant, insofar as it identifies honesty (*Redlichkeit*) as a virtue foreign to Socratic and Christian thought, a virtue "in the making": "one of the youngest virtues, still quite immature, still frequently mistaken and misconstrued, still barely aware of itself" (*D* §233).

Nietzsche makes frequent use of substantivized adjectives, a common feature of German philosophical and scientific writing. Among the most frequently occurring is the antithetical pair *angenehm/unangenehm*, translated here as "pleasant" and "unpleasant." The word's translation merits discussion because prior to Nietzsche it had been a central topic in eighteenth-century aesthetics, particularly in the works of Baumgarten, Herder, and Kant. In English translations of those works and in English-language scholarship on them, the word pair is often translated as "agreeable" and "disagreeable." The difference of course is one of shading and not of kind. "Pleasant" and "unpleasant" are used here because of their direct link with "pleasure." Pleasure, rather than agreement or agreeableness, is what Nietzsche takes to be the ruling criterion in judgments of value and taste.

A second frequently appearing term, again a substantivized adjective, is "the useful" or "the advantageous" (*das Nützliche*). While no friend of British utilitarianism, Nietzsche did not indulge the late nineteenth-century fashion of holding use values in contempt. On the contrary, the useful, like other values, has a qualitative scale ranging from the more cultivated (*gebildet*) to the less. For Nietzsche it is, to use a musical analogy, a value's pitch that matters and not the value as such — for example, the useful, the pleasant, the dissimulating. For the same reason, Nietzsche eschews the antithetical use of key concepts: utility and liability, the pleasant and the unpleasant, dissimulation and honesty are not opposed states but variations on a scale.

Neologisms and other instances of unconventional usage are concisely explained in the endnotes. Otherwise, with one exception, Nietzsche's core conceptual vocabulary does not require comment. That one exception is the word "power" (*Macht*). The difficulty in this case does not lie with Nietzsche's German but with sometimes fuzzy English usage. Nietzsche makes occasional use of the German words *Kraft* and, less often, *Gewalt*. *Kraft* is translated here, according to context, as "force," "strength," or "faculty," but in no instance as "power." Given the weighty significance of the concept of power in Nietzsche's work, translation of *Kraft* as power is at best confusing. *Gewalt* is translated, according to context, as "authority," "violence," or "power."

Regarding their content, the notebooks' entries can be divided into four groups: first, free drafts of reflections on the history of morality and related topics, e.g., contemporary mores and educational ideals; second, reflections on historical figures, thinkers, and artists; third, notes on the books

Nietzsche was reading at the time; fourth, reflections of an intimate or personal nature. There is of course overlap between these groups, especially between the first two. Most, if not all, of the longer notebook entries belong to the first two groups. Nietzsche's notes on his reading are often in the nature of incidental remarks, personal asides, and quick observational judgments. Many are on the order of marginalia: fragmentary sentences, single words or phrases, exclamations, short polemical aphorisms.

Entries from the first group are those which most often get worked up into sections of *Dawn*. The historical figures, thinkers, and artists who appear most often in the notebooks are virtually the same as throughout Nietzsche's corpus: the Apostle Paul, Luther, Pascal, Kant, Napoleon, Schopenhauer, and Wagner. Although they are important figures for Nietzsche, Plato, Spinoza, and Goethe appear less often here. During the writing of *Dawn*, Paul, Pascal, Napoleon, and Schopenhauer still were absorbing Nietzsche's attention, with Wagner in the background. Nietzsche's remarks in *Dawn* range over much of Western philosophy, but the notebooks suggest his philosophical reading at the time was targeted at John Stuart Mill and Herbert Spencer. This accords with the pattern of Nietzsche's writing overall. Nietzsche's treatment of the philosophical tradition does not proceed through close dialogue with individual texts but rather through broad typification of philosophical schools and doctrines. His reading of Mill and Spencer was more a function of his desire to assess influential contemporary doctrines than to engage philosophical scholarship. The one signal exception to this is Hermann Lüdemann's *Die Anthropologie des Apostels Paulus und ihre Stellung innerhalb seiner Heilslehre: Nach den vier Hauptbriefen dargestellt* ("The anthropology of the Apostle Paul and its place in his doctrine of salvation: As represented in the four major letters"). Although this text is not cited in *Dawn*, the notebooks, especially the fourth (N V 3), show that Lüdemann's book was foundational to the view of Paul Nietzsche developed in *Dawn* and in later writings.

The notebooks also reveal how intently Nietzsche was reading the three-volume *Mémoires* of Madame de Rémusat, his chief source for his knowledge of Napoleon as a personality. He was also reading, though with no immediate consequence for the text of *Dawn*, the non-fictional works of Stendhal: *Rome, Naples and Florence*; *On Love*; *Racine and Shakespeare*; *History of Italian Painting*, and Stendhal's correspondence. References to these works begin in notebook 6 and occur throughout notebook 7 but are brief and do not rise to the level of a preliminary sketch for a section of *Dawn* or another work. The abundant references to Rémusat in notebook 6 are close paraphrases without comment. Because Nietzsche was reading these works concurrently, one may be inclined to seek interior connections between them proceeding from the central importance of Napoleon to both. Nietzsche himself, however, does not take that step.

The fourth group of entries noted above, reflections of an intimate or personal nature, are not only among the briefest texts but also the fewest in number, and for that reason perhaps all the more intriguing. The subjects of these entries are usually left unnamed, though one often, or even always, wonders whether they are not forms of self-address. They are scattered throughout the notebooks, though the greatest number appear in the seventh. Nietzsche seldom uses the first person singular pronoun. Notebook entry 3[140] may serve as an example: "Is not our freethinking to be understood as an exaggerated, one-sided behavior that has lost its counterweight? Is not the artist frequently thrown from his center by his artistic creativity? Are not self-concealment, self-forgetting, self-denial the dangers of the fruitful solitary man?" This notebook entry reads like an aphorism *in nuce*. It seems to proceed from personal experience, and yet its significance is more than personal. To anticipate some of what follows, it reveals in a distilled manner Nietzsche's uncompromising critical spirit. Here it is the arch-freethinker who discerns an unwarranted conceit in free thought; here it is the model of the fruitful solitary man who warns of the dangers of solitude.

II.

The ground note of the notebooks of 1880–81 is what Nietzsche called the necessity of "unlearning" conscience and morality (3[97] and 4[5]). A majority of the entries read like rehearsals of *Dawn*'s central claims and arguments: that there is no basis for morality's normative status in European thought and culture; that it is above all Christian morality which has presumed to claim this normative status; that its claims are not disinterested but predicated on a deep suspicion of and hostility to bodily instincts and pleasures as well as to science and critical thought in general; that Christian morality has held onto its normative status in modern bourgeois society less because of any genuine belief in its truth than because of the inertia of social custom and habit; that the inherited psychological and social force of Christian morality is therefore what has to be uprooted if European humanity is to know a new dawn. But a new dawn can only break with the appearance of true individual spirits, for which nineteenth-century individualism, e.g., the Romantic and post-Romantic cult of the artist as genius and hero, is a poor counterfeit (3[81]). The dubiousness of the would-be individual's position is not, in Nietzsche's view, the dilemma of a subset of individuals or of a certain type of individual but, much rather, a symptom of the modern age. The modern age is, in this sense, a duplicitous phenomenon: on the one hand, it is the occasion for a rethinking of the culture's most cherished values; on the other hand, when provoked, it evinces huge resistance to the kind of rethinking that would have to take place for a true individualism to emerge.

These arguments are familiar by now even to those who have only a second-hand knowledge of Nietzsche's thought. This afterword focuses on the last, the problem of the individual. The problem of the individual, in what sense and under what conditions there can be such a thing, is the problem in which Nietzsche's critique of morality issues and comes most clearly into focus. Several recurrent topics in the notebooks bear upon this issue and come together to form a nodal point. These are dissimulation (*Verstellung*), honesty (*Redlichkeit*), and the question of adequate models for the individual.

The story of how *Dawn* came to be the title for Nietzsche's collection of new thoughts from 1879 to 1881 has its own illustrative point to make. Nietzsche's working title for the manuscript had been *Die Pflugschar*, "The Plowshare," though in between he momentarily considered calling it "*the need for truthfulness*" (6[261]). "The Plowshare" was the title inscribed on the draft he sent to Peter Gast on 25 January 1881 (see *CW* 5, 285). By the time the book was published by Ernst Schmeitzner Verlag in Chemnitz in 1881 it bore the new title by which it has been known ever since, *Morgenröthe*, or *Dawn*. The original title page, and every title page since, has included a brief quotation from the *Rig Veda* glossing the title: "Es giebt so viele Morgenröthen, die noch nicht geleuchtet haben" ("There are so many dawns that have not yet broken"). The origin of the new title is well known. Heinrich Köselitz, better known under his artist name Peter Gast, was doing Nietzsche the service of diligently reading, correcting, and producing clear copy of the manuscript. In February of 1881, struck by the newness of Nietzsche's thinking in the manuscript he had received, Köselitz sent a copy back to Nietzsche accompanied by the above quotation. Nietzsche was so taken with the saying that he immediately adopted it as the book's new title.[3]

Nietzsche's biographer Curt Paul Janz points out, however, that Köselitz not only delivered the quoted phrase without citing a specific passage in the *Rig Veda* but that the phrase corresponds to no passage in then existing translations of the *Rig Veda*. This discrepancy is not in itself of great moment. Unlike Schopenhauer, Nietzsche was not a proficient reader of the *Rig Veda* and would have had no motive to make a connection of his own work to that text beyond the aptness of this single phrase. At the same time it is important to remember that dawn is a distinct and rather long-lived motif in German literature and

3. See Curt Paul Janz, *Friedrich Nietzsche. Biographie*, 3 vols. (Munich: Carl Hanser, 1978), Vol. II, 65–66.

art, above all from the time of the German Romantic reception of Jacob Boehme, the early seventeenth-century Lusatian shoemaker and mystic whose own work of the same name, *Aurora, oder die Morgenröthe im Aufgang* (1612), was closely studied by Novalis, the brothers A. W. and Friedrich Schlegel, and the artist Philipp Otto Runge, to name only the most prominent. Notable in the motif's Romantic reception is that it especially took hold in the wake of the French Revolution, a time in which German artists and thinkers, including the philosopher Fichte, sensed epochal change afoot.[4] More notable yet perhaps is the fact that for Runge, an art theorist as well as a painter, the new dawn is not a singular event but a cyclical event. That there is not one dawn but returning dawns accords with Nietzsche's emphasis, especially in notebook 6 (N V 4), that humanity has many goals and not one goal and accords as well with how the phrase "there have been so many dawns" resonated with him. His choice of *Dawn*, rather than *The Dawn*, as the work's title is decisive, for it points to a profound temporal indeterminacy running throughout this work and beyond.[5]

4. "If I am not wholly mistaken, this is the point in time of the breaking of a new dawn, and the full day will follow upon it in its time" ("*Wenn mich nicht alles täuscht, ist jetzt der Zeitpunct der hereinbrechenden Morgenröthe, und der volle Tag wird ihr zu seiner Zeit folgen*"). Johann Gottlieb Fichte, as cited by Gerhard Schulz in "*'Potenzierte Poesie,' zu Friedrich von Hardenberg's Gedicht* An Tieck," in *Gedichte und Interpretationen*, Vol. 3 *Klassik und Romantik*, ed. Wulf Segebrecht (Stuttgart: Reclam, 1984), 248. Significantly, the statement cited is from the preface to an essay entitled "*Beitrag zur Berichtigung der Urtheile des Publikums über die französische Revolution*" ("Contribution to the correction of the public's judgments on the French Revolution") (1793). Fichte presents himself as a prophetic historian, instructing on the meaning of a past event for the future.

5. On Runge, see Christiane Hertel, "Raphael's *Sistine Madonna* and the search for language in Phillip Otto Runge's art theory and practice." *Word and Image* Vol. 9, No. 4 (1993): 320–48. Raphael's relevance to Nietzsche is discussed in section IV below. For a detailed, comprehensive treatment of myth and prophecy in German Romanticism, see Manfred Frank, *Der kommende Gott. Vorlesungen über die neue Mythologie* (Frankfurt: Suhrkamp, 1982). Frank discusses Nietzsche's thought in relation to the theme of "the coming god" in *Gott im Exil. Vorlesungen über die neue Mythologie* (Frankfurt: Suhrkamp, 1988).

Nietzsche was barely acquainted with early German Romanticism, and the notebooks as well as his published writings reveal that he was influenced by the later nineteenth century's prejudicial view of it as a conservative, if not reactionary, movement marked by a sentimental view of German folk culture and of the Middle Ages. The object in calling attention to the title's precedents is not to suggest an alternative source for Nietzsche's title but rather to lay out a relevant historical context. Nietzsche's announcement of a new dawn comes at the end of an eighteenth- and nineteenth-century prophetic tradition most fully exemplified by William Blake in England and in Germany by Novalis and Hölderlin. Relying on tropes of inversion and reversal, hyperbole, and paradox, this tradition espoused a syncretistic, if not heterodox, appropriation of the Christian religion in which present prophecy and future vision tend to merge and in which the prophetic voice is typically an isolated voice.[6] Strictly speaking, *Zarathustra* is Nietzsche's unique work in the prophetic mode. Yet the prophetic strain is a constant throughout his work. As this brief typification of the prophetic mode states, the prophetic mode has two facets, the loneliness of the prophetic voice and its new, even revolutionary stance towards a tradition. That said, the voice's loneliness is not the loneliness of a self-invented persona, for it stems from a unique dialogue with a tradition. That the prophetic voice hears the tradition in a way it had not been heard before is what defines the voice's individuality. Moreover, its individuality differs from the modern sense of the individual as personality or

6. This is not to say that Nietzsche stands under the influence of this line of thought, but rather that his writing, with its cognate tendency to reversal, hyperbolic expectation, and non-closure, engages a similar rhetoric of prophecy. Nietzsche admired what he knew of Hölderlin but would have had no access to the great hymns of 1801–5 that contain his prophetic vision. The first critical edition of Hölderlin's works, begun by Norbert von Hellingrath, dates to 1913–23. Interestingly, Nietzsche's one positive connection to this tradition was through Ralph Waldo Emerson, who was widely read in English and German literature of the Romantic era, albeit not in the works of Blake, Novalis, and Hölderlin.

character. Finally, the prophetic voice is primarily receptive. Its freedom consists in its capacity for making room for illumination, for the appearance of what is as yet unheard but at the same time always already there.

III.

Dawn is a clarion call for a new kind of individualism. At the same time, it is an anatomy of the obstacles mid to late nineteenth-century European culture, and German culture in particular, presented to the realization of an authentic individualism. In this anatomy is an abiding strand of pessimism that persists through, and not in spite of, Nietzsche's taking leave of Schopenhauer after *The Birth of Tragedy*. Schopenhauer's pessimism was all-encompassing; Nietzsche's by contrast is a pessimism focused more and more on the fate of the individual in modern societies. An expatiatory entry in the sixth notebook condenses Nietzsche's criticism of late nineteenth-century culture as diluted bourgeois Christian morality: "*Prudence* has taken the place of pride. Science enters into *its* service. A more common species of humans acquires authority (instead of the *noblesse* or priests): first the merchants, then the workers. The masses emerge as dominant: the individual must *dissimulate* as part of the masses" (6[31]). So, while dissimulation may have been initially a tactic of the weak, once in place it becomes the effective moral, and immoral, rule: "One praises and blames according to a model (call it moral or immoral) First comes the *submission* to a model" (7[69]).

Perhaps more important, although dissimulation may begin as a calculated tactic, with repetition and time it becomes something ingrained and therefore a deep-seated habit and convention. Above all, it is reciprocal. As an acquired habit, the practice of dissimulation is self-reinforcing for agent and recipient alike. The social-conventional dimension of dissimulation constitutes its peculiar significance for morality. Hence Nietzsche's claim that dissimulation is inherent in morality, as in *Dawn*, §248 (*CW* 5, 172–73): "*Dissimulation as duty.* — For the most part, goodness has been developed by extended dissimulation that sought to appear as goodness: wherever great power has taken hold one has recognized the necessity of precisely this type of dissimulation — it exudes certainty and confidence and increases hundredfold the sum of real physical power. The lie is, if not the mother, then the wet nurse of goodness. Honesty [*Ehrlichkeit*] too has, for the most part, been reared to maturity on the requirement that one seem honest and upright . . ."

It must be said straightaway that dissimulation and honesty do not compose a simple antithesis, as in Christian morality, whether the strict traditional Christian morality or Christian morality as it was assimilated in an increasingly secular post-Reformation culture. Nietzsche specifies, in fact, that the functional opposite of honesty is not dissimulation but imitation. It is far easier, he notes, to imitate an existing model, and thus to betray oneself, than to invent with one's own ingenuity a new model.

Nietzsche mainly associates dissimulation with the conduct and thought of weaker individuals. Already in the 1873 unpublished essay "On Truth and Lies in an Extra-moral Sense," he defined the central importance of *Verstellung* as dissimulation: "The intellect, as a means of preserving the individual, reveals its greatest strengths in dissimulation; for this is the means by which weaker, less robust individuals preserve themselves [. . .] In the natural condition of things, insofar as the individual wants to preserve itself against other individuals, it largely uses its intellect only for dissimulation" (*KSA* 1, 876, 877; *CW* 1). But if self-preservation in the face of others is at first a defense mechanism, it is also, or even simultaneously, the means of accommodating oneself to others. In 3[23], Nietzsche lays down his basic argument that morality is pre-eminently the form of dissimulation that enables a social existence, morality being the pretense that humans require in order to secure a tolerable level of co-existence with others free of fear. The social calculus of dissimulation informs the ordinary relation between individual and group: the individual presents himself as similar and usable ("*sich benutzen läßt*"). According to Nietzsche, this is so much the case that the habit of dissimulation becomes physically absorbed; it becomes part of our blood, a second nature. Over time, he observes, the habit of dissimulation has grown so interwoven with social intercourse that it has effectively become imperceptible. We come to resemble our world, we disappear into it. Today we speak matter-of-factly of adapting to an environment. Just so, following custom, one becomes moral; following authority, one becomes believing and trusting; and in the process one forgets how great a part dissimulation plays. For Nietzsche, this is the nature of the social dynamic from the beginning, so that even when we imagine we achieve independence we are necessarily returning to that which we have adopted from our environment, whether in reconciling ourselves to it or rebelling against it:

> That morality which is most strictly demanded, honored, and sanctified by everyone, the foundation of social life: what else is it but that dissimulation which people need in order to be able to live with one another *without fear*? (So that the single person presents himself as the other's equal and lets himself be used, just as he uses that other.) The greatest part of this dissimulation has already passed over into flesh, blood, and muscle; we no longer sense it as dissimulation, as little as we think of words of greeting and polite gestures as dissimulation: which they nevertheless are. The commonest kinds of dissimulation are: *first*, one assimilates to one's surroundings, one conceals oneself in them as it were; *second*, one imitates another human who enjoys respect and success, and dissembles as something higher than one is. In the first case one follows custom and becomes "moral," in the second case one follows authority and becomes "faithful": at all events one no longer arouses fear — for we have now many "peers." (3[23])

Reading through the notebooks suggests that the vision of a new dawn for the individual, if not for all of humanity, is encumbered with the weighty task of unlearning the insidious logic of dissimulation, if such is to be unlearned at all. In 3[97], he writes: "We must unlearn [*verlernen*] conscience, just as we have learned it," conscience being perhaps the most insidious means morality has of insinuating itself. And in 5[34]: "Not only do we have to relearn [*umlernen*] but to *rehabituate* our valuations — *practice* is needed!" Unlearning morality is not its mere rejection but an acquired discipline. Hence, the intention to escape dissimulation by cultivating a solitary life apart, or among a chosen few, is also a form of dissimulation: it shares with other social forms of dissimulation the goal of self-preservation, only in an inverse manner. The longing for others, for the like-minded (*Seinesgleichen*, as he likes to say) substitutes for fear of others.

In 3[145], Nietzsche gives an instance of how the dynamics of dissimulation work: "Lying and dissimulation, which within the community are cultivated to produce equality, yield in the end a free surplus that discharges itself in the generation of poets and actors. Let us think how much pleasure a community takes in abusing, cursing, sleights of hand, and similar original arts." This already represents a modification of his view of dissimulation toward a dynamic understanding of it as a necessary and finally ineliminable component of social discourse and behavior.[7]

Even more instructive in this context is notebook entry 6[367], a rare combination of personal confession with a concise formulation of principle: "If he earnestly bade me or I guessed that he very much needed me, I would, against all better knowledge, take his side. This would be my weakness. Better to abandon *ourselves* and those who need us! And we are capable of a great

7. At the same time, Nietzsche speaks of the noble as those who do not need to dissimulate: "The noble ἐσθλοί the truthful, who do *not need to dissimulate*! As the powerful and individuals!" (8[78]). But this describes an ideal, or limit, condition and not the conventional moral world.

deal of dissimulation: and, consequently, of much reeducation and a *second honesty*." The note addresses itself to Nietzsche's fraught relationship with Richard Wagner. Although the friendship had already ruptured, at this point the rupture was recent enough that Nietzsche still acknowledges to himself a residual tie. In the same moment, however, he abjures the tie as sentimental; that species of compassion serves neither the other nor oneself. Dissimulation as shifting informs the Nietzschean trope of masking. More than mere disguises, masks are the means of achieving a finer, more discriminating grasp of motive and desire. However paradoxically, honesty is inseparable from the achievement of a refined level of dissimulation.

Nietzsche does address more familiar forms of dissimulation. In 3[8], he addresses dissimulation in the sense of hypocrisy or pretense: "The presumptuous person poses as proud, but pride is precisely free of pretense (in contrast to the vain person); to this extent presumptuousness is the hypocrisy of a kind of absence of pretense, and wherever it is masterfully simulated it is confused with pride." This fragment gets fully developed in *Dawn* §291, though without any qualification of the basic thought that presumption (*Anmaßung*) is the hypocrisy of being without pretense (*Verstellung*). In 6[227], "Infinite dissimulation is required in order to become a loving person." In the case of passionate love, Nietzsche says we want to believe we are being honest with ourselves because when we feel strongly about something we believe that it is our true passion. In §335 of *Dawn* he gives the thought another turn: "We need to be honest with ourselves and to know ourselves very well in order to be able to practice toward others that philanthropic dissimulation that goes by the name of love and kindness" (*CW* 5, 199). Dissimulation, in other words, is a constant, even, or above all, when we think that we know perfectly well what we believe or feel. While that thought may be familiar enough, Nietzsche's peculiar consequence lies in his further claim that dissimulation is not limited to the sphere of passion and belief but extends to science and reason as well.

> Rash inclination and disinclination, dissimulation, etc. has been *molded* into our whole organism: gradually truthfulness too can be molded onto it and grow ever deeper roots, with what effects? For the time being it is a moving net of falsehood and deception and their tentacles: entirely animal-useful. The education toward truth — is it an improvement of the animal, a higher adaptation to reality? — Our benevolence compassion, our self-sacrifice, our "morality" rests upon *the same foundation* of falsehood and dissimulation as our evil and selfishness! This is to be shown! The unpleasant, yes, tragic impress of this discovery is initially unavoidable. But at first all our drives must become more anxious more distrustful, gradually incorporate more reason and honesty, become shrewder and thus ever more lose the *reason* for *distrust* of one another: so can one day a greater, more fundamental joyfulness emerge: for the time being this *joyfulness* would only be *possible for the dishonest. Resignation and that heroic pleasure in defiance and victory are the only forms of our joyfulness: if we are cognitive beings. NB NB NB*!!! How then does it happen that we struggle against the *profound mendacity and dissimulation*? A feeling of *power*, which in our mind's development and operation becomes free, compels us: it whets the appetite. (6[274])

The exclamation marks and the triple *nota bene* with emphasis suggest that Nietzsche set store by this notebook entry, even if it was not taken up as such into the text of *Dawn*. Significantly, the concept of power adduced here is the consequence and not the cause of the mind's development. If it is not even remotely like Schopenhauer's blind will, it also does not resemble a transcendental ground. The grammar of agency in Nietzsche's phrasing is instructive. It is not we, as autonomous agents, that become free but rather the feeling of power by which we are driven (*treibt uns*). The implicit thesis is that the development of the human mind is instrumental to but not therefore the end, or destination, of a process that traverses us but does not stop with us. To this extent at least Nietzsche's provisional concept of power must be tied to the new importance he was attaching to the concept of the drives. Dissimulation is not, as in traditional morality, an intentional act subject to determination by a conscious will, but rather a manifestation of a complex interplay of drives for self-preservation and for acceptance by others, but also of drives for submission and control. When we posit goals for ourselves we do not do so, as we may imagine we do, according to our own intents and mortal purposes, but only as far as the drives allow us to see.

Nietzsche specifies that the drives are of an indeterminate scope. What is useful (*nützlich*) is not their final goal, as little as what is pleasurable. As he notes in 6[18], no one knows how far drives develop: what people strive for, what they posit as the good or as the ideal, is highly divergent and aligns accordingly on a scale ranging from the original and individual to the merely imitative and slavish. It is only custom and habit, reinforced by authority, that lend to these ideals a normative status. Were individuals left for once to their own drives, a different picture would emerge. That we fail more from our strengths than our weaknesses is an index of the fact that we do not know how to act in our own interest or to our own advantage. In addition, it is in the nature of the drives that there is always something afoot, something developing of which we are not aware. Development is towards a different, colorful future, as Nietzsche sometimes says, although it is not clear whether this development is something naturally destined to come about on its own or will be the result of human decisions. In the main Nietzsche leans toward the latter, for he posits that the coming of a new dawn will be the consequence of a dissolution of the force of customs (*Sitten*) and of a greatly enhanced honesty. In contrast with Christian morality, this honesty will not be in the first place an honesty about our failings and weaknesses but an honesty about how and why our failings and weaknesses are so judged. For all his typification of cultures and traditions, on the whole Nietzsche refrained from predicting where such "a different, colorful future" might emerge.[8]

Some of Nietzsche's phrasing in notebook entry 6[274] quoted above, e.g., "it is a moving net of falsehood and deception and their tentacles," echoes the phrasing of "On Truth and Lies in an Extra-moral Sense" where, in a much-cited remark, Nietzsche argues that truth is a moving army of rhetorical figures which, through long use, have grown fixed and acquired for a people (*Volk*) who use them as a binding force. But what then are the limits of dissimulation, whether in its form as a deliberate practice, as a rhetorical and political strategy for gaining influence and power over others, or in its form as a passive, more or less conscious accession to the lies we tell ourselves for the sake of maintaining communal belief in things like truth, justice, the individual soul, the common good? On the one hand, Nietzsche speaks of dissimulation as the recourse weaker natures have in order to preserve themselves in the face of others. And this is the way dissimulation is often treated in the notebooks. On the other hand, however, at least by virtue of its psychological and rhetorical inescapability, dissimulation is a behavior and aspect of thought that stronger natures, too, cannot and do not avoid. Their practice, being simply more subtle and more resourceful, is also more powerful. Nietzsche says the strong individual wants to rule, is indeed driven to rule.

For Nietzsche it is axiomatic that morality and intellect-science are opposed (3[169]). And yet it does not follow from this that the future of culture lies in the mere severance of intellect and science from morality. If, for Nietzsche, there is no morality that does not rest upon the prejudices of custom and convention, he also makes a telling and striking concession in this regard. In 3[172], the notebook's final entry, he remarks that the perfect morality would be justice, i.e., a judgment not motivated by reward and punishment, by praise or

8. Notebook seven, however, shows that at least for a time he foresaw a special role for Russia; cf. 7[111, 205, 283].

blame. A judgment of this order would be perfect cognition (*Erkenntnis*) and thus perfect morality. But the existence of such a judgment is purely hypothetical. Nietzsche concludes the fragment with the exclamation that there is only ever deficient cognition, hence only ever defective judgment and therefore no judgment free of prejudice. Just as the wholly just judgment is conceivable but does not exist, so also there is no thinking or use of language that would be wholly free of dissimulation. In the notebooks, Nietzsche's working through of this gambit leads to the provisional conclusion that dissimulation is not the contrary of truthfulness, or honesty, but rather a necessary moment in the achievement of honesty. It does not follow from this, however, that the relationship of the two is a dialectical progress. The moment of dissimulation is never definitively surpassed, much less is the achievement of honesty ever something complete. Things being what they are, though, joyfulness belongs for the time being to the dishonest, the dissembling (cf. 6[274]).

Nietzsche's complex conception of honesty is quite remote from its sense in contemporary everyday English usage, where it often signifies little more than a blunt straightforwardness or even an undisguised egoism. The notebooks show him working toward a conception of honesty far beyond the naked confession of feelings and facts. To begin with, honesty for Nietzsche is something to be achieved and not a starting point or a mere disposition to truthfulness. Its complexity owes to the fact that he does not make honesty the simple opposite of deception, or dissimulation. The standard of truthfulness is an honesty (*Redlichkeit*) that does not presuppose a "true self" or any other kind of inner substance that could be wholly clear to itself. It is, instead, a discipline and practice rather than a cognitive possession: "It is mythology to believe that we will find our true self after we have dropped or forgotten this and that. In this way we unravel ourselves back into the infinite: instead *to make ourselves*, to *create* a form from all elements — is the task! Always that of the sculptor! Of a productive human! *Not* through knowledge but practice, and we become *ourselves* a model! Knowledge has at best the value of a means!" (7[213]).

The first thing requiring honest reflection is the fiction of purpose and purposiveness: that the human decides and acts according to clear conscious purposes; that nature has purposes, or a purposive structure. "Generally, one considers no action as intelligible unless it is aimed at purposes: and absolutely no movement in the world. For that reason, all earlier thought intended to explain all motion in the world as purposive and purposeful (God). Philosophy's greatest turning point is that action according to purposes was *no longer found comprehensible*; with that all earlier tendencies are invalidated" (6[250]). To the illusion of purpose belongs the illusion that our words and thoughts are somehow fitted to the real: "The thought, just as much as the word, is only a sign: there is no question of any congruence of thought and the real. The real is some movement of a drive" (6[253]).

Nietzsche's reflections on the interdependency of dissimulation and honesty are animated by and follow from his genealogical method, concisely defined in 6[140]: in the past one asked whether a thought was true, now one asks how it came to be regarded as true — what purpose or intention, conscious or unconscious, does it serve?[9] The genealogical method does not consist alone in the unmasking of past claims to truth. If that were the case, then at some point its ground clearing work would be done and the method itself would be history. The genealogical method depends on a new unbounded need for truthfulness, or honesty (*Redlichkeit*), on a will and an ability to pierce outworn models of truth and integrity, including one's own: "Practice in cognition has produced in the end a

9. See 6[140]: "Formerly one asked: Is the thought true? Now: how did we come upon it? What was its driving force? Let's discover it —." The grammar of this notebook entry is ambiguous on account of the dash at the end. We have read it as an imperative and translated it accordingly. However, it can also be read as the beginning of a conditional statement left incomplete ("if we discover it, then . . .") or as a question ("will we discover it?").

need for truthfulness, which now is a new great power, with dangers and advantages" (6[261]).[10] Yet the ability to take pleasure in this cognitive acuity is rare and new, a mark of a dawning acuity that is only won gradually and laboriously, likewise the pleasure in exercise of this cognitive acuity.[11] Most relevant here is Nietzsche's stirring sense of the theme's timeliness. Philosophy's future, he implies, is dependent upon the development of a new sense of honesty.[12]

And yet this new sense of honesty is not a landing point but, like the new individual, something as yet indeterminate. As he says, it entails dangers as well as a new power. As a technique of cognition this honesty bodes new iterations of the ancient precept *nosce te ipsum*, "know thyself." Among its dangers is confusion, not only the general culture's but also the individual's, about the nature of the path forward. What kind of a day is it to which this new consciousness awakes? This is the inception of Nietzsche's intention throughout the mature phase of his thought to furnish a revision of the ancient precept that would rend it of the entire weight of its Christian reception, not only the Christian ascetical tradition, which Nietzsche singles out for its victimization of the individual, but also the Christian humanist tradition, which for Nietzsche is finally an unpersuasive attempt at the appropriation of classical sources.[13]

The genealogy of human beings' dishonesty with themselves leads back to the genesis of Christianity, itself a complex of distrust of the intellect and passions coupled with an overvaluation of conscience and associated feelings of guilt, remorse, and repentance. For Nietzsche the Christian ideal of humility and holiness deriving from a message of guilt and repentance constitutes its

10. 6[261] is the source for N's note to himself, cited above, on "the need for truthfulness" as a possible book title.

11. See 6[265].

12. In the Afterword to *Dawn*, Keith Ansell-Pearson notes the centrality of a new sense of honesty to Nietzsche's arguments there. See *CW* 5, 378.

13. Nietzsche credited only a few seventeenth-century Frenchmen — Francis de Sales, Fénelon, and Pascal — with a plausible form of Christian humanism. See 5[37].

own "sublime kind of pride" (6[229]). In this longer speculative note on the origin of the Christian mentality Nietzsche observes that "his honesty with himself is very slight" (6[229]). The antecedent for "his" here is the figure of Christ, but it is telling that everything Nietzsche says here about the psyche of Christ is predicable of virtually every Christian believer. Here Nietzsche is bringing to the surface a level of indiscernibility between the figure of Christ and the religion to which his person gave rise. Nietzsche postulates an identity of the two: the Christian psychology is a specious form of egoism appealing to the marginal, the despised, and the weak. Significantly, this generic typification of Christ and the Christian as the same cultural and psychic formation does not enter into the text of *Dawn*. Instead, Nietzsche concentrates there on the long-term effects of the psycho-cultural formation represented by the Apostle Paul.[14]

In the text of *Dawn* Nietzsche takes the instructive tack of referring only indirectly to Christ, as in §113 where he speaks obliquely of "a god of love . . . even of holiness and sinlessness." In this aphorism the tactic of indirection serves to focus the reader's attention on what Paul, Dante, and Calvin have drawn from the Christian teaching rather than on the person or psyche of Christ himself. The significance of this tactic lies precisely in the fact that Nietzsche leaves the figure of Christ alone, less out of deference or respect for the person than out of deference to our ignorance finally of what and who that figure really was. It is surely significant that aphorism §68 from Book One, which is Nietzsche's initial core diagnosis in *Dawn* of the personality of the Apostle Paul, runs under the heading

14. The notebooks show Nietzsche taking tentative steps toward the kind of diagnosis of the figure of Christ that he performed at greater length on Paul, Luther, Pascal, Schopenhauer, and Wagner. See, for example, 6[143]: "Christ bore not only God but Satan too in his bosom: that is the counterclaim with this moral hyper-idealism: the absolute damnation of the human being, the *odium generis humani* [hatred for the human race]. — For humanity to feel worthy of such a sacrifice by a god, one had to despise humanity to the depths and degrade it in its own sight."

"The First Christian," for it is in this same aphorism that he establishes one of *Dawn*'s basic genealogical motifs, namely, that the ostensible Pauline renewal of Christianity by Luther and Pascal would turn out to be, for anyone capable of reading it, the exposure of the Pauline deceit perpetrated upon the Jewish law and turn out to be not Christianity's renewal but its final demise. Later, in a much-cited passage from §39 of *The Antichrist* (*CW* 9, 170–71), Nietzsche would revise his view of who the first Christian was: "Even the word 'Christianity' is a misunderstanding — at bottom there was only one Christian, and he died on the cross" ("*Das Wort schon 'Christentum' ist ein Mißverständnis — im Grunde gab es nur einen Christen, und er starb am Kreuz*"). Coming from a later phase of Nietzsche's thought, this verdict bears an important retrospective significance for *Dawn*. For in this statement Christ has become for Nietzsche, in an ironic inversion of the Christian apostolic mission, the model of the individual: he is not to be imitated.[15] For Nietzsche Christ's notable failure was that although a thorough individual, he was an individual who nevertheless imputed his own standards to others. Christ's precedent is the example Nietzsche expressly refuses: "I want to socialize only with humans who have their own model and do *not* see it in *me*. For this would make me responsible for them and a slave" (7[70]).

15. In 6[175], Nietzsche assigns Christ to a subset of the individual. According to the distinction he draws there, Christ is a higher nature, yet not the highest because he lacks a true grasp of the common person and the individual alike. Nietzsche accuses Christ of a blindness towards himself and the world: "A sub-species: *higher natures* who *everywhere* presuppose their own individuality and their standard of feeling, thus their own history — and do *not* recognize the individual, *just as little* as they understand the *common* (e.g., Christ). *They know themselves* not as individual." At the end of this entry Nietzsche contrasts Christ to another subspecies of the individual: higher types who know themselves as individual and who understand individuals, but only with difficulty commonness, and then adds "*this they have to learn*" (N's emphasis). This seems to be a telling self-reflection. See also 10[E89] "Moral prescriptions are stopgaps for the indiv⟨iduals⟩ who cannot recognize themselves as strictly individual and must have a norm external to themselves."

IV.

The word "model" appears in the later notebooks of 1880–81, especially the sixth and seventh. It is applied both to conduct and to persons, but the accent is squarely on conduct as index to an exemplary or a deplorable personality type. Accordingly, Nietzsche thinks of models in two ways: as the prevailing models, or what have heretofore served as paradigms of morality, and as future models, or what has yet to be devised and brought into being. The difference in usage reflects the inevitable tension between the expectant, or prophetic, side of Nietzsche's thinking and its pessimistic side. Beyond that tension, however, a further ambiguity arises which is the ineluctable result of Nietzsche's singular conception of the individual. The setting in place of models for the individual's development presupposes a minimally integral conception of the individual as a self or ego. As will be seen, Nietzsche's slant throughout the notebooks runs towards a multiple and non-integral conception of the individual life.

In 8[15], Nietzsche confides: "I am fortunate not to have had a moral education (except that by role models)." Unless this is an inconsistency, we must assume that Nietzsche is thinking of role models who not only allowed him to develop independently of prevailing social norms but who themselves did not conform to norms. In this light it is not surprising that Nietzsche seems to hesitate between a view of the individual as something incommensurable and a view of the individual as something in need of an adequate model. This is not an inconsistency but a tension inherent in his effort to imagine a culture that is the product of individual happiness, in stark contrast with a culture that produces happy individuals. The following passages from the notebooks illustrate this tension:

> Some humans are simpler, but most often though the individual is *unrecognizable* and ineffable. *Consequently*, the *model* is necessarily an illusion! If I do not know the

> construction materials in terms of mass and kind, what are architectural designs! And how constrained this eternal brooding about the ego makes us! We would have no time for knowledge of the world! And if even this knowledge were first of all the means to cognition of the ego, then we would *never* arrive at the task itself! And ultimately this infatuation with our own model is one more bondage! (7[54])

> I want to help all who seek their model by showing *how* one seeks a model: and my greatest joy is encountering the individual models that do *not* resemble me. The devil take all the imitators and followers and panegyrists and admirers and devotees! 6[50]

The notebooks reveal that Nietzsche saw Goethe as the paradigmatic model but that his paradigmatic character did not consist in the things that education and social custom, or morality, think of as models. As Nietzsche writes in §497 of *Dawn*, one should only speak of genius in persons where "spirit" (*Geist*) appears only lightly attached to temperament and character.

For Nietzsche the figure of Goethe was always a standard, if not the standard. The word "figure" is not used casually here but in preference to alternatives, like artist, person, model, certainly thinker. The phenomenon, the figure, of Goethe exceeds all of these. In 4[213], Nietzsche goes so far as to say that "Goethe knew what it takes to be a scientific person: he is an ideal in whom all human competencies unite like all the streams in the sea." If this sounds hyperbolic, we should recall a late section of *Dawn*, §540, where, taking up the contrast Michelangelo drew between himself and Raphael as that between study and nature, i.e., between learning and talent, Nietzsche rejects the distinction as a piece of pedantry, asking what else talent is but an older piece of learning, experience, appropriation, incorporation. Learning, by Nietzsche's lights, means optimal openness, hence the ability to experience and absorb without the artist's customary envy or pride. For him, this open, unprejudiced receptivity is what set Raphael apart as an exemplary learner and exemplary artist. Goethe's name appears in this text only parenthetically, yet weightily: Raphael, "like Goethe," Nietzsche writes, was a great learner, unencumbered by the defensiveness and resentment other artists display at what is unknown or foreign. In other words, the sea-like quality Nietzsche notes in Goethe is an expression not of some primordial originality but more precisely of a profound receptivity. This thought is at one with Nietzsche's other distinction between an illusory, purely suppositious moral freedom and artistic freedom. The latter has no need to claim a pretended autonomy or independence.

This discussion raises perhaps unexpected, though not surprising, questions about the meaning of individualism in Nietzsche's thinking around 1880. Paradoxically, what matters most to Nietzsche in the phenomenon of the individual is precisely not what one usually thinks of as the earmarks of individuality, namely, temperament, personality, and character, but rather this other thing he calls spirit (*Geist*). Although this spirit is not restricted to artists — interestingly, Nietzsche names Plato and Spinoza as other exemplary instances — it is principally an aesthetic manifestation rather than a matter of individual liberty, belief, or, to be sure, profession. Of course, the word "aesthetic" must be understood here in a broad sense and may not be confused with the cultic individualism of late nineteenth-century aestheticism. On the contrary, the paradox inhering in Nietzsche's ideal conception of the individual is that the artist, a Raphael or a Goethe, is the highest specimen of the individual, and yet it is their endowment to be more than individual. This "more than" does not signify the empty concept of artistic or philosophical universality but instead the very concrete and singular path by which the artist became a seer and thinker. The artist is inimitable, not because he has attained a mythical peak beyond the reach of others but for the far more tangible and proximate reason that he has learned his own way of using the past.

Nevertheless, Nietzsche is occasionally critical of Goethe, as in the aphorism "the Germans' hostility to the Enlightenment" (*D* §197, *CW* 5, 142–43). This same section can be taken to explain why for Nietzsche Goethe is not the definitive noble type. The aphorism concludes with Nietzsche's affirmation that the Enlightenment must be carried on, yet not in the terms ordinarily used, namely, the steady progress of critical reason and steady emancipation from dogma. Instead, Nietzsche notes that the "great Revolution" of the Enlightenment, having been succeeded by a "great reaction," has not been replaced by that reaction but continues to exist alongside it. The antiquarianism, sympathy with the past, and fascination with origins that had been the insignia of German opposition to the (French) Enlightenment became, Nietzsche observes, the instruments or means by which the Enlightenment has been carried forward. Nietzsche lays down here a more complex because conflicted and interrupted view of historical development that anticipates a later, more familiar "dialectic of enlightenment."[16] The aphorism concludes with a sea image that ought to be read as an equivalent of the light imagery of dawn. Great revolutions and great reactions, Nietzsche writes, are mere surface ripples compared to "the truly great tide in which *we* surge and want to surge!" (*CW* 5, 143).[17]

The dilemma as well as the distinction of the individual is that this tide is unapparent except to the few discerning spirits who are the harbingers of a better and different future. This is presumably a nobler future, but is it Goethe's future? In this respect Erich Heller was right to say that Nietzsche always also had misgivings about Goethe.[18] Heller refers here to a note by Nietzsche

16. Theodor Adorno and Max Horkheimer, *Dialectic of Enlightenment*, trans. John Cumming (New York: Herder and Herder, 1972).

17. This passage reflects Nietzsche's predilection for water imagery, particularly seas and rivers. Much has been said about his symbolic use of animal imagery. A good deal could also be said about his use of sea- and landscapes. Analysis would show that their significance is not limited to their use as illustration or background setting.

18. Erich Heller, "Nietzsche and Goethe," in *The Importance of Nietzsche: Ten Essays* (Chicago: University of Chicago Press, 1988), 35.

on Goethe's rejection of Kleist. That rejection, which characteristically took the form of a standing aloof, is Goethe's own avoidance of tragedy. For Nietzsche, Goethe had to take this stance: "What Goethe sensed in H. Kleist was his feeling for the *tragic*, from which he turned away: it was the incurable side of nature. He was himself conciliatory and curable" (*CW* 4, 322, 29[1]). For Nietzsche himself, however, there is no standing aloof, however much he elsewhere professed admiration for Goethe's "Olympian" nature, as his own metaphors attest. The new dawn's spirits ride a great tide.

In order not to posit false oppositions or to impute to Nietzsche an inconsistency of vision, we can draw a distinction between retrospective and prospective vistas in his thinking. Goethe and Raphael, with their learners' ability to make free use of the past, correspond to the former. For a while Nietzsche imagined Schopenhauer and then, especially, Wagner as harbingers of the latter. Neither availed, and then the prospective vista became the wholly open vista. Essential here is that the distinction between the two not be seen as a distinction between earlier and later, developing and mature phases of his thought but rather as his thought's constitutive tension, the ability to maintain both vistas at once.[19]

The problem of individuality was manifold. Its challenge did not lay simply in overturning a Christianity that victimized the individual while espousing under the mask of humility and self-abnegation a perverse individualism. The challenge was complicated by what Nietzsche considered the nineteenth century's counterfeit individualism, whether the exotic individualism of the Romantic era or the sober individualism of bourgeois liberalism.

19. An analogy can be drawn here to "On the Utility and Liability of History for Life" from *UO* (*CW* 2), where Nietzsche distinguishes between the antiquarian, monumental, and critical approaches to history. The distinction can initially be read as qualitative: the critical approach supersedes the antiquarian and monumental approaches. But it is more just to read the three as interdependent and mutually informative.

This places Nietzsche in the tradition of Emerson and John Stuart Mill, both of whom he had read with varying degrees of approval.[20] Nietzsche's agreement with Emerson and Mill consists in their common questioning of a social and psychological model of the self that proceeds from the Christian concept of the individual soul. Under a qualified Romantic influence, nineteenth-century thought tended to preserve the egoistic conception of the individual that informs Christianity: each person is endowed with a special soul, a kind of inborn spirit, with which it enters the world and, once there, wants its proper development. Nietzsche's own objection to the Christian concept of the individual is precisely its egoism, namely, the, for him, preposterous notion that every person born into the world is the object of a solicitous divine care. "Christianity gave each person the right to take himself unspeakably *seriously*: he is an 'eternal being!' a 'genius,' a 'personality'" (5[24]).[21] Whether Emerson and Mill go as far as Nietzsche in abjuring this egoistic definition of the individual is a question in its own right.[22] Whereas Mill wished to rescue individuality by ensuring individual consciousness a free space within the parameters of modern culture, Nietzsche asks what kind of individuality is now even possible within those parameters. As far as Nietzsche is concerned, the

20. Ansell-Pearson observes in the Afterword to *Dawn* that Nietzsche fails to acknowledge that Mill was a champion of individual liberty and autonomy (*CW* 5, 393, n51). He points out that Mill, like Nietzsche, inveighs against the pressures of conformist, majoritarian opinion. This is surely correct, and yet it is also the case that Mill's disposition was to conceive of the individual in the privative terms of liberty. Ultimately, that was not Nietzsche's tack. For him this was not, or would not have been, enough.

21. In *Dawn*, §132, Nietzsche criticizes the Christian conception of the individual for tying the individual's worth to salvation and eternal life (*CW* 5, 99).

22. Stanley Cavell is the most forceful advocate of a Nietzschean, or at least Nietzsche-like, reading of Emerson. See *In Quest of the Ordinary: Lines of Skepticism and Romanticism* (Chicago: University of Chicago Press, 1988); *Emerson's Transcendental Etudes*, ed. David Justin Hodge (Palo Alto: Stanford University Press, 2003); and *Philosophy the Day After Tomorrow* (Cambridge, MA: Belknap Press of Harvard University Press, 2006).

appearance of a new individual freedom within nineteenth-century culture was merely that, an appearance. The reality for him was that prospects for a true individual freedom were actually shrinking.[23] In an entry toward the end of the third notebook Nietzsche ties the future of education to the critique of morality: "In truth, though, present education appears miserable because a great task has arisen before it on the horizon, namely the revision of all valuations; but that requires, even before all the things can be laid on the scale, the scale itself — I mean that utmost fairness of the utmost intelligence which has in fanaticism its mortal enemy and in the present 'well-rounded education' its ape and master of ceremonies" (3[158]).

The tendency of nineteenth-century bourgeois thought and culture was either to subtract the concept of a providential God from its model of individual development or to let it become so attenuated as to allow for a secularized Christian *Bildung*. There is no doubt that Emerson, Mill, and others like them took up a less guarded and more variegated view of the individual as a thing admitting of multiplicity. Still, Emerson and Mill did not venture as far as what Nietzsche projects in the notebooks, namely, a concept of individualism that, paradoxically, does away with the individual in the sense of a single unique self and replaces it with a constellation of forces. This is an individualism that no longer consists in the realization of an essence, or personal genius, but rather in an individual's readiness to hold himself open to a multiplicity of perspectives and forces, however contradictory and conflicting.[24] If this alternative view of

23. This line of thought in Nietzsche was amplified and most fully developed in the next generation of German thought by Max Weber. Against the view that material and scientific progress would be the seedbed of freedom and individualism, Weber augured that this progress would simply foster new kinds of servitude. To this extent Weber carried forward Nietzsche's stance of defiant pessimism, a pessimism quite distinct from Schopenhauer's.

24. Nietzsche sketches this eccentric or, to use a more recent term, decentered view of the self in 6[70] and 6[80]. He anticipates in this respect Sigmund Freud, who is said to have avoided deeper acquaintance with Nietzsche's writings for fear of being unduly influenced and diverted from his own path.

individuality were to hold sway, it would disqualify not only any notion of a generally valid culture (*Bildung*) but would also seem to entail a drastic revision, if not elimination, of conventional notions of individual freedom and autonomy. "All moralities thus far have proceeded from the prejudice that we know *for what purpose* the human being exists: hence knows his ideal. Now we know that there are many ideals: the consequence is the individualism of the ideal, the denial of a general morality" (4[79]). By abjuring the idea of a generally valid morality Nietzsche opens the possibility that the individual morality, or immorality, that he recommends is an incommensurable that has no scale and thus is hardest to come by and least intelligible: "Should not conversely every individual be the attempt to *attain* a *higher species than the* **human being** on the strength of his most individual things? My morality would be this, *to remove* more and more from the human his general character and to specialize him, to make him less intelligible to a degree for others (and thus into an object of experiences, wonder, instruction for them)" (6[158]). Nietzsche's basic conviction is that the individual is incommensurable (6[175]), a singularity that stands apart and consequently appears irrational to the common person. For morality as we have known it, this conception of individuality signifies an intolerable variety of standards.

See, for example, *The Ego and the Id*: "Now I think we shall gain a great deal by following the suggestion of a writer who, from personal motives, vainly asserts that he has nothing to do with the rigours of pure science. I am speaking of Georg Groddeck, who is never tired of insisting that what we call our ego behaves essentially passively in life, and that, as he expresses it, we are 'lived' by unknown and uncontrollable forces." Sigmund Freud, *The Freud Reader*, ed. Peter Gay (New York: Norton, 1989), 634–35; Sigmund Freud, *Gesammelte Werke*, Vol. 13, *Jenseits des Lustprinzips, Massenpsychologie und Ich-Analyse, Das Ich und das Es, und andere Werke aus den Jahren 1920–1924* (Berlin: S. Fischer Verlag), 251. Freud goes on to say that he will take up Groddeck's "discovery" into his own systematic distinction between Ego (*Ich*) and Id, or It (*Es*), and adds the following footnote: "Groddeck himself no doubt followed the example of Nietzsche, who habitually used this grammatical term [i.e., "*Es*"] for whatever in our nature is impersonal and, so to speak, subject to natural law."

In the tenth and final notebook of 1880–81 Nietzsche staked out this problem in addressing himself to Spencer's prognostication of a social condition in which the individual's being consists in his becoming a functioning member of a social whole:

> Such an adaptation as Spencer envisions is imaginable, but so that each individual becomes a useful instrument and also perceives himself only as such: thus, as *means*, as *part* — hence *with annulment of the individualism* according to which one wants to be *purpose* and *a completeness*, namely in both a *uniqueness*! This transformation is possible, indeed perhaps history is taking its course toward that! But then the individuals will become **ever weaker** — it is the history of the *demise of mankind*, where the principle of disinterestedness, the *vivre pour autrui*, sociality rule! If the individuals are to become stronger, then society must remain a *state of emergency* and always must expect changes: to lead a *provisional existence perpetually* (10[D60]).

These notes are taken up and greatly expanded into §132 of *Dawn*, "The last gasp of Christianness in morality" (*CW* 5, 99–101).[25] There Nietzsche no longer makes reference to Spencer but names Voltaire, Comte, Schopenhauer, and Mill as instances of the transmutation, in the wake of the French Revolution, of Christian moral ideals into a secular ethic of sympathetic and compassionate action. His focus in §132 is emphatically on the subordination of the single individual to the social whole, to what he calls an effective "cancellation of the *individual*" (*CW* 5, 100).

The finished aphorism does not take up the notebook entry's call for an indefinite state of emergency. That is appropriate, for the aphorism's accent is not on the future of the individual but rather on the malign aftereffects of Christian morality in

25. The neologism "Christianness" translates Nietzsche's *Christlichkeit*, also a neologism, albeit more natural in the German than in the English.

the progressive social ideals of the nineteenth century.[26] The irony, however, if irony it be, is that the text of *Dawn* is mainly a ground clearing for a future conception of the individual that remains outstanding. Though it would be too clever to object that Nietzsche's quest for a new conception of the individual is condemned to failure by the rigorousness of his own criteria, the objection does serve to remind us that the individuality and sense of truth he has in mind had few if any imitable precedents outside of ancient Greece. He says poets have not yet begun to explore the possibilities of life, that unlike Greek poets, they have not yet discovered the earth. And yet in this endeavor the ancient Greeks can only serve as a negative model, for their path to the earth — by which they would have meant the native element, or what is most original and intimate to us and, as a result, what is most concealed — is categorically different from our own.[27]

In the remark cited above from 3[158], Nietzsche notes that a revaluation of values is the task lying on the horizon but that the scale necessary for such a task is wanting. A scale, however, implies an objective standard, the possibility of which Nietzsche had already abjured. Nietzsche's thinking in the notebooks suggests that the idea of a scale is finally unrealizable. His paradigmatic examples of the individual life are all exemplary, in the end, for their failure: the Apostle Paul, Pascal, Schopenhauer, Napoleon, Wagner. Even Goethe, whose life Nietzsche singles out at times as a life that succeeded in rising above the ideological vicissitudes of its era, does not always rise far enough to instantiate the future individual. Notable here is §481 of *Dawn*, "Two Germans," where Nietzsche singles out Kant and Schopenhauer

26. Indeed, the aphorism's conclusion contains the exceptional positive reference by Nietzsche to Kant. Kant, unlike the others named, stipulated that moral judgments not be tied to the affections.

27. If a historical anachronism be allowed, Nietzsche anticipates here Hölderlin's substantive rethinking of Greek poetry's exemplarity. On Hölderlin's internal dialogue with the Greeks, see Peter Szondi, "Überwindung des Klassizismus: Der Brief an Böhlendorff vom 4. Dezember 1801," in Szondi, *Schriften I* (Frankfurt: Suhrkamp, 1978), 345–66.

against Plato, Spinoza, Pascal, Rousseau, and Goethe for the fact that their "thoughts do not comprise a passionate history of the soul [. . .] their thinking is not at one and the same time an involuntary biography of the soul" (*CW* 5, 242). Their thinking, in other words, is not truly individual; not being individual, it is not pathbreaking, it does not show a way forward. Thus, when Nietzsche says, in 3[54], that all value judgments would have to be overthrown in order to have a clear path forward and in 3[70] that the future lies in an extra-moral form of thought, he is describing a path that does not yet exist, just as the individual who would tread that path does not yet exist. However unexpectedly, Nietzsche's thinking displays in this respect a strict and relentless Kantian consequence. Kant could say that the moral law always obtains, whether or not there is anyone who upholds it. Nietzsche contends that the space for the individual life must be held open, whether or not there is anyone who instantiates it.

The riddle of the individual life occasionally yields notebook entries of an intimate and personal stamp. A common facet of these passages is the isolation of the individual. Notebook entry 3[32] is one of these confessional asides: "His bright head often drove him onto lonely paths where he was rid of humans; but his heart was too anxious for this and pounded unbearably against his ribs. When he yielded to his heart, he mingled again with humans and now his head felt miserable."[28] The oppositional tension of heart and head here may reflect Nietzsche's internal dialogue with Pascal. In any case it does reflect a method Pascal employed, that of objectifying internal questions, dilemmas, disputes in a hypothetical third person. It is important neither to pathologize nor heroize the acute isolation these reflections bespeak but to see it instead within

28. Perhaps Nietzsche's most self-transparent reflection is that in 6[182]: "The most embarrassing thing for me is having to defend myself. With that I become aware that I first have to compare my way of being with that of others and that I have to *supply* for it *intelligible motives*: not being accustomed to this I know that I will fail. Yes, every presentation of my image by others causes me confusion. '*That* I am certainly not!' is my feeling; if I wished to express thanks, I would appear to myself *dishonest*."

the parameters of N's larger project. Within this project one may become accustomed to seeing Nietzsche's preferred objects of discussion — the Apostle Paul, Luther, Pascal, Napoleon, Schopenhauer, Wagner — inside the context of his dual critique of Christian morality and contemporary German culture. As certain as that context is, however, it can also overshadow the fact that Nietzsche's motivating interest in these figures was equally in the example they afforded of the drama of individual determination, or vocation. The depth of that interest is epitomized in his acute remark that the Christian religion's canonization of the Pauline writings effectively served to bury out of sight the tremendous internal dialectical struggle to which those writings give witness.[29] And when he speaks of Napoleon he does so twice in the company of Byron, suggesting in one passage that Napoleon in fact was the origin of the Romantic cult of the adored genius and hero (*D* §298, *CW* 5, 188).

What is striking in all of this is that Nietzsche always returns to the case of the individual in isolation. In notebook entry 4[45] he remarks that the isolation which is prematurely sought in fact defeats the individual: "Humans living in solitude often torment themselves to an astonishing degree over their character: but ⟨it⟩ is not character, rather solitude, from which they suffer. Let anyone who does not wish to accept this go back into the stream of the world where 'one's character is formed': whereas solitude consumes it. Let us become accustomed to intercourse with the dead; that preserves character. No, one should only enter into solitude with a *formed character* — not too early!" Isolation is a refuge only for the mature, i.e., the cultivated, for the one who has a "formed character." Nietzsche's original model for the solitary individual thinker was Schopenhauer. His eventual

29. See 4[220]: "As soon as something counts as true, any more refined understanding comes to an end, e.g., for its edification all of Christendom has read its Paul word for word, sentence for sentence, but has *not at all* grasped the true dialectic, the conflicting thought processes, his true distress and crux; thus, the suffering and struggling Paul: he was dead, i.e., he spoke inspired, as God's mouthpiece." The note is thoroughly ironic. The insinuation is that the inspired Paul is a dead Paul masking the living, suffering Paul.

reproach to Schopenhauer, however, was that he was only a solitary, that his thinking had only one string to play: "To feel strongly, to be able to let a strong feeling last long and to play many melodies on one string — that defines the great pathetics among the great writers, to whom Schopenhauer too belongs: they are distinct from the philosophers, although Schopenhauer counted himself among these: for they do not want to know at all costs but rather to sing *their* song at all costs." (3[136]). Nietzsche seems to have this note in mind when he writes, in a later entry, "If you have made it your practice to think of others and to do something for them, a good deal remains when it is impossible for you to achieve your goal: namely, to promote that of others. It is good and prudent to have these two strings to play. To comprehend the other and to look closely at *ourselves from his point of view* is indispensable for the thinker" (6[259]).

These complex reflections ought to be enough in themselves to invalidate the image of Nietzsche's thought as another nineteenth-century heroization of the individual. By Nietzsche's lights what we take for individuality is often enough a phantom, a favorite illusion; what we think of as self-knowledge is a deflected self-knowledge because mediated by the interference of another. The self I presume to know is really the image of myself in the mind of another (3[60]). This is of a piece with Nietzsche's regret for the intellectual weakness of much of what passes for individualism, a weakness that lies first of all in overestimation of the conscious intellect and underestimation of bodily drives. Nietzsche hints in fact at the plausibility of a physiological reduction of much, if not all, of intellectual and moral life. Physiology is the ground of morality: the latter shrinks in inverse proportion to increase in our knowledge of the former.[30] That said, Nietzsche is sparing

30. In 6[7], Nietzsche ventures the thought that "Perhaps all of morality is an *interpretation* of physical drives" (N's emphasis). In 6[144], he calls morality "a sum of errors that have been fused onto the drives." In the same entry he impugns the "presumptions" (*Anmaaßungen*) of the intellect over against the drives and the "basic prejudice" (*Grundvorurtheil*) that "the moral alone is true."

in the notebooks of specific remarks about physical weakness and sickness. He who sees practically nothing, therefore writes constantly (*homo scribens*); he who is embarrassed by and at the appearance of others, therefore speaks constantly in an internal dialogue, at times with the present but largely with the past and the dead; afflicted by migraines, he requires darkness and silence. Instructively, Venice, at that time still a customarily dark and quiet city, qualified for Nietzsche as the closest spatial analog to music, in his mind the highest art form.[31] All of this could arouse the sympathy, or compassion (*Mitleid*), for a solitary life. But Nietzsche would remind us that compassion is dissimulation in the bad, or worst, sense of self-deception.

The notebooks from the period of *Dawn* occupy a cusp lying between Nietzsche's prior publications' critique of contemporary German culture, German educational institutions, and inherited Christian morality and his later writings' projection of a way of life and thought that is still, even by contemporary standards, barely imaginable. At the same time a continuous thread runs through his writings, namely, the exemplarity of the philosopher as an individual spirit and, thus, as the exemplification of true freedom. This thought is increasingly developed and refined in the writings after *Dawn* where Nietzsche's critique of the tradition is the springboard for the projection of a revolutionary daybreak. In §212 of *Beyond Good and Evil* (*CW* 8, 115) Nietzsche will write: "It seems more and more to me that the philosopher as *necessarily* a human of tomorrow and the day after tomorrow has always found himself to be in contradiction to his today and *must* be: his enemy has always been the ideal of today." This distills his conviction that the true philosopher is at one and the same time untimely and revolutionary. That conviction was not entirely new. Already in the conclusion to *Schopenhauer as Educator*, where it embeds a quotation from Emerson's essay "Circles," Nietzsche fundamentally expresses

31. "*L'Ombra di Venezia*," "The Shadow of Venice," stands as if a book title at the head of the third notebook.

the same thought: "Let an American tell them about the significance of a great thinker who arrives upon this earth as the center of tremendous powers" (*CW* 2, 254).

Singular and striking in this thought is the discordant historicity it implies. That the philosopher is necessary, and his thinking revolutionary, implies that the philosopher answers and completes a historical development to which he is especially, if not uniquely, sensitive: Emerson's and Nietzsche's thinker "arrives upon this earth as the center of tremendous powers." If the thinker stands at the center of tremendous powers, then the thinker qualifies as a historical focus. And yet the thinker is also untimely. He does not conform to today, to his time, because he answers the call of a time that is tomorrow's, or the day after tomorrow's. Hence a permanent degree of indeterminacy shadows the thinker's historical appearance. That is the peculiar temporal and historical constellation that stares out at the reader from the notebooks of 1880–81, where Nietzsche's obsessive concern is less the plight of the individual than the very possibility of such — the individual being a thing whose dawn has still not broken. That that dawn might never break in a way we would be prepared to see is an irony that was not lost on Nietzsche:

> The bird Phoenix showed the poet a flaming scroll turning to ashes. "Do not be terrified!" it said, "it is your work! It does not possess the spirit of the times and still less the spirit of those who are against the times: consequently, it has to be burned. But this is a good sign. There are many types of dawn." (*D* §568)

Index of Persons

Subject Index

The Complete Works of Friedrich Nietzsche

IN NINETEEN VOLUMES

1 The Birth of Tragedy/Unpublished Basel Writings (Winter 1869/70–Fall 1873)
2 Unfashionable Observations
3 Human, All Too Human I
4 Human, All Too Human II/Unpublished Fragments from the Period of *Human, All Too Human II* (Spring 1878–Fall 1879)
5 Dawn
6 The Joyful Science/Idylls from Messina/Unpublished Fragments from the Period of *The Joyful Science* (Spring 1881–Summer 1882)
7 Thus Spoke Zarathustra
8 Beyond Good and Evil/On the Genealogy of Morality
9 The Case of Wagner/Twilight of the Idols/The Antichrist/Ecce Homo/Dionysus Dithyrambs/Nietzsche Contra Wagner
10 Unpublished Fragments from the Period of *The Birth of Tragedy* (Fall 1869–Spring 1872)
11 Unpublished Fragments from the Period of *Unfashionable Observations* (Summer 1872–Winter 1874/75)
12 Unpublished Fragments from the Period of *Human, All Too Human I* (Winter 1874/75–Winter 1877/78)
13 Unpublished Fragments from the Period of *Dawn* (Winter 1879/80–Spring 1881)
14 Unpublished Fragments from the Period of *Thus Spoke Zarathustra* (Summer 1882–Winter 1883/84)
15 Unpublished Fragments from the Period of *Thus Spoke Zarathustra* (Spring 1884–Winter 1884/85)
16 Unpublished Fragments (Spring 1885–Spring 1886)
17 Unpublished Fragments (Summer 1886–Fall 1887)
18 Unpublished Fragments (Fall 1887–Winter 1888/89)
19 Editors' Afterwords/Chronology of Nietzsche's Life/General Index

Library of Congress Cataloging-in-Publication Data

Names: Nietzsche, Friedrich Wilhelm, 1844-1900, author. | Baker, J. M. (Jay M.), Jr., translator, writer of afterword. | Hertel, Christiane, 1958– translator. | Nietzsche, Friedrich Wilhelm, 1844-1900. Works. English. 1995 ; v. 13.

Title: Unpublished fragments from the period of Dawn (winter 1879/80-spring 1881) / Friedrich Nietzsche ; translated, with an afterword, by J. M. Baker, Jr. and Christiane Hertel.

Description: Stanford, California : Stanford University Press, 2023. | Series: The complete works of Friederich Nietzsche ; volume 13 | "Translated from Friedrich Nietzsche, Sämtliche Werke: kritische Studienausgabe, ed. Giorgio Colli and Mazzino Montinari, in 15 vols. This book corresponds to Vol. 9, pp. 7–439, and Vol. 14, pp. 625–644." | Includes bibliographical references and indexes.

Identifiers: LCCN 2023007565 | ISBN 9780804728867 (cloth) | ISBN 9781503636989 (paperback) | ISBN 9781503636996 (ebook)

Subjects: LCSH: Nietzsche, Friedrich Wilhelm, 1844–1900—Notebooks, sketchbooks, etc. | LCGFT: Notebooks.

Classification: LCC B3312.E5 N33 2023 | DDC 193—dc23/eng/20230424

LC record available at https://lccn.loc.gov/2023007565